WITHDRAWN BY THE
UNIVERSITY OF MICHIGAN

NOUAKCHOTT by Benoît Vollmer and Jérôme Chenal

CHICAGO by Chris Bennet

SAO PAULO by Mario Novas

DUBAI by Ramon Prat Homs

MUMBAI by Ibai Rigby

LONDON by Javier Bravo

MEXICO CITY by Pablo López Luz

CHICAGO by Ibai Rigby

SINGAPORE by Siyuan Ma

BARCELONA by Jon Tugores

HONG KONG by Volker Heinze

IMMINENT COMMONS: URBAN QUESTIONS FOR THE NEAR FUTURE

SEOUL BIENNALE OF ARCHITECTURE AND URBANISM 2017

EDITED BY ALEJANDRO ZAERA-POLO AND HYUNGMIN PAI

028	**BIENNIAL GOVERNMENTALITY** Hyungmin Pai	
038	**IMMINENT URBAN COMMONS** Alejandro Zaera-Polo	
046	**AIR**	
054	**AIR INFRASTRUCTURES FOR THE COMMON** Nerea Calvillo	
060	**AIR DESIGN** Maider Llaguno-Munitxa	
078	**WATER**	
088	**DISSIDENT WATER** Lindsay Bremner	
102	**THE RECREATION OF THE COMMONS** Gunter Pauli	
114	**FIRE**	
120	**SKINS AND SOURCES:** **TOWARD A THERMODYNAMIC MATERIALISM** Iñaki Ábalos and Renata Sentkiewicz	
132	**FIRE IN URBAN GENESIS** Aleksandar Ivančić	
144	**EARTH**	
152	**PROTEST LANDSCAPES:** **SCENES OF UPHEAVAL ON THE GROUND** [1] David Gissen	
162	**TOWARDS A "NEW HELIOMORPHISM"** Charles Waldheim	
170	**SENSING**	
180	**SENSE AND THE CITY.** **TOWARDS A NEW DIGITAL COMMON** Carlo Ratti with Daniele Belleri	
192	**TELEPATHICALLY URBAN** Jennifer Gabrys	
204	**COMMUNICATING**	
212	**CAN CITIES HELP US HACK FORMAL POWER SYSTEMS?** Saskia Sassen	

224	**A TALE OF THREE CITIES, OR: THE SMART CITY AS WILL AND CATEGORY ERROR**	

Adam Greenfield

230	**MOVING**
238	**ACCESSIBILITY IN CITIES: TRANSPORT AND URBAN FORM**

Philipp Rode and Graham Floater

266	**THE RESTLESSNESS OF OBJECTS**

Jesse LeCavalier

282	**MAKING**
294	**REALITY MATTERS. THE ROBOTTIC TOUCH**

Fabio Gramazio, Matthias Kohler and Jan Willmann

302	**REPUBLICS OF MAKERS**

Mario Carpo

310	**RECYCLING**
318	**THE END OF WASTE? TOWARDS A SOCIO-ECOLOGICAL COMMONS**

Mitchell Joachim and Christian Hubert

334	**BUILDING FROM WASTE: THE WASTE VAULT[1]**

Dirk E. Hebel, Felix Heisel and Marta H. Wisniewska

346	**IMMINENT COMMONS: STORYLINES**

Edited by Mahgol Motalebi

404	**SHARING AND THE URBAN COMMONS**

Duncan McLaren and Julian Agyeman

416	**LIVE PROJECTS SEOUL**
	PRODUCTION CITY

Jie-Eun Hwang, SoA, and Hyungmin Pai

420	**URBAN FOODSHED**

Hyewon Lee

424	**WALKING THE COMMONS**

Soo-in Yang, Kyung Jae Kim, and Hyungmin Pai

430	**AUTHOR BIOGRAPHIES**
438	**IMAGE CREDITS**

BIENNIAL GOVERNMENTALITY
Hyungmin Pai

The world does not belong to one person; it belongs to the whole world. The harmony of the Yin and Yang forces does not favor growth in only one species of thing, the sweet dews and seasonable rains are not partial to one thing, and so the ruler of the myriad people does not show favoritism toward a single individual. ... Heaven and Earth are so great that while they give life they do not raise anything as their own, and while they bring things to completion they do not possess them. The myriad things all receive their blessings and obtain their benefits, but no one knows whence they first arose.[1]
—*The Annals of Lü Buwei*, 239 B.C.E.

Ecological crisis ... is the slow and painful realization that there is no outside anymore. It means that none of the elements necessary to support life can be taken for granted. To live under a huge inflated Globe you need a powerful air-conditioning system and powerful pumps to keep it inflated. ... So here is the question I wish to raise to designers: where are the visualization tools that allow the contradictory and controversial nature of matters of concern to be represented?[2]
—Bruno Latour, "A Cautious Prometheus?: A Few Steps Toward a Philosophy of Design," 2008

The Seoul Biennale of Architecture and Urbanism is driven by a sense of crisis. It is not only a crisis of our physical and social environment but also of the words and ideas with which we deal with this reality. Though a small part of an expansive and fluid condition, the Seoul Biennale is part of an ongoing transformation, both global and local, that requires us to question our political, economic, and technological systems. Not initially conceived as a goal of the biennale, working through a series of ideas in the midst of transition will, I believe, nevertheless come to be a key contribution of this biennale. The first idea to be questioned is the concept of the biennale. The birth and transformation of the biennale during the past 120 years has been part and parcel of the changing political economy of art and architecture. In the manner of the world expositions of the nineteenth century, the pavilions in the exhibition grounds and the art and products exhibited in them were identified with nations, peoples, and corporations as organized within nineteenth-century colonialism and capitalism. Based on the contradictory foundation of nationalism and the Romantic notion of autonomous art, the Venice Biennale and its national pavilions were born from a Eurocentric notion of a "world art." As part of "the exhibitionary complex," the exposition, museum, and biennale emerged together with modern representation.[3]

1. Lü Buwei, *The Annals of Lü Buwei*, trans. John Knoblock and Jeffery Riegel (Stanford: Stanford University Press, 2000), 71–73. At the time of its compilation, Lü Buwei was prime minister to the ruler of the state of Qin. He would later become the first emperor of a newly unified China. Lü retained a group of scholars whose aim was to encompass the world's knowledge in one great encyclopedia.

2. Bruno Latour, "A Cautious Prometheus?: A Few Steps Toward a Philosophy of Design with Special Attention to Peter Sloterdijk," in Willem Schinkel and Liesbeth Noordegraaf-Eelens, eds., *In Media Res: Peter Sloterdijk's Spherological Poetics of Being* (Amsterdam: Amsterdam University Press, 2011), 159–163. The text is based on Latour's keynote lecture for the Networks of Design meeting of the Design History Society Falmouth, Cornwall, 3 September 2008.

3. Tony Bennett, *The Birth of the Museum: History, Theory, Politics* (London: Routledge, 1995), 60–63.

Since the advent of the Havana Biennale and the explosion of biennales after the 1990s, the biennale took a major turn as it began to fly the banner of the global contemporary. Justified in its progressive stance against the conservatism of established museums and the promotion of a global, expansive notion of art, the art biennale has now become a dominant cultural form. As I write, there are 207 biennales listed on the Biennial Foundation website, with many more, including the Seoul Biennale, not registered in this listing.[4] Even as an architecture and urbanism biennale, the Seoul Biennale adheres to the following general and quite pertinent definition of the art biennale: "Often grandiose in scale, sometimes dispersed across several locations in a city, at times locally imbedded through site-specific commissions while being global in ambition, and often involving discursive components such as symposia, extensive publications, or even accompanying journals alongside a group show featuring, for the most part, a panoramic view of a new generation of artists."[5] Within this definition provided by the editors of *The Biennial Reader*, the only point to be changed for the Seoul Biennale would be to substitute the last phrase with its thematic of the urban commons.

What, then, is the justification of my claim that the Seoul Biennale provides a moment to question the idea of the biennale? Wouldn't the fact of its sponsorship by the Seoul Metropolitan Government, one of the largest municipal bureaucracies in the world, only give more credence to such skepticism? Bureaucracies are, by definition, conservative. Working through regulations, official documents, and hierarchical organizations, maintenance, rather than innovation, is their inherent nature. It is not that public sponsorship of biennales is rare. Most biennales in Korea and many biennales around the world are supported by state and public entities. However, in almost all such cases, the official position of both the bureaucracy and the biennale is that the former does not interfere with the art displayed in the latter. For example, while Seoul also supports a major art biennale, Media City Seoul, neither the municipality nor the biennale would confess to a symbiotic relation in its content or thematic. In contrast, for the Seoul Biennale, both the sponsoring municipality and the biennale have staked a position that the latter will serve as an experimental laboratory of urban governance, not just of Seoul but also of the major cities of the world. It is a position that urbanism-focused biennales, such as the Rotterdam and Hong Kong–Shenzen Bi-City biennales, have also staked out. With its urban agenda and the "live projects" that connect with municipal projects and policies, the Seoul Biennale has sought no refuge in the idea of autonomy. It invites the inevitable criticism that it will restrict itself by merging itself too deeply into the requirements and politics of local governance. The Seoul Biennale and the governance systems of Seoul will challenge, frustrate, and assist each other in their expectations and definitions. It is a marriage that is not only immediate in the thematic focus on the commons but also can be traced to the political lineage of Korea and the East Asian region.

4. "Directory of Biennials," Biennial Foundation, http://www.biennialfoundation.org/home/biennial-map/, accessed 10 May 2017.

5. Elena Filipovic, Marieke van Hal, and Solveig Ovstebo, *The Biennial Reader* (Bergen: Bergen Kunsthal, 2010), 14.

Suseonjeondo, Map of Hanyang (Seoul during the Joseon Dynasty), 1846-49

The scholarly and professional literature on the commons, if less so for the urban commons, is vast. This introduction to the conceptual issues of the Seoul Biennale is not the place to reiterate the debates of the past fifty years. I will rather discuss the context in which the commons became its central thread and the issues that were raised in the process. Early conversations with Alejandro Zaera Polo on the thematic direction of the Seoul Biennale included a debate on the nature of ecological elements, the emergence of posthuman conditions and the idea of the posthuman, and the search for a new urban cosmology. In setting the basic parameters of the commons, I suggested a comparison between the Taoist Five Elements—water, fire, earth, metal, and wood—and the Four Elements established during ancient Greece—water, fire, air, and earth. My first point was that the Taoist "element" is an inaccurate and misleading translation of *hsing* (in Chinese) or *haeng* (in Korean). *Haeng* more properly designates "actions" or "movements," and has at times been translated as "forces" or "powers." The most striking aspect of the Five Elements, for me as well as for many commentators on East Asian cosmology, is the inclusion of metal and wood. It has been suggested that "the grouping of these elements was not originally associated with primordial matter or substances of the world but with the practical, productive activities of agriculture." In the *Book of Documents*, for example, Emperor Yu is quoted as saying, "Virtue is seen in good government. Good government is proven by its [capacity] to nourish the people. There are water, fire, metal, wood, earth, and grain. These must be properly regulated."[6] Hence, the five *haeng* are not elements of nature but pre-humanized and institutionalized technologies incorporated in a system of governance. Nature and technology, in all its disruptive force, were never distinct from the human but were viewed as an inherent part of governance. This world view stands in contrast to the Western genealogy of humanism, first emerging as a radical challenge to the transcendent absolute and subsequently becoming a political, technological, and social mechanism. It may be argued that the politico-religious arena in China and East Asia never entertained the idea of the absolute. In human history, very few societies had the power and arrogance to view humans (themselves) to be the masters of a separate nature. Beyond this specific tradition, posthumanism is at once obvious, a contradictory misnomer and, in the case of its most naïve forms, once again self-delusional.

In East Asia, governmentality, to use a Foucauldian term, has an expansive history. Modernity, industry, and capitalism in the region emerged not through the mechanisms of the bourgeoisie and the market but through the state and its guidance of capital. Generally designated as "late industrialization" and the "strong state," they are characteristics confined not just to South Korea but to most economies of East Asia.[7] From the Western perspective, it would seem strange to talk

---

6. Cited in Benjamin I. Schwartz, *The World of Thought in Ancient China* (Cambridge, MA: Harvard University Press, 1985), 358. Schwartz is in turn referring to the work of the Chinese scholars Hsu Fu-kuan and Li Te-yung.

7. The classic English text on late industrialization in Korea is Alice Amsden, *Asia's Next Giant: South Korea and Late Industrialization* (Oxford: Oxford University Press, 1989). See also her more recent global discussion in *The Rise of "The Rest": Challenges to the West from Late-Industrializing Economies* (Oxford: Oxford University Press, 2001). For a more recent Korea-specific study, see Kim Yoon Tae, *Bureaucrats and Entrepreneurs: The State and the Chaebol in Korea* (Seoul: Jimoondang, 2008).

of the state in the context of a municipality such as Seoul. We must hence be reminded that local self-government based on democratic representation was de facto established in Korea only after the first modern local elections in 1995. If industrialization came late to South Korea, civil society, in all its fluid variations, appeared even later. As Seoul's governance now evolves into more horizontal forms, governmental apparatuses continue to provide the context of the Seoul Biennale. Its thematic direction is played out in the fact that in 2012 the Seoul Metropolitan Government announced the "city of commons" as official policy. This new policy has disrupted not only the internal workings of the municipality but also its relation to elements of civil society working with the commons. The Seoul Biennale emerges from this re-organization of governmentality. Rather than work to ward off its controlling forces, my approach as director has been to engage directly with them, intensifying their logic and commitments. *Live Projects Seoul*, a major sector in the Seoul Biennale, in particular function less as exhibition installations and more as interventions, instigating projects and steering policies that extend beyond the time frame of the biennale.

In the limited space of this essay, I point to the background and approach of *Production City*, one of the three thematic sectors of the *Live Projects Seoul*. As a theoretical project, *Production City* is an exploration into post-capitalism and the future of work, essential aspects of the commoning process. The history of work tells us of its changing nature, of its spatial distribution in local and global networks. "The end of work" is one of the fundamental issues not only of post-industrial societies but of emerging economies. *Production City* takes the position of economists, sociologists, and urbanists such as Jeremy Rifkin, Ulrich Beck, and André Gorz that, as mass work declines in all sectors of the economy and new technologies accelerate the disappearance of existing jobs, a radically new form of work must find a place within an evolving urban fabric. Production, as described by André Gorz, "takes place not only in the work situation but just as much in the schools, cafes, athletic fields; on voyages; in theatres, concerts, newspapers, books, expositions; in towns, neighbourhoods, discussion and action groups—in short, wherever individuals enter into relationships with one another and produce the universe of human relationships."[8] Gorz is articulating why a radical redefinition of production is key to the urban commons. In contrast to private, insulated urban spaces, production in the city requires all the modalities of sharing, connecting, and making. In this system, knowledge and space, the two commons that are enhanced through intense use, must be shared. As the transformation of production in the city is not an abstract process, it will play out in the specificities of local and global conditions; and in the case of the Seoul Biennale, in the streets and back-alleys of central Seoul.

Seoul is estimated to have around 270,000 people working directly in manufacturing.[9]

8. André Gorz, *Strategy for Labor: A Radical Proposal* (Boston: Beacon Press, 1967), 117.

9. Bong Choi, Mook-Han Kim, and Jai-Ho Kim, *Current State and Future Outlook of Geographical Concentrations of Small-sized Manufacturing Enterprises in Seoul* (Seoul: Seoul Institute, 2014).

It is a small percentage of the working force of Seoul and is not significantly larger than the employment figures of a similar sized metropolis such as London. What is peculiar with Seoul is that significant manufacturing sectors still exist in its central areas. Whereas most of the world's major metropolises have agglomerated into centers of business and consumption, historical Seoul sustains a complex ecology of traditional and cutting-edge production. These areas include the fashion and garment districts of the Dongdaemun and Changsin-dong areas and the electronics, printing, and machinery clusters of the Euljiro-Sewoon Sangga area, all key sites of the Seoul Biennale. The historical background to this condition lies in the fact that Seoul's industrialization, led by national economic policy, came late in the twentieth century; and peaked around the mid-1960s, a moment when most major cities in Europe and the United States had already lost most of their manufacturing functions. Zoning was a key mechanism for managing and controlling the different functions of Seoul, and presently the semi-industrial zones still take up 5% of the land area of Seoul. Even as neo-liberal policies sought to disassemble this bureaucratic system of control, the rigidity of zoning delayed what once seemed to be an inevitable elimination of all manufacturing capacities. When the global economic crisis triggered a fundamental shift in the real estate dynamics of Seoul, the retention and development of the manufacturing sector became a key policy of the Seoul Metropolitan Government. Production City, as a strategic agent, consists of a range of interventions, installations, and interpretations: historical overviews of the nature and distribution of work in the city, analytic and creative documentation of sites and activities, interventions into manufacturing districts in Seoul, and proposals for new modes of work and productive spaces. The point of Production City is to coalesce the different agents in the landscape towards a moment not only of visibility but also of engagement.

The great attraction of modern curatorial work is the fact that it can work in a realm that moves between thinking, showing, and acting. The Seoul Biennale takes full advantage of the global mandate that the biennale privileges as well as the particular governmentality of a large municipality. It assumes a worldview in which nature, technology, and politics are inseparable. In its thematic, on the one hand, the Seoul Biennale follows Bruno Latour's thesis "that there is no outside anymore." In its curatorial approach, on the other hand, I must question and refine Latour's subsequent logic that the role of the designer lies primarily in representation. Even as I acknowledge Latour's understanding that to represent is a "verb" that includes "artistic, scientific and political representation techniques," we must understand that the idea of representation is itself part and parcel of the modernist divide of interior reality and exterior appearance.[10] If there is no outside, the very idea of representation must be questioned. The search for a different kind of biennale is, then, a search for a renewal of representation and engagement as political practices. The Seoul Biennale brings the element of the stage into the urban fabric, a stage that is "simultaneously a locus of public activity and the exhibition-space for 'fantasies.'"[11]

10. Latour, "A Cautious Prometheus?," 163.

11. Jacques Ranciere, *The Politics of Aesthetics: The Distribution of the Sensible* (London: Continuum, 2004), 15.

It is a stage that is specific to Seoul but one that invites an array of diverse agents to engage in a specific biopolitical performance . Rather than an exhibition enclosed within gallery walls, the Seoul Biennale seeks to be part of the everyday fabric of the city. It is interested less in putting up a show and more in bringing a multitude of agents into the existing city. This is the *architecture* of the Seoul Biennale of Architecture and Urbanism. It is an architecture less of representation and more of organization and performance. It involves aspects of architecture as a building practice but divests from the fundamentalist notion of architecture as work. For, is not architecture the discipline where "the sense of self-realization, in the sense of 'poiesis,' of the creation of work as oeuvre," to again borrow Gorz's characterization, is strongest, and is not this kind of work "disappearing fastest into the virtualized realities of the intangible economy"?[12] This open-ended transformation is never a one-way street. As much as architecture is mandated to redefine itself, this transformation affects the way urban societies function. The point of the Seoul Biennale is neither to preserve nor to throw away the efficacies of terms such as "the commons," "architecture," "production," and "representation." It enters into the fray of the politics of aesthetics not in the dichotomy between artistic autonomy and bureaucratic control, but as a performative engagement in a mechanism of biopolitical production.

12. André Gorz, *Reclaiming Work: Beyond the Wage-Based Society* (Cambridge, UK: Polity Press, 1999), 2.

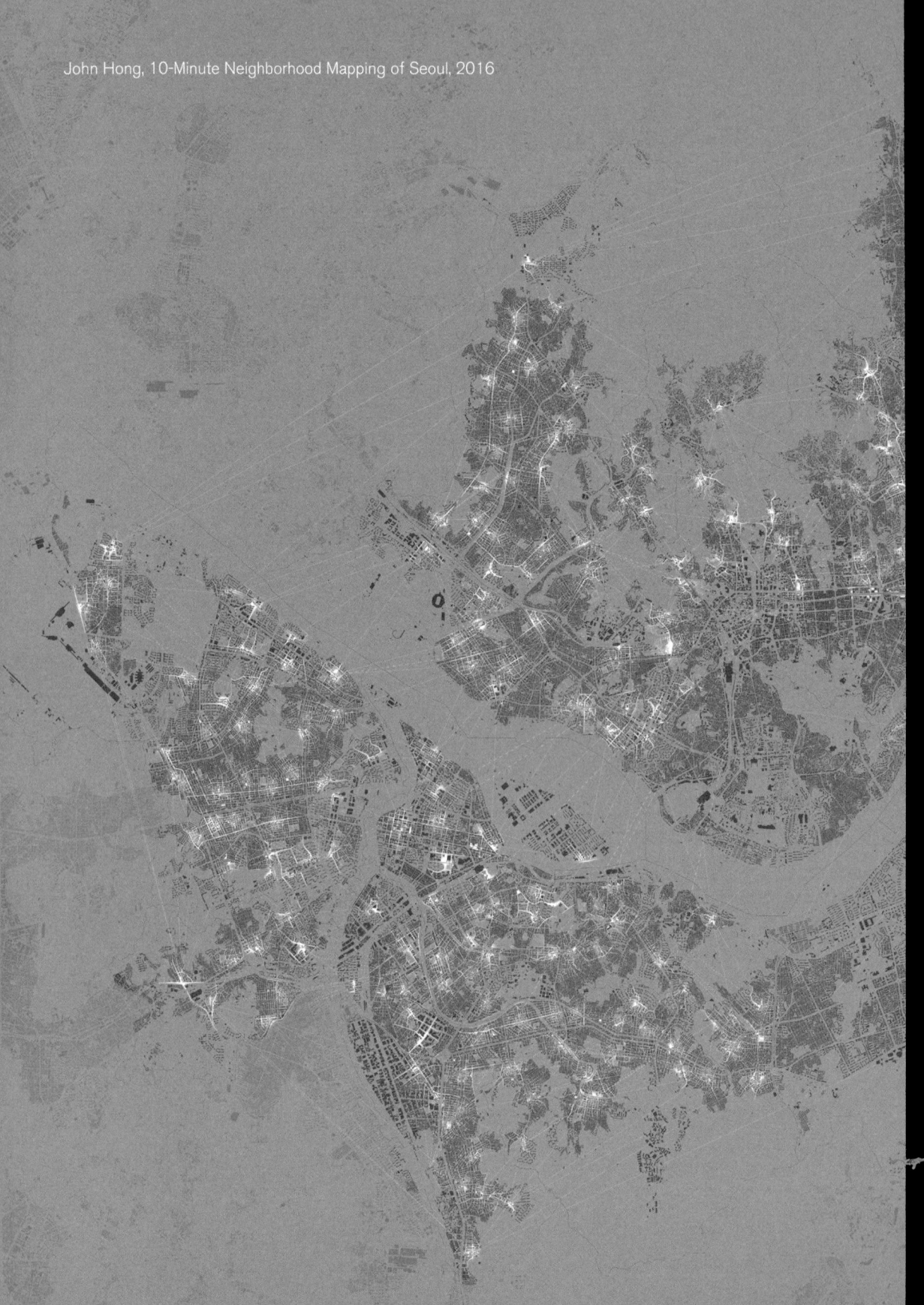

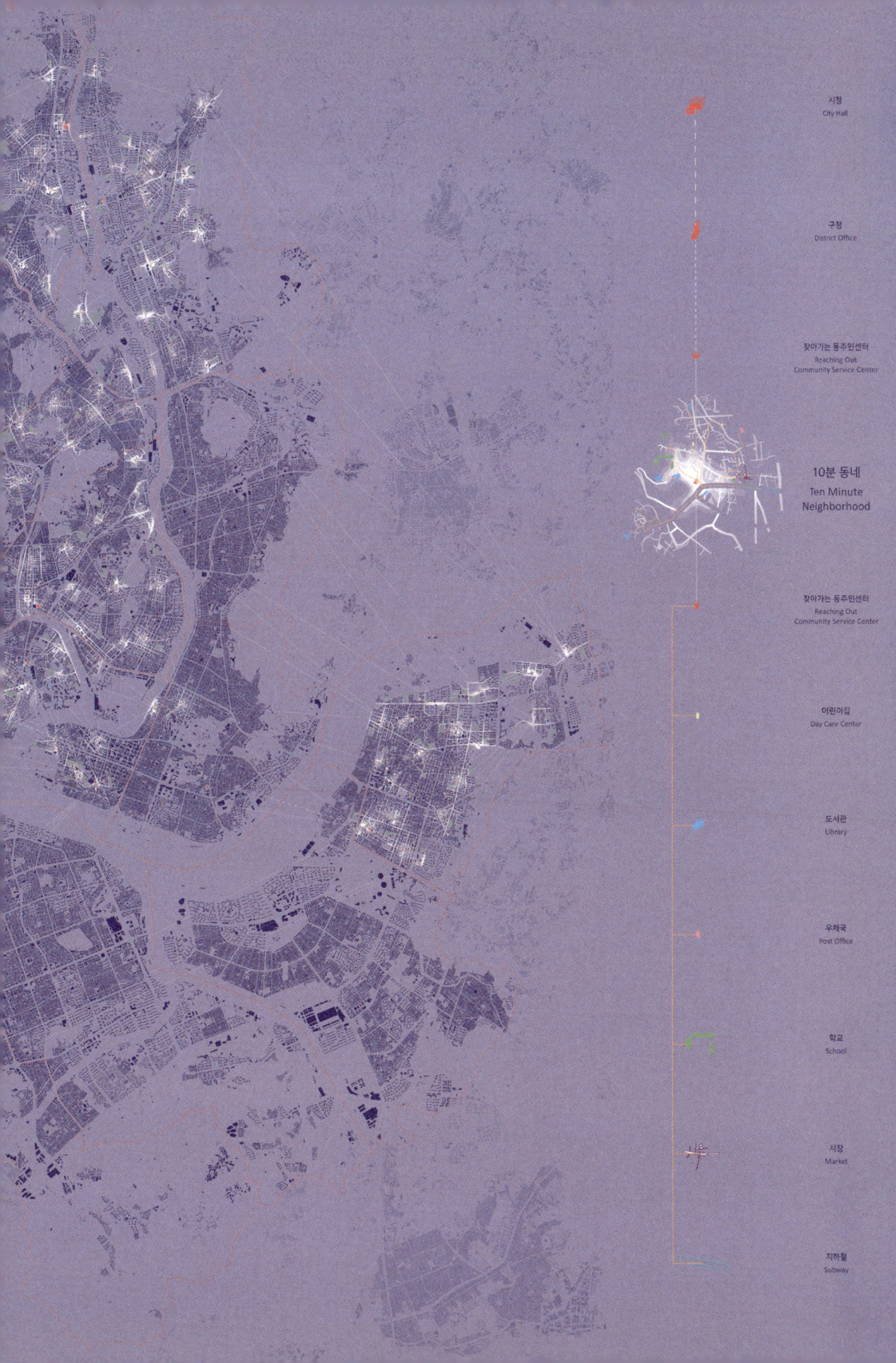

IMMINENT URBAN COMMONS

Alejandro Zaera-Polo

AIR
WATER
FIRE
EARTH
SENSING
COMMUNICATING
MOVING
MAKING
RECYCLING

Since the eighteenth century when the Western world became human-centered, humankind has not ceased to evolve, and so too has the very concept of the human. In 1933, Le Corbusier and a few other members of the CIAM issued *The Athens Charter*, a document aimed at orchestrating the emerging technologies of the built environment into a proposal for the future of cities.[1] A classification of human activities became the vertebral spine of this proposal, structured around four urban functions: work, residence, leisure, and transport. This functional classification has structured urban planning policies ever since, but its human-centered approach appears now to be unable to address the problems of our age.

In the Anthropocene, humans have become capable of modifying natural ecosystems, geological structures, and even the climate; we have become so powerful that it is increasingly difficult to delimit the natural from the artificial. As the most populated human environment, cities are a central focus of these transformations, and yet, none of these concerns seems to have permeated the tools that we use to plan cities. The urban planning disciplines remain primarily conceived around human functions, despite the fact that the crucial questions they need to address—air pollution, rising water levels, drought, the heat island effect, deforestation, biodiversity, food security, automated work, inequality…— are primarily driven by concerns that, for the first time in history, transcend human societies and threaten the very survival of the planet. The economic, political, and technological drivers of modern urbanism—the mass integration of production, employment, and consumption; the separation of work, dwelling, recreation, and transportation; the division between the natural and the artificial—are no longer effective at addressing the urgent questions cities are facing today. Likewise, the traditional urban instruments such as plazas, streets, and neighborhoods have been commodified by neo-liberal practices and have become ineffective at addressing the new urban collectives and constituencies, both human and nonhuman, which populate contemporary cities.

1. Le Corbusier, Jean Giraudoux, and Jeanne de Villeneuve, *La Charte d'Athenes* (Paris: Plon, 1943).

POSTHUMAN COSMOLOGIES

The agency that cities have in the construction of the Anthropocene is something that can no longer be ignored. We are assisting in a veritable paradigm change, one that requires a reformulation of the cosmologies upon which the contemporary tools of urbanism have been constructed. Arcane technologies and rituals of the urban were often based on mythological references. Ancient cosmologies were mechanisms of comprehending the natural world which enabled cultures to understand and operate within the natural environment. The oldest ones predated human settlements and were aimed at explicating natural phenomena and regulating the modes of relation between humans and nature. As the urban environment became increasingly controlled by human agency, cosmologies were discarded as systems of urban knowledge and governance. Typology and monumentality became primary tools for urbanism, with the structure of human relations prevailing over the physical and material determinations of the environment. The *affairs of cities* (*politika*) became an entirely artificial endeavor.

The current prevalence of artificial environments and politics—cities—has tended to naturalize technology while de-politicizing nature. However, the pressing nature of ecological concerns and the scale of technological developments call for the imminent city to re-politicize both nature and technology and construct new urban cosmologies which can support the development of new urban sensibilities. An entirely new set of urban technologies have since appeared, radically transforming urban protocols and experiences: smartphones, GPS, electromobility, and biotechnology. Yet, these technologies still remain largely outside the practices of urban planners and designers, which remain trapped in the humanistic precepts of modern urbanism.

Far from producing urbanity, urban functionalism has dismantled the *commons* and undermined urban democracy. Clichés, such as the relevance of public spaces as guarantors of urban communities and urban democracy, are as problematic as the inability of architects and urban planners to quantify the implications of density and urban form in the energy consumption or the determination of urban micro-climates. The idea that architects and urban designers can find effective agency in the distribution of human functions—such as work and domesticity—is at best naïve. Cities have become sources of extreme inequality and environmental degradation (in contempt not only of the *demos*, but also of all of the nonhuman constituencies that exist in cities), and these are even threatening the subsistence of cities and are pointing at insurmountable contradictions at the core of the current modes of economic integration. Theorists like Jeremy Rifkin and Paul Mason argue that we are already entering a post-capitalist world in which politics are shifting from a focus on capital and labor to a focus on energy and resources, and they have proposed new economies: shared economies of zero marginal costs driven by new technologies: peer-to-peer organizations enhanced by pervasive computation, sustainable energy sources, and carbon-neutral technologies.[2]

As the largest human habitat, cities have become the epicenters of global warming, air pollution, and a variety of ecological malaises. Naomi Klein has pointed at the fundamental opposition between capitalist growth and the limited natural resources of the earth, and questioned the capacity of capitalist regimes to resolve an imminent ecological catastrophe.[3] The decline of capitalism has loaded urban ecologies and technologies with unprecedented political relevance. Cities have now become a crucial intersection between ecology, technology, and politics where the equation between wealth, labor, resources, and energy has to be reset to address the shortcomings of neo-liberal economies.

2. Jeremy Rifkin, *The Zero Marginal Cost Society: The Internet of Things, the Collaborative Commons, and the Eclipse of Capitalism* (London: Macmillan, 2014. Paul Mason, *Post Capitalism: A Guide to Our Future* (London: Allen Lane, 2015); and Paul Mason, "The End of Capitalism Has Begun," *The Guardian*, 17 July 2015, http://www.theguardian.com/books/2015/jul/17/postcapitalism-end-of-capitalism-begun.

3. Naomi Klein, *This Changes Everything: Capitalism vs. the Climate* (New York: Simon & Schuster, 2014).

ECOLOGIES AND TECHNOLOGIES RATHER THAN FUNCTIONS

Does this scenario, determined by the rise of the Anthropocene and the crisis of neo-liberal capitalism, imply that the work of urbanists and architects has become futile? That the new commons will be entirely developed within social media? Has urbanism been expelled from politics, and is it now at the mercy of securitization and capital redistribution? On the contrary, some economists[4] argue that urban planning, housing, and real estate hold the key to resolving urban inequality.[5] Cities precede the installation of political systems, and have systematically outlasted them, often constituting themselves in mechanisms of resistance to power. For cities to become devices for the common good rather than instruments producing and implementing power structures (and often inequality or ecological destruction), urban practices need to locate resources and technologies at their core. Rather than splitting urban life into functions easily captured by power, we should try to identify first where the *imminent urban commons* are and how to reconstruct them as instruments of devolution and ecological awareness, constructed transversally across technologies and resources. We have tried to outline what those might be, and how they may become the source of a revision of urban practices.

It appears inevitable that urban practices of the immediate future will address these emerging fields to locate the new urban commons. Urban planning based on human functions has now become a mechanism to divide and to exert power rather than to produce urbanity. A new set of urban instruments will need to be developed to address these imminent posthuman commons, which we have tried to identify and classify. Like any other classification it probably

---

4. Matthew Rognlie, "Deciphering the Fall and Rise in the Net Capital Share," BPEA Conference draft, March 19–20, 2015; http://www.brookings.edu/~/media/projects/bpea/spring-2015/2015a_rognlie.pdf, accessed 5 October 2016.

5. Thomas Piketty, *Capital in the Twenty-First Century* (Cambridge, MA: Belknap Press: An Imprint of Harvard University Press, 2014).

Mumbai by Ibai Rigby

has lacks and contradictions, but it also serves as a basis for further discussion and development. For the purpose of the structuring of the Seoul Biennale 2017, we have identified commons that relate to natural resources and their ecologies, and other commons which emerge from technological developments which will imply new urban collectives, regulations and governance.

The other five commons that we propose here are related to the technological developments which are opening alternative forms of urban community. These commons become opportunities for new urban practices to pervade institutional, bureaucratic, and market mechanisms, and operate mostly on a micropolitical scale. Technologies can be considered extensions of human capacities, which have developed a posthuman life on their own—or as McLuhan writes in *Understanding Media*, "technologies are self-amputations of our own organs."[6] *Sensing, communicating, moving, producing, and consuming* have developed disembodied, collective *modes of existence*,[7] which have transcended their human origin. The "human scale" of the city planners resembles a nostalgic reference to something that does not matter any longer.[8] With the emergence of these technologies we seem to be engaging on a *micropolitical* scale of operation.

6. Marshall McLuhan, *Understanding Media* (London: Routledge Classics, 2001).

7. Thie idea of the *modes of existence* of technical objects is taken from Gilbert Simondon's definition. Gilbert Simondon, On the Mode of Existence of Technical Objects: Part One, trans. Ninian Mellamphy, University of Western Ontario, June 1980, Duke University.

8. "With the arrival of electric technology, man extended, or set outside himself, a live model of the central nervous system itself."
"It is to the railroad that the American city owes its abstract grid layout the nonorganic separation of production, consumption and residence. It is the motorcar that scrambled the abstract shape of the industrial town, mixing up its separated functions to a degree that has frustrated and baffled both planner and citizen. ... Metropolitan space is equally irrelevant for the telephone, the telegraph, the radio, and television. What the town planners call 'the human scale' in discussing ideal urban spaces is equally unrelated to these electric forms. Our electric-extensions of ourselves simply by-pass space and time and create problems of human involvement and organization for which there is no precedent." McLuhan, "The Gadget Lover," in Ibid., 127.

We live in an age marked by vast technological developments and ecological concerns which need to be incorporated effectively into the conception and design of cities, taking into account wider global ecologies. The micropolitical scale of new technologies and the cosmopolitical scale of new ecologies will replace the *human* scale of traditional urban politics. The arcane natural elements and the artificially enhanced sensibilities, collectivities, logistics, and metabolic processes enabled by emerging technologies should become the central concern of a posthuman urbanism: an urbanism that is focused on the ecologies and economies of elements and milieus, where cities are designed to engage with much broader concerns than the delivery of organizations that are merely responding to human activities, as if independent from the milieus, the climates, the topographies where they take place , and the tools through which they become implemented. An update of the modernist human-centered functionalities that still form the vertebral spine of urban practice is now urgently needed.

BEIJING by Kevin Frayer

AIR

Air is, as Naomi Klein has stated, the element that most intimately binds all humans on earth together. While the ozone depletion from CFCs represented a shocking and imminent threat, the effects of other airborne pollutants have been less conspicuous. Seven million people die every year from exposure to air-induced diseases.[1] Despite increased awareness of these problems, air quality in cities seem to have gotten worse over the last few decades. According to an October 2016 UNICEF report, "300 million children live in areas with extremely toxic levels of air pollution" and "approximately 2 billion children live in areas where pollution levels exceed the minimum air quality standards set by the World Health Organization."[2] With this exposure comes increased instances of respiratory disease, asthma, and other ailments. The risk of airborne disease outbreaks is a constant threat in transportation centers, a location which could help infections to spread globally, and the threat to cities of global warming and the associated sea-level rises is a constant reminder of the importance of managing air.

But increasing air quality and decreasing polluted air conditions requires regulation. With cities as the densest location of human populations, cleaning air, moving polluted air away from city streets, preventing air stagnation, and improving airflow between buildings are central to preserving the rights of urban citizens to common resources. Since the early twentieth century, buildings and cities have developed the ability to delimit, filter, and qualify air. However, as toxic emissions continue to rise every year, these abilities are becoming ever more urgent and politically charged. While air is a universally needed resource, it is extremely difficult to quantify, visualize, sense, and model. For this reason, it has been historically difficult to regulate, and policies

---

1. World Health Organization, news release, March 2014, http://www.who.int/mediacentre/news/releases/2014/air-pollution/en/, accessed 5 October 2016.

2. UNICEF, *Clear the Air for Children*, October 2016, http://www.unicef.org/publications/files/UNICEF_Clear_the_Air_for_Children_30_Oct_2016.pdf.

for improving urban air quality are still in their infancy. Quantifying air movement and quality has been an obstacle historically to creating policies to regulate its use, and the lack of regulatory frameworks on air quality has led to rampant pollution. The freedom to sacrifice clean air essentially functions as a corporate subsidy. Naomi Klein has called this "the theft of the sky."[3] The emerging technologies of sensing and computational modelling will enable the development of effective tools to manage the air common.

Historically, an intuitive understanding of airflow drove much of related urban policies. Planners could guess that larger street widths and breaking up monolithic street fronts would improve airflow and reduce urban canyons. However, years of improvement in simulation and airflow modeling are beginning to show scientifically how air moves through cities, what prevents it from doing so, and how to improve urban air quality conditions through planning. Besides improving regulatory conditions on industries which impact global air quality on the whole, the rights of citizens to improved air quality need to be addressed through planning and building regulation.

The ability to sense pollution with scientific instruments came long after the ability to sense phenomena such as airflow, barometric pressure, and wind speed. However, the threat of sick air was long known and long feared. Prior to the development of germ theory, the accepted belief was that diseases such as cholera or the black death could be spread through "bad air" that emanated from rotting organic matter.[4] This "miasmatic theory" remained popular from the Middle Ages until the late nineteenth century, when it became accepted knowledge that outbreaks of microorganisms lead to disease. Whatever the cause, air was seen as both a bringer of life and a potential harbinger of disease, epidemics, and other pathogens. Since the chlorine and mustard gas attacks of World War I, the danger of toxic air and the threat of air

3. Klein, *This Changes Everything*, p. 60.
4. John M. Last, ed., *A Dictionary of Public Health* (Oxford: Oxford University Press, 2007).

contamination became well known and widely feared.[5] At that moment, air became vividly understood as a dangerous milieu subject to weaponization and a carrier of disease and pollution.[6]

The first legislation to regulate urban smog and air pollution emerged in the late nineteenth century. In the United States, municipal legislation appeared in 1881 in Chicago, Illinois, and Cincinnati, Ohio; the first state legislation appeared in 1910 and 1912 in Boston, Massachusetts, and Providence, Rhode Island. But the first federal air pollution law did not appear until 1955.[7] In London, the first attempt to regulate smog dates from the early twentieth century, with the introduction of the 1926 Public Health Act and the Clean Air Act of 1956 (following the deadly 1952 "Great Smog" in London, which was blamed for thousands of deaths).[8]

These regulations were followed closely by visionary urban proposals: around the time of the first legislation for smoke abatement, Sir Ebenezer Howard published *To-morrow: A Peaceful Path to Real Reform*, republished in 1902 under its more popular title: *Garden Cities of To-morrow*.[9] These Garden Cities would promote healthy airflow by limiting industrial growth and spacing development to provide open spaces and public parks as well as wide boulevards. Howard's original text was partially focused on alleviating social divisions, improving health conditions for the working class who were forced to live and work in unhealthy urban environments.

5. During World War I, it was realized that "the enemy's environment, the space occupied by him, could be destroyed" through the poisoning of the air itself. See Peter Sloterdijk, "Atmospheric Politics," in Bruno Latour and Peter Weibel, eds., *Making Things Public* (Cambridge, MA: MIT Press, 2005), 945.

6. Peter Sloterdijk, *Terror from the Air*, trans. Amy Patton, and Steve Corcoran (Los Angeles: Semiotext(e), 2009), p. 16.

7. Arthur C. Stern, emeritus professor, University of North Carolina, Chapel Hill, NC, "History of Air Pollution Legislation in the United States," *Journal of the Air Pollution Control Association* (March 2012): 44.

8. B. Goodall, *Dictionary of Human Geography* (London: Penguin, 1987).

9. E. Howard, *Garden Cities of To-morrow* (London: S. Sonnenschein & Co, 1902), 2–7.

Luke Howard's *The Climate of London*, first published in 1818, was one of the first books which connected urban planning to meteorological phenomena in a comprehensive way. Howard described three factors which climatically differentiate the city from the country: convection, radiation, and evaporation. These three factors remain today some of the most relevant concerns for cities combating urban heat island effects.[10]

Consolidating the path initiated by Howard, the second edition of *Das Stadtklima* (*The Climate of Cities*), published in 1956 by Dr. P. Albert Kratzer, was perhaps the first accessible and comprehensive book dedicated to urban airflow and microclimatology.[11] This book was a compilation of research completed over the last half century, mostly conducted by German architects, climatologists, and urban planners. In the foreword, Kratzer stated that he hoped the book would "prove not only a useful tool in the hands of city planners and builders but also a lucid and instructive work on their climate for all interested city-dwellers"—illustrating his dedication to making the topic of urban microclimatology accessible to all. Kratzer understood the importance of the air common and dedicated the book —and his career as an urban planner in Stuttgart—to urban airflow, the heat island effect, downdrafts, and other common air concerns.

But neither Howard nor Kratzer had the tools to visualize, measure, and model these phenomena so that policies could be established. The possibilities we have today to make CFD models of air movement in cities or to visualize heat with thermal cameras will certainly enable us to

---

10. "[T]he country presents for the most part a plain surface, which radiates freely to the sky, — the city, in great part, a collection of vertical surfaces, which reflect on each other the heat they respectively acquire: the country is freely swept by the light winds of summer, — the city, from its construction, greatly impedes their passage, except at a certain height above the buildings: the country has an almost inexhaustible store of moisture to supply its evaporation — that of the city is very speedily exhausted, even after heavy rain." Luke Howard, *The Climate of London* (1818; repr., The International Institute for Urban Climate, 1833), 9–10; http://www.urban-climate.org/documents/LukeHoward_Climate-of-London-V1.pdf.

11. Albert Kratzer, *Das Stadtklima* (Braunschweig: Friedr. Vieweg and Sohn, 1956).

set up policies for cities to improve air quality and environmental comfort, giving design an active role in the management of this common.

The destructive consequences of increasing atmospheric carbon dioxide levels on our planet have been slow to materialize and have been manifested in subtle ways. According to NASA's Goddard Institute for Space Studies, average global temperatures have risen roughly 0.8 degrees Celsius since 1880 (with almost two-thirds of the warming having occurred since 1975), mostly due to heat-trapping greenhouse gasses such as carbon dioxide.[12] While this may not seem like much, the threat of further warming outlines an existential crisis for the human species. While governments around the world attempt to limit our warming to 2.0 degrees Celsius, the World Bank has stated that we are on track for a 4.0 degrees Celsius of global average temperature increase by the end of the twenty-first century, stating that there is "no certainty that adaptation to a 4°C world is possible."[13]

As the most concentrated human habitats, cities are at the center of these concerns. Besides using massive amounts of energy which contribute to global warming, some of the most fundamental issues for cities today are mitigating the effects of smog on urban inhabitants and dealing with rising sea levels and other effects of climate change. Not only will major metropolitan areas be at risk for serious flooding in the near future due to rising sea levels, but these cities will be hubs for populations displaced by global warming. As discussed earlier, the effects of smog on urban populations has been well known since the dawn of the Industrial Revolution, and legislation to mitigate it, as well as architectural and urban strategies for dissipating it, have been developing for over a century.[14]

12. NASA Goddard Institute for Space Studies, https://www.giss.nasa.gov/, accessed 5 May 2017.

13. World Bank, "New Report Examines Risks of 4 Degree Hotter World by End of Century," 18 November 2012, http://www.worldbank.org/en/news/press-release/2012/11/18/new-report-examines-risks-of-degree-hotter-world-by-end-of-century.

14. For example, the Coal Smoke Abatement Society (CSAS) was formed in 1898. See Peter Thorsheim, *Inventing Pollution: Coal, Smoke, and Culture in Britain since 1800* (Athens, OH: Ohio University Press, 2006), 103.

New technologies being developed enable cities to increase air exchange rates and natural ventilation, both at the scale of buildings and city-wide. Climate-altering technologies such as pollution mitigation, cloud seeding, carbon sequestration, and adiabatic cooling are some of the instruments being developed to mitigate anthropogenic effects on climate and to forge a contemporary *cosmopolitics* of air to bring about both new cultural constructs and design opportunities. Filtering and purifying technologies such as HEPA filters, activated carbon filters, titanium dioxide photocatalytic air purification, and gas phase advanced oxidation are developing on a scale to address air pollution. However, addressing the source of many of these toxins remains a contentious issue in a legal vacuum.

As instrumentation to model and visualize air has developed, air regulation has increased. The greater the degree to which we can see the effect we are having on air, the more precise the regulations will become. Air regulation has always been intimately connected to its visualization, which provides evidence to phenomena which we could understand only intuitively a few decades ago.

AIR INFRASTRUCTURES FOR THE COMMON

Nerea Calvillo

INTRODUCTION

Since the Industrial Revolution, urban air has been an artificial environment, the space where the gases and particles released by combustion processes to generate energy and power merge with the atmosphere. This is the reason it has been identified as one of the indicators of the Anthropocene. According to Peter Sloterdijk, it was not until World War I, when the Germans used toxic gas as a weapon, that the air was actually designed (2005, 2009). However, as architectural historian Reyner Banham explored in *The Architecture of the Well-Tempered Environment* (1969), the air—and, even more, air pollution, it could be argued—has been mostly absent from debates over architecture and urban design from architecture and urban debates. How can we, as architects, start dealing with it? What do we need to know about the air in order to operate in it? Can we think about "air design" (Sloterdijk 2009), and if so, which tools need to be developed? To respond to these questions, and drawing on Science and Technology Studies (STS) and feminist literature, I have been thinking about urban air as a complex sociotechnical assemblage (Farías and Benders 2010) in order to acknowledge its materiality, its effects, its bodies, and politics. If, as a heuristic, we considered this aerial sociotechnical assemblage as a city, what would its urbanisms be?

COMMON INFRASTRUCTURES

The atmosphere is the (sometimes) invisible dump of capitalist practices, but it is also a fundamental component of human and more than human life, that which makes us breathers. We inhale and exhale thousands of times a day, and still we take the air for granted. However, the more polluted the air is becoming globally, the more its image is shifting from an infinite, resilient space with never-ending waste-absorption capacities to a limited resource that needs to be taken care of. For this reason it has been conceptualized as one of the global commons (see Helfrich 2008; Klein 2014). And, as this book's introduction also suggests, we need infrastructures to deal with the global commons, as part of the "imminent urban commons."

When thinking about urban air infrastructures, some practical difficulties emerge. The air is a relational entity, with components that react among themselves, with the weather, or with any material that gets suspended in it. This implies that the air is different at neighborhood, national, and global scales. It may operate at the same time as a large-scale set of actors and spaces, such as the aviation space—which has been conceived as a "cosmopolitan commons" (Disco and Kranakis 2013)—and as spaces produced through the collaboration and communication of local communities, such as community gardens—named as "urban commons" (Eizenberg 2012). The air is also (mostly) invisible, inapprehensible, uncontrollable, and unlimitable—qualities that pose difficulties for conceptualizing and managing it. It also travels with the wind, very far away, carrying seeds, ashes, microbes, dust, or radiation to places where they may not be expected or wanted.

Very often, in our times, the air is polluted, which makes palpable its pharmakon condition of being a cure or a danger depending on its concentrations. One immediate response to this fact would be to advocate for air-cleaning infrastructures. But how does one clean a global circulating entity when the economic system that has set up this situation does not seem to be changing soon? Understanding that this endeavor is almost impossible, would it not be more effective to aim for a nonpolluting approach instead? Deep structural changes are needed to shift from a cleaning approach towards a nonpolluting situation, and that is what we should aim for. But as Lauren Berlant has argued (2016), in the meantime we need forms to deal with the transition, which may involve, among other things, inhabiting polluted sites.

There is also a conceptual difficulty when having to think about the infrastructures required to engage with a commons. What kind of infrastructures are we talking about, and what do we exactly mean by "commons"? Infrastructures are not only technological devices—bridges, roads, sensors, or satellites, for instance—but, as STS have well demonstrated, they are also sociotechnical assemblages composed by hard, soft, human, and nonhuman entities, situated and networked in different ways (Graham and Marvin 2009; Leigh and Bowker 2006; Schick and Wintherik 2016; Star 1999). Here we will focus on the infrastructures able to engage with the different materialities of air, which also take into consideration and engage openly with their social implications, and which allow us to manage the "terms of transition that alter the harder and softer, tighter and looser infrastructures of sociality itself" (Berlant 2016: 394).

The commons is also an unruly concept, as it takes various forms and approaches depending on the context and author. It usually brings together resources, property rights, and regulations, but one of the problems of relating the commons to limited resource management is that the discussion ends up being about economy and costs. Frequently, the infrastructures designed to deal with toxic air are framed from this perspective, from monitoring technologies to understand "how much more" it can be polluted, to infrastructures to clean the polluted air, such as carbon sequestration or titian dioxide paint. These approaches may partially contribute to remediating the particles' concentrations, but they are clearly not addressing the causes, the emission of pollutants. Carbon markets were set in place to regulate emissions, but they are not achieving the desired effects: on the one hand, global emissions have not been reduced; and on the other, the highest-emitting companies, mostly multinationals, are continuing to pollute at the same amount and are even making money through the carbon market (Banner 2008). So maybe we need to amplify our idea of the commons from an economy-based management of resources to include cultural, social, and political values, to initiate "the transformation of some fundamental aspects of everyday life, social practices and organization, and thinking" (Eizenberg 2012: 779). Then, in which other ways can an infrastructure *of* a common (the air) also be an infrastructure *for* an expanded idea of the common, one that addresses other forms of being together?

With this last question comes another problem, because as Berlant (2016) argues, the incontestable desired common often reinforces an idea of the collective based on agreement (or at least on dialogue) and belonging (to a community, a state). Considering the challenges that these idealistic approaches imply in terms of who belongs and how they belong to that common—inspired in nonsovereign critiques, for instance—I follow Berlant in her proposal of focusing instead on proximity and detection, as "the experience of affect, of being receptive, in real time" (2016: 402). In our context of industrial toxicity, financial insecurity, and permanent war, how do we start thinking about infrastructures to deal with the air that will also enable these other forms of cohabitation?

Philosopher Marina Garcés (2013) argues that due to the complexity of this context, thinking about "what to do" can be paralyzing. Therefore, she suggests thinking instead about how to change our modes of dealing with things, with each other, and with the world. Whereas previously these modes were focused on representation and action, she proposes to shift towards attention and treatment (Garcés 2013). Following Garcés, we may want to conceive infrastructures that deal with the toxic air in a common world, and instead of asking what to do with the polluted air, aim to test whether there are other modes of paying attention to it that involve forms of treatment other than cleaning. But again, as Berlant (2016) argues, while infrastructures for the commons acknowledge a broken world, they also trigger new ways of living in it. I take this as an invitation to speculate, which is the only possible way of dealing with our troubled times, as Donna Haraway (2016) also suggests. So overall, I'm interested in speculating on what air design can do to engage with the urbanisms of the air, what it can mean to care for the environment, and more specifically, to care for air pollution. In other words, I intend to speculate through any possible format what "air design" can do to deal with the Anthropocene.

"In the Air", 2008

TOPOGRAPHIC INFRASTRUCTURES TO SENSE THE AIR/ENVIRONMENTAL INFRASTRUCTURES

Some scholars, including architects, geographers, sociologists, and anthropologists, have been thinking about the infrastructures of the air and commons. Geographer Derek McCormack (2016) coined the concept of "stratospheric infrastructures" as a means to understand the stratosphere as an infrastructure itself (as the space through which other elements such as balloons can navigate), but also to name infrastructures that operate in the stratosphere. This aerial space is more or less stable and homogeneous, quite different from the urban air that is in contact with the ground, the troposphere layer of the atmosphere. This air, the one which surrounds us, is messier, dirtier, more volatile, and performs as the mirror of our daily lives. Maybe, in alignment with McCormack, we could refer to this air/infrastructure entity as a "tropospheric infrastructure" to help us better think about its qualities.

Other scholars have proposed different forms of thinking about infrastructures that suggest other ways of living together. Some have focused on infrastructures' capacity to make controversies public, and therefore to raise matters of concern (Latour and Weibel 2005). Along these lines, Domínguez Rubio and Fogué (2013) have suggested that it is the visibility of the infrastructure itself that provides its political capacities. And yet, both of these approaches require some sort of dialogue—even if agonistic—among humans. For anthropologist Alberto Corsín (2014), a different approach to make infrastructures common is to open their hardware, an approach inspired by the software open source movement, where the common is achieved by collectively designing and/or building infrastructures. All of these approaches so far involve belonging to some sort of community or neighborhood, or require participants' being socially entitled to speak. And therefore, as Berlant (2016) reminds us, these proposals potentially leave some humans and other entities on the side.

Understanding the potential and capacities of these proposals, I would like to speculate on another one, one of infrastructures of sensation. Instead of making visible, let's say, a controversy about the concentration of air or gases, these infrastructures would make us pay attention to other aspects of the air through embodied practices or forms of sensation. They may not require dialogue or discussion, but would necessitate recognizing the differences in the air and in what surrounds us, human or more-than-human. These differences would reflect the uneven distribution of pollution, in spaces and in bodies, and its different effects across agents.

An infrastructure of sensation is just one of the many proposals that could be envisioned from this framework. This approach provides us with other forms of knowing the air which, even if not quantitative, are fundamental for our practice as architects. And it reminds us that the different neighborhoods that compose the urbanisms of air are made out of air, people, plants, and buildings, and with them, power relations and politics. Maybe speculating on common infrastructures could help us to test other forms of redistribution of the excess of some gases and particles suspended in the air.

REFERENCES

Banham, R. 1969. *The Architecture of the Well-tempered Environment*. London: The Architecture Press.

Banner, S. 2008. *Who Owns the Sky? The Struggle to Control Airspace from the Wright Brothers On*. Cambridge, MA: Harvard University Press.

Berlant, L. 2016. "The Commons: Infrastructures for Troubling Times." *Environment and Planning D: Society and Space* 34(3): 393–419.

Corsín Jiménez, A. (2014) The Right to Infrastructure: A Prototype for Open Source Urbanism, *Environment and Planning D: Society and Space*, 32 (2), pp. 342–362.

Disco, N., and Kranakis, E., eds. 2013. *Cosmopolitan Commons: Sharing Resources and Risks across Borders*. Cambridge, MA: MIT Press.

Domínguez Rubio, F., and Fogué, U. 2013. "Technifying Public Space and Publicizing Infrastructures: Exploring New Urban Political Ecologies through the Square of General Vara del Rey." *International Journal of Urban and Regional Research* 37(3): 1035–52.

Eizenberg, E. 2012. "Actually Existing Commons: Three Moments of Space of Community Gardens in New York City." *Antipode* 44(3): 764–82.

Farías, I., and Benders, T., eds. 2010. *Urban Assemblages*. London, New York: Routledge.

Garcés, M. 2013. *Un mundo común*. Barcelona: Ediciones Bellaterra.

Graham, S., and Marvin, S. 2009. *Splintering Urbanism: Networked Infrastructures, Technological Mobilities and the Urban Condition*. London and New York: Routledge.

Haraway, D. 2016. *Staying with the Trouble: Making Kin in the Chthulucene*. Durham, NC: Duke University Press.

Helfrich, S., ed. 2008. *Genes, Bytes y Emisiones: Bienes Comunes y Ciudadanía*. Mexico: Fundación Heinrich Böll.

Klein, N. 2014. *This Changes Everything: Capitalism vs. the Climate*. New York: Simon & Schuster.

Latour, B., and Weibel, P., eds. 2005. *Making Things Public: Atmospheres of Democracy*. Cambridge, MA, and Karlsruhe, Germany: MIT Press.

Leigh, S., and Bowker, G. C. 2006. "How to Infrastructure." In L. A. Lievrouw and S. Livingstone, eds., *The Handbook of New Media*, 230–45. London: Sage.

McCormack, D. P. (2016) Elemental infrastructures for atmospheric media: On stratospheric variations, value and the commons, *Environment and Planning D: Society and Space*, pp. 1–20.

Schick, L., and B. R. Winthereik. 2016. "Making Energy Infrastructure: Tactical Oscillations and Cosmopolitics." *Science as Culture* 25(1): 44–68.

Sloterdijk, P. 2005. *Esferas III*. Barcelona: Siruela.

———. 2009. *Terror from the Air*. Cambridge, MA, and London: The MIT Press.

Star, S. L. 1999. "The Ethnography of Infrastructure." *American Behavioral Scientist* 43(3): 377–91.

AIR DESIGN
Maider Llaguno-Munitxa

As described by Sloterdijk in *Terror from the Air*, "the discovery of the 'environment' took place in the trenches of World War I." On 22 April 1915, a specially formed German gas regiment launched the first large-scale chemical attack against French-Canadian troops in northern Ypres Salient, using chlorine gas as their means of combat. Chlorine-filled cylinders were positioned facing prevailing north-northeast wind and released the liquefied chlorine into the air, producing a cloud nearly 6 kilometers wide and 600 to 900 m deep. It is estimated that 15,000 people were poisoned and 5,000 died in this terrorist act, which Sloterdijk describes as "'atmotechnic' innovation […] a sort of regional atmospheric design." Sloterdijk introduces the concept of "air-design" as "the technological response to the phenomenological insight that human being-in-the-world is always and without exception present as a modification of 'being-in-the-air.'" And he continues, "Since there is always something in the air, advances in atmosphere explication throw up the idea that, by way of precaution, we might put something in it ourselves."[1]

1. P. Sloterdijk, *Terror from the Air* (Cambridge, MA: MIT Press, 2009), 23 and 93.

Chai Jing's *Under the Dome*, documentary from 2015
Al Gore's *An Inconvenient Truth*, documentary from 2006

The atmosphere is progressively transformed through anthropogenic emissions as a form of "slow violence" that is dispersed across time and space.[2] Through vehicular, household, and tertiary activities, the chemical composition of our atmosphere is constantly under transformation, and in many cities around the world air quality is being severely compromised, seriously affecting urban health. A recent report from the WHO stated that "in 2012, around 7 million people died—one in eight of the total global deaths—as a result of air pollution."[3] Various newsletters and documentaries, such as *Under the Dome* by Chai Jing or *An Inconvenient Truth* by Al Gore, have reached large audiences that exceed the boundaries of scientific research, and thus air pollution has become a topic of general concern. Hence, regulatory bodies to improve the air quality conditions in our cities are becoming more in demand every day.

2. R. Nixon, *Slow Violence and the Environmentalism of the Poor* (Cambridge, MA: Harvard University Press, 2013).

3. WHO, *World Urbanization Prospects 2014* (United Nations, 2014).

The mask emoji is among the most popular emojis
Air Quality Index graphics by the Shanghai Environmental Monitoring Centre

However, air phenomena has proven to be very hard to regulate. Airflow is an irregular medium and, as such, its regulation is conceptually problematic. The nonlinear characteristics of turbulent flows make a deterministic approach to resolve them analytically intractable; therefore, it is challenging to formulate simplified modelling approaches for urban flows. In addition, quantitative predictions about the influence of environmental policies on local air quality are hard to prove and difficult to argue for. Air is also a continuum with no physical boundaries, and thus geopolitical friction over regulatory policies is often unavoidable. Consequently, while the anthropogenic transformation of our atmosphere has been ongoing for over two centuries already, curating this "design process" through the implementation of regulatory strategies has proven challenging.

Not surprisingly, the governance bodies that handle environmental policies have also often proven unsuccessful or insufficient in addressing the problem at the required spatio-temporal scales, which account for the variability in the phenomena[4]. The phenomena in the atmosphere are classified according to temporal and spatial scales [5], which within the Urban Boundary Layer (UBL) range from the study of meso- to local and micro-scale climates.[5] And thus, in order to reflect upon the locally specific concentration levels, the governance bodies that implement environmental policies have to effectively address the spatial variability of air quality in cities.

As of today, the responsibility to draft atmospheric regulations generally falls in the hands of high-level regional or federal governance bodies, occasionally complemented by city-scale regulations. Not surprisingly, such high-level governance bodies fail to account for the atmospheric variability that characterizes local and microclimate scales. While "small-scale" atmospheric variability has been scientifically understood since the nineteenth century (refer, for example, to the pioneering work of meteorologist Luke Howard from 1838),[6] it remained within the realm of environmental sciences and was not discussed in public forums. However, especially in the last decade, with the spread of sensing technologies and the Internet of Things (IoT), the local variability in air quality concentrations is being acknowledged and the role of architecture in the design of the atmosphere is starting to be recognized.

In this context, the physical boundaries of architecture are to be revisited to consider the design of natural systems as part of the disciplinary domain. Since adverse air quality tends to be primarily an urban problem, incorporating the measures to guarantee good air quality in built areas is critical. And so through architectural design strategies, we have the opportunity to become active agents in the remediation of this common.

4. Kundu PK, Cohen IM. Fluid Mechanics. Burlington, MA: Elsevier; 2008. 904 p.

5. The urban boundary layer is a mesoscale phenomenon. Its characteristics are affected by the urban surface. Oke, T.R. 1987. Boundary Layer Climates. York, UK: Methuen & Co. Ltd.

6. L. Howard, *The Climate of London, Deduced from Meteorological Observations Made at Different Places in the Neighbourhood of the Metropolis* (London: C. Baldwin Printer, 1838).

DIVERGING GLOBAL AIR POLICIES

Concerns about air quality have been present for centuries, as have regulations for emission controls. Since King Edward I's ban on burning sea coal in London in 1306, through the Glasgow smog in 1873, to the London smog in 1952, households were forced to reduce the use of coal, eventually leading to the formulation of the 1956 clean air act in the United Kingdom. Similarly in the United States, following the 1881 Chicago and Cincinnati smog, and the 1939 extreme smoke days in the city of St. Louis, among other events, the U.S. Congress passed the Air Pollution Control Act of 1955 to solve the problems associated with air quality.[7]

By the second half of the twentieth century, hand in hand with economic globalization, environmental policies acquired regional and global scales. Influenced by contemporary theories such as the ecosystem approach addressed in *Silent Spring* by Rachel Carson,[8] the formation of environmental think tanks such as the Club of Rome (1968)[9], or the formulation of concepts such as "sustainable development" addressed in the Brundtland report (1987)[10], a global environmental consciousness was recognized and global environmental consensus on issues such as pollutant emission controls started to be sought. Thus, while the intensification of global economic activity contributed significantly to environmental deterioration, globalization also enabled increased public awareness of environmental issues around the world.

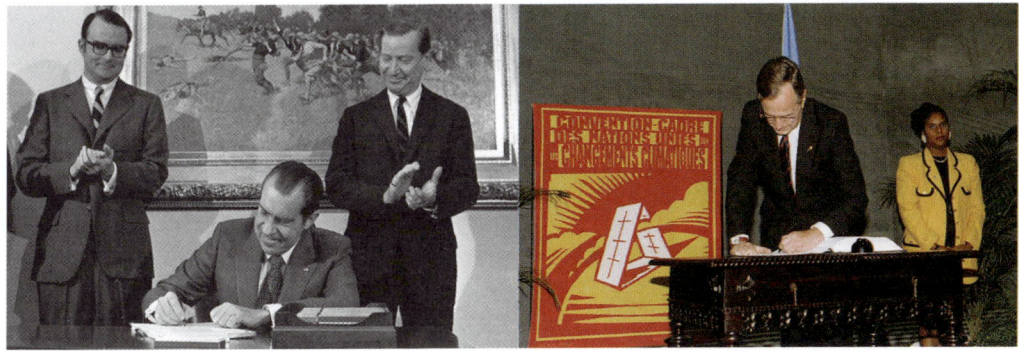

7. CCPS-AIChE, *Safe Design and Operation of Process Vents and Emission Control Systems* (Hoboken, NJ: John Wiley & Sons, 2006). 326 p.

8. R. Carson, *Silent Spring* (Boston, MA: Houghton Mifflin, 1962).

9. https://www.clubofrome.org/   In 1972 the The Limits to Growth(the first study to question the viability of continued growth in the human ecological footprint was published).

10. N documents url: http://www.un-documents.net/our-common-future.pdf.

U.S. President Richard Nixon signing the Clean Air Act in 1970

U.S. President George H.W. Bush signing the first climate change agreement in the UN conference on the Environment in Rio de Janeiro in 1992

Global initiatives to stabilize greenhouse gas (GhG) concentrations were first introduced as an issue of global concern at the United Nations (UN) Conference on the Environment and Development held in Rio de Janeiro in 1992.[11] Since then, and as part of the Annual UN Framework Convention on Climate Change (UNFCCC), various international conferences have followed, with the Paris UN Conference of partiers (COP 21) held in 2014 and the last one (COP 22) being held in Marrakech in November 2016, committing its members by setting internationally binding GhG emission reduction targets. On the other hand, regional-scale pollutant release regulations such as the EU VI or the U.S. emission standards set by the EPA introduce limits for vehicle exhaust or industrial emissions.

In the table shown below, the concentration standards such as those established by the National Ambient Air Quality Standards (NAAQS) for the United States or the European Commission of Pollutant Standards are compared against the guidelines suggested by the World Health Organization (WHO). While these standards are not legally binding, they offer an outlook on the criteria followed in the different countries and reveal a missing coherent approach on the definition of air quality criteria. Similarly, the commitment of different stakeholders to global and regional pollutant emission regulations has historically proven to be challenging, and thus such policies become a recurrent domain for geopolitical confrontation.

Furthermore, neither the global nor regional regulations reflect the concentration peaks observed in urban environments for which municipal-scale emission controls are implemented. That is the case, for example, with the newly approved anticontamination protocol in the city of Madrid,

11. UNFCCC, Rio Convention 1992, http://unfccc.int/essential_background/convention/items/6036.php, accessed 28 March 2016.

U.S. EPA Director Scott Pruitt, on taking a "humble" approach to regulating the CO_2 emissions, 28 March 2017

U.S. President Donald Trump officially withdraws from the Paris climate accord during a speech at the White House Rose Garden on Thurs. June 1, 2017. Screenshot from White House video

	WHO	EU	US	Canada	Australia	China
Ozone 8 hour, ppb	50	60	75	65	80	80
Fine Particulate 24 hour, μg/m³. PM2.5|10	25 | 50	25 | 50	35 | 150	30 | -	25 | -	75 | 150
Sulfur Dioxide 24 hour, ppb	8	48	140	115	80	60
Nitrogen Dioxide Annual, ppb	21	21	53	53	30	21
Carbon Monoxide 8 hour, ppm	9	9	9	13	9	-

or with the Low Emissions Zone (LEZ) regulation established in 2008 in London.[12] Similar policies are also being implemented in other cities around Europe, such as Paris or Zurich.

However, municipal regulations fail to reflect local concentration levels. Air quality is generally measured in idealized sites (often located in suburban contexts) where the concentration levels don't resemble those observed in urban street canyons.[13] Furthermore, recent findings have shown that the concentration levels of ultrafine particles are approximately six times higher in urban street canyons.[14] Since air quality is therefore not a homogeneous phenomenon, municipal regulatory bodies generally fail to address the concentration gradients present in urban environments, and prove unsuccessful in incorporating the necessary remediation strategies.

Thermal pollution and chemical pollutant concentrations peak in cities as opposed to the countryside, due not only to high and localized anthropogenic emissions, but also to the topographical and surface material properties of the urban fabric.[15] A building can affect its

12. Transport for London, "Low Emission Zone" (2015), https://tfl.gov.uk/modes/driving/low-emission-zone, accessed 15 June 2016.

13. T. R. Oke, "Siting and Exposure of Meteorological Instruments at Urban Sites," in C. Borrego and A. L. Norman, eds., *Air Pollution Modeling and Its Application XVII* (New York: Springer Science+Business Media, LLC, 2007), 615–31.

14. R. E. Britter and S. R. Hanna, "Flow and Dispersion in Urban Areas," *Annual Review of Fluid Mechanics* 35(1) (2003): 469–96.

15. Kumar P, Fennell PS, Hayhurst AN, Britter RE. Street Versus Rooftop Level Concentrations of Fine Particles in a Cambridge Street Canyon. Boundary-Layer Meteorology. 2008;131(1):3-18.

Comparison of Ambient Air Quality Standards and Guidelines

local wind speed, wind direction, air pollution, driving rain, radiation, or daylight,[16] and so by adjusting its geometrical or material attributes, a reduction in the local concentration levels can be induced. Therefore, in order to achieve effective air-quality remediation strategies, not only must international, regional, and municipal policies be incorporated, but domestic scale (street and neighborhood scale) strategies must also be integrated where local urban structures (topography, architecture, etc.) play a crucial role.

CONVERGING LOCAL AIR POLICIES

The period of time between the second half of the nineteenth and the first half of the twentieth century was particularly interesting for the study and implementation of urban environmental initiatives which included air quality remediation strategies. At that time, the disciplinary boundaries of architecture, planning, and urban sanitation were not yet clearly drawn, and hence the architect had to think holistically about architectural, social, and environmental considerations. Architecture was therefore often designed to comprise its surrounding microclimate and air quality.

The role of passive architectural considerations such as building morphology and materiality in urban health were discussed in various climate forums and were incorporated at urban policy levels. To ensure solar access and fresh air to streets and communal areas as well as to building envelopes, many cities in Europe and in the United States introduced a variety of building codes between the 1850s and the 1930s. Interestingly, these codes, while pertaining to urban scale regulations, also introduced indications for architectural-scale geometrical aspects such as roof geometries.[17]

Ildefons Cerdà's masterplan codes also introduced environmental architectural parameters for the Eixample in Barcelona planned in the late 1850s. Besides including building height H to street width W ratio indications, Cerdà introduced regulations to constrain building frontage heights and set back distances for the terrace levels. This criterion was intended to promote a continuous urban frontage while limiting the massing to enable the access of direct sunlight to urban street canyons and building envelopes. His considerations in regard to urban ventilation were proposed in the form of block consolidation. That is, block permeability was encouraged to favour street ventilation, and the consolidation of more than two façade frontages was deemed undesirable for courtyard ventilation.[18] While the measures proposed by Cerdà to guarantee the access of direct

---

16. B. Blocken and J. Carmeliet, "Pedestrian Wind Environment around Buildings: Literature Review and Practical Examples," *Journal of Thermal Envelope and Building Science* 28(2) (2003):107–59.

17. W. Atkinson, *The Orientation of Buildings, or Planning for Sunlight* (New York: John Wiley and Sons, 1912).

18. A. Doerr, "Behind Four Walls: Barcelona's Lost Utopia" (2014), http://www.failedarchitecture.com/behind-four-walls-barcelonas-lost-utopia/, accessed 10 May 2016; A. Soria y Puig, *Cerdà: The Five Bases of the General Theory of Urbanization* (Madrid: Sociedad Editorial Electa Espana, 1999); J. Busquets, *Barcelona: The Urban Evolution of a Compact City* (Rovereto: Nicolodi; Cambridge, MA: Harvard University Graduate School of Design; distributed by Actar, 2006).

sunlight to the building facades and streets were generally successfully adopted, his proposal for the limiting block consolidation to guarantee urban ventilation was less successful. As opposed to the open courtyards Cerdà had envisioned, urban blocks are mostly enclosed today.

The London Building Act of 1894, on the other hand, prescribed slanting roofs instead of flat or curved ones to maximize the access of natural light in urban street canyons.[19] Likewise, building codes established in 1902 for the city of Paris not only described the requirements for street width and building height, but also introduced indications to regulate roof geometry. With the same philosophy, William Atkinson, an advocate of passive solar design, in *The Orientation of Buildings, or Planning for Sunlight* from 1912,[20] criticized the limitations of most of the building codes that only constrained street H/W ratios. Atkinson instead proposed strategies to compute direct sun ray incidence and shadow casting on public areas or neighboring buildings, and suggested such measures should also be incorporated in planning policies. Among his considerations we can find studies on the effect of cornice details, the influence of roof designs on street daylight conditions, and neighbor shadow-casting studies.

The 1916 Standard Zoning Act in the United States also addressed the role of passive design strategies on sun incidence and ventilation. The building code aimed at stopping the erection of massive buildings such as the Equitable Building in New York which would prevent light and air from reaching the streets below.

The increasing concerns about urban sanitation, coupled with the ongoing aerodynamic investigations in early-twentieth-century Paris, awakened local architects' awareness of the interaction of buildings and airflow and, in particular, the role of building geometry in urban ventilation.

Little is known about the meteorological investigations performed by Gustave Eiffel, however. Fascinated by the interactions of land and airflow, Eiffel developed one of the first urban weather stations: the Eiffel Tower. From his *pied à terre* located 285m above the city in the Eiffel Tower, Gustave Eiffel monitored weather conditions in the city of Paris. Between 1903 and 1914, beginning with the drop test studies performed from the tower,[21] and culminating with the wind tunnel tests developed at the Champ-de-Mars laboratory located at the base of the tower, the Eiffel Tower became a platform where various meteorological and aeronautic experiments that

19. F. Banister, *The London Building Act, 1894: A Text-book for the Use of Architects, Surveyors, Builders, etc. Containing the act printed in extenso together with a full abstract, giving all the sections of the act which relate to buildings, set out in tabular form for easy reference and an introd. showing the leading alterations made by the act* (London: B. T. Batsford, 1896).

20. Atkinson, *The Orientation of Buildings*.

21. A. Angot, "Les Observations meteorologiques de la Tour Eiffel," *La Nature* (869) (1890): 117–8; G. Eiffel, *Nouvelles recherches sur la résistance de l'air et l'aviation, faites au Laboratoire d'Auteuil* (Paris: E. Chiron, 1919).

I. THE ENVELOPE AS DEFINED BY LAW.
Assumed a city block 200 x 800 feet. The number and position (but not the volume) of the Dormers, likewise the shape and position (but not the area) of the tower, are optional with the designer. Otherwise this perspective is simply a pictorial representation of the maximum mass allowed by the present laws.

II. THE ENVELOPE MODIFIED BY A PLAN.
Its appearance after having assumed a plan, and having passed this downward through the original envelope.

III. THE MODIFIED ENVELOPE FILLED WITH RECTILINEAR FORMS.
Its appearance after having substituted for the sloping planes, set-backs occurring at every second floor; tentative limitation being placed upon the tower.

IV. THE MASS MODIFIED BY THE STEEL CONSTRUCTION.
Its appearance after conforming the set-backs to the steel grillage and truncating the pinnacles to the highest floor level, which contains a practicable area. The mass is now ready for architectural articulation.

Drawings by Hugh Ferriss illustrating the impact of the 1916 New York City Zoning Code. Exhibited at the 37th Annual Exhibition of the Architectural League of New York, 1922

Voorhees Walker Smith & Smith,. *Zoning New York City: A Proposal for a Zoning Resoluition for the City of New York* (New York: The City of New York, 1958)

focused on the study of airflow were developed.[22] Such experiments enabled Eiffel to identify the urban boundary layer, which described the interaction between the rough urban surface and the incoming airflow, as well as the influence of building geometries on the surrounding pressure gradients. Such investigations inevitably echoed in the work of designers concerned with the contemporary problems of urban health and air quality in particular.

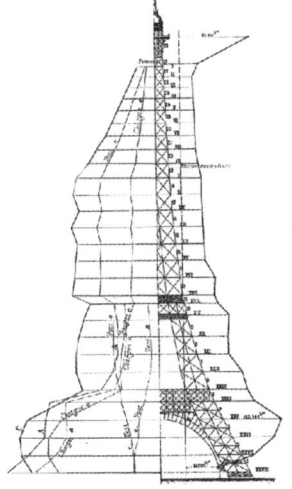

Soon after the recently adopted French law "L'hygiene des Habitations a Bon Marché (HBM)" of 1894,[23] Adolphe Augustin Rey designed the winning entry for the Rothschild housing competition located between the rue Charles Baudelaire and rue Teophile Roussel in Paris. In response to contemporary concerns about tuberculosis, the main goal of Rey's proposal was to introduce architectural strategies that would enhance urban ventilation, an ambition that is reflected in Rey's words: "L'air est devenu le premier élément dont vit l'habitat."[24] In his proposal, Rey refused to resort to the traditional closed courtyard massing strategy and instead proposed fragmented housing layouts designed to promote urban ventilation and access of fresh air to the communal areas as well as to all rooms in the residential units. Rey's entry for the Rothschild

22. G. Eiffel, *The Resistance of Air, and Aviation: Experiments Conducted at the Champ de Mars Laboratory* (London: Constable & Co., 1913).

23. The "Habitations à bon marché" from 1894 is the first French law on social housing, and is considered the first in the world.

24. C. Simonnet, *Breve histoire de l'air* (Versailles, France: Quae, 2014).

Gustave Eiffel's private apartment in the Eiffel Tower
Analysis of force of wind load on the Eiffel Tower

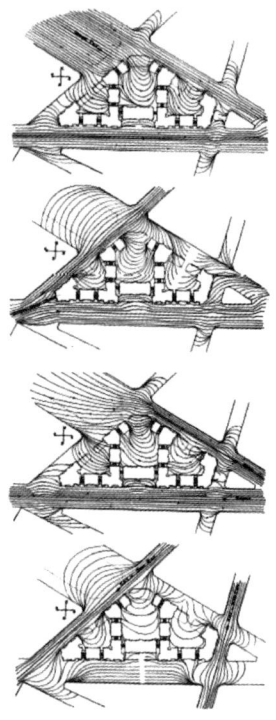 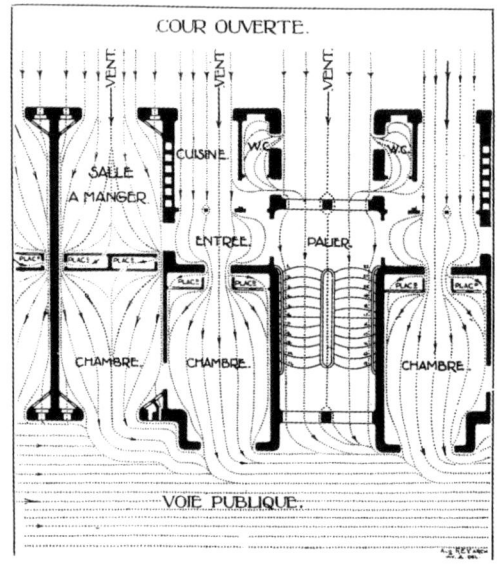

Foundation competition proposed an aerodynamic urban block design. In his diagrams, all overlaid with airflow streamlines and arrows, Rey describes the interaction of the proposed block layouts with variable angles of attack to argue that the proposal would enable a ventilated urban environment no matter what the predominant wind direction would be.

While the urban and household ventilation considerations of Augustin Rey's entry were welcomed by the jurors, the design that was ultimately constructed suffered many compromises and ended up resembling the traditional courtyard typology. Possibly, the lack of understanding of the phenomena of airflow and the impossibility of introducing an analytic strategy to quantify the influence of the building's geometry on neighboring air quality prohibited Rey from proposing a detailed argument. Once again, Rey's proposal resorted to a reduction of building units to enhance building permeability to airflow. Not surprisingly, this criterion produced friction with the speculative forces that urban areas were subject to, and compromised the suggested strategies to promote urban ventilation.

Augustin Rey's Rothschild competition entry. Airflow diagrams showing variable angles of attack
Augustin Rey's Rothschild competition entry. Interior space ventilation

From A. Rey, "Concours de la Fondation Rothschild: etudes preliminaries des plans—determination du parti adopte par la question de ventilation generale," *L'Architecture: journal hebdomadaire de la societe centrale des architectes francais* 18(36) (1905). Reprinted in E. Ramirez, *Airs of Modernity* (Princeton: Princeton University, 2013)

As opposed to airflow analysis, the geometrical representation of sun rays, as well as the physical understanding of the phenomena of sunlight from an architectural and urban design perspective, enabled sunlight considerations to be analytically studied and subsequently incorporated in architectural design processes as well as in the formulation of urban policies. The phenomena of airflow, on the other hand, cannot yet be resolved analytically. Therefore, airflow in architectural drawings has generally either been introduced as a qualitative atmospheric representation or through diagrammatic sketches.

Lewis Leeds, lithographs of a glass room showing the qualitative effects of stale air

Thus, given the lack of analytic tools for airflow analysis in urban areas, the formulation of detailed architectural-scale measures to improve urban ventilation has been historically problematic. Instead, general strategies such as the reduction of F.A.R (Floor Area Ratio) or limitations to the block consolidation were suggested. While sun ray studies offered concrete guidelines that could be more easily implemented at an architectural level, urban ventilation proposals compromised building density, and so limited the chances to prevail over the social and economic pressures that were favoring dense cities. Therefore, although an intuitive understanding of the phenomenon has been present since ancient times, criteria to favor strategies such as street ventilation were generally ignored because the effect of such strategies couldn't be quantified.

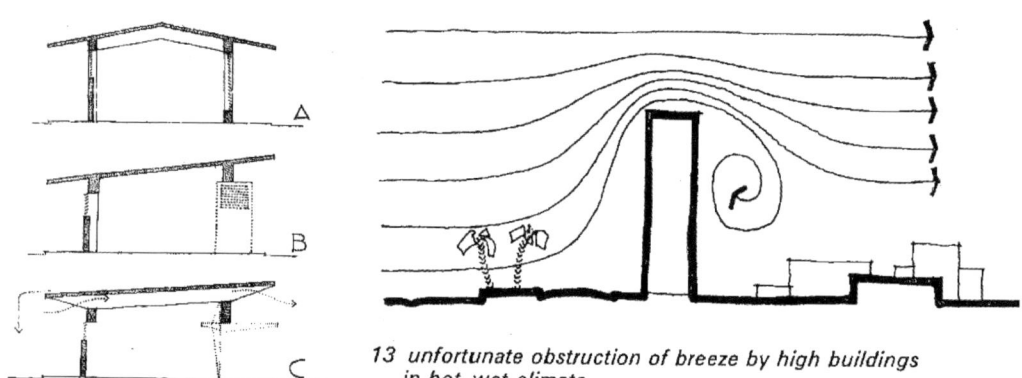

13 unfortunate obstruction of breeze by high buildings in hot-wet climate

IN SEARCH OF EVIDENCE ON AIR QUALITY

The scientific search for evidence on the interaction between architecture and local air quality has been ongoing since the nineteenth century. Meteorologist Luke Howard's pioneering 1838 work *The Climate of London*, mentioned earlier, reflected upon urban pollution based on meteorological records. Albert Kratzer's seminal publication *Das Stadtklima* from 1937 also offered a comprehensive description of the relationship between urban characteristics and urban climatology.[25] His standpoint was shared by succeeding peers such as Helmut Landsberg, who emphasized the benefits of introducing microclimatic considerations in architectural design processes: "One of the surest ways of improving the performance of individual buildings and

---

25. A. Kratzer, *Das Stadtklima* (Braunschweig, Germany: Vieweg & Sohn, 1937).

Sketches from Richard Neutra on school room ventilation. From R. Neutra, *Architecture of Social Concern in Regions of Mild Climate* (Sao Paulo: Gerth Todtmann, 1948)
Maxwell Fry and Jane Drew described the disadvantageous conditions (lack of ventilation) produced behind large buildings

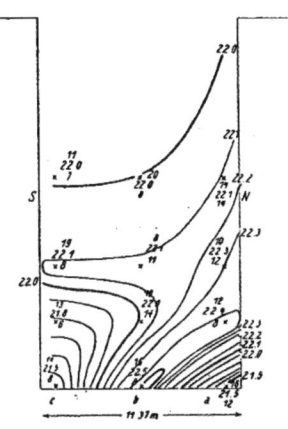 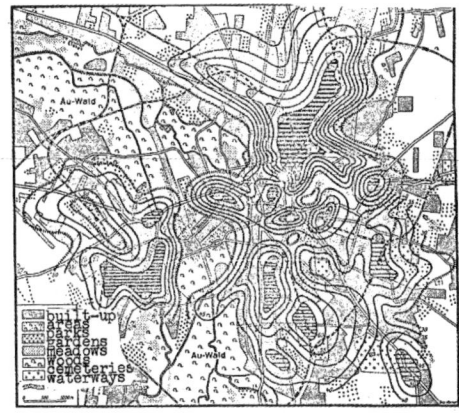

Temperature distribution in a courtyard in Berlin-Charlottenburg, July 27, 1931, 6 p.m.

The colder air at the lower left and right is outgoing cellar air, i.e., from the entrance to the courtyard. One can see very clearly the effect of the house wall which is in the sun (N) [3, 96].

whole cities, would be to incorporate microclimatic knowledge into their design […] buildings should blend harmoniously with the visible landscape but they should also recognize the invisible but important configuration of their microclimate."[26] That is, the role architecture plays in its surrounding microclimate must be acknowledged.

Today, investigations on the influence of urban structures on local pollution levels are confirming the strong dependence of local air quality on the neighboring architectural parameters.[27] However, given the uncertainties associated with numerical simulations and wind tunnel experiments, as well as the ongoing lack of a sufficiently extensive body of research on the topic, the results are yet to be validated against field experimental data. There is thus a growing need for urban meteorological data to support air pollution research and management. Nevertheless, urban weather stations are generally costly to implement and rarely provide sufficient information on neighborhood- and street-scale microclimate and air quality.[28] Therefore, while the number

26. H. E. Landsberg, "Microclimatology," *Architectural Forum* 86(3) (1947): 114–9.

27. Britter and Hanna, "Flow and Dispersion in Urban Areas."

28. Oke, "Siting and Exposure of Meteorological Instruments at Urban Sites."

Temperature distribution in a courtyard in Berlin, Charlottenburg, July 27, 6 p.m.
Dust distribution in Leipzig

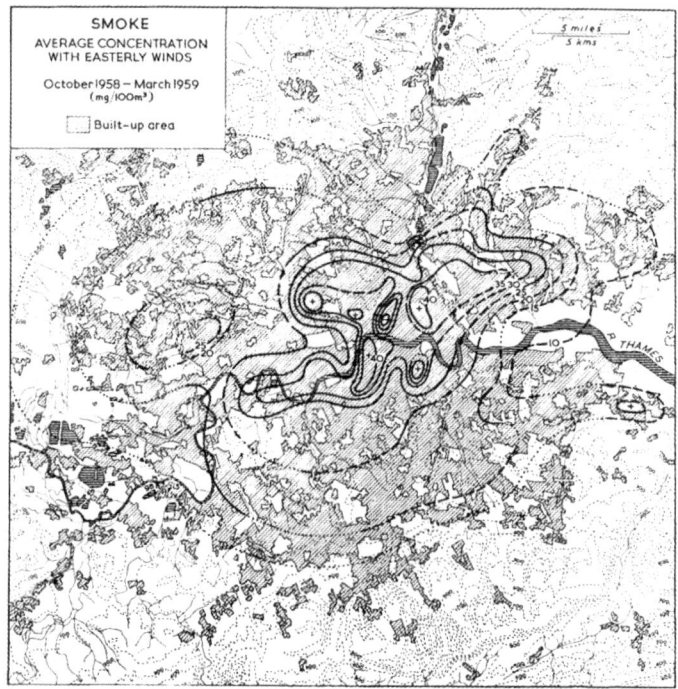

of weather stations for measuring urban air quality is growing, the space resolution obtained from these networks is generally insufficient to analyze the effect of architecture on urban microclimates and air quality. This means that when operating at the building and neighborhood scale, or when data is required for specific sites, weather stations generally provide the necessary temporal resolution to capture the steady and unsteady flow characteristics; however, the spatial resolution of the data obtained from weather stations generally proves insufficient.

In recent years, with advancements in sensor technologies, it has become possible to acquire environmental data at fine spatial and temporal resolution. In upcoming years, it is expected that vast quantities of data will be gathered by autonomous sensors that will cover large spatial extents. That is, with the spread of the Internet of Things (IoT) and the availability of relatively cheap meteorological sensors, it will become increasingly possible to observe the spatial pattern of atmospheric variables with much more detail than in the past.

In this context, aiming for a higher acquisition of spatial air quality data, the use of sensor networks and remote sensing technologies is becoming more widespread. Furthermore, the increasing accessibility of easy-to-use and low-cost sensors is also motivating citizens to engage with urban

Map of the average smoke concentration over the City of London

sensing projects through citizen science initiatives, as well as promoting their incorporation in everyday objects. And thus our capacity to understand the phenomena of airflow to an increasingly higher spatio-temporal resolution is providing us with the necessary evidence to address the problem of air quality locally and quantitatively. Such data is starting to enable us to prove the effect of architecture and urban features on local microclimates and air quality, and thus to argue for urban- and architecture-scale strategies that can contribute to the remediation of local air quality.

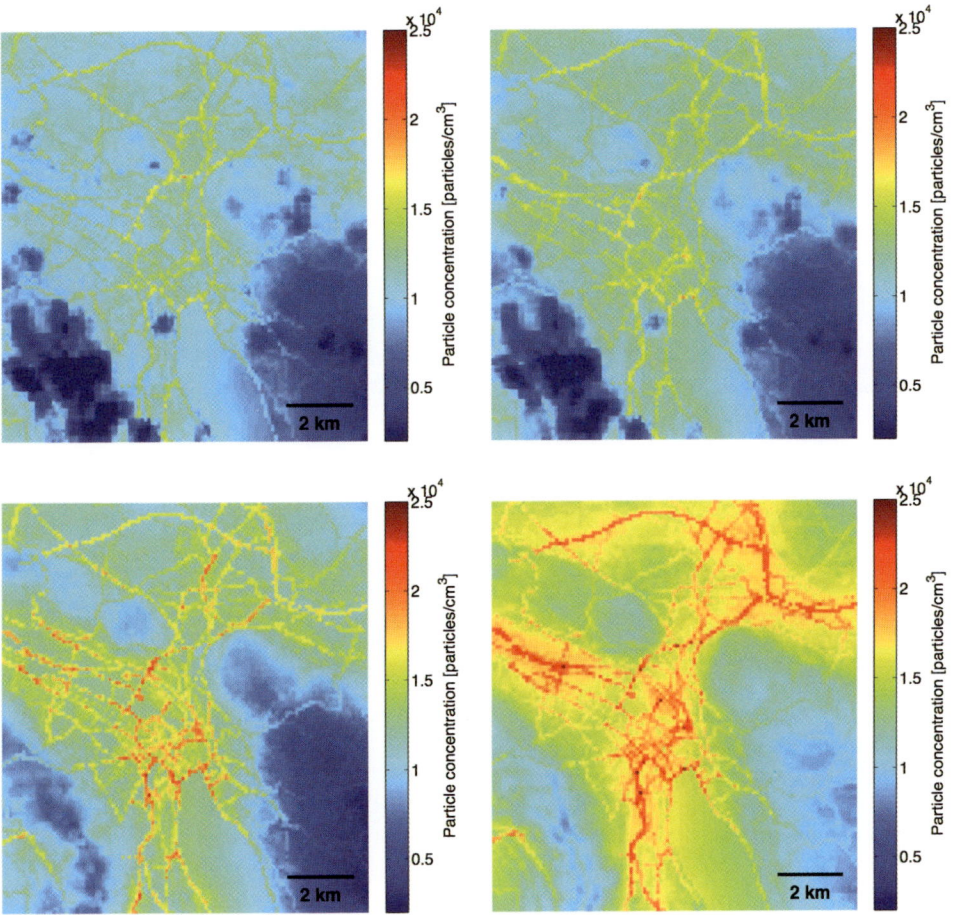

Ultrafine particle concentrations in Zurich, based on the OpenSense measurements of one year (from left to right: spring, summer, fall, winter)

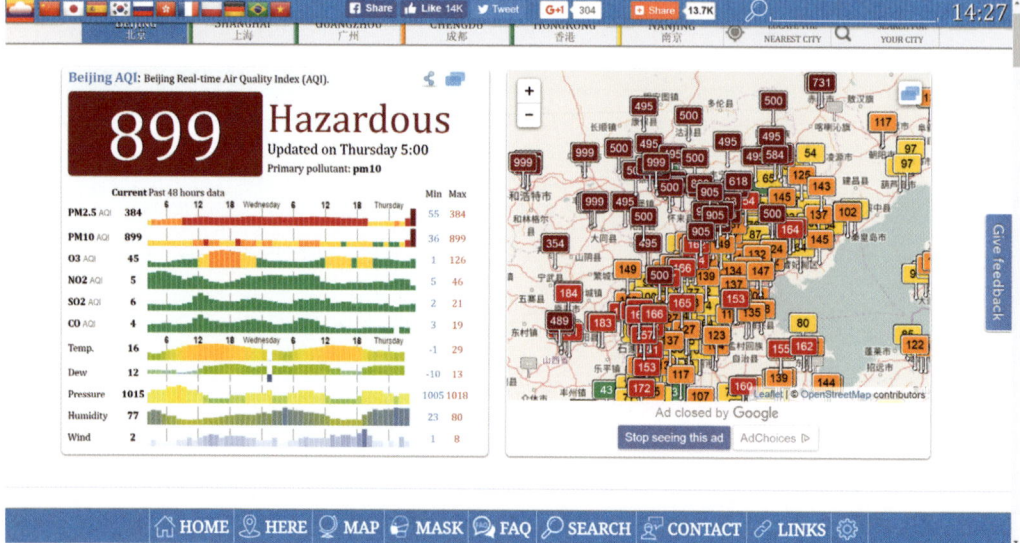

LOCAL RESISTANCE IN THE FACE OF ENVIRONMENTAL DEREGULATION

In the current political situation, where global environmental agendas are often neglected by questioning the validity of international goals, and governmentally funded environmental research is often not made available to the public, it seems critical to empower local urban environmental remediation strategies.

In this context, initiatives such as ICLEI – Local Governments for Sustainability (the global cities network) focus on exploring the possibilities of establishing local governance structures to enable sustainable water, air quality, or urban soil management.

While still rare, air quality assessment regulations that pertain to urban planning and architectural design considerations are also starting to be implemented in some cities, such as Hong Kong.[29] Instead of incorporating top-down and generalized building restrictions, these regulations capitalize on local environmental studies to design architecture and its immediate microclimate

29. E. Ng, "Policies and Technical Guidelines for Urban Planning of High-density Cities: Air Ventilation Assessment (AVA) of Hong Kong," *Building and Environment* 44(7) (2009):1478–88; and E. Ng, "Towards Planning and Practical Understanding of the Need for Meteorological and Climatic Information in the Design of High-density Cities: A Case-based Study of Hong Kong," *International Journal of Climatology* 32(4) (2012): 582–98.

Aqicn.org sensed air quality data for the city of Beijing

cohesively. Further strategies to improve the thermal environment and pollutant concentration in cities via cool roofs and green roofs are also being researched and deployed.[30]

Strategies at the building scale are also starting to be revisited. Today buildings are subject to local-scale environmental assessment proposals. That is, in order to obtain building permit or planning approval, environmental assessment processes that involve the fulfilment of a building certification system such as LEED also must be undertaken. Once again, given the complexity of airflow phenomena, such international certification processes often fail to incorporate airflow considerations in their rating processes. And thus, the need to complement such global assessment structures with locally informed microclimate strategies is starting to be discussed.

Citizen science initiatives are also beginning to reframe the role of citizens in environmental policy making. Especially in city- and neighborhood-scale initiatives, citizen science and participatory democracy mechanisms are enabling the empowerment of communities by involving them in research as well as in local political debate.[31]

While the results obtained from locally driven air quality policies are still to be seen, in times when high-level governance bodies are failing to undertake the steps required to heal the insalubrious air quality conditions present in many cities around the world, local action becomes critical. And thus, local power relationships must be established in the air common.

---

30. T. Susca, S. R. Gaffin, and G. R. Dell'Osso, "Positive Effects of Vegetation: Urban Heat Island and Green Roofs," *Environmental Pollution* 159(8–9) (2011): 2119–26.

31. K. Rowland, "Citizen Science Goes 'Extreme,'" *Nature* (2012).

LAGOS by Heinrich-Böll-Stiftung

WATER

Global warming and climate change are not only distorting traditional climate patterns, but also reshaping the earth itself. While rising sea levels are expected to have a massive impact on cities around the world in the coming decades, their impact is already being felt through disasters and plummeting real estate values.[1] Urban waterfronts and riverfronts, traditionally key territories of urban life, are now threatened by climate change, but the lack of access to clean water for urban populations is a growing humanitarian problem too: by 2050, a third of the people on earth may lack a clean, secure source of water. Of the resource-based commons, none is so intimately tied to urban ecologies as water. Cities grew in the proximity of adequate water supply, and the first urban policies appeared in relation to the use of water: the Hammurabi Code included provisions for the distribution of water based on the area of the fields farmed, dictated responsibilities for farmers to maintain canals, and distributed administration responsibilities for canals. Cities function like a mediator between water-dependent organisms—humans— and hydrological cycles driven by the evaporation, condensation, collection, and flow of water.

One of the primary responsibilities of a city is to provide infrastructure to deliver potable water to its citizens. The Roman Empire was famous for its aqueducts and initiated the idea that providing free, clean water to all urban citizens was a right. Citizens need clean water to survive, and providing it as a free resource to public areas was a governmental responsibility. These extremely complex networks of water infrastructure were massive investments for the Roman Empire.

1. See Laura Parker, "Climate Change Economics," *National Geographic* (May 2016).

Equally important to the health of a city is the ability to remove large amounts of water supplied by rains and flooding, but also that produced by human waste. Ancient Mesopotamian, Greek, and Chinese cities all had extensive drainage networks, typically composed of ditches or channels that ran next to the streets to direct water.[2] Romans improved and advanced these technologies, developing drainage layers under roads, curbs, elevated sidewalks, under-street sewers, and gutters.[3] The central sewer in Rome, the *Cloaca Maxima*, and the system of *cloacae* which fed it, was originally designed to drain the swampy area between the hills of the city.[4]

Until the mid-twentieth century, it was considered perfectly acceptable for sewers to carry off untreated sewage directly into water systems such as rivers, lakes, and oceans. In the United States, it was not until the Water Pollution Control Act of 1952 and the Clean Water Act of 1972 that sewage treatment plants became required by law around major metropolitan areas, wherever sewage flowed into water supplies. Because these sewage plants required large amounts of energy and resources to properly function, it became the norm for cities to develop a double sewer system to keep storm water away from sewage water and prevent the sanitation plant from having to treat all the water that flows through a city.

The expedient removal of household waste from cities and away from underground aquifers was responsible for significant reductions of disease in cities. Indeed, the development of centralized sewer systems for waste removal in cities was far more influential to the history of urbanism than any architectural or planning achievement, as significant increases in the average lifespan and wellbeing of urban populations

2. S. J. Burian et al., "Historical Development of Wet-Weather Flow Management," *Journal of Water Resources Planning and Management (ASCE)* 125 (1) (1999).

3. D. Hill, *A History of Engineering in Classical and Modern Times* (Beckenham, Eng.: Croom Helm, 1984).

4. David Sedlak, *Water 4.0: The Past, Present, and Future of the World's Most Vital Resource* (New Haven: Yale University Press, 2014).

were achieved almost immediately after every historical water treatment campaign, from the introduction of the sand filter to chlorination to government subsidization of sewage treatment plants.

Due to the growing scale of urban populations in the nineteenth century, human waste began to be seen as a valuable resource for agriculture, rich in nitrogen and phosphorus that could be used as fertilizer. In *Das Kapital*, Karl Marx bemoaned the enormous waste produced by the capitalist economy and described "excretions of consumption" as holding the "greatest importance for agriculture."[5] Marx described the city of London as having no better use for the excrement of its massive population than to contaminate its own river, the Thames. In fact, around this time in the nineteenth century, the cities of London and Paris were wondering what to do with their human waste, and the city of London commissioned Sir Edwin Chadwick to find a solution to excessive pollution in the Thames River. Probably inspired by the work of Justus von Liebig,[6] Chadwick proposed to pipe sewage from London to sewer farms outside the city. The goal was to take advantage of the sewage as a nutrient-rich resource.[7] However, due to the expense of this solution, the city decided to simply dump its waste further downstream from the city.[8] Paris, on the other hand, was able to implement a nutrient-reuse system similar to Chadwick's plan for London. Engineers proposed a sewage farming system which could utilize the city's human waste to produce fertilizers: beginning in 1889,

5. P. Burkett, *Marx and Nature: A Red and Green Perspective* (New York: St. Martin's, 1999).

6. The early-nineteenth-century German chemist Justus von Liebig is credited with founding the discipline of organic chemistry as well as creating the modern fertilizer industry, as he identified nitrogen, phosphorus, and potassium as the essential nutrients for plant growth. Liebig also popularized the Law of the Minimum, which establishes that the growth of plant matter is controlled by the scarcest resource available rather than by the total amount of resources, demonstrating the need for careful management of nutrients in agriculture. See William H. Brock, *Justus von Liebig: The Chemical Gatekeeper*, 1st ed. (Cambridge, U.K.: Cambridge University Press, 1997).

7. Cooper, "Historical Aspects of Wastewater Treatment," in Piet Lens, Piet N. L. Lens, Grietje Zeeman, and Gatze Lettinga, eds., *Decentralised Sanitation and Reuse: Concepts, Systems and Implementation* (London: IWA Publishing, 2001).

8. Sedlak, *Water 4.0: The Past, Present, and Future of the World's Most Vital Resource.*

sewage farms were built along the banks of the Seine to grow crops such as cabbage, artichokes, and sugar beets.[9] The Parisian engineers were aware of the process through which sewage could become purified through percolation through the soil. Thus, the sewage farms served not only as a nutrient delivery system for agriculture, but also as a primitive water-purification system in which microbes in the soil could remove some of the contaminants from the water before it made its way to the Seine.[10] In order to dispose of the sewage generated by thousands of people through sewage farming, about 2.5 acres was required, necessitating massive hinterlands around a city simply to dispose of its daily waste.[11] This solution was unfortunately limited to Paris in its implementation because the city had the farmland that was required to dispose of the waste of a very large population.

This very limitation of needing expanses of land was what drove the treatment of sewage away from its use as a fertilizer, and triggered the development of mechanical and chemical systems of purification. At the turn of the twentieth century, in an attempt to replicate and control the process through which percolation through soil purified water, scientists began researching biofilms that developed in gravel and sand filters. The goal was to harness the power of microbes to reduce the footprint of natural purification processes, significantly accelerate these processes, and apply them at the urban scale.[12] Because rivers near cities were suffering from oxygen depletion due to microbe growth caused by sewage dumping, these sewage treatment systems were systematically applied to cities in Europe and North America throughout the twentieth century. In 1948, the United States Government passed

9. Ibid., 38.

10. Ibid., 39.

11. G. E. Waring, "Out of Sight, Out of Mind," *Century Illustrated Magazine* (1894).

12. Two main approaches characterized the sewage filtration technology developed in the 20th century. The first was the trickling filter, a gravel pit onto which sewage was applied and through which the sewage drained. The other system works by bubbling air through sewage in order to oxidize reduced compounds without the need for an attached biofilm, requiring much less space in order to complete the purification cycle.

the Water Pollution Control Act. When this act was reauthorized by Congress in 1956, it began providing financial support for sewage treatment plant construction and expanded its enforcement of water standards.

With urban growth, groundwater became more and more contaminated, creating a demand for rapid water purification. MIT engineers discovered that sand filters using aluminum sulfate, inventing a fast and reliable water treatment system.[13] This "rapid sand filtration," developed around the turn of the twentieth century, is still the most common method for purifying water and preventing the spread of waterborne diseases in cities, and very quickly led to an increase in life expectancy. In the first half of the twentieth century, the average life expectancy of Americans increased from forty-seven to sixty-three years, and approximately half of that increase has been attributed to the treatment of drinking water.[14]

Centralized water purification and sewage treatment systems allowed modern cities to flourish, greatly increasing populations, human health, and average lifespans. However, overreliance on centralized systems has come to threaten water security. Additionally, there is a threshold of efficiency for centralized systems which is often overreached. Large amounts of energy are dedicated to sending water through extensive, corroded pipe networks. The energy required to pump water along these huge, centralized systems accounts for around 25% of the energy used after water reaches the treatment plant.[15] On the other hand, the decentralization of urban water infrastructure allows a city to consume less energy and become more resilient, and it may also diminish the costs of water infrastructure: for example, London's Thames Tideway Scheme, a 25km tunnel running out of London which will capture

---

13. Sedlak, *Water 4.0*, 54.

14. D. Cutler and G. Miller, "The Role of Public Health Improvements in Health Advances: The Twentieth-Century United States," *Demography* 42, no. 1 (2005).

15. Electric Power Research Institute, *Water and Sustainability*.

and transport the sewage and rainwater discharges that currently dump into the Thames River during floods, has a cost estimate of 4.2 billion pounds. Once completed, water utility customers in London will be charged a monthly fee for use of the tunnel. This singular water management solution allows for a universal taxation on its use, as opposed to distributed systems which could target problematic areas, but which may not be as easily distributed.

Yet, distributed systems, which rely on small-scale water purification, greywater reuse, and small-scale bioreactors for waste and drinking water treatment, are becoming increasingly appealing options for water purification, as they consume much less energy. The relationship between energy and water runs deep in the history of urbanism and civilization itself. At first, the kinetic energy in flowing water itself was harnessed to perform work such as turning mills or even lifting water. In contemporary water systems, the energy of water is still captured in hydroelectric power plants; however significant energy resources are also dedicated to pressurizing water, filtering water, and lifting water. Water is used as a coolant for coal or nuclear energy plants. The relationship between important resources of power plants and water purification systems has formed a complex material entanglement which is embodied in all water-to-energy and energy-to-water infrastructures.

But water is also critical for cities in other ways. The hydrologic cycle of cities involves more than preventing damage from rising sea levels. Water retention for urban comfort, water collection, and water treatment systems are equally important areas of development for urban water infrastructure. Water is a crucial element of the urban microclimate. For example, Los Angeles is facing serious droughts while also experiencing inundations of rainwater. The city's flood prevention system directs all the rainwater dumped on the city out to sea rather than into groundwater aquifers where it could be reclaimed and added to drinking water reserves. Because of the large amount of impervious surfaces in the city (especially asphalt), the earth is parched even while experiencing inundations of rainwater. Meanwhile, Singapore, whose water problems can be thought of as a microcosm for an even more heavily urbanized future earth, has evolved into a city of high porosity by building seventeen reservoirs and a sophisticated urban drainage system designed to increase the amount of time that water spends within its borders. In addition to expanding the country's effective catchment area by 10,000 hectares, it also provides a barrier to seawater intrusion from sea level rise and extreme storm events.

Cities modify radically hydrologic cycles. Because the earth is paved over in urban areas to create buildings, roads, parking lots, and other surfaces, the way water runs off the land during flood events has been dramatically altered. The earth that used to absorb water and slowly return it to aquifers has been covered with impervious surfaces, making more water run through the permeable areas. This greater volume of water flow has led to soil erosion, periods of drought and flood, and high-velocity water flows which can strip away earth and destabilize foundations, the walls of watercourses, and living matter. The erosion of sediments from the walls of streams reverberates through ecosystems with a compounding effect: as more sediment is carried away by the water, these sediments scour the bottom of streams, making them deeper, which then further destabilizes their walls, exacerbating the problem.[16] As a tangential effect, vegetation around the edge of the stream is destroyed, affecting the whole ecology of species living within the stream.

New strategies for designing large paved surfaces with permeable or planted areas to absorb and slow the flow of water are becoming common in the United States and Europe. "Low-Impact Development," "Sustainable Urban Drainage Systems," and "Water-Sensitive Urban Design" are some of the practices developed to retain runoff from rainstorms. These all aim to use soil and vegetation to solve urban

16. Sedlak, *Water 4.0*, 128.

drainage problems and reduce harmful runoff by respecting the existing drainage patterns in areas that are being developed. The ecological repercussions of water runoff around human habitation are finally beginning to be incorporated into planning technologies that are not so univocally driven toward the satisfaction of human needs. The replacement of impervious/non-osmotic pavements—such as asphalt surfaces covering a large percentage of urban land—the introduction of bioswales, the recovery of buried streams within cities, or the development of water-retaining materials for building envelopes, are some of the current possibilities for urban practices likely to change the landscape of future cities toward decentralized water systems.[17]

17. National Geographic *Water: A Special Issue* Accessed 10/05/2016. http://ngm.nationalgeographic.com/2010/04/table-of-contents/.

DISSIDENT WATER
Lindsay Bremner

INTRODUCTION

The discovery of gold on the Witwatersrand in South Africa in 1886 gave rise to the exploitation of the world's largest gold reserves. This turned the earth inside out, inaugurating new associations of air and earth, science and politics, humans and nonhumans. Very rapidly, these relations were organised into two apparently distinct realms: an above-ground world of capital, labour, commerce, politics, and culture (the city) and a below-ground world of minerals, rocks, and science (geology). Cartographic representations constructed these two worlds as separate and as having little if any relation to one another, while for those who worked underground, of course, geology was palpable and felt in the body. Nevertheless, it was not until rising acid mine water, a toxic by-product of mining operations separated, or dissented, from the underground place assigned to it and rose to the earth's surface, that geology became a vibrant force in the political life of the city.

This essay lays out the consequences of this liquid intrusion of the underground into above-ground affairs. It echoes Maria Kaika's critique of modernity in *City of Flows, Modernity, Nature and the City* (2005), in which she argued that when a city's invisible networks such as storm water drains, electrical conduits, or Internet cables malfunction, the "contradictions of the commodification of nature by multiple socio-ecological processes of domination/subordination and exploitation/repression that feed the capitalist urbanisation processes" are exposed (Kaika 2005: 49). My essay argues that acid mine water not only made the commodification of nature visible and generated protest on its behalf, it also opened up possibilities for new modes of political, spatial, and aesthetic practice. I make this argument by aligning Jacques Ranciere's (1999) notion of *politics* as occasions when those who previously had no right to be counted as speaking beings demand to be heard, with Bruno Latour's (1999, 2004) notion of a *proposition* as an occasion when entities, human or nonhuman, bring about conditions of uncertainty, mobilising collectives in search of articulation.

THE POLITICS OF DISSIDENCE

Ranciere identifies the foundation of politics as the staging of conflict over the distribution of bodies: "those that one sees and those that one does not see, those who have a logos— memorial speech, an account to be kept up—and those who have no logos, those who really speak and those whose voice merely mimics the articulate voice to express pleasure or pain" (Ranciere 1999: 22). He illustrates this with a story by Livy, retold by Pierre-Simon Ballanche, of the secession of the Roman plebeians on Aventine Hill. Faced with a situation in which they were denied symbolic enrolment in the city, the plebeians established another parallel order by conducting themselves as speaking beings who shared the same properties as those who denied them their voices. In doing so, they found that they too were endowed with intelligent speech and were the equals of those in higher power. This violated the space of the city and gave them a place in the symbolic order of speaking beings. Politics exists, Ranciere argues, when those who "have no right to be counted as speaking beings make themselves of some account, setting up a community by the fact of placing in common a wrong that is nothing more than this very confrontation, the contradiction of two worlds in a single world: the world where they are and the world where they are not, the world where there is something between them and those who do not acknowledge them as speaking beings" (Ranciere 1999: 27).

For Ranciere, politics belongs by definition to human subjects; nonhumans do not qualify to participate in the demos, for the disruption of a symbolic order must be accompanied by engagement in reasoned discourse. Bennett (2010) challenges this view, arguing that Ranciere's model suggests possibilities for a more vital materialist account of democracy. Nonhumans, she argues, are able to act or argue against the partitioning of the sensible and catalyse a public able to engage, on their behalf, in reasoned discourse. Ranciere seems to hint at this in his discussion of questions of identification and representation, of who speaks for whom and how this is interpreted in political discourse. In this arrangement, the third person is essential. Politics is never a simple dialogue between two equal parties, but rather a situation where their very equality as speaking beings is at stake. Politics arises when the distinction between who speaks and who does not speak is uncertain, thus "creating a stage around any specific conflict on which the equality or inequality as speaking beings of the partners in the conflict can be played out" (Ranciere 1999: 51).

For Latour (1999, 2004), this is the idea to make relations between humans and nonhumans. He replaces the opposition between nature as mute objects and society as speaking subjects with the idea of human and nonhuman "actants," or "propositions," which "are not positions, things, substances or essences, made up of mute objects facing a talkative human mind, but occasions given to different entities to enter into contact" (Latour 1999: 141). Propositions are associations of humans and nonhumans before they are fully articulated or constituted as members of a collective. Through contact over the course of an event, propositions perform in certain ways, their definitions are modified, and their attributes and competencies in relation to one another are played out. While he expressly denies equivalence between human and nonhuman propositions, writing, "Inanimate things, do you then have a soul? Perhaps not; but a politics, surely" (Latour 2004: 87), Latour establishes an equivalence between them. The door is thus opened for nature to enter the political arena and for political life to be reformulated. The nonhuman becomes a "scandal at the heart of an assembly that carries on a discussion requiring a judgment brought in common" (54).

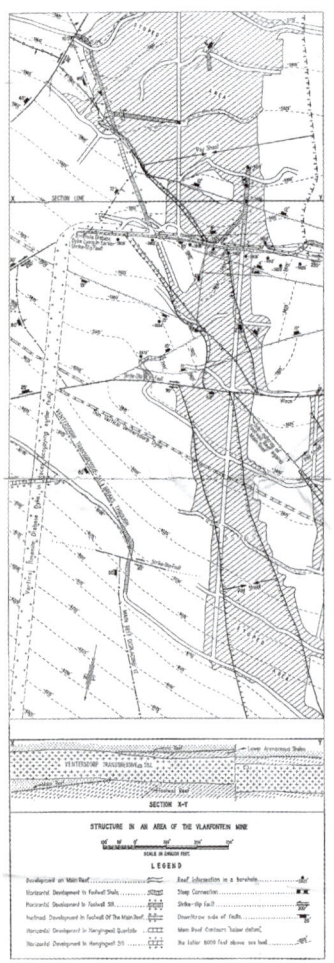

It is these conceptions of the political that rising acid mine water, by decanting, staged. While it was underground, its politics were only immanent; by dissenting from its spatial disposition, by gaining visibility and materially entering the world of human affairs, it became a proposition, mobilising heterogeneous publics to speak on its behalf and laying out new political, spatial, and aesthetic agendas.

GOLD MINING AS A REGIME OF INVISIBILITY

The act of wresting minerals form the earth has historically required the subjugation and the demeaning of both nature and humankind, as faceless pairs of hands and unseen labouring backs descend into the dark, inhuman hell of tunnels to strip away the organs of nature. (Mumford 1934 in Bridge 2009: 45)

The transformation of the underground into a frontier for capital accumulation is both an unimaginable technological feat and an unprecedented debasement of humans and nonhumans alike. The deep-level South African gold mine is one of the most extreme forms of this exploitation of nature. It is a vast infrastructural network of shafts, tunnels, pumping stations, conduits, vents, pipes, ropes, and cables that continuously move water, air, electricity, dynamite, equipment, ore, and people between surface and depth.

Section through the Vlakfontein gold mine, Nigel, East Rand, South Africa

Underground, humans drill holes into the walls of narrow, inclined stopes using hand-held machines, exposing their bodies to heat, silica dust, and other toxins. Rock faces are dynamited. Fractured ore is gathered and dropped down ore-passes, then hauled by rail or truck to shafts where it is hoisted to the surface. Here it is crushed, milled to dust, and dissolved in a solution of cyanide. Zinc or carbon is added to the solution to precipitate gold, which is then smelted and purified. The waste generated by this process is discharged onto slimes dams—vast metabolic mountains of toxic sludge that leach into groundwater and emit radioactive contaminants into the air. For the broad public, the underground and mining processes are visible only in the form of these slimes dams piled up on the surface of the earth and the mineshafts that mark thresholds into the underground. In South Africa, such invisibility was enhanced by a number of mechanisms, including the allocation of rights (the law) and the representation of space, (cartography).

Before the discovery of gold, the Zuid-Afrikaansche Republiek (ZAR)'s *grontwet* (ground law) gave ownership of any minerals found under a piece of land to the owner of that land; mining

Slimes Dam, Soweto, South Africa
Mine headgear, Randfontein, South Africa

these minerals was permitted without permission from the state. However, by the time gold was discovered on the Witwatersrand in 1886, a policy of state control over mining through proclamation had been instituted. This meant that once the precious metal was discovered, a piece of land was proclaimed a goldfield. This gave the state control (not ownership) over the land and its underground minerals, and licensing provisions entitled the state to grant a title (a *mynpachtbrief*) to a third party to mine the land. The landowner retained ownership over the land and its minerals until they had been severed from the earth, when they became the property of the party that had mined them. This preserved the common-law rights of land and mineral ownership, while those with the skills, expertise, and capital to mine gold were given the rights and incentives to do so (Stott 2008). This allocation of extractive rights as separate from land rights established the relations of production underpinning the modern South African political economy and the legal, governmental, and cartographic practices that supported it (Van Onselen 1982a, 1982b).

In 1886, the city of Johannesburg came into being as a mining town on a triangular site at the centre of the eight farms that had been proclaimed as public diggings after gold had been discovered. This site was called an *Uitvalgrond*, an Afrikaans word meaning "surplus ground," the definition the ZAR gave to land leftover between farm portions whose perimeters were determined by the distance a farmer could ride in a day from his or her farmstead. The surplus ground that became the city of Johannesburg was crossed by a line of mining claims in the south and was therefore considered by the ZAR to be a mining camp, managed by the state through a Mining Commissioner and a Diggers Committee. The state granted *Voorkeurrechte*, or preferential rights, for use of its urban stands in much the same way that it granted *mynpachtbriefe* to mine for gold. This meant that the city and the mine were part of a legal, institutional, and spatial continuum. In December 1887, however, Johannesburg was given permission to elect a Sanitary Board, and in 1897 it was granted a limited form of municipal government (Beavon 2004). This inaugurated the legislative separation of town and mine, consolidated from 1900 onwards, when the British occupied the city and granted formal municipal powers (Beavon 2004). From then on, the city was subjected to one legislative regime and mining to another.

This schism is apparent in two maps dating from 1897. In the first, titled *Plan of Johannesburg City and Suburbs*, street grids, railway lines, and townships clearly designate a town in the making. One can read the faint register of the original *uitvalgrond* triangle, but the city has already exceeded this boundary, spreading east and west along a valley and northwards over the Witwatersrand ridge. Early signs of the future racialisation of urban space are evident in names like "Coolie Location," "Kafir Location," and "Native Location," though at this time the city was still a site of racial cohabitation (Bremner 2005). South of the city, mines are named and drawn as surface areas, with no registration of their underground topography or even of the location of their shafts or surface workings. A locational map on the bottom left-hand corner of the document omits the mining properties altogether and simply overlays township portions on farm portions. The only indication that this was a mining town is a table in the bottom right-hand corner that shows quantities of gold produced between 1887 and 1897.

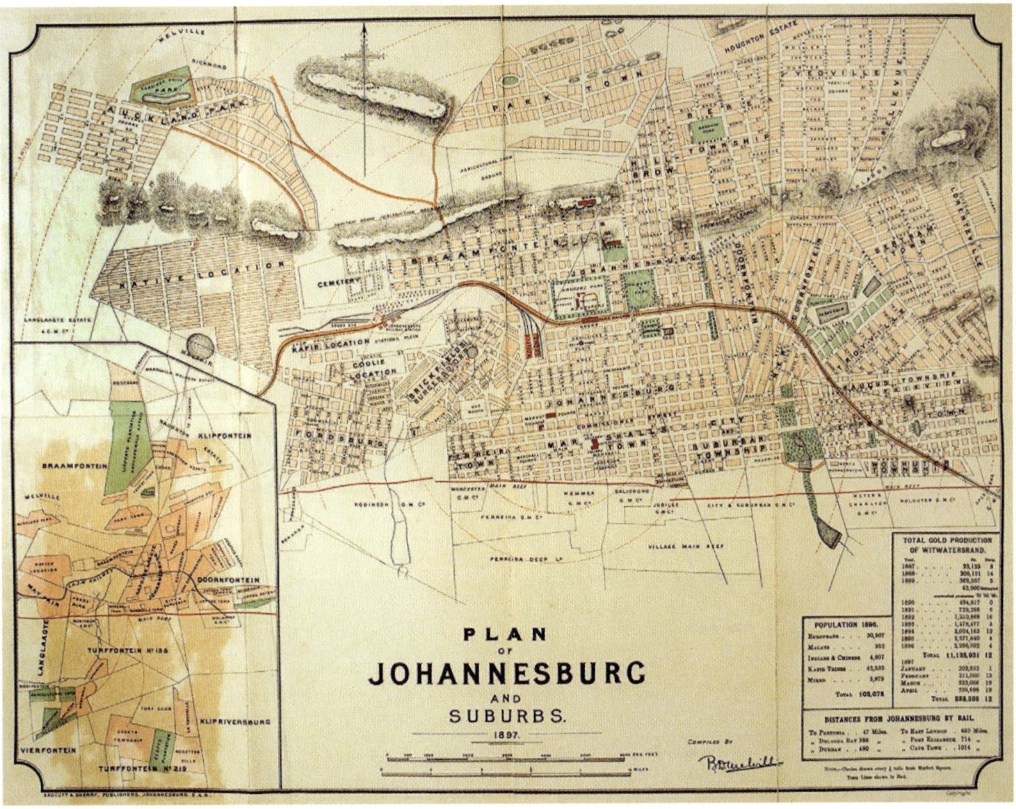

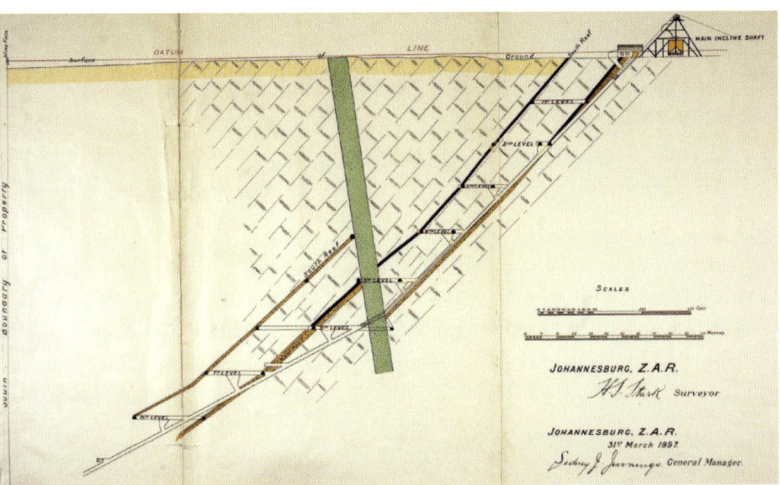

Plan of Johannesburg and Suburbs, 1897. William Cullen Library, University of the Witwatersrand, Johannesburg
Johannesburg Z.A.R, 31st March 1897

The second map, titled *Johannesburg, Z.A.R.* is a sectional drawing of a mine, which shows two inclined gold reefs, a geological fault, a mineshaft, and eight underground mining tunnels. No indication of the identity or location of the mine is given other than that it is approaching its southern property boundary. The ground surface is a wavy line subsumed by a firm, level datum from which subterranean levels are plotted. Whereas on the first map the city was only drawn in plan, on the second the mine is only drawn in section. Where mining maps do make use of the plan, as in *A Map of the Witwatersrand Goldfields* published for the *South African Mining Engineering Year Book* of 1927, cities and towns vanish, appearing only as underlined names (i.e., Johannesburg, Benoni, Roodepoort) subsumed by a patchwork of mining claims.

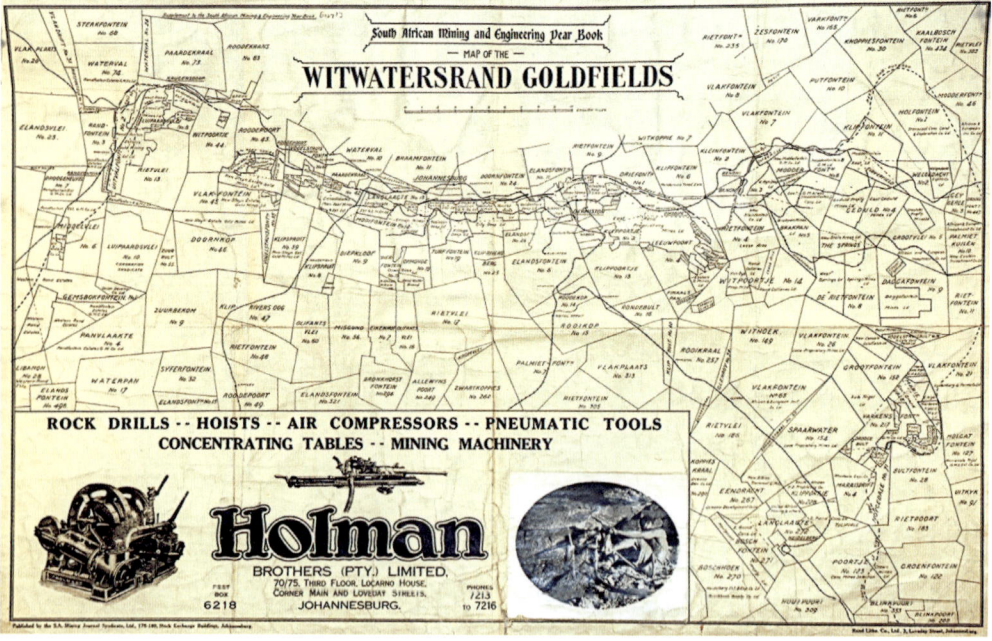

These examples reveal that urban maps and underground maps privilege different views and offer different readings of space, and bear little if any relation to one another. The underground, though extensively surveyed and mapped, was kept firmly out of sight. The above ground was constructed as a tumultuous human world of social re-production: a world of modern economic, political, and social life, mapped and spoken for by artists, administrators, health authorities, legislators, lobbyists, planners, politicians, professionals, unionists, writers, etc. The below ground, on the other hand, was an apparently mute, nonhuman geotechnical world, the province of engineers, professionals, scientists, and seismologists who spoke its recalcitrant depths in the language of measureable data

Map of the Witwatersrand Goldfields, 1927

and scientific fact. Evidence that the two realms existed in "a set of relations in which each relies on the existence of the other, in which they are entwined or enfolded, suggestive of the other, interpenetrating, (though) separating out at different points" (Nuttall 2009: 83) was eradicated.

THE POLITICAL LIFE OF RISING ACID MINE WATER

Water is both indispensable to mining and yet dramatically transformed by it. Early in the history of gold mining in South Africa, water was used primarily for dust suppression after blasting. Mines were shallow enough to be ventilated through airshafts opening directly onto the earth's surface. However, as mines became deeper, air circulation had very little cooling effect, so water began to be used as a coolant. Mines penetrated the aquifer, meaning that operations were effectively taking place under water and voids had to be drained. Water was mediated by and subjected to multiple modes of engineering. A complex network of discourses, practices, technologies, skills, trades, and materials was deployed to alter its behaviour and spatial disposition. It was evaluated, modelled, and tested. Scientific laboratories, associations, and journals were set up to study it, discuss the problems associated with it, evaluate new technologies, and propose more effective ways of managing it. Complex systems of dams and pressure-reducing valves were introduced underground. Later, water was refrigerated on the surface, dropped down shafts, circulated through cooling coils, sprayed onto rock faces, pooled, and then pumped to the surface again. Different types of water, some of which was contaminated by sulphides and other minerals, and other types, which were less contaminated and drove machinery, travelled on their journeys through mines in separate pipes (Stephenson 1983).

On these journeys, water was chemically transformed. Mining introduced oxygen into deep geological environments where it had never been before. This led to the oxidisation of underground minerals, the most widespread of which was pyrite (FeS_2), commonly known as fool's gold. As it oxidized, pyrite produced acids and released heavy metals and sulphates. The water in mine voids leached these out, producing a highly acidic, saline solution. This was compounded by the presence of toxic metals (arsenic, cadmium, copper, cobalt, uranium, and zinc) in mining voids, which were mobilized in the acidic water (Akcil and Koldas 2006). While mines were operational and water levels stabilised by pumping, little pyrite oxidation occurred below them and few metals were leached from above. When mines closed and pumps were turned off, however, contaminants were leached out and water levels rose (Johnson and Hallberg 2005; McCarthy 2010). This is what occurred on the Witwatersrand goldfields after 2002. Mine closures and a number of socio-environmental, legislative, and political recalibrations created the conditions for water to seek its pre-mining piezometric level. Rainwater filled abandoned mine shafts, and unmaintained underground water reticulation systems began to leak. Toxic underground water rose and eventually decanted onto the surface and into the political spotlight. This provided me the opportunity to reflect on the political ecology that had been kept out of sight in the first place, and what new modes of political, spatial, and aesthetic practice it had made possible.

Acid mine water first became visible on the Witwatersrand in 2002, when it decanted from two abandoned mine shafts on the Randfontein Estates Gold Mine west of Johannesburg and flowed via a seasonal stream into a nearby nature reserve. Here it filled a hippo dam, turning its water yellow, and killed all aquatic life in addition to causing a number of animal fatalities. These localised calamities received little attention until media reports in 2005 revealed that the Cradle of Humankind, a significant World Heritage Site just downstream from the game reserve, was under threat of acidic water pollution. At the same time, Robinson Lake, a nearby mine-waste site was found to have water with a pH of 2.0 (equivalent to that of lemon juice or vinegar) along with elevated levels of uranium and heavy metals. The lake was declared a radiation hotspot and fenced off. Nearby, a luxury retirement village was abandoned when it was found to be exposed to radioactive airborne dust, and residents of Tudor Shaft, an informal settlement located on top of a neighbouring mine dump, were found to have inhaled or ingested dangerous amounts of radioactive material (Hervieu 2012; Mathews 2011; National Nuclear Regulator 2010).

By 2010, scientific and political studies on the water's radioactivity, heavy metal content, and archaeological impact, and on communities at risk from radiation and toxicity, had begun to identify the water's attributes and make it more knowable (Dugard et al. 2011; Winde 2009; Oelofse et al. n.d.; Adler and Rasche 2007). Its status and the threats it posed were debated in the public media (Funke et al. 2012; Pressly 2011.). Activists brought the acid mine water and those

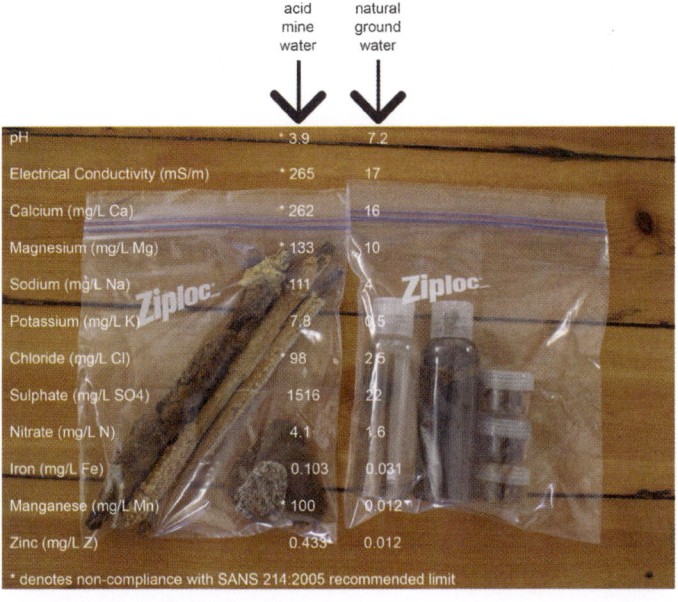

Toxicity of acid mine water. Data source: Oelofse et al. (no date)
Known sites affected by radioactivity on the West Rand, South Africa

Page 96: The polluted Tweelopies Stream, Krugersdorp Municipal Nature Reserve, South Africa
Robinson Lake, Randfontein, South Africa

affected by it to the attention of the public in public fora (Funke et al. 2012); artists visualised its impact on aquifers, dams, crops, and human health (Kritzinger 2012); and architects investigated whether the water could be viewed as a positive economic, political, infrastructural, and cultural proposition (Bremner et al. 2010; Coetser 2012).

What had occurred was that after the water became visible and began to circulate in expanding networks with other actants—streams, hippos, fish, farmers, the media, tour operators, scientists, mining companies, property developers, radioactive monitors, shack dwellers, venture capitalists, artists, architects, and others—uncertainty about its status abounded. Was it about mining, about waste, about water resource management, about air quality, about human health, about economic development, about land values, about legal liability, or about ecological rehabilitation? To whom or to what was it a matter of concern—the government, current mining companies, former mining companies, taxpayers, municipal authorities, shack dwellers, developers, farmers, people who live far downstream, people not yet born? If it was of concern to all of these and more, how did one put together an assembly that spoke a common language to discuss it, account for it, call it to order, assess its contradictory scenarios, and make decisions about how to deal with its consequences? Should this be in parliament, in appointed committees, in public gatherings, in scientific journals, in art galleries, in the media, or all of the above—or more? Its regime of visibility—its yellow and black metallic coating, white salt scum, acidic taste—and its practices—the dead aquatic life it left behind, the pipes it corroded, the itchy skin it produced, its radioactive sludge—mustered a riotous assembly of "policy entrepreneurs" (Turton n.d.: 13) or what Latour (2004) calls spokespeople or witnesses, operating in the spaces opened up in South Africa's post-1994 constitutional, legal, moral, and political environments, to articulate it across multiple registers.

In 2010, the water had become a national political crisis. Towards the end of that year, a Parliamentary Portfolio Committee visited the contaminated sites. A team of scientists was appointed to appraise, assess, and report on the situation. Their report, *Mine Water Management in the Witwatersrand Goldfields with Special Emphasis on Acid Mine Drainage* (South African Council for Geoscience 2010), acknowledged the toxicity of the water and recommended immediate steps to neutralise it, pumping it to prevent surface decant, and a long-term strategy to neutralize acidity and remove salts. A state-owned entity, the Trans-Caledon Tunnel Authority (TCTA), was issued a directive to undertake the pumping, neutralisation, and discharge of the water into the Tweelopies Stream and to dispose of its residual heavy metal sludge into an existing deep surface excavation, the West Wits Pit. Given that the water would still have elevated levels of sulphate, manganese, iron, and uranium—some of these up to 1000% of the South African operational limits (Oelofse et. al n.d.)—and that these heavy metals would continue to leach into aquifers, scientists, farmers, and environmental activists viewed the steps as far from adequate. Voices of dissent were heard at the public meetings conducted as part of an environmental-impact assessment scoping exercise in July 2012. Attendees protested that solutions should be deferred until all entities impacted by the water were gathered into a coherent whole (Personal attendance at a public meeting, July 2012).

The government's subsequent proposal to address the environmental and political problems raised by the acid mine water did not attempt to hold its many entities and propositions together in an all-encompassing spatio-temporal envelope. Instead, it curtailed and rearticulated the water's trajectories and rearticulated by "amicable agreement" (cf. Adler et al. 2007: 34) between just three players—central government departments, select scientists, and state-owned companies. The water's multiplicity of clamorous attendants and associations were silenced and its propositions were translated into technical processes of partial treatment, piping, and discharge, to be conducted in private by certain government officials, engineers, scientists, and company employees. This shedding of its wider gamut of collaborators and associations divested the water of its politics and made it less real (Latour 1999). What it had brought to the surface was channelled into treatment plants, engineering works, and pipes and made to disappear.

CONCLUSION
The dissent of rising acid mine water between 2002 and 2010 in Johannesburg, South Africa, transgressed the institutions, practices, and discourses that had assigned it to its place. It became a "scandal at the heart of an assembly that carried on a discussion requiring a judgment brought in common" (Latour 2004: 54), making visible what apparently had no business being seen, and revealing a discourse where once there was only place for noise (Ranciere 1999: 30). In redistributing geology across the surface of the earth, into the air, and into the metabolism of plants, animals, and humans, the water made what had been invisible (except to those who daily came into contact with it) clearly visible and knowable—not as hidden abstractions or scientific facts, but as forms of above-ground experience and matters of concern. It reorganised surface and depth into a fluid, contested continuum and made it impossible to pretend that what had formerly been distinct realms—geology and city, science and politics, humans and nonhumans, the visible and the invisible—did not belong to the same sphere—an assemblage of associations between heterogeneous actants, events, matters of concern, and points of view. The water revealed that mining displaces geology not only in terms of the matter it extracts and commodifies, but also in what it discards and leaves behind. Much of this is polluted, toxic, and unstable. It metabolises into groundwater, air, and flesh. Geology becomes biology, and toxicity becomes a condition of daily life. Engaging with these conditions through documenting, visualising, and mapping reveals new ways of seeing and understanding them, exposes new ethical and aesthetic challenges, and suggests new sites for political, practical, spatial, and aesthetic intervention.

Note: A longer version of this essay was published as L. Bremner, "The Political Life of Rising Acid Mine Water," *Urban Forum* 24(4) (2013): 463–83.

REFERENCES

Adler, R., M. Claassen, L. Godfrey, and A. R. Turton. 2007. "Water, Mining and Waste: A Historical and Economic Perspective on Conflict Management in South Africa." *The Economics of Peace and Security Journal* 2(2): 32–41.

Adler, R., & Rascher, J. (2007). A Strategy for the Management of Acid Mine Drainage from Gold Mines in Gauteng. Council for Scientific and Industrial Research Report No. CSIR/NRE/PW/ER/2007/0053/C. Pretoria: Council for Scientific and Industrial Research.

Akcil, A., and S. Koldas. 2006. "Acid Mine Drainage (AMD): Causes, Treatment and Case Studies." *Journal of Cleaner Production* 14: 1139–45.

D. Pressly, "Cabinet Given Acid Ultimatum," *AMD in SA* (February 4, 2011).

Beavon, K. 2004. *Johannesburg: The Making and Shaping of the City*. Pretoria: University of South Africa Press.

Bennett, J. 2010. *Vibrant Matter: A Political Ecology of Things*. Durham and London: Duke University Press.

Bremner, L. 2005. "Remaking Johannesburg." In S. Read, J. Rosemann, and J. van Eldijk, eds., *Future City*. London: Spon: 32–47.

Bremner, L., D. Doepel, H., Judin, and M. Sorkin. 2010. Masterclass at the AZA Congress in Johannesburg, September 25–28.

Bridge, G. 2009. "The Hole World: Scales and Spaces of Extraction." *New Geographies* 2: 43–49.

Coetser, D. A. 2012. "Remining Johannesburg: Urban Redevelopment through the Treatment of Acid Mine Drainage." Master in Technology, University of Johannesburg.

Dugard, J., J. MacLeod, and A. Alcaro. 2011. "Rights Mobilization in South Africa in the Context of Acute Environmental Harm: The Case of Acid Mine Drainage on the Witwatersrand Basin." Human Rights and the Global Economy Conference, Center for Public Scholarship, The New School, New York, 10 November. Copy from Mariette Liefferink.

Funke, N., S. Nienaber, and C. Gioia. 2012. "An Interest Group at Work: Environmental Activism and the Case of Acid Mine Drainage on Johannesburg's West Rand." http://hdl.handle.net/10204/5841. Accessed July 2012.

Haughton, S. H., ed. 1964. *The Geology of Some Ore Deposits in South Africa*. Johannesburg: The Geological Society of South Africa.

Hervieu, H. 2012. "Poor South Africans Living on Toxic Remains of Defunct Gold Mines." *World Crunch*, 15 November. http://www.worldcrunch.com/culture-society/poor-south-africans-living-on-toxic-remains-of-defunct-gold-mines/tudor-shaft-radioactive-spoil-tips/c3s9958/#.ULUHvuOTv88. Accessed November 2012.

Johnson, D. B., and K. B. Hallberg. 2005. "Acid Mine Drainage Remediation Options: A Review." *Science of the Total Environment* 338: 3–14.

Kaika, M. 2005. *City of Flows, Modernity, Nature and the City*. London: Routledge.

Kritzinger, L. 2012. *Insidious Waters*. Master in Fine Arts, University of Pretoria exhibition, Van Wouw House, Pretoria, 29 September–21 October.

Latour, B. 1999. *Pandora's Hope: Essays on the Reality of Science Studies*. Cambridge, MA, and London: Harvard University Press.

———. 2004. *Politics of Nature: How to Bring the Sciences into Democracy*. Trans. C. Porter. Cambridge, MA, and London: Harvard University Press.

Mathews, C. 2011. "Pouring Poison." *PEA Public Environmental Arbiters*, 29 August. http://www.pea.org.za/latestnews/news.php?n_id=438. Accessed October 2012

McCarthy, T. 2010. "The Decanting of Acid Mine Water in the Gauteng City-Region: Analysis, Prognosis and Solutions." *Provocations Series*. Johannesburg: Gauteng City-Region Observatory.

Mumford, L. 1934. *Technics and Civilization*. New York: Harper.

National Nuclear Regulator. 2010. *Surveillance Report of the Upper Wonderfonteinspruit Catchment Area*. Report No. TR-NNR-10-0001. Pretoria: National Nuclear Regulator.

Nuttall, S. 2009. *Entanglement: Literary and Cultural Reflections on Post-Apartheid*. Johannesburg: Witwatersrand University Press.

Oelofse, S. H. H., P. J. Hobbs, J. Rascher, and J. E. Cobbing. No date. "The Pollution and Destruction Threat of Gold Mining Waste on the Witwatersrand: A West Rand Case Study." http://www.anthonyturton.com/admin/my_documents/my_files/983_SWEMP.pdf. Accessed February 2012.

Ranciere, J. 1999. *Disagreement: Politics and Philosophy*. Trans. J. Rose. Minneapolis, MN: University of Minnesota Press.

South African Council for Geoscience. 2010. *Mine Water Management in the Witwatersrand Goldfields with Special Emphasis on Acid Mine Drainage*. Report to the Inter-ministerial Committee on Acid Mine Drainage. Pretoria: Council for Geoscience.

Stephenson, D. 1983. "Distribution of Water in Deep Gold Mines in South Africa." *International Journal of Minewater* 2(2): 21–30.

Stott, J. 2008. "Preservation or Exploitation? A Study of the Development of the Mining Rights Legislation on the Witwatersrand Goldfields from 1886 to 2008." Master of Economics thesis, Rhodes University, Grahamstown, South Africa.

Turton, A. R. No date. "South African Water and Mining Policy: A Study of Strategies for Transition Management." http://www.anthonyturton.com/admin/my_docume nts/my_files/The_Evolution_of_SA_Mine_Policy.pdf. Accessed July 2012.

Van Onselen, C. 1982a. *Studies in the Social and Economic History of the Witwatersrand 1886–1914*. Vol. 1, *New Babylon*. Johannesburg: Ravan Press.

———. 1982b. *Studies in the Social and Economic History of the Witwatersrand 1886–1914*. Vol. 2, *New Nineveh*. Johannesburg: Ravan Press.

Winde, F. 2009. "Uranium Pollution of Water Resources in Mined-out and Active Goldfields of South Africa: A Case Study in the Wonderfonteinspruit Catchment on Extent and Sources of U Contamination and Associated Health Risks." http://www.imwa.info/docs/imwa_2009/IMWA2009_Winde.pdf. Accessed July 2012.

THE RECREATION OF THE COMMONS
Gunter Pauli

The future of air, water, health, topsoil, biodiversity, clean energy, and soil, based on design principles for a city that lives and lets live, uses all that is locally available, moves, recycles, senses, and shares.

Author of *The Blue Economy* and Founder of the Zero Emissions Research and Initiatives (ZERI)
February 27, 2017.

When I presented in April 2009 the core concepts and findings on local economic development as a possible report to the Club of Rome under the title "The Blue Economy: 100 innovations, 10 years, 100 million jobs," I sketched out a vision. This vision was based on a clear understanding that nature in general and a wide range of ecosystems in particular have overcome nearly every imaginable challenge over the past millions of years, and therefore provide an inspiration for how we as a society can chart a pathway towards the future. We can build on the ingenuity of ecosystems that provide the wealth of products and services on which life depends, and then strengthen the social systems that build up culture, tradition, and social capital. This approach provides resilience in adverse times and joy during the better moments of our lives. It also permits us to learn how to live within obvious limits while evolving from scarcity to abundance.

Observing ecological and social systems for decades can guide our quest towards a world where nature regains its evolutionary path and society strengthens its social web, enhancing the quality of life of all by empowering everyone to know how to respond to their basic needs with what is locally available. This challenge has become even more relevant in an urban context.

The past six years have taught me many lessons. How could we achieve a fast transition from traditional business and economic development, based on the logic of globalisation and the drive to cut costs by enterprises searching for ever higher economies of scale, to a Blue Economy in cities and rural zones that would perform better and transform industries faster than often has been considered viable?

These past six years have permitted me to better understand the fundamental shortcomings of the existing economic model, where practice differs greatly from theory, and where a simple focus on a core business based on a core competence has blinded many to seeing the wide portfolio of opportunities that we could pursue. The management of companies with their short-term objectives, translated into financial terms void of social and environmental considerations, considers the commons a place to exploit (as we do with excessive consumption of water) or a place to release our excesses (as we do with the release of greenhouse gases into the atmosphere). How can we believe in the "invisible hand" where self-interest faced with scarcity is bound to lead to destructive behaviour?

The logic of enlightened self-interest whereby "an individual who intends only to improve his own gain, is, as it were, led by an invisible hand to promote the public interest" (Adam Smith, 1776) has been too easily explained through the price fluctuations determined by the supply and demand of commercial goods and services. A high demand with constant supply leads to a higher price, which will allocate resources to the most efficient operator. True, if there is a well-functioning market with transparency to all players. However, this enlightened self-interest turns into destructive behaviour when it is deployed in the realm of *the commons*, as we call the services and systems that are supplied freely by nature and which have—to date—no commercial value. The commons include biodiversity, the continuous provision of drinking water, the supply of oxygen in the air, the availability of grazing land for herds, the evolutionary and symbiotic path of biodiversity, the cycling of nutrients, the build-up of topsoil, and so much more.

ECOSYSTEM SERVICES, OR THE COMMONS
Whereas a few economists have made an effort to calculate the value of all these factors, business and society have embraced the commons to be privatized for commercial exploitation by a few through an exclusive license to operate, as we have done with the permission to bottle water and sell it, thus depriving ecosystems of water through depletion of water tables. The commons have also been exploited through a selfish approach that undermines the very premises that guarantee the conditions of life. The critique against the invisible hand—which Adam Smith never meant to be something that would always function—was already successfully argued in the nineteenth century, but was conveniently omitted from any further economic teachings.

William Forster Lloyd, an amateur mathematician, wrote a pamphlet in 1833 that could well have been called "The Tragedy of the Commons" because it conveys a remorseless situation. Picture a pasture open to all. Each herdsman will try to keep as many cattle as possible on these commons. A rational individual seeks to maximise his gain and asks, "What is the utility to *me* in adding one more animal to the herd?" Since the herdsman receives all the proceeds from the sale of this additional animal, he is prepared to neglect the fact that there is additional overgrazing. After all, this adverse effect is shared by all herdsmen who—at first—would hardly notice. Worse, when the problem of overgrazing is finally recognised, the herdsman who has added extra animals does not feel responsible, since all herdsmen apply the same rationale with a compelling logic to increase without limit on a pasture that is clearly limited.

Modern society has believed in the freedom to exploit the commons, and has offered companies a license to act accordingly. We have confused the "free market" with the free exploitation of the commons. Now we realize that there is not only over-grazing, but this "freedom to add extra sheep to graze on public land" leads to soil erosion, loss of water retention, and desertification. Thus, the freedom to pursue one's own interests leads to the destruction of the very basis of the ecosystem that supports life. This laissez-faire approach that has been applied to the market is unknowingly applied to the commons as well. This reality is widely recognised for ecosystems, but few have noted that the commons in cities suffer even more, because space is so limited, the air is so dense, and the water is so scarce.

The decisions of the herdsmen are also taken by fishermen, by miners pursuing gold, by petrochemists exploiting more fossil fuels turned into plastics, by polluters who use water or air to carry away their toxic waste or particles, and by the individuals and institutions that pursue this blind goal of "more for me." This attitude of "me" brings ruin to everyone from irreversible climate change, as well as dramatically changing health (with respiratory diseases topping the list), the accumulation of toxic waste in dams built by mines, the depletion of topsoil, and the permanent loss of biodiversity—all of which makes it impossible to live a quality life in the cities. This mistreatment of the commons by the pursuit of "more for me" goes hand in hand with a permanent display of our free market's incapacity to respond to the basic needs of all living on Earth. It is no surprise that poverty is rampant in inner cities and that it's impossible to eliminate it, since we are continuously undermining the ecosystem services that make life on Earth viable. Who has access to free fruit in the center of town?

The key for business is not to grasp the latest strategy for cost reductions, the newest technology of the Internet of Things, nor the return on investment that pleases shareholders beyond expectations; rather, business urgently needs to rethink its model of operations. Following the same logic, cities need to rethink the way we design the commons so that its use can be ensured to everyone in an urban environment. We need business models that enhance and secure not just "the functioning of the market"; we need to strengthen the very conditions on which life depends. How could we ever have given license to a company that destroys—often unknowingly—the very environment in which life exists? For the past few decades, the search has focused on how to design a business that is capable of responding to basic needs while ensuring that the commons thrives, and while still offering a return. We do not have to pretend that the invisible hand will guide us; rather, we should make a conscious decision to curtail the freedom to exploit the commons following the same logic with which we deal with thieving. Stealing less is still stealing. Polluting less is still polluting.

Destroying the commons more slowly is still destroying the commons. When one decides not to add an extra sheep to graze, all of the other herdsmen combined are still opting to overgraze! So the environmentalist who wants to preserve the grazing land is considered the "stupid" one in the eyes of all the others, because he or she loses out. Where has the invisible hand of Adam Smith gone?

This leads to the obvious question: Can we still build on a market system and apply capitalist principles while ensuring a better quality of life for everyone living on Earth? Or does the present system predestine societies in which 1% of the population can accumulate as much wealth as is owned by the other 99%? It is clear that the market which considers the commons as a free-for-all leads to recognition that we go (and have gone) beyond the limits, and that the benefits have gone to very few individuals. Thus, there is a need to curtail the freedom to operate as a business with limited liabilities. Now, if there are millions of operators on the market and the exploitation of the commons could be regulated, could we then steer business and society towards sustainability? If power is concentrated in the hands of a few super-corporations and super-rich people who pay no taxes anywhere, how does anyone value the chances of 200+ governments to guide the process of redesigning the business model? We know that the opposite will be true: those few global operators will tell governments what to do. Within this context, how can we ever expect that the commons on which the very life of all depends will prevail?

This question inspires me to search for better solutions, driven by a new generation of entrepreneurs. While inspirational writers like David Korten and Bill McKibben rightly point to the adverse effect of control by a few, we need to focus on how disruptive technologies and disruptive business models could transform the present production and consumption system into a market economy that considers the role and importance of the commons, and transforms our living space into one that promotes life and strengthens resilience. The last we need is to put a value on the ecosystem; first we need to respect it, knowing that we can never fully understand it, but that without it the whole system would degenerate and ultimately collapse. While there is a need to revisit the logic of economics, and especially the effects of the "Tragedy of the Commons," we therefore need to rethink our management models.

The principles that guide management today—like supply chain management, outsourcing, and core business—are not only out of date but are outright destructive, and yet management does not realize it. These concepts are a perfect copy of the herdsmen's decision to overgraze without ever feeling responsible. These management concepts, widely taught at all business schools around the world, culminate in the most commercial and profitable diploma ever sold: the MBA. How can we pretend to have efficient management when it depletes the commons beyond repair, and when of our limited natural resources, only 10% of all material processed is allotted any value, and 90% ends up as waste? In this oversimplified approach to production and sales, cost cutting and controls determine everything, and day-to-day operations are run by the desire to offer ever cheaper products without considering the full impact on people's lives. How will managers ever face the absurdity of shipping butter and milk around the globe to bake cookies, which are then also shipped around the world?

The present management model of production, distribution, and consumption not only squanders resources and infringes on the commons, but the worst aspect is that this linear approach focused on one core business has blinded everyone in the process to recognizing a vast portfolio of opportunities. How can we continue to focus on only one activity, when it is obvious that through cascading and clustering activities we can increase material efficiency and the creation of value-added by a multiple, provided we are prepared to depart from this obsession with well-defined niche markets built on very narrowly defined core competences?

THE KEY IS WATER

Life on Earth evolved from a few single-cell bacteria to a wealth of biodiversity thriving in the most distinct ecosystems nestled in every corner of our planet. Natural systems inspire us with their capacity to evolve from scarcity to abundance, using available resources ranging from the leaves dropping from a tree in the fall and converted to humus by micro-organisms, fungi, ants, and earthworms, to the dust particles from one continent deposited into the Amazon rain forest and contributing to the thin layer of soil that characterizes this lush tropical region, which emerged as an explosion of biodiversity after the rising Andes Mountain range cut off the flow of rainwater to the Pacific and forced water through thousands of miles of continental shifts towards the Atlantic.

Natural systems cascade endlessly, not by eliminating waste and weeds but rather by turning what seemingly has no value for one into a desired item for another. This creates the continuous flows on which life on Earth depends. This observation inspired me to write in 1991 for the first time about the design of business models that have no residue and no emissions. This observation also led to my involvement in the creation of the first ecological factory (1991–1993) which led to the creation of ZERI (Zero Emissions Research and Initiatives) with the support of the United Nations and the Japanese government (1994–1997). This proposal for the environmental strategies of the future was not a call to close the loop and make material flows circular, or to stop making waste; it was a vision on how much more we can produce if we imagine value in everything we have. I went so far as to propose that the time had come to ban the concept of waste. After all, it seems that humans are the only species capable of producing something no one desires.

Nature is also an inspiration for me because, in spite of the fact that the laws of physics offer predictable results, there are always exceptions that confirm the rule. There is one simple molecule that fascinates us: H_2O or water, or should we write H_3O_2 as Professor Gerald Pollack suggests?[1] Water is called the "universal" solvent because it dissolves more easily and broadly than any other liquid by disrupting the attractive forces that hold molecules together. It is the only substance we know that has four phases: solid, liquid, an exclusion zone, and gas. This means that whenever water is in the air, soil, or our bodies, it takes valuable chemicals, minerals, and nutrients along.

---

1. For more background on the fourth phase of water and the work of Dr. Gerald Pollack, see "Dr. Gerald Pollack and Structured Water Science," Structured Water Unit, LLC, http://www.structuredwaterunit.com/articles/structuredwater/dr-gerald-pollack-and-structured-water-science (accessed 7 April 2017).

Here is a first exception: in the exclusion zone, water transforms into a pure state and deposits all "impurities." Water has a polar arrangement of oxygen (negative charge) and hydrogen (positive charge), which allows water to be attracted to many different types of molecules. Water is the solvent that cleanses our kidneys of all possible metals and minerals we have in excess, such as potassium. Water creates the positive and negative charges that reshape red blood cells and make them flow effortlessly through our capillary veins.

Once we embrace nature as our inspiration, we transform our perception of the realities around us. This includes revising logic to rely on solutions derived from chemistry (designing new molecules) and biology (designing new forms of life) to a better understanding of the laws of physics and how geometry determines almost everything in life; transforming the logic of this linear cause-and-effect into a nonlinear complex reality; searching for an optimum for a whole system, rather than maximizing the result of one parameter; setting the goal of strengthening the resilience of society and the economy by promoting more diversity; and finally going beyond organics as a standard. These insights, all inspired by natural systems, offer a first set of principles that allow us to achieve results that traditional logic and management cannot even imagine. The key is to evolve from these general reflections and this philosophy to taking action on the ground in the city. It should all start with farming.

FARMING IN THE CITY
The key revolution we need is to make a jump from rural to urban farming, designing food and energy systems for high-density living areas. To fully understand the potential, I organized field trips to China, the United States, Brazil, and Cuba. The visit to Qingyuan (清远) in Guangdong Province (广东;) organized by Professor Shu-ting Chan, then the dean of the Faculty of Biological Sciences at the Chinese University in Hong Kong, was an eye-opener: a city with the same area as San Francisco employed 250,000 people in inner-city mushroom farming. Our network of scientists view mushroom farming as one of the greatest potential applications of urban farming. The thousands of initiatives we witnessed and inspired in mushroom farming offer us a first-hand perspective on how to possibly feed 75% of the citizens of the world who are packed on a few square meters in shanty towns. While this essay will not go into detail about mushroom farming, which is the subject of separate writings, it is important to point out that ZERI teams and Blue Economy practitioners around the world have designed programs for food security in villages, towns, and megalopolises, each time starting from a simple mushroom farming unit that converts readily available fibrous waste into food and feed. It was the logic of the Five Kingdoms of Nature that inspired us to look at plants as food (coffee grounds) for mushrooms, then to use the spent substrates enriched in amino acids as animal feed, and finally to collect manure for composting, thus using four of the five kingdoms of nature in a local system.

The second field trip was to Wuxi (无锡) in Jiangsu Province (江苏省). Our host was Professor Li Kangmin, who had participated in the ZERI World Congresses in Namibia, where he visited the beer brewery site, and in Colombia, where he saw the inner-city farming of mushrooms in the city of Manizales. I have returned four times to Wuxi: first because of the interesting inner-city farming techniques, then because of the IFFC, and finally because my first fables in Chinese were published in cooperation with the Wuxi Association for the Promotion of Science and Technology. This fast-industrializing region has a GDP in excess of one trillion dollars—half of California's and 50% bigger than India's—and has maintained its farming component of the local economy within an urban context. This may have a historic reason: the population of Wuxi was saved during the early 1960s from hunger by its inner-city farming of water spinach, azolla, chlorella, and its integrated fish-farming technique, which are centuries-old traditions and part of their water management. While this approach to food security is only viable in cities with abundant water, it has been pointed out that every large city, even when there is a (perceived) shortage of water, has an excess of waste water. This water is considered polluted by some and excessively rich in nutrients by others, but remains unused for productive purposes by most. Professor Li showed me how the city's biological waste system in Wuxi could create a large food

production system. Although he never trained as a biologist, as a junior military officer he was concerned with the livelihood of people in Wuxi and initiated the farming of water spinach when hunger reigned. Without biological waste rich in nutrients, spinach would not grow. When spinach grows, its roots provide outstanding feed for grass-feeding carps. The more carps would nibble on the suspended roots, the better the spinach would grow. Professor Li saw this symbiosis unfolding. It was in line with the proposals of Professor George Chan, another inner-city waste water management expert, who started his career as the City Engineer for Water Management in Port Louis (Mauritius). According to him, a high biological oxygen demand (BOD) is not a problem; it implies a high concentration of nutrition and therefore the need to design intensive removal of these nutrients through plants (floating gardens), algae (azolla and chlorella), and fish (at every trophic level).

Inner city mushroom farming in Belgrade

URBAN FARMING AND SELF-SUFFICIENCY

The third field visit to study urban farming brought me to Brasilia, the capital city of Brazil. Cassio Taniguchi, who was formerly mayor of Curitiba and the Brasilia Minister of Planning, showed me how city planners in the 1960s had allocated land around the newly created city to immigrant farmers, mainly from Japan. This farm land, combined with an ample supply of water, today secures 90% self-sufficiency in fruits and vegetables for the two million city inhabitants. Food is cheap in Brasilia, not because of the efficiency of large-scale farming in the Mato Grosso or cheap imports from Chile, but because of the ingenious design of the founding fathers of the new capital to include food and water security. The only other city in the world that matches this level of food security within its city boundaries is La Habana, Cuba, our fifth field study. Its food security was not by design, but by necessity. Deprived of fertilizers and food due to the boycott by the United States and the demise of the Soviet Union, the determined and creative citizens of Cuba imposed a fresh start in farming. The results are equally impressive: not only has the city been able to provide food security, but the diet of the people changed for the better, as can be seen from the health indices. The limited availability of dairy and meat put the population on a healthy diet which translated into a significant drop in heart diseases and diabetes.

These experiences from different continents, and the expert insights provided by ZERI's network of scientists, stimulated us to advance on the challenge of urban farming. Our young research team at the United Nations Environment Programme offices in Geneva documented many additional cases through desk research. By the beginning of the third millennium, we knew that every corner of a city, be it a balcony, roof, kitchen, or bathroom, could be turned into a green oasis. We envisaged the creation of a "vegetable city" as the design team of the Politecnico di Torino, under the leadership of Professor Luigi Bistagnino, demonstrated that it would be an opportunity to make cities self-sufficient in food as well as carbon-neutral, mitigating climate change risks, and allowing residents to enjoy full employment and improved, healthy living conditions.

The ZERI network goes beyond replacing one "input-output" model with another and sees through the simplicity of "food in, meat out." We implement the cascading of nutrients and energy and use existing infrastructure for a new purpose, as Jan Willem Bosman Jansen did by converting the old greenhouses of flower bulbs in the city of Egmont, the Netherlands, into mushroom farming units, or Siemen Cox and Mark Slegers, who converted an old swimming pool (Tropicana) in Rotterdam into a mushroom farming and training center. These initiatives are inspired by the work of Ivanka Milenkovic in Belgrade, and combined, they have created more than one thousand inner-city farming initiatives that reduce the waste going to landfills, and offer fresh and healthy food for immediate consumption without the need for drying, packing, refrigeration, or transport, but for a bicycle.

The greenhouse is of interest for urban farming in a temperate climate. Encouragingly, former New York City Mayor Michael Bloomberg strongly promoted urban farming because it captures storm water and diverts it from the sewer, plus reduces the number of trucks on the road, which

cuts greenhouse gases. Today, New York is the leader in urban farms in the United States, which in America doesn't necessarily mean that there is a huge volume, but that there is capital flowing into commercial ventures. To name a few: Gotham Greens (gothamgreens.com) was founded in 2008 by Vijay Puri and Eric Haley; Brooklyn Grange (brooklyngrangefarm.com) was set up by Ben Flanner, Anastasia Cole Plakias, and Gwen Schantz; Bright Farms (brightfarms.com) was established by Ted Caplow and run by Paul Lightfoot, the CEO who raised $20 million in capital and supplies major supermarkets for an annual food sales value of $130 million. The City of New York is pushing to the next level, and decided to initiate a 20,000-square-meter rooftop farm on its food distribution hub in the Bronx.

INNER-CITY FARMING IN THE FUTURE

The Blue Economy is all about changing the paradigm. The urban farming program offers a solution to certain societal problems. It is unique to find corporate headquarters that have introduced urban farming, and exceptional when it is used to transform staff. Here the case clearly demonstrates that new business models cannot be fully captured in a classic business plan. We are convinced that urban farming will move from its more than one thousand large-scale initiatives around the world to at least ten thousand initiatives in a decade.

Cities will change building codes, and investors will search for economies of scale in urban farming, which is constrained in size by the erratic building space available on rooftops, especially on commercial and industrial buildings. For every 1,000 square meters of urban farms, there is potential to generate 12 direct and indirect jobs, reducing the miles traveled by people to get to work as well as miles the food travels. This implies that we see worldwide a potential of at least 25 million jobs in urban farming in a decade. However, with all the breakthroughs we have witnessed, we still want to accelerate speed and scale, and therefore we have been looking for other opportunities to shift the management of water, food, and health. We decided that the best way to progress is by focusing on the needs of infants.

IT ALL STARTS WITH MOTHERS' MILK

When a mother breastfeeds, the baby's urine and feces are of an extraordinary quality and quantity. A great variety of micro-organisms and substances are released after digestion, and these

Inner city mushroom farming in Belgrade

contain energy, or life force. This is, after all, the core nutrition for building an immune system that is to protect a person's health for his or her entire lifetime. It also allows for new life to emerge. Therefore, one should never denigrate this rich source of materials (used diapers and their content) as a waste problem: diapers that end up in landfills. We are committed to reorienting the flow of this high-quality mix of materials and to transforming it. We hope to transform it in such a way that it will provide families with an abundance of fresh fruit—for generations to come, within the city's boundaries. How will that work?

THE FROM-THE-BOTTOM-UP PROJECT

The From-the-Bottom-Up Project empowers us to redesign a city by creating a remarkable fruit belt surrounding an urban environment, providing—within a single generation—millions of tons of a rich variety of highly nutritious, seasonal fruit, adding to the biodiversity of the region. The supplies of fruit, berries, and nuts will be rolled out with planting and harvesting in tune with the cycles of nature. This will attract more bees and more birds, and offer more joy. At the same time, this project will allow for the creation of a spirit of community in an urban context seldom seen in modern history: everyone in the area will get to know each other, and will know the names of every baby who is contributing in their area. Can you imagine what it means when a baby hears its name pronounced by fifty couples that meet regularly around a productive initiative?

This may seem like a vast undertaking. However, the start is very simple. The process requires a business model that has all the elements needed to redesign a city over time—starting with the creation of a community. This will require a fresh look at the reality of both the problems and the needs of citizens. The ecosystem allows for the design of an initiative that is so effective and efficient that diapers—yes, this modern expression of comfort and massive pollution—can be offered for free. We envision this project for a minimum of one thousand babies in any city. The impact is beyond imagination. This kind of initiative, described below, will generate jobs while money is created by the sale and planting of trees on land provided by citizens and by the city. How is this *überhaupt* possible (how could this ever be possible)?

COOPERATIVES AT THE CORE

We envision that at the core of this positive yet radical transformation lies a small nucleus of citizens, consisting of no more than one hundred families. Mapping software has indicated that in vibrant cities, in every circle 800 to 1,000 meters in diameter, there will be approximately 100 babies with parents ready to work together for the comfort of their offspring. This measuring process can be repeated hundreds—and in a megalopolis—even thousands of times. We create the network of the networks based on babies and their families. Parents and grandparents who participate in the "Free Diaper Initiative" agree to pick up their free supply of four ingredients: a mix of bamboo dust, bamboo charcoal, and coffee grounds, and a double film of biodegradable plastics. And, key to the initiative is that the parents also agree to drop off used diapers at a central point every Saturday. Parents are also encouraged to bring organic kitchen waste in biodegradable plastic bags, as both materials are needed to convert these natural resources into black earth, also known as *terra preta*—the secret of highly productive farming by the Incas and the Vikings. Each of the families will have at home a "diaper waffle machine" which basically produces diapers in the same way that waffles are made: after the four ingredients are mixed together, the warm waffle iron is used to seal and shape the diapers."

Parents are encouraged to change diapers as often as is needed, and not to wait an extra hour to save on diapers. Yes, parents will be encouraged to get up for diaper changes frequently at night, according to their baby's feeding and weaning cycle, to ensure their baby has a bottom that is clean and dry but without reliance on the super-absorbent diapers that only wither and hardly degrade. In this way, the risk of an infant getting a urinary infection, which is painful and may even lead to infertility, is minimized.

COMMIT TO PLANTING 1,000 TREES
There is no cost for the new diapers that families receive when they return the soiled ones. All that is required is that every family commits to selling and planting one thousand fruit trees every year. Everyone receives the necessary training to do so. The total mass generated and the amount of black earth produced in a year (from the combination of diaper, human waste, and biomass waste) amounts to an astounding one ton per baby. This will provide enough carbon-rich soil to plant one thousand fruit trees. Thus, in summary: each baby produces enough organic waste to provide the nutritious soil that offers a growth basis for one thousand trees—each year!

During the trial phase in Berlin, Germany, families offered to pay for the diapers even when not required to do so. We encourage people who want to pay to donate the money to the *100 Babies Cooperative* (or *The Fresh Fruit Generation*). These funds are not to be used for the project, but rather are allowed to accumulate to serve as a guarantee for investments in the future. On the basis of our pilot study, a cooperative of one hundred families can accumulate approximately €1.2 million within twenty-five years … and this amount of cash in the community is obtained only through voluntary contributions for the diapers.

FROM SCARCITY TO ABUNDANCE
All city officials we have approached are keen to contribute to the process. There are two reasons for this. In the first place, the project decreases the amount of diapers that end up in landfills (as diapers currently form 5-6% of landfills), and secondly, the conversion of soiled diapers to black earth saves money, retains storm water, and produces an abundance of fruit. The simple collection system used cuts down on transport costs, reducing the excessive load of trucks shipping diapers in and out of the urban zone, nearly all imported from overseas. Available land is used to grow large numbers of trees that will offer fruit for many decades, even for generations to come. If one thousand families pursue these goals over twenty-five years, 25 million trees will be planted. If each tree offers on average 50 kg of fruit, the yield will be more than one million tons of fruit every year within a quarter of a century. We have clearly shifted from scarcity to abundance. We have embraced a new era for the commons, where what is good and necessary is also free.

PARTNERSHIP WITH THE CITY

Now if this is the impact 1,000 babies and their families can have … imagine the impact 100,000 families can have if they undertake to produce fresh local fruit in a capital city with a million or more inhabitants. It now becomes obvious that cities need to incorporate this remarkable opportunity to include a fruit belt in their master plans. Fruit growing on this scale is not new. The Prussian emperors had orchards of thousands of fruit trees planted around their Sanssouci castle in the outskirts of Berlin, including apples, pears, and plums. They even had greenhouses for growing oranges, melons, and bananas. We are returning to that wisdom, one of securing healthy soil that will ensure abundance for decades to come.

THE NETWORK ECONOMY

The responsibility for selling and planting fruit trees goes beyond only the parents. Mothers and fathers will mobilize their networks of friends and family, organizing tree planting days. They will make use of corporate sponsors, ones that are keen to contribute to a worthwhile cause. Service clubs like Rotary will gather the funds. We are transforming the city; we are creating abundance.

WHO ARE WE?

We—the think tank of the ZERI Network, which was created in 1994 in Japan at the United Nations University with the support of the Japanese government in preparation for the Kyoto Protocol, and the "do tank," known as the Foundation for the Blue Economy, which emerged after the publication of my Report to the Club of Rome in 2009 under the same title, harvesting the insights and experience of fifteen years of academic and field research—have learned that community can be created, and that sharing is possible.

We clearly see the radical transformation and the creation of an economy that embraces the commons, where the technologies may be patented, but the business model is shared as an open source. In this economy, jobs are created in the city, and waste turns into one of the most precious sources of life: soil from which life regenerates more life, food, and indeed abundance. And while we are aware that this approach is disruptive for existing businesses—who may well react in traditional ways to this threat to do much better with what we have—we are convinced that there is no stopping the wisdom of the people and that there is no stopping the unleashing of entrepreneurship because, yes, we need to wake up the innovator within us, and and know that we are the ones who make the decision.

FIRE

Fire—the elemental placeholder for energy—is one of the vital questions that cities need to address imminently. Fossil fuel consumption is not only depleting natural resources, but, most importantly, liberating carbon to the atmosphere and producing climate change, which is in turn producing pollution health hazards and raising water levels. Buildings consume 40% of global energy and 60% of global resources, and produce 48% of carbon emissions, with large energy use concentrated in urban centres.[1]

The spatial distribution of energy sources, energy processing, and energy demand are a solid basis upon which different urban systems can be studied, historically or parametrically. The history of energy and cities is driven through a sequence in which urban energy systems evolve progressively toward highly concentrated forms of energy, often obtained from fossil fuels, which can be easily transported.[2] The large industrial metropolises would have never been possible without the availability to reach out for energy resources that were not available on site, coupling large scale populations and large energy resources in order to develop unprecedented productive capacities. Ralph Waldo Emerson famously wrote that coal was like a portable climate, providing a very graphic image of the geographical distortion being affected by the industrial

1. United Nations Environment Program. Accessed 10/05/2016. http://www.unep.org/sbci/AboutSBCI/Background.asp.

2. Vaclav Smil, *Energy in World History* (San Francisco: Westview, 1994).

revolution through the transport of coal.[3] Because of its light weight and high energy density, coal could be brought anywhere, eliminating the attachment between territory and energy resources. The development of fossil fuels as energy sources enabled the deterritorialization of energy needed to sustain the large industrial metropolises which would have never been possible without the availability of energy resources.

In the 1960s, an increased environmental consciousness initiated the development to sustainable energy sources, which was intensified with the 1970s energy crisis. The development of solar, wind, tidal and ground-sourced energy sources able to power cities without resorting to the combustion of fossil fuels will profoundly redefine the new urban cosmopolitics. Fossil fuel ecologies triggered massive geopolitical conflicts in the Middle East, Central America and Southern Russia, but the shift to sustainable sources will trigger politics articulating consumption patterns with sustainable energy source potentials. As sustainable energy is primarily mediated through electricity, it needs to be resolved with locally responsive strategies as the potentials of sustainable energy sources vary depending on climate and geology. A new cosmopolitics of sustainable sources would do away with global geopolitics and national energy standards and take into account climatic variations.

Comparing to densities of population and their energy requirements we can understand the type of energy system that characterizes a particular urban environment. From the over 18,000 kg of oil equivalent of energy use per capita which is consumed in Iceland and Qatar to the around 600 kg of oil equivalent of energy use per capita consumed in India, the energy profiles of cities vary widely.[4] Population density, for

3. "We may well call it black diamonds. Every basket is power and civilization. For coal is a portable climate. It carries the heat of the tropics to Labrador and the polar circle: and it is the means of transporting itself whithersoever it is wanted. Watt and Stephenson whispered in the ear of mankind their secret, that *a half-ounce of coal will draw two tons a mile*, and coal carries coal, by rail and by boat, to make Canada as warm as Calcutta, and with its comfort brings its industrial power." Ralph Waldo Emerson, "Wealth," chapter 3 in *The Conduct of Life* (1860), collected in Emerson's *Complete Works* (Boston: Ticknor and Fields, 1860).

4. The World Bank, "Energy Use (kg of oil equivalent per capita)," IEA Statistics © OECD/IEA 2014, http://data.worldbank.org/indicator/EG.USE.PCAP.KG.OE?year_high_desc=true, accessed 5 May 2017.

example is one of the parameters that contributes most effectively to lower energy consumption patterns, with the densest cities in the world widely outperforming energy consumption in low density populations. But energy is not only related to heating, cooling, and transportation, it also relates to water consumption and food production. For example, one of the most energy intensive industries today is the synthesis of ammonia, which is now used in more than half of the fertilizers consumed in the world, which are crucial for food production.[5] Increased meat consumption, coupled with intensive livestock production systems account for a substantial amount of energy consumption and greenhouse gas emissions.[6]

The progressive shift toward a civilization based on sustainable energy sources which no longer rely on fossil fuel combustion, and the emergence of an urban environment in which DC devices are increasingly widespread suggests that there may be opportunities for an even more intense reterritorialization of energies. One of the characteristics of this new energy paradigm is the convergence of all energy supplies and consumptions toward electricity, which is now becoming the main source of energy for everything, including transport, with the rise of electromobility.

The proliferation of computers, smartphones and other low-voltage devices which run on DC stored on batteries suggest that solar panels could be feeding directly onto these devices or their batteries, without the need for long distance transportation. The development of energy systems which directly link the energy sources to the energy consumption devices without the need to transport may have crucial implications for the spatialization of energy. The current development of batteries with increasing capacity, which can serve as temporal —rather than spatial— bridges between the time of production and the time of consumption is likely to have a huge impact in the architecture of future cities.

5. Vaclav Smil, "Nitrogen Cycle and World Food Production," *World Agriculture 9* (2009).

6. Danny Harvey, *Energy and the New Reality 1: Energy Efficiency and the Demand for Energy Services* (New York: Routledge, 2010).

Tesla Motors and its subsidiary Solar City's pioneering efforts to develop technologies able to power homes and cars directly from solar energy are now some of the technological developments with a direct impact on cities. Paradoxically, it may be that Tesla Motors' efforts may be reversing Nikola Tesla's efforts toward alternate current. If AC proved superior for a paradigm where energy needs to be transported and delivered on large quantities, DC may be more adequate for a localized form of energy to deliver a diminishing amount sourced from solar panels or geothermal loops.

The development of solar, wind, tidal and ground-sourced energy sources, able to power cities without resorting to the combustion of fossil fuels will profoundly redefine the future urban cosmopolitics. As sustainable energy is primarily mediated through electricity, supplies will need to be driven locally, driven by sustainable energy sources vary depending on climate and geology. The ubiquity of energy resources provided by fossil fuels will be phased out toward a reterritorialization of energies.

The thermodynamic concept of exergy is a central notion in this more eco-centric context, as it expresses energy with a built-in measure of quality. Exergy measures the combined energy of natural resources and captures the available work on any system, converting energy and matter in a metabolic process. Ecosystems consume energy, and an exergy flow through the system is necessary to keep the system functioning. Exergy analysis is commonly performed in the field of industrial ecology, in order to quantify the energy efficiency of a process and combines properties of a system and its environment, jointly. The current interest and investment in "Low-Exergy" building systems may entirely change the relationship between buildings and cities: unlike other energy forms, buildings are static and in permanent physical contact with the earth's energy. The possibility to tap into large volumes of matter with small temperature differentials (or low-exergy sources) may in the future deliver a substantial amount of energy to buildings, and increase the re-embodiment and re-localization of urban energy.

SKINS AND SOURCES:
TOWARD A THERMODYNAMIC MATERIALISM
Iñaki Ábalos and Renata Sentkiewicz

The abdication of concern with the architectural *interior* is a subject of considerable historical impact. Deflection of interest to the currently faddish idea of the "envelope" has resulted in a systematic deformation of thought, concept, and imagination in the field. By way of example, most discussions of an architectural "interior" imply the admission of a basic aspect: the concept of the interior varies with climatic regions and leads to differentiated modus operandi linked to two broad climatic areas (cold and warm), which generate two primal architectural prototypes. The first involves the construction of a compact, technified, parameterized, artificial ambience based on the artificial management of comfort using environmental strategies designed for seasonal cycles in cooler countries. The latter, projected from more "solar" geographies—the tropical and subtropical belt, including the Mediterranean—is based on the skillful, sensualist management of various elementary resources (described by Claude Lévi-Strauss as the method of the *bricoleur*) within predominantly daily, rather than seasonal, thermodynamic cycles. Obviously, these two modus operandi are open to every possible gradient of convergence, but their definition (or caricature) permits the identification of the original reference types in both cases: the greenhouse and the shade house, or better still, an updated version of Marc-Antoine Laugier's primitive hut: Richard Buckminster Fuller's modest glass dome and the shady beach bar. These two simple *Cabanes*, frivolous as they may seem, reflect two distinct approaches to a culture-based relationship between the physical environment and architecture.

Using these domestic typological archetypes, or caricatures, we can distinguish between different ways of materializing the interior-exterior dialectic on the basis of the thermodynamic relationship between matter, thermal "sources," and "sinks." In northern climates, the center—traditionally the fireplace/stove—is a basic resource, especially in homes with low thermal mass and high emissivity such as wooden structures. The interior core is the source of heat gains that compensates for the losses in the perimeter with different strategies that depend on the properties of the material: conduction and emission, thermal lag, etc. Thus, the interior is compact and activated by a solid core which provides thermal comfort. In the domestic environment, this point is located close to the stairs in order to centralize the heat source and to use buoyancy to store the nocturnal warmth on the upper floor.

In warm and temperate climates, the interior is always a heat sink, its most obvious manifestation being the courtyard house and the ubiquitous use of the patio at multiple scales. Shady courtyards, often passively conditioned by water surfaces, produce cross-ventilation and buoyancy generated by the lower weight of warm air to dissipate heat into the atmosphere. So the idea of the interior changes: the architectural interior is not occupied, but instead is a void; it is not a source but a sink, it is not a machine but an architectural space with a specific configuration and materiality, which is often the focus of social life at different scales. In turn, the external perimeter is not used as a solar collector but rather to shield the glazing from direct radiation and to maximize the porosity of

Interior of Jay Balwin's dome

the opaque material, using the air trapped in the material (adobe or clay) as insulation. Houses are attached to each other to create narrow streets and throw shadows on the walls. In contrast, houses have historically been set apart in cold climates in order to maximize solar gains, thus creating a lower-density urban fabric. Architecturally shaped interiors and exteriors are thus a "natural" mode in climates that require sinks, while the interior, which is occupied and treated as a thermal machine or source, is the particular or prototype form in areas where the climate defines long periods outside the range of thermal comfort.

These truisms would have no greater impact than a technical observation if the typologies in question were linked only to limited material resources. However, this duality of the interior as a heat source or sink is in fact the enunciation of an exemplary principle which illustrates the way that basic thermodynamic factors induce certain forms, geometries, and material properties. From the perspective of what I have called a "thermodynamic materialism," this way of working with passive parameters is still relevant and valid today, given the scarcity of energy resources and the growing social awareness of energy waste and its global consequences.

The skyscraper, the canonical symbol of modernity, was designed in and for early twentieth-century metropolises, which at the time were overwhelmingly located in the cold north. With its rings around a compact, machine-like, and mechanical core, the skyscraper is efficient in

Jean-Charles Adolphe Alphand, Buttes-Chaumont Park, Paris, France, 1867

such climates. However, it is a mistake to extrapolate this typology to other climates without revision: the current shift of the world's metropolis to tropical and subtropical zones, coupled with the feasibility of vertical extrusion above the twentieth or thirtieth story, require changes to the typologies and the organization of resources, with a much greater focus on maximizing ventilation and minimizing radiation. The Mediterranean interior is essentially an exterior climatized passively by the architecture, which is given different configurations depending on the specific climate, materials, and thermal loads generated by the interior activity. The courtyard is undoubtedly one of the most characteristic and recognizable configurations, but by no means the only one. The most extreme version of the passively conditioned interior is the "grotto" with its maximized stability thanks to the inertia of the earth (geothermal energy) and other strategies such as the combined action of radiation and ventilation. While the courtyard is one of the most widespread "thermosocial" devices—but also the most variable in scale and proportions—grottos are organized by means of horizontal or transversal perforations in the built mass to facilitate cross-ventilation and they are often built completely underground and to prevent direct sun lighting, to facilitate radiation from the human body to the building material, and to use the geothermal stability to reduce daily and seasonal peaks of heat and coldness.

Another recurrent mode, particularly suitable for public and large-scale buildings, is what could be described as "thermal baths." These are the large conglomerate of thermal mass, courtyards, and

Alejandro de la Sota1, houses in Alcudia, Majorca, 1984

grottos in combination with water and fire, used in cases such as the Caracalla baths in ancient Rome—a prodigious example of the efficient combination of form, matter, and energy in the construction of an essential public facility for Roman social and cultural life. This mode is a configuration of a hybrid, cellular thermodynamic conglomerate. Its calibrated cavities are deployed at different scales (from millimeters to hectometers) using specific techniques to regulate heat sources and sinks with highly varied ranges and scales. This conglomerate is largely automorphic—that is, self-similar across scales—and can give rise to ambiguous structures, anywhere between a single building and a cluster (what in modern times has been described as "mat buildings") created by the multiplication of porosities in the form of courtyards, grottos, and lanes organized as a single whole.

While the term "thermal bath" seems appropriate to this type of organization when applied to sunny Mediterranean climates, in cold climates, compacted interiors give rise to landform buildings, a term used by Stan Allen to describe large business, cultural, and infrastructure complexes, the heirs to the mat buildings and the mega structures of the 1970s.[1] This type also employs passive geology and places some emphasis on the use of natural materials, but falls short of the thermal bath concept, which exhibits a more complex organization of heat sources and sinks and a better adaptation to mild climates.

A redirected focus on the interior would lead today to the construction of a contemporary alternative to the modern project; which was based on the tectonic and thermo dynamic behavior of built spaces and would reject the misguided division between envelope and structure and the resulting proliferation of "commercial products" that belong to the triumphant pattern inherited from modernity. A material and formal review of modern assumptions, adapted to the local climate and contemporary material culture—including digital tools and the new understanding of thermodynamics—would accrue numerous financial and material benefits—both individual and collective, from health to hedonistic pleasure—and would have a powerful technical potential that

1. See Stan Allen and Marc Mc Quade, eds, *Land form Building* (New York: Princeton Architectural Press/Baden: Lars Müller Publishers, 2011).

Caracalla thermal baths, Rome, Italy, 3rd-century

is only now starting to be fathomed. Socially, it could enrich community life and the sensorial experience of citizens who would discover relatively undetermined spaces ready for them to appropriate in creative ways.

The principles of this redirection of priority away from the often one-dimensional values at the basis of the modernist project are those associated with what we might, for the purposes of argument, call a new "quadrivium" for the current age. They make up a considerable part of the thermodynamic materialism that contemporary work must address.

MATTER
Buildings and cities are an accumulation of matter and energy, organized systematically in relation to natural resources in order to create specific ecosystems that develop over time with varying degrees of self-organization. The matter that builds up—the set of materials that compose the building—constantly interacts with the physical environment through energy flows that take on different forms, depending on the sources (electromagnetic waves, air movements, and molecular movement in the mass, depending on whether we are talking about radiation, convection, or conduction).Matter organizes these flows simultaneously, while organizing the potential energy that underpins the structural work (and directs the gravitational forces, the wind, and the seismic movements into the ground to maintain the stability and compatibility of the various components).Ideally, the built artifact's matter and geometry collaborate syncretically in all three subsystems—spatial organization, tectonics, and thermodynamics—and with the natural elements on the basis of their integration as a choreographic system of automorphic porosities at different scales: the scale of the rooms that compose the spatial system, the full/empty scale that transfers the mechanical stress to the ground, and the scale of the internal porosity that defines their degree of conductivity/emissivity and their ability to insulate and/or organize convective flows. In its physical order, the building is a full/empty organization with different scales and a hybrid composition that forms a "conglomerate" which is able to negotiate energy flows and internal life (metabolism)to achieve relative stability in time.

Thermodynamic matter is the set of physical elements involved in the construction of the artifact as a comprehensive energy negotiation system. A separation into differentiated times and responsibilities (structure, internal partitions, and enclosures) is a left-over from the specialized mechanical paradigm of modernity, which gave rise to the general inefficiency of the modern building, the unnecessary proliferation of layers and single-purpose subsystems, and the difficult management of the staggered lifetimes of its endless list of hard-to-employ components. Thermodynamic materiality is thus synthetic and multi-area, but it is also hybrid. It is not only composed of voids and mass, but also has a binary organization: an inert part for the storage and regulation of heat gains, and an active part which is responsible for capturing energy and instantly adapting it to extraneous variations. In turn, the arrangement of the gaps or pockets transforms the air and organizes its flows in vital parts of this hybrid.

Thermodynamic materiality thus tends towards a new passivity (to avoid the need for mechanical devices and heat engines) and the abolition of specialized multilayered systems and commercial products (insulation, fibers, sound barriers, waterproofing, pipes, sluice gates, drop ceilings, etc.), which are replaced by a small, specialized, organic set of components that form a system which combines flows and matter as required by the design of the organization. *The engine is the building itself.*

Although it benefits from the beauty and the performance of certain historic, vernacular types of construction, this concept is not a nostalgic return to primitive mass. On the contrary, it tries to steer knowledge about material properties, scientific advances, and innovation towards a refined use of physical elements, depending on desired insulation, conductivity, emissivity, and diffusivity properties, integrating the system's tectonic-structural capacity, its availability and economy, and also its compatibility, to work in symbiotic organizations.

Thermodynamic materiality does not focus on the "construction detail" as an expressive moment, or the "envelope" as the primary manifestation. Instead, it aims to abolish them in favor of a 3D ensemble, ideally constituted as a set of natural and artificial materials, both visible and invisible, combined in a performative system with maximized compatibility and hence minimized complexity in its optimal expression.

The transformation of these ways in which the city can perceive matter requires a scalar leap in porosities and flows. It is automorphic in respect to the molecular and typological scales and is therefore analogous to the system described on the architectural scale.

FORM

The advocacy of form as the transcendental principle of all thermodynamic concepts has many implications for design protocols. The form factor, in its role in the energy performance of the exchanges of fluid between the building and its surroundings, is a major decision and, precisely for that reason, should be considered from the outset, given that any divergence from the basic principles of the adaptation of the form to each climatic context weighs irreversibly on the design process. Numerous tables and manuals provide quite simple explanations of the basic principles of adaptation between form and climate. Their diagrams are so obvious that they are often ignored, often hiding the cultural dimension of this advocacy of thermodynamic form.

The articulation of Stephan Behling's well-known *diagram of the present and future* is a lucid summary of the recent situation. Historically, however, this is a blind articulation that illustrates the inherent weakness of positivist approaches to time, which always focus on the future. If we want to incorporate this broader diachronic perspective, we need another type of organization, adding an initial triangle like the one for the future, in which the area used for Active Systems (with nuances), labeled as "past," is removed, and the initial labels "today/future" are changed to redefine the "past/20th-century/present" triangles. This gives rise to a

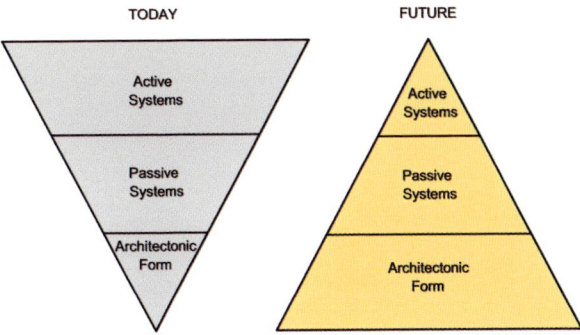

Stefan Behling. 2002

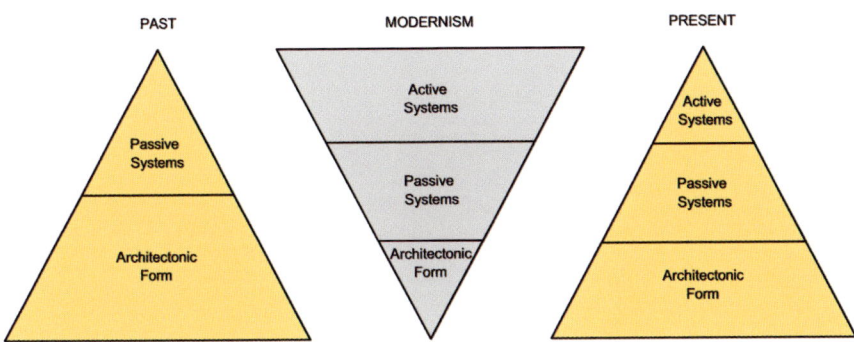

Iñaki Ábalos, Renata Sentkiewicz. 2013

new approach to the program to be deployed, and also the political and technical critique of modernity, postmodernity, and its "sustainable" epiphenomenon.

The triangles illustrate the potential authority of architects in the thermodynamic concept, given that the two most important base segments lie in their domain. They also show the limited efficacy of active systems, relegated, as they are, to resolving extreme or initially ill-conceived situations, including concepts that are spatially sealed off and isolated from their context. The most obvious conclusion is a vigorous defense of the validity of passive approaches (in both qualitative and quantitative terms), along with an affirmation of the responsibility of design techniques in the production of this program. This diagram also shows that not all typologies or locations can be resolved with passive strategies alone; that the parameterization of the physical environment plays a key role in identifying how far we can go in each case; and when innovation and invention, more closely tied to the realm of engineering, are indispensable. This is not a nostalgic advocacy of the past but a call for knowledge in all its forms, particularly the most advanced types.

Finally, the base and the centroid of the triangle—which sum to form the major responsibility of thermodynamics—permit the conclusion that there is a one-to-one relationship between form and matter: the form of matter and the matter of form are intertwined in a dialectic field of calibrated automorphism and porosity, a core issue in thermodynamic design.

Although this diagram is designed to explain the sustainability of buildings in thermodynamic terms, its scope can easily be expanded to the city, thus illustrating its pan-scalar potential. It also explains the role of typology as a historical system of empirical improvement over time, based on trial and error through the dual relationship between our social structures and adaptation and innovation.

To put it descriptively: form can be described now as both typical and prototypical, the former with a historical basis, the latter with an experimental scientific basis.

TIME

The inclusion of time in the body of scientific knowledge is one of the clearest triumphs of thermodynamics over the classical sciences. Since the earliest hominids' caves—or, if one prefers, since the first primitive huts and group settlements—down to the present day, the thermodynamic perspective has required an appreciation of architecture and the city as phenomena subject to constantly evolving fluctuations and processes, forming clusters of matter, energy, and culture that occasionally crystallize into stable structures during certain periods. These crystallizations now inform our work, regardless of their physical or historic location, and facilitate our understanding of the architecture that runs parallel(neither the same nor different) to the chronological, stylistic, ideological, iconographic, etc., sequences of conventional historiography. This vision, with its interpretation of the material culture, biology, and thermodynamic strategy in the city and its buildings as the same thing, is largely consistent with the anthropological vision of Claude Lévi-Strauss, who regarded the city as the "quintessential human thing."

Thermodynamic materiality permits countless ways to review the experience and legacy built up over time, and to expand the role and the techniques of historiography, in contrast to the modern prejudice of interpreting time as an ongoing positivist process of optimization and the postmodern bias that bases historiographic methods on suspicion and the questioning of their simplifications and instrumentalizations. A *redescription* of the contents of what—and how—we have learned can affect the humanist basis of historical perspectives and hinder their ability to interact with a reality that works from other positions. It is no coincidence that the digital and thermodynamic change of course converges in a total reconceptualization of time and its value as a design tool. This perspective helps us to understand the modern episode as a surrender of architecture, reflected in the huge amount of waste that has accrued despite so many heroic examples of outstanding talent, and verifiable in phenomena such as the abolition of the architectural interior and the universalization of the insulated, sealed envelope. In other words, we are witnessing a global dissolution of matter and the traditional tectonic concept without a parallel consolidation of alternatives, despite the massive use of material and energy during the twentieth century while our population was already growing at an unprecedented rate.

A new historiography of modernity that is neither apocalyptic nor moral, one which is the result of a reappraisal of the material culture in that experience occasioned by the thermodynamic change of course, should play a decisive role in the diachronic review of the past and its influence on the present, evaluating the acquired legacy and knowledge by using updated parameters.
In the case of modernity, this may happen when we evaluate great achievements such as the skyscraper as a typology, without focusing exclusively on its visual features, and instead relating it to the work done and the energy consumed at the private (building), collective (city), and global (world) scale. From a thermodynamic perspective, narrating the story of modernity is a necessary way of moving forward towards other ways of viewing and understanding architecture.

We doubtlessly see different things now when we look at the Pantheon, Pompeii, and the Caracalla thermal baths; when we see the heritage of Swiss, Basque, and Chinese domestic architecture, Europe's Gothic cathedrals and cities, the Crystal Palace, and the nineteenth-century bourgeois city. Time, culture, and the way we design have largely changed due to the parallel spread of science being applied to our everyday lives.

From the perspective of the digital and thermodynamic change of course, time is the invisible material that performs the updating processes—i.e., the integration, organization, and coordination that steer the transition from virtual to real in complexity theory—substantial to both changes; an " exfoliation of actualizing diagrams," in the words of Sanford Kwinter. In this situation, architecture seems to be a sort of human-designed biotechnology (similar yet different from spontaneous natural design) which operates with these actualizing processes and is shaped by time—that other real but incorporeal material. This concept is the one that can be articulated historiographically, because architecture is the means by which the productivity of these processes is revealed to us:

Joseph Paxton, Crystal Palace, London World Exhibition, United Kingdom, 1851

Architecture plays, or could and should play, a privileged role in bringing these processes of organization, integration and co-ordination not only to the foreground of public and cultural appearance but also to the more subtle arena of experience itself, to the place where time of things and the time of the body are one, to the space of intuition. Through the materialization of actualization, architecture has the capacity to free the imagination from three-dimensional experience—to free it from the curse of so-called" invisible processes" and hidden diagrams and to show us that the processes and events which give form to our world and our lives have shapes of their own.[2]

BEAUTY

It is tempting to idealize thermodynamic materialities as sources of an aesthetics that will revive the principles of organic unity inherent to a natural philosophy, and overlook the more essential aspects of thermodynamic change, imbalance, and flux and its status as a cultural and technoscientific construct that is no less provisional than a "mobile army of changing metaphors," which is how Friedrich Nietzsche characterized the history of philosophical thought. Despite its focus on matter and form, thermodynamic beauty has no stability or canon. It derives from the combination of new parametric ways of calibrating matter with the imperfection of the ordinary and the pragmatic, a subjective aspiration to make buildings and cities look and breathe like the citizens who inhabit them, and at the same time be an expression of their most cherished desires. The hypothesis of a thermodynamic beauty is based on the assumption that culture and knowledge lead the species to moments of order in the midst of chaos.

The design processes of thermodynamic materialism follow protocols that divide their moments between those that are initially objectifiable and additive—which give rise to the assembly processes of "thermodynamic monsters"[3]—and subjective, synthetic moments that negotiate the relationship between the prototypical built monsters and the substantial imperfections of the real world, its practices, and its material culture. While the idea of the monster is conventionally associated with ugliness, and imperfection is linked to faults or failures, thermodynamic beauty considers—as was the case with the picturesque aesthetics that it draws on—that a new idea of beauty can be achieved only through and by accepting large doses of ugliness. Monsters are the very catalysts of beauty; the moment when a formal and material base can be construed, distanced from clichéd languages.

---

2. Sanford Kwinter, "A Materialism of the Incorporeal," in AAVV, *Documents of Architecture and Theory*, vol.6 (New York: Columbia University, 1997), 85–89. *Documents* is a collective of collective essays published by Columbia University, in the vol. 6 the text of Stanford was included.

3. Iñaki Ábalos and Daniel Ibáñez,eds., *Thermodynamics Applied to Highriseand Mixed Use Prototypes* (Cambridge, MA: Harvard Graduate School of Design, 2013).

Thermodynamic beauty also understands and shares with the picturesque aesthetics the idea that imperfection, limitations, and chance are a stress field with just as much, if not more, aesthetic fecundity than the fields impregnated with certainty and assuredness. Thermodynamic beauty means that the old divisions between nature and culture have ceased to be operative at the same time that knowledge has ceased to be linked to isolated experiments, and now invades global society and life. As Bruno Latour accurately wrote about *Weather Report*, Olafur Eliasson's installation at the Tate Modern in London:

Since the sciences have expanded to such an extent that they have transformed the whole world into a laboratory, artists have perforce become white coats amongst other white coats: namely, all of us. We are all engaged in the same collective experiments. Both (Peter) Sloterdijk and (Olafur) Eliasson are exploring new ways of escaping the narrow constraints of modernism. They benefit from the rich humus provided by the sciences, but they turn scientific results upside-down, not to tell a great narrative of progress, but simply to explore the nature of the atmospheres in which we are all collectively attempting to survive.[4]

---

4. Bruno Latour, "Atmosphère, Atmosphère," in Olafur Eliasson, *Weather Report*, exh.cat. (London: Tate Publishing, 2003), 30.

FIRE IN URBAN GENESIS
Aleksandar Ivančić

*The chief function of the city is to convert **power into form, energy into culture**, dead matter into the living symbols of art, biological reproduction into social creativity.*
—Lewis Mumford, The City in History

ENERGY PASTS AND FUTURES

The city, the product of civilization par excellence, has emerged as an object of desire among rich and poor alike due to its ability to offer opportunity, be it economic, cultural, or social. As humans have found new ways to increase energy flows through society, an increasingly sophisticated control of energy has been occurring in quantum leaps of urban-evolutionary progress, leading in turn to more and more consumption.

In his pioneering work on evolutionary thermodynamics, Alfred Lotka postulated a theorem on energy as a catalyst for self-organization and increasing complexity among living organisms. In many aspects, and precisely in those of self-organization and complexity, cities can be seen to behave similarly to living organisms. The dynamics and evolution of the city are closely related to the energy that flows within its urban tissue. In *A Thousand Years of Nonlinear History*, Manuel de Landa wrote, "Urban morphogenesis has depended, from its ancient beginnings in the Fertile Crescent, on intensification of the consumption of nonhuman energy."[1]

1. **Manuel de Landa,** *A Thousand Years of Nonlinear History*. (Brooklyn, NY: Zone Books, 1997), pg 28.

Cities of more than a million inhabitants were a rare exception before humanity mastered control of fossil energy. The capability to efficiently direct and process energy within a city has always been highly dependent on available technology. The unprecedented population explosion of metropolitan areas in modern times is the direct result of a radical change in access to energy resources, a change that has accelerated hugely over the last two centuries.

In the second half of the eighteenth century, the steam engine enabled industrial activity to break free of a dependence on hydraulic mechanical power, enabling its relocation away from rivers. This first-level decoupling of city location from energy source proximity meant a greater overall regional isotropy in the accommodation of productive activities.

FOUR GREAT BUT UNKNOWING TWENTIETH-CENTURY URBANISTS

The last quarter of the nineteenth century was a period of massive scientific and technological change. Innovation in the field of energy during the second industrial revolution led to changes in both the physical and the socio-economic landscape, especially in the urban environment, since the rapid introduction of technology provided novel capabilities for everyday activities. Cities could evolve, develop, and thrive thanks to an increased availability of energy.

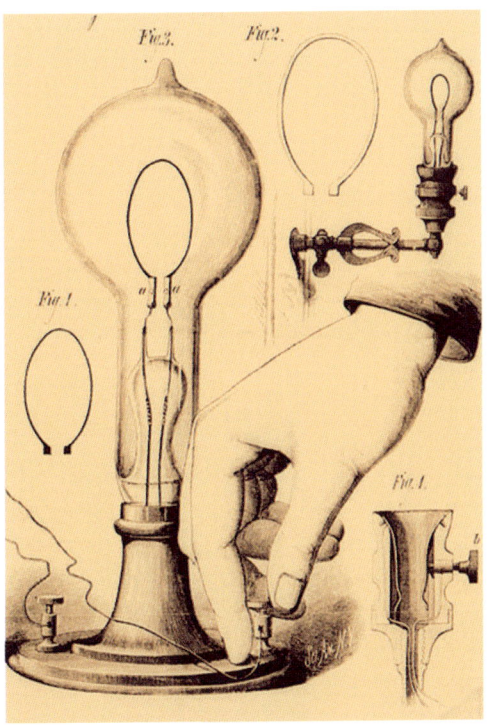

Edison's Light Bulb

At that time, four radical energy-related technologies were invented that particularly shaped the modern city. Curiously, despite contributing decisively to the present image of the city, none of the four inventors was an architect, urban planner, or city maker of any kind. Yet, each of them was simultaneously an engineer, inventor, and entrepreneur dealing with energy.

In 1880, Thomas Alva Edison, holder of over a thousand patents, illuminated Christie Street in Menlo Park, New Jersey, using fifty-three incandescent light bulbs, thus inventing the long-life, utility-scale urban electric lighting system. The conceptual novelty that Edison introduced, in comparison to similar devices from the same period, was that of a large robust system capable of illuminating entire cities. This signified the end of night-time as an inactive and passive period for cities of the epoch, opening the way for the non-stop city that operates twenty-four hours a day.

Soon after, Nikola Tesla, a Serbian-American inventor, engineer, and still to this day unsurpassed futurist, presented humanity with the transmission of an alternating current over a long distance to electrical motors that would eventually power elevators, subways, and other devices in cities. Vertical architecture became commonplace thanks to this invention, fostering the growth of cities in the third dimension.

Henry Ford, while chief engineer with the Edison Illuminating Company between 1893 and 1899, started experimenting with gasoline-powered engines, developing two prototype vehicles during that period. In the early twentieth century, Ford mastered the moving assembly line that allowed for the mass-production of cars, transforming the motor car from an expensive luxury item to a practical and affordable transportation medium for the middle-class citizen. The horizontal growth of cities was now possible, eventually leading to what we now refer to as urban sprawl. The city became virtually infinite in its reach.

But even if Edison had not invented the light bulb, Tesla the elevator, or Ford the automobile, by improving these devices and greatly enabling their massive use, the role of Edison, Tesla, and Ford in shaping the contemporary city became enormous.

Due to the energy-based inventions of urban lighting, efficient electrical power, and individual mobility, the expansion of the city in four dimensions was assured: the city became ready for space-time endlessness. With a technological basis established, the way was paved not only for urban utopias such as Le Corbusier's Ville Contemporaine or Ville Radieuse, Ludwig

Tesla's AC motor

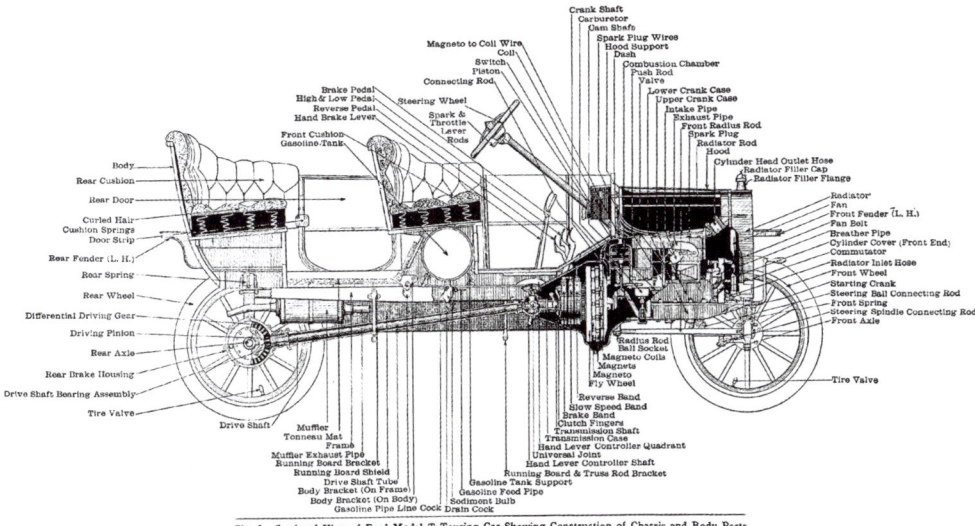

Fig. 2.—Sectional View of Ford Model T Touring Car Showing Construction of Chassis and Body Parts.

Hilberseimer's Großstadtarchitektur, or Frank Lloyd Wright's Broadacre City, among others, but also for new urban realities such as central business districts, edge cities, dormitory suburbs, etc.

Only one frontier remained, namely that of ubiquity. Inhospitable climates may not be a barrier for small vernacular settlements, but it was unimaginable for a modern metropolis to be situated in a place of extreme climatic conditions. This last barrier could be conquered only once total climate manipulation could be achieved. A distinguished personality in this regard was Willis Carrier, proclaimed the father of air conditioning or, as he called it: "man-made weather": a technology that helped "liberate designers from conventional methodologies of location of buildings in relation to the sun or by ventilating them with practicable windows, making them functionally dependent on air conditioning."[2] In other words, Carrier facilitated the proliferation of an architecture alien to its climate. The city becomes weather-proof, definitively unbound from environmental constraints despite the expense of enormous amounts of energy.

Le Corbusier adopted the idea of manmade weather shortly afterward, envisaging hermetically sealed buildings, the interiors of which would be kept at a constant temperature of 18 ºC, be they in Moscow or Port-Saïd. In his Ville Radieuse, he advocated using *respiration exacte* (exact air), *mur neutralisant* (neutralizing wall), and *brise soleil* (sun control). Referring to *respiration exacte*, or air conditioning, he reflects on climate diversity: "But then where is Utopia, where the temperature is 18ºC? [...] And why the devil do men insist on living in difficult or dangerous

2. http://www.willliscarrier.com.

Sectional View of Ford Model T Touring Car Showing Construction of Chasis and Body Parts

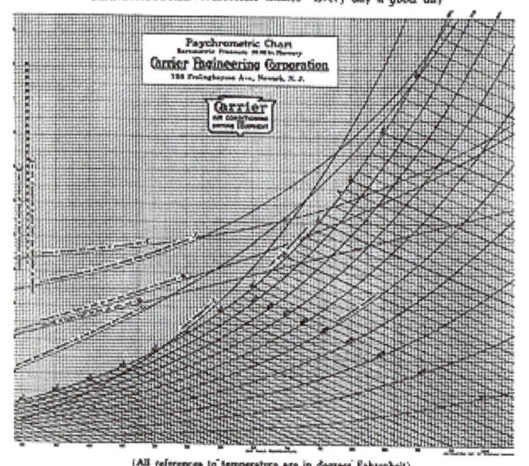

climates? I've no idea! But I can observe a worsening situation: The variety of climates had forged races, cultures, customs, dress, and work methods suited to the obtaining conditions."[3]

Le Corbusier expects technology to provide the solution for extending the 'promised land': "Since the machine age, the product of progress has disturbed everything, couldn't it also give us the means to salvation?" He thus concludes: "I seek the remedy, I seek the constant; I find the human lung. With adaptability and intelligence, let's give the lung the constant which is the prerequisite of its functioning: exact air. Let's manufacture exact air: filters, driers, humidifiers, disinfectors. Machines of childish simplicity. Send exact air into men's lungs, at home, at the factory, at the office, at the club and the auditorium: ventilators, machines so often used, but so often used badly!"[4]

He also comments that "Man resists extremes of cold more easily than extremes of heat."[5], and seems to be aware that the abundant use of glass may cause the overheating of buildings, requiring yet more air conditioning: 'Let's give man the solar rays which will penetrate the all-glass facades. But it will be too hot in the summer and terribly cold in the winter! Let's create 'neutralizing walls.' (And 'sun control')"[6]

The inventions of the motorcar and electricity caused the formerly clear frontier between countryside and city to become blurred, producing as a result major urban growth. Thus, the great reshaping of the twentieth-century city, of urban forms and architecture, did not come from the tectonic disciplines. It came not from shaping volumes, but from mastering and governing energy.

ENERGY IN THE NEXT SOCIO-ECONOMIC PARADIGM CHANGE

We are presently aware that humanity is capable of affecting the planet unlike any other biological species to date. In the Anthropocene, the power of human action has become greater

---

3. Le Corbusier, *The Radiant City: Elements of a Doctrine of Urbanism to be Used as the Basis of Our Magine-Age Civilization.* (Orion Press, 1967 1933), pg. 42.

4. Ibid.

5. ibid.

6. ibid.

Carrier's Psychrometric chart

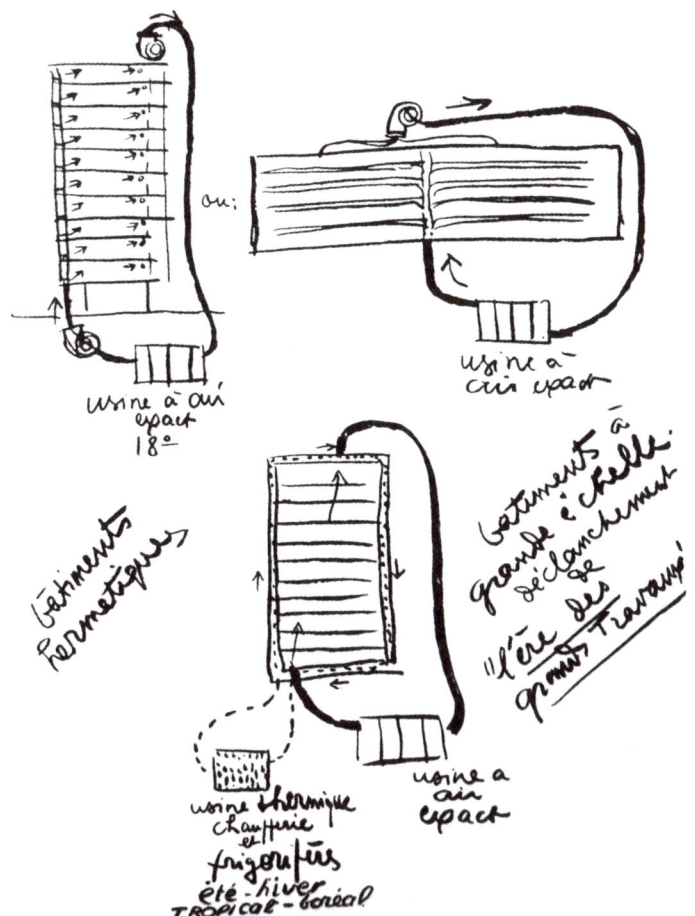

than that of geological forces. One of the main characteristics of the Anthropocene is the domination of carbon-based fossil energy and its massive use. The combustion of fossil resources that accumulated over long periods in remote times releases large quantities of carbon dioxide into the atmosphere. The greenhouse effect of this gas is one of the principal factors keeping our planet within a liveable threshold. Without it, all water on earth would be frozen and no life would be possible. Yet, the emissions released from the combustion of fossil fuels are dangerously raising the global atmospheric CO_2 concentration and causing smog formation in metropolitan agglomerations to the degree that the planet is warming and cities are drowning.
Buckminster Fuller, in his *Operating Manual for Spaceship Earth*, warned us of this eventuality with his brilliant reflection on the role of fossil fuels:

Le Corbusier's *respiration exacte*

"We can make all of humanity successful through science's world-engulfing industrial evolution provided that we are not so foolish as to continue to exhaust in a split second of astronomical history the orderly energy savings of billions of years' energy conservation aboard our Spaceship Earth. These energy savings have been put into our Spaceship's life-regeneration-guaranteeing bank account for use only in self-starter functions."[7]

The contemporary city is witnessing a significant change in energy-demand patterns as new forms of consumption expand quickly. Space cooling and power for computation are two kinds of electrical demands that are growing at a particularly rapid rate.

In an era of global warming and perturbed climate in densely built areas, the global demand for space cooling is estimated to grow significantly in the coming decades. Power consumption for space cooling already grew worldwide by 60% between 2000 and 2010. In 2010 alone, Chinese consumers purchased some 50 million air conditioning devices. Electricity consumption to satisfy cooling demand in India is placing major pressure on power systems, causing regular blackouts during peak cooling periods. Approximately 40% of Mumbai's power consumption is estimated to be due to air conditioning. Additionally, indoor space cooling requires that thermal energy extracted from buildings be dissipated into the environment. The next frontier of urban pollution could easily be the waste heat.

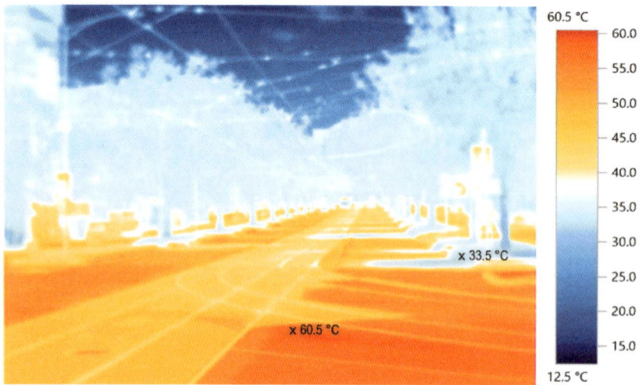

In the near future, cooling demand will likely rise most in the densely populated tropical regions of emerging economies such as China, India, Southeast Asia, or South America. According to optimistic forecasts by the International Energy Agency, global cooling demand is set to climb six-fold by 2050 with respect to current figures. Research undertaken by the Netherlands Environmental Assessment Agency predicts that cooling demand for the residential sector could surpass heating demand around the year 2060.

On the other hand, energy consumption for modern electronics and ICT systems is growing significantly due to increasing information gathering, processing, and transformation activity. The amount of energy that globally powers data centers quadrupled from 2007 to 2013, and is expected to nearly double again over the next 15 years.

7 Buckminster Fuller, *Operating Manual for Spaceship Earth*. (Zurich: Lars Muller Publishers, 2008), pg 128.

Melbourne's Elizabeth Street: Thermography showing heat island effect

The computer processors are each time more efficient. After the Koomey's law the number of computations per unit of energy dissipated has been doubling approximately every 1.57 years. But the global computation demand is evolving approximately three times quicker than the processors energy efficiency improvement. Following this pattern, the power demand for computing will reach the present value of total global power generation at some moment between 2035 and 2045.

With challenges of such magnitude in front of us, what kind of global energy landscape can we expect?

Actually, one of the most challenging questions for our society at the beginning of the twenty-first century is how to achieve a much-needed paradigm shift regarding energy. This challenge is more social and intelectual than technological. Finding the right answer is going to require covering a number of topics within a complex matrix that is holistic in its approach and offers an integrative view of the city, overcoming the divisions that often separate the social from the technological realm. The proper use of energy in buildings and in urban systems becomes paramount in a socio-political context increasingly concerned with environmental sustainability.

Actually, the next energy transition is already knocking at our doors. It can be found at the cross-section of the energy-information technology hybrid and the service-oriented platforms, or collaborative economy.

The collaborative economy is starting to prove that it is easier, cheaper, and more effective to involve a wider range of participants in value creation. Thus, new services are frequently being built based on partnerships between a variety of players rather than by a single giant company. In parallel, information and communication technologies are increasing the capability to control, gather, and analyze data at decreasing expense.

However, changes are also noticeable on the demand side: in affluent countries, users are more willing to take control in their exercise of the best choice regarding cost, service, and environmental impact. In a more ambitious or maybe extreme interpretation, this translates into so-called *energy self-sufficiency* in technical terms, or *energy sovereignty* as a political position. In any case, the most concise way to describe these new trends on both the supply and demand side is probably to use the term *energy democratization*.

This trend, in the first stage, is necessarily going to provoke a clash between incumbent "fossil" players and the "new kids on the block," as is already happening in the United States or in Spain. We should not forget that globally, the energy business is one of the most profitable legal businesses. But the incumbents are going to be forced to evolve and to adapt to the new situation, as is already happening in the German power sector, for instance.

So far, even if we would like to make quick and ground-breaking changes in the world's energy economy and in its consumption patterns, this will not be a short-term process; it will most probably take decades. The more affluent Western society typically determines the paths that the rest of the world follows, and the cultural *inertia* of an imaginary based on consumerism, which is particularly present in the urban environment, is so strong that it will take time for it to change.

In any case, the coming energy transition, which seems unstoppable, entails the opportunity of rethinking the relationship between energy and the city.

IMMINENT ENERGY FUTURES: FROM THE COMMODITY TO THE COMMONS
Unlike Edison, Tesla, Ford, or Carrier, the next game changers should help cities to make better use of better energy. What we see nowadays and what we can envisage for the immediate future is that the main drivers behind the energy (r)evolutions are the four Ds of Democratization, Decarbonization, Decentralization, and Digitalization.

The democratization of energy is becoming possible due to an important technological evolution, and especially due to the appearance of different soft and digital technologies. Soft technologies are ones that may be produced, purchased, used, or controlled by an individual or a small organization, and include small-scale energy-harvesting technologies such as solar, wind, and heat recovery. In the near future, we should be able to include small next-generation heat pumps, and eventually kinetic energy–harvesting devices and high-density energy batteries, among others.

In the past decade, solar PV technology has reached considerable maturity, with the cost of PV panels decreasing 10% per year over the last thirty-five years. Nowadays, the cost per energy unit produced by PV is equal to or even cheaper than conventional electricity generation in many countries. The International Renewable Energy Agency foresees that this cost could decrease by as much as 59% by 2025, meaning that PV electricity cost could become as much as three times cheaper than conventional generation. Next-generation PV, based on organic polymers, promises a further cost reduction and even better building integration, eventually becoming embedded within transparent glass suitable for windows. Battery storage costs are also expected to decrease by around 50% over the next five years, which may enable even stronger PV deployment in cities in the immediate future.

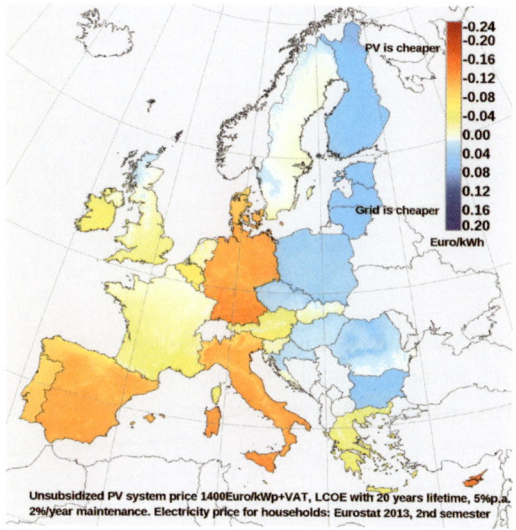

PV technology is becoming competitive in more and more countries

Unfortunately, the power density of solar radiation—the useful energy that may be harvested per unit area—is too low to satisfy the energy hunger of our cities. Thus, it is vital to reduce energy demand as much as possible and to supplement PV with other energy sources that cannot be as easily integrated within the city.

The objective of reducing building demand, as visualized in the net zero energy building (NZEB) concept, is being promoted globally—particularly in Europe, where it will become compulsory in 2020 for almost every kind of new building. It is particularly important to understand that an NZEB should not be conceived as an autonomous or autistic building in terms of energy, but as one that dynamically interacts with both its natural and its technological environments. Thus, the aim should not be to disconnect buildings from utility infrastructures but to turn them into active nodes in energy networks. Here, the capability of infrastructure to respond to this new network architecture is critical.

The concept of a smart grid, which is presently in rapid development, corresponds to this new architecture of a digitally enabled and integrated system with bi-directional energy and informational flows. The same basic idea is being applied to both electricity and thermal—heating and cooling—networks.

The ultimate objective of these smart systems is to make better use of existing and future energy infrastructures, which does not necessarily mean having less infrastructure. Our present utility infrastructures were built over decades as layers, each one upgrading the capacity or the functionality of previous layers. Thus, in a majority of cases, smart grids are going to be a next-generation upgrade of existing infrastructures. But a further potential for energy infrastructure evolution resides in a convergence of energy carriers and networks: electrical, thermal, and eventually hydrogen infrastructures have great potential to gain efficiency if interconnected. Electricity is much more efficient for energy transmission, while heat or hydrogen is much more efficient for energy storage.

Barcelona's Forum Area: co-siting and integration of different service infrastructures

Another emerging trend in urban energy efficiency is utility infrastructure coupling. This concept applies the field of industrial ecology, also known as industrial symbiosis, to urban systems. Whereas the conventional approach treats the three flows of water, energy, and waste separately, and thus considers the design of the corresponding infrastructures independently, an integrated or unified approach to these flows may significantly improve service performance. Both water cycle and waste treatment systems demand energy, while at the same time they may also potentially be sources of energy. An integrated approach seeks synergies between the infrastructures related to these three flows, with the aim of reducing the consumption of the resources in question. This new complex and promiscuous relationship between infrastructures demands interdisciplinarity (even antidisciplinarity) between more comprehensive urban planning and new-generation engineering. The first spatial consequence of such coevolution of infrastructures is co-siting of different systems. This means placing key elements of different systems together in order to facilitate the synergies between them.

In Stockholm's Hammarby Sjöstad district, the infrastructure systems were designed using this concept: infrastructures for water, waste, and energy feed from each other, thereby reducing the overall amount of energy and resources needed. The waste water from the housing is used as a heat source, while the biogas produced in the sewage treatment is used within a district heating system. Similarly, in Barcelona's Besòs area, a synergetic relationship is established between an organic waste treatment facility, an urban waste-to-energy plant, and a district heating and cooling plant in order to improve overall environmental efficiency.

Waste heat harvesting uses a complementary approach. Waste thermal energy abounds in urban environments, originating from different infrastructures but also from tertiary buildings, data centers, and industries, among other sources. In many cases this energy has a low exergetic value, meaning a low capacity for performing tasks due to the small difference in comparison with the temperature of the environment. It can nevertheless be used, in some cases directly but in most cases by means of a heat pump. A heat pump may actually become a kind of energy router, downloading and uploading energy to and from grids. Thus, the dissipated heat from industrial processes, electric and electronic equipment, and even from human bodies should evolve to become the main energy source for heating indoor space and water.

London's Bunkhill 2 Energy Centre: waste heat recovery from the subway tunnels, Cullinan Studio

An example of this is London's Underground subway, which is experimenting with recovering heat from the ventilation of tunnels. Between the Old Street and Angel stations, the abandoned station of City Road is now used as a mid-tunnel ventilation shaft. The Northern Line tunnel ventilation system extracts air at 18 to 28 °C year-round; the plan is that this waste energy will be recovered by heat exchangers and then upgraded to approximately 80 °C by means of a heat pump booster. Once upgraded, the energy will supply the existing Bunhill district heating system.

The massive use of low-grade waste heat is also being intensively promoted in the Netherlands. Waste heat from industrial facilities in the port of Rotterdam area is pumped through the *Warmterotonde* (heat roundabout) to greenhouses, industrial buildings, and housing in South Holland. The system is expected to cover The Hague and Delft and to reach the Leiden Region, and to supply heat to around 350,000 homes and 1000 ha of greenhouses by the year 2020.

A further urban energy challenge is to push the net zero energy concept in order to extend it from buildings to other urban objects. The question becomes: to what extent would it be possible to conceive of net zero energy infrastructures (NZEI) for our cities? Devices like traffic tunnels, metro lines, airports, water treatment plants, public space lighting, and many other city infrastructures are heavily dependent on an exogenous energy supply. Making them NZEI would significantly improve urban energy efficiency.

Up to the present moment, changes are being produced by strong progress in technology and constantly louder social demand. Yet, we still need to have a much deeper discussion of energy transition and a new socio-economic positioning of energy as a commons. This debate should not be reduced to encounters among experts, but should take place in a much wider political forum. After all, energy transition is about political change: when we begin to perceive energy as a commons rather than a commodity, the ground for this transition will be in place.

Current heat network of Rotterdam: waste energy recovery and long distance transport, *Warmtebedrijf* Rotterdam, 2017

MEYMAND by Sebastian Bullinger

EARTH

The *earth common* addresses the organic resources which make up the biosphere. Earth processes in cities relate fundamentally to the synthesis and resilience of life—human and otherwise—within urban environments. Life on Earth would be impossible without incessant cycling of key elements that make up biomass. Three cycles—those of carbon, nitrogen and sulphur—are particularly noteworthy: carbon is, of course, the dominant constituent of all living matter (typically 45-50% of dry weight). These three cycles are remarkable because of their complexity, the importance of microbes in their functioning, and because the cycled elements are transported by both air and water away from their sources. How these cycles interact with urban cycles is the key to the perpetuation of non-human life in the city.

The birth of urban civilizations was aligned with the ability of human communities to increase the productive capacity of land to feed larger densities of people. The management of these organic resources was related to the birth of writing, mathematics, astronomy, calendars, and many other disciplines. The ability to predict when environmental conditions would change allowed early civilizations to take advantage of the harvest, produce more food and other organic resources for their citizens, and vastly increase their population and security. Because most arcane citizens were farmers, there was a direct relationship between the productive capacity of the land, and the population which could be sustained in a city. This balance changed with advanced agricultural techniques and animal labor, as well as machines and synthetic fertilizers.

While vegetation and organic matter appear to be the nemesis of architecture, destabilizing architectural matter and leading to deterioration and failure, plant matter, soil, and other organic elements are increasingly being re-incorporated into city fabrics and building design for a number of reasons. For example, organic matter as a percentage of surface area coverage affect reflectivity, humidity, thermal mass, heating and cooling cycles, and water runoff.

Because most arcane citizens were farmers who were designated plots of land, there was a direct relationship between number of laborers, the productive capacity of the land, and the population which could be sustained in a given region. This relationship changed with advanced agriculture techniques and animal labor, as well as machines and chemicals like synthetic fertilizers.

After a long exile from the city, plant matter, soil, and other organic elements are increasingly being re-incorporated into city fabrics and building design. Organic matter as a percentage of surface area coverage affect reflectivity, humidity, thermal mass, heating and cooling cycles, and water runoff. Cities depend on the synthesis and resilience of life—human and otherwise. Urban land cannot be determined exclusively by functional assignments in respect to human functions: it involves topography, climate and the bioactive layer of the soil. Cities depend the synthesis and resilience of life -human and otherwise- within urban environments. And life is only possible through the incessant cycling of key elements that make up biomass: carbon, nitrogen and sulphur.

Nitrogen is one of the most important elements to organic life, accounting for 6.25% of the dry mass of a given organism on average.[1]

1. Hermann Bothe, William Edward Newton, and Stuart Ferguson, eds., *Biology of the Nitrogen Cycle* (Amsterdam: Elsevier Science, 2006).

This element is essential to organic growth, however, most of the nitrogen on earth is in a gaseous form unusable by plant and animal matter.[2] In order for this element to be used by living organisms, it must be "fixed" in usable form. In 1909, Fritz Haber, a German chemist, synthesized ammonia (NH_3), a compound of nitrogen and hydrogen. By 1913, Carl Bosch, a German chemist and engineer had developed a commercial process for producing large amounts of ammonia to be used as fertilizer and BASF, a German chemical company, began using the "Haber-Bosch process."[3] In the following decades, fertilizers with ammonia from the Haber-Bosch process would be mass produced. By 2011, synthetic nitrogen fertilizers provided "just over half of the nutrient received by the world's crops."[4] As a result of the Haber-Bosch process and the extensive cultivation of legumes in agriculture, humans have vastly increased the nitrogen cycle's transfer of nutrients into biologically usable forms, more than doubling the annual nitrogen transfer over the last century.[5] Due to human intervention in the natural processes of nutrient transfer, human population has increased exponentially, and synthetic ammonia accounts currently for roughly 45% of the human population, at great energy expense.[6] Obviously, this situation is entirely unsustainable, and cities need to reconstruct their original relationship with the biosphere, if food security needs to be ensured. The relationship between urban land and its bioactive layer needs to be retrieved in order to be able to sustain urban populations, reduce global energy consumption, absorb carbon dioxide and improve generally the urban microclimates.

2. Steven B. Carroll and Steven D. Salt, *Ecology for Gardeners* (Portland, OR: Timber Press, 2004).

3. Smil, "Nitrogen Cycle and World Food Production."

4. Ibid.

5. P.M. Vitousek, J. Aber, R.W. Howarth, G.E. Likens, P.A. Matson, D.W. Schindler, W.H. Schlesinger, and G.D. Tilman, "Human Alteration of the Global Nitrogen Cycle: Sources and Consequences," *Issues in Ecology* 1(3) (1997): 1–17.

6. Smil writes: "Without the use of nitrogen fertilizers we could not secure enough food for the prevailing diets of nearly 45% of the world's population, or roughly three billion people." Smil, "Nitrogen Cycle and World Food Production."

Therefore, biotechnologies have developed increasingly effective urban applications—urban farming, hydroponics, and algae cultures with the ability to produce food, biofuels and even lit cities—are some of the fastest growing urban applications. High-tech farming technologies such as hydroponics and aquaponics are constantly improved to increase the efficiency and yields. The deployment of such technologies will become increasingly relevant to urban practices and assemblages.

Urban land cannot be determined exclusively by functional assignments in respect to human functions: it involves topography and the bioactive layer of the soil. A new type of land determinations, such as biomass rates, nitrogen contents, carbon footprints and land surface energy budgets establish equivalences between land and space-measuring units and the capacity to produce energy from sustainable sources, to emit carbon or nitrogen to the atmosphere and perform within the hydrological cycles. We can imagine that some of these parameters will become the urbanist parameters of tomorrow, just as the floor-area ratios, the land use or the building footprint.

Some recently developed technologies for managing dense collections of organic matter include bioreactors using algae cultures, carbon dioxide, sunlight and water to produce foods, oxygen and biofuels. New closed loop, vertical bioreactors have greatly increased the efficiency and reduced the environmental impact of open-pond biodiesel production, and allowed them to enter into urban areas because of their small footprint. Green building envelopes—roofs and walls—are capable of not only increasing a building's *albedo*,[7] but also retaining natural humidity in the urban microclimate, absorbing carbon dioxide, producing oxygen, reducing the heat island effect, and even contribute to the production of food. These technologies have yet to be incorporated into buildings as an integral part of the earth's surface, an intrinsic component of the imminent urban cosmologies.

7. Albedo is the earth's reflectivity, another parameter derived from meteorology and energy budgets commonly applied to building envelopes. *Environmental Encyclopedia*, 3rd ed. (Farmington Hills, MI: Thompson Gale, 2003).

The earth common also involves the non-organic and physical entities of urban land, and of buildings as part of the artificial crust of the earth. According to the World Metrological Organization, on average, every square meter of the earth's surface is struck by 164 Watts of energy per day. How this energy is reflected or absorbed has profound effects on the local microclimates. Subtle changes in the surface composition of urban pavements and building envelopes can have dramatic effects on the local microclimate. The Urban Heat Island (UHI) effect is a phenomenon that describes climate change in urban areas, leading to significantly hotter temperatures compared to neighboring rural areas. High concentrations of dark materials which absorb solar radiation, thermally massive and impervious materials, such as those that make up our road infrastructure, and a lack of materials which absorb and evaporate water can lead to this effect. Higher surface temperatures and reduced airflow due to buildings acting as a wind trap, have relevant impacts on the UHI effect. Some unexpected consequences of UHI include monthly rainfalls which tend to be higher downwind of UHI cities due to warming effects, pollution becoming concentrated due to a lack of airflow, and further losses of vegetation due to changes in climate which affect the biomass cycles.

The Surface Energy Budget of an entity on the surface of the earth is the amount of solar energy which it absorbs which is then balanced out through different forms of energy dissipation. Typically, around 48% of incoming solar energy is absorbed by the surface of the earth, with 29% being reflected by particles in the upper atmosphere or reflective ground sources and 23% being absorbed by the atmosphere itself. That 48% of net solar energy absorbed by materials on the surface of the earth then has to be dissipated through evaporation, convection, or thermal radiation (in the form of infrared radiation). The infrared radiation emitted by the surface of the earth is one of the primary drivers of the greenhouse effect the source of energy driving climate change. While gasses such as oxygen and nitrogen are transparent to both visible and infrared radiation, other gasses present in the atmosphere such as carbon dioxide and methane are transparent to visible radiation but opaque to infrared energy, absorbing the thermal radiation emitted by the earth and re-radiating it back down to the surface, intensifying the UHI.[8]

The more energy is absorbed in the physical fabric of a city, the more energy has to be dissipated through other means. Higher percentages of heat-absorptive materials in urban pavements or building envelopes lead to higher net thermal infrared radiation, which leads to an increase of infrared-opaque materials in the atmosphere and increased re-radiation back to the surface of the earth and even further warming. By manipulating the overall *albedo* of an urban surface—for example by removing vegetation and adding materials such as concrete or dark roof tiles—significant changes in the urban microclimate can take place. This not only has an effect on global warming, it also can have serious negative local effects, making air in city streets stagnant or blustery, making temperatures uncomfortably hot or subject to wild temperature swings, or manipulating city wide humidity levels. Furthermore, these subtle microclimatic changes can have large economic impacts on cities. Raising the average temperature of a city (where large numbers of people are concentrated) by even one degree Celsius increases urban energy consumption by elevating cooling loads on air conditioners. Transferring Surface Energy Budgets from geophysics and microclimatology to architecture can account for the relationship between land, hydrology, energy and airflow. Some of these parameters invented to capture environmental parameters on a continental scale, can become effectively used to plan cities in respect to the earth common.

---

8. NASA Earth Observatory, "Surface Energy Budget," NASA, https://earthobservatory.nasa.gov/Features/EnergyBalance/page5.php, accessed 30 March 2017.

PROTEST LANDSCAPES:
SCENES OF UPHEAVAL ON THE GROUND[1]

David Gissen

Citizens of Madrid and Lisbon leaving large piles of garbage at the entryway to the city's banks, French farmers dumping manure in front of Parisian government buildings, Peruvian farmers blocking city roadways with enormous piles of rocks … These seemingly unrelated formations made in recent years are the latest manifestation of "protest" landscapes. They are forms of protest because they are made as statements that agitate for an alternative political future; and they are landscapes because their authors fashion them as both things and potential scenes made with materials on the ground. In many iterations, these protest landscapes might be one of the more provocative realizations of landscape in the contemporary city and its surroundings, but one that has not been named as such or closely examined as a genre. Made during moments of revolt and protest, these barricades, mounds, and heaps are typically positioned *against* the existing iconography and utility of the city and countryside. These landscapes, which can be traced to early modernity, are a critical component of recent contemporary culture, and several offer another physical manifestation of the early twenty-first-century networks of revolt within the contemporary city.

Within the long and contemporary history of landscapes, the protest landscape offers both a compelling counterpoint and a surprising extension of the aesthetic politics and disciplinary concerns of those who make claims to the urban and ex-urban ground more generally. While the word "landscape" has become generalized to describe any assemblage of things,

1. Research for this article was aided by Samuel Garcia Perez in Paris and Madrid and Tiago Lopes Diaz in Lisbon. Thank you to Fabrizio Gallanti for assistance in locating researchers.

what I call "landscape aesthetics" and "disciplinarity" are a set of practices and sensibilities that have origins tied to eighteenth- and nineteenth-century architecture and art practices and that have extended into virtually every conception of urban space.[2] Within this particular history, landscapes—whether one speaks of picturesque landscapes in eighteenth-century England, nineteenth-century parks such as Central Park, or contemporary parks in Madrid—are places for specific instrumental activities tied to scenes and objects that create arguments out of the ground. "Landscape" is thus a term of use and politics as much as it is a term of topography and nature. I believe protest landscapes offer a confrontation to this tradition from within, as their authors and planners must operate within the conceptions of ground and nature formulated within an older disciplinary history and that permeate any city or given landscape.

Things which we might call "landscapes" that were made as acts of modern protest have an even longer history, traceable to the early modern history of the large town and city. In Paris, for example, barricade construction as a radicalized extension of urban political bargaining commenced in the sixteenth century; the fabrication of mounds as a form of urban protest and agitation can be traced quite early in France and reached a monumental moment in the years following the 1789 revolution. But what I see as the conjunction between modern protest and

2. See e.g. Malcolm Andrews, *Landscape and Western Art* (New York: Oxford University Press, 1999). For a competing definition of "landscape," see W. J. T. Mitchell, ed., *Landscape and Power* (Chicago: University of Chicago Press, 2002).

Protesters blocking the road to a mining project with boulders, Yorohoco, Desaguadero, Peru-Bolivia border, May 16, 2011

modern notions of landscape are further entangled with their mediation and mass representation, and are thus tied to a more recent and modern history, sometime between the end of the nineteenth century and the beginning of the twentieth century. Numerous European historians describe the 1871 revolt *La Commune de Paris* as the origins of modern revolt, and examining the numerous productions and photographic representations of its landscapes of barricades, debris, and rubble, its destruction of urban iconography, its appropriation of urban networks to radically different and expressive ends, one might consider it the origin site of the modern protest landscape. The activities of the Commune overturned and subverted the Second Empire's vision of the city. And the photography of the ruins and rubble from this revolt enabled a type of reflection on the Commune's actions—a type of reflection seemingly impossible within the parameters of revolt itself. This photographic documentation further enabled the repetition of and association with certain key contemporary acts within the Commune—for example, within the pamphlets of the Situationist International to the more recent events of the Occupy movement.

In terms of politics, one can locate the contemporary manifestations and production of protest landscapes across a wide political range. While many protest landscapes are certainly produced as

A barricade during the Paris Commune, boulevard Voltaire and boulevard Richard-Lenoir, 1871

politically leftist acts against State and municipal governments, if we accept the definitions above, we must also acknowledge their appearance in a more ideologically diffuse political anarchism and rightward leaning libertarianism. Nevertheless, virtually all of the examples examined in this essay were made in response to the continual reach of neo-liberal economics via state-level policies that led to often acute transformations in the relationship to nature and the ground more generally—in agricultural enterprises, urban waste, or resource mining. And while calling these things "protest landscapes" implies roots in the cities and spaces of continental Europe, the protest landscape is found across a global geography of various cities and towns. But rather than simply offer an overview of or ultimatum on the protest landscape's geographic and political character, my goal here, as is clear already, is to identify it as a category of landscape in the first place. I believe this statement contains its own political possibilities, and I ultimately wish to position it in such a way that we can rethink those disciplines that make claims for the future landscapes of the contemporary city.

The Vendôme Column in ruins, Paris, 1871. Hippolyte-Auguste Collard

AESTHETICS

Protest landscapes are disruptive; they offer moments of anti-iconography and—most critically—the sublimity of repulsion as a form of revolt. In January 2014, Thierry Borne, the manager of a stable complex in the Rhône-Alps, parked a large semitrailer in front of the French National Assembly in Paris with the words "Hollande et toute la classe politique dehors!" (Hollande and the entire political class out!) painted on its side. He then proceeded to dump several tons of horse manure out of the back of the truck into a large pile adjacent to the monumental steps of this government building.[3] This action was an urban version of a type of protest landscape that has appeared in numerous iterations in French rural capitals. In recent years, French farmers and agricultural workers have resorted to dumping manure at local state administrative buildings as a method of protest that brings the fetishized labor of the countryside to the attention of the city centers where changes in legislation that impact their enterprises are made. In 2014, the entryway to a government office in rural France was literally buried in manure by the local farming cooperatives.

In conducting this absurd action at the National Assembly, Borne constructed a temporary and visceral landscape that figuratively associated politicians with "shit," while introducing a stench familiar in the countryside and that wafted through the political center of the city. In photographs of his arrest, one sees police officers and guards wrinkling their noses in the presence of the enormous pile—a contemporary and more fantastical iteration of what historian Vittoria di Palma describes as the key experience of "disgust" that drove a more polite pastoral aesthetic within the notion of proper landscapes.[4] Such notions of disgust in this context also create a potential entryway into the more explicitly *anti-pastoral* experience fashioned by Borne, in which the labor of the countryside is presented as a noncommodifiable aspect of urban experience—a disruption both in the urban view of the countryside and in the mechanics of urban ecology. One must acknowledge these aesthetic aspects of the landscape of protest as a critical component—a confrontation with by-products of a contemporary urbanism.

In this particular iteration—representative of others—the protest landscape also becomes a regurgitation of the eighteenth-century concept of the "sublime" as political expression. Within the landscape sublime, one felt the unsettling pleasure embedded within one's experience of a frightening landscape, and this experience could be equally conveyed in art and literature. The romantic notions embedded in such aesthetic theories are related to the aforementioned confrontation with fetishization; one hypothetically engages in a sublime confrontation with what fell out of view—the space of the factory, the ecological waste products of the industrialization of food and agriculture. But the sublimity of several protest landscapes extends beyond this romanticist politics of revelation, beyond simply seeing massive amounts of waste; they also offer opportunities to engage in disruptive acts—blocking traffic, introducing piles of offensive matter

3. See e.g. "Fumier devant l'Assemblée: Thierry Borne porte plainte contre les policiers," France Info, 18 January 2014, http://france3-regions.francetvinfo.fr/rhone-alpes/2014/01/18/fumier-devant-l-assemblee-thierry-borne-porte-plainte-contre-les-policiers-397611.html (last accessed on 25 January 2015).

4. Vittoria Di Palma, *Wasteland: A History* (New Haven, CT: Yale University Press, 2014).

as a symbol against power in bureaucratic spaces, and explicit uses of humor against the self-seriousness of urban monumentality. We can understand the protest landscape as a "landscape" not only because of its form, not only because people make protest landscapes out of matter that lies on the ground and represent them as landscapes, but also because the reactions they are meant to convey in those viewing these landscapes and the representations of individuals as they view them offer a parallel realm of sense that overturns a more traditional conception of landscape. While these protest landscapes can be strange—seemingly too far outside the genre "landscape"—they nonetheless resonate with the historically conceptualized aspects of landscape experience.

REPETITION

Protest landscapes are seemingly, and often endlessly, repeated. We might understand barricades or heaps as repetitive unauthored social acts, but that might deny the self-awareness of the various movements and individuals who create these protest landscapes. As stated above, photography plays a critical role in enabling us to understand protest landscapes as realms for reflection and contemplation, but photography also enables these structures to inspire imitators. The protest landscape becomes radical not only through the radical actions of their creators but through interrelated repetitions and photographic distributions of them that position these landscapes as real and potential threats to urban order. The circulation within media of these landscapes remains a critical component of their contemporary representation. The recent Instagram/Twitter hashtag "#tubasuraalbanco ("your garbage to the bank") accompanied photographs of the very large piles of trash dumped by people in Madrid at various banks, and these photos were a critical factor leading to the repetition of this action in several locations around the city.

#Tubasuraalbanco has its roots in the November 2012 garbage worker strike that followed the state-mandated layoff of 1,143 garbage workers and a 40% proposed pay reduction as part of a measure to privatize garbage collection. As garbage collectors went on strike in Madrid, trash quickly amassed in overflowing containers and became strewn around numerous streets and public spaces. In response to the crisis, the collectives that had formed around the socialistic 15M protests of 2011 responded to the escalating trash problem by dumping trash at banks—because the banks were blamed for promoting policies that led to the initial economic crisis. The groups posted photographs of the trash piles accompanied with statements such as "Put it in the safe with the rest." Hundreds of photos of trash piles at Spanish banks emerged in the ensuing days on Instagram, Twitter, and Facebook, and the action played a role in the favorable labor agreement reached between the workers and the garbage companies two weeks after the strike. In February 2013, when garbage workers went on strike in Lisbon due to similar reasons, activists used photos of the original Madrid action to call for an action in Lisbon, named #OLixoAosBancos, where it enjoyed a similar mass appeal and representative power. Again, numerous images of garbage piled at bank entryways appeared in various forms of social media networks.[5]

5. See TuBasuraAlBanco http://ccaa.elpais.com/ccaa/2013/11/13/madrid/1384333518_867444.html and https://www.facebook.com/TuBasuraAlBanco?fref=ts (last accessed January 25, 2015).

Like Thierry Borne's action, #Tubasuraalbanco befouls urban spaces as an act of association and damning critique. But what makes #Tubasuraalbanco so compelling is that its propagators understood that photographing these piles of garbage in numerous locations would visualize both the actual reality and an alternative, fantastical urban ecological reality. The participants in #Tubasuraalbanco subvert the function of a bank, but in so doing, they also subvert the perverse and late-modern urban ecological frameworks of the modern city, which historian Antoine Picon once mockingly characterized as an "anxious landscape" extending from shopping mall to the landfill.[6] #Tubasuraalbanco brought the most hidden aspects of this ecology (garbage and refuse) into the "clean" iconographic and instrumental sites of finance that underpin the relationship between consumerism and trash. One can view #Tubasuraalbanco as an abject confrontation against finance and a performative act of solidarity with labor as much as a landscape montage that juxtaposed two spaces at opposite ends of the urban spatio-financial structure—the bank and the dump.

ACTION

When such protest landscapes are realized, they represent a compelling notion of landscape formed through action as much as a protest created through a transformation of the conditions of landscape—the surface through which economic realities are mobilized. This variant of the "production of nature" potentially challenges not only how we understand the production of

6. Antoine Picon, "Anxious Landscapes: From the Ruin to Rust," *Grey Room* (2000): 65–83.

Tweet posted during protests in Madrid with the hashtag #TuBasuraAlBanco
(Your Garbage to the Bank), February 1, 2014

protest but also the character of the urban landscape in production.[7] Beginning in the mid-1990s and continuing today, a series of protests have swept Peru, Argentina, and Bolivia in response to a range of governmental reforms, from changes in government workers' pay, privatization efforts in national rural electrical utilities, and changing environmental practices among the countries' numerous foreign and state mining conglomerates. These seemingly diverse causes share a concern over shifting neo-liberal policies of governance and their economic and environmental effects, and are intimately tied to the types of economic transformations railed against in the protests in Madrid and Lisbon. One of the key examples of such activity was the action in 2004 by a group of northeastern Peruvian farmers who fashioned large fields of stones across the roadways around Cajamarca, effectively forming impassible barricades to automobile traffic. This was a protest against the government's plans to issue the U.S.-owned Newmont mining company a permit to mine the nearby Cerro Quilish mountain, which would have had a devastating impact on the farmers' water supply. In the face of the protest's intensity and the extent of the barricade construction, the government interceded and denied Newmont a license to mine the mountain.[8]

As political theorist Moisés Arce has noted, in addition to the content of these various Peruvian protests, what made these protests unique was that they entailed a shift from traditions of strikes and street protests to barricade construction. More specifically, they extended the action and activity of protest from the workplace to the landscape. Typically, the Peruvian barricades were built from rocks strewn across rural roadways often 50 to 100 yards deep, which effectively made roads impassable by truck and therefore shut down country to city trade. Like #Tubasuraalbanco, the barricades were the result of earlier actions across a wide geography. Between 1997 and 2002, 4,676 road blockades were formed on roadways throughout Argentina—an incredible figure.[9] In both countries, the road blockade has emerged as a key and surprisingly effective manifestation of economic protest and negotiation due to the way it disrupts *all* activity along the roads. Such actions represent a considerable shift in understanding the techniques of political action and negotiations for environmental and workplace reform. They also more directly represent key shifts in our understanding of the potential politics of ecological activism. Against the very real possibility of their farmland being transformed into unproductive land as a result of the environmental fallout from mining operations, the farmers surrounding Cerro Quilish briefly transformed the area's roadways into an analogous landscape—a temporary wasteland. As in the other examples cited above, the late-modern urbanized space "of flows" is transformed into a more stagnant reality.

7. Neil Smith, *Uneven Development: Nature, Capital, and the Production of Space* (Athens: University of Georgia Press, 2008).

8. See Moisés Arce, "The Repoliticization of Collective Action after Neoliberalism in Peru," *Latin American Politics and Society* 50(3) (2008): 36–7. See also Gaston R. Gordillo, *Rubble: The Afterlife of Destruction* (Durham: Duke University Press).

9. Arce, "The Repoliticization of Collective Action," 40–41.

LANDSCAPE

"Landscape"—broadly defined—is a realm that presents particular obstacles to the rather impressive *expressive* politics and actions throughout this short essay. In the context of landscape, I use the term "expressive actions" to describe those activities and formations that can be realized both alongside and potentially outside of preconstruction, representational instruments.

This includes technical drawings and plans and bureaucratic planning, not to mention the biggest preconstruction representational instrument of them all—money. I would argue that the expressive limitations of our understanding of landscape are primarily due to both the considerable infrastructural scales at which the word "landscape" tends to be utilized in the English language and how it is realized as a public discipline—the labor and capital involved in working with its materials. And yet, without overstating the point, action and activity are what appear to rival representational instruments so well in the range of actions that I call protest landscapes.

Today, numerous landscape architects argue that the political future of the urban landscape is to be found either in explicitly ecological projects or in what is termed "landscape urbanism," where land-

Farmers spraying liquid manure on riot policemen during a protest over soaring fuel prices, Dijon, France, June 2, 2008

scape becomes embedded in a city's or countryside's infrastructural network.[10] In the South American context, Harvard University's Graduate School of Design has engaged in an ambitious effort to use landscape urbanism concepts to address many of the environmental concerns over land use, water, and resource allocation which were voiced in the protests briefly described above.[11] Both ecological landscape and landscape urbanism offer clear appeals to the profession, as they mark shifts away from the decorative roles that nature often takes in cities and its surroundings, and they place the designers and producers of landscapes in a position to have a determining influence on urbanization.

But the protest landscape suggests that the political expressiveness of the ground might lie in additional possibilities—additional practices that are outside these disciplinary self-reflections. Again, this idea requires some more thought, but a group of Peruvian farmers rolling rocks down a hill to form a highway barricade, a group of students turning several cars over on their side, and the explosive force of a monument falling into a pile of detritus outside Kiev represent an idea of politics found in landscape. I doubt one could easily incorporate these manifestations into one discipline, but that tension offers another moment for disciplinary reflection—not at all unique to landscape. In the late 1960s, early 1970s and more recently, architects and organizations found a certain expressive, serial architectural action and politics via the creation of inflatable architecture, deployable furnishings, and other forms of quickly made experimental structures. In landscape, the analogous object to such forms of "instant" architecture is the heap. The protest landscape, which is formed through the intersections of nature-matter, action, repetition, and mediation, differs from other political landscape formations found within both a discipline that lays claim to the urban landscape and our understanding of what the experience of landscape might become in the contemporary city. Nevertheless, those of us reading this essay may not be the actors who reproduce these artifacts; we may not all literally be on the barricades, so to speak, but we must all understand these creations as belonging to both a category of thought known as politics and a category of thought called landscape. Protest landscapes are arguments for a different type of realization of nature both within and outside the city—one that speaks of a larger representational territory and those tied to it. The productions that can be realized from the explicit intermingling of politics and landscape have an outline somewhere on the ground and somewhere in the immediate future.

10. Charles Waldheim, ed., *The Landscape Urbanism Reader* (New York: Princeton Architectural Press, 2012)
11. See The South America Project, http://www.sap-network.org/ (accessed 25 June 2015).

TOWARDS A "NEW" HELIOMORPHISM
Charles Waldheim

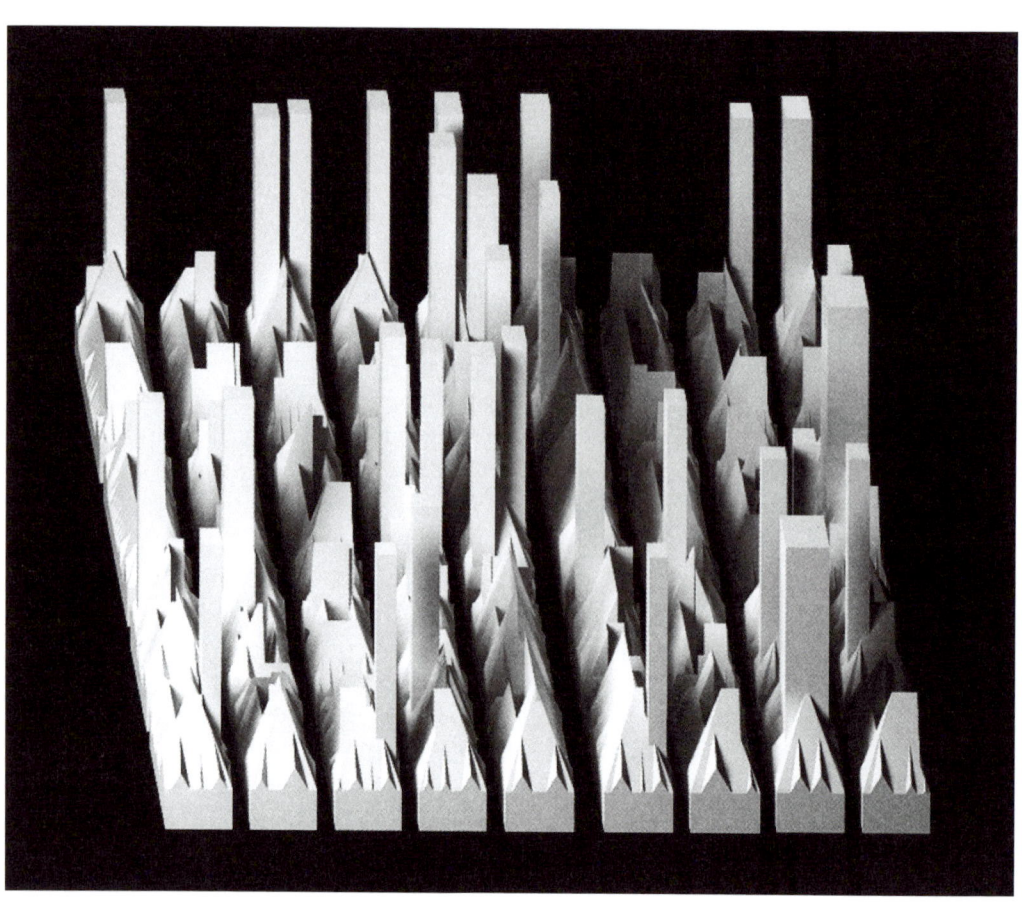

Contemporary discussions of the status of the city in design culture tend to bend towards one of two self-referential and ultimately irreconcilable logical loops. On the one hand, many discussions of the contemporary city in relation to design devolve into an obsessive preoccupation with the social and political abstractions of policy, participation, and governance. On the other hand, it is equally common for these discussions to be delimited to the description of individual sites, projects, and protagonists as singularities in the history of the city. In between these two scopes and scales of urban agenda, we seem to have lost the potential for describing the design of the city as a collective cultural project. This broad statement clearly oversimplifies the situation, and runs the real risk of overstating the case. Yet, it remains true that in the vast majority of cases the discourse and practices of design associated with the contemporary city trend towards the scales, sites, and subjects associated with either policy on the one hand or individual development projects on the other.

It has become commonplace to situate a critique of an urban proposal in the broader failings associated with a lack of political leadership, an absence of robust regulatory mechanisms, or ineffectual public participation (... if only we had the right mayor, an enlightened governance model, progressive tax incentives, a better educated public, etc.). It has become equally commonplace to locate this critique in relation to the specifics associated with a single parcel of land, individual development interest, or singular architect's identity (... a once-in-a-lifetime opportunity, unlocking a singular urban site, the Olympics are coming, the world's most famous architect is attached, etc.). While there remain perfectly reasonable and necessary dimensions to both of these scales of critique, what is most often absent in contemporary design discourse on the city seems to be the capacity to articulate interests or values beyond the singular project, operating at the scale of collective urban form of some dimension, yet not at the scale of the city itself. In short, we seem to have withdrawn from the sites and scales at which urban form manifests itself in collective and cultural terms.

There are many well-founded historical reasons behind this atrophy of urban propositions. In both instances, we witness a retreat into alibis and explanations associated with the lack of a larger political economy or those specific to the self-interests of those directly and immediately invested in the project in material terms. Surely much of this stems from the relative autonomy of realms enjoyed by urban planning and architecture since their professionalization in the academy post-1968. Equally, much of this stems from our broader political economy and civil discourse in which the potential for collective consideration of shared interests and mutually beneficial outcomes seems harder and harder to come by. In the wake of planning's radicalization around the social, and architecture's radicalization around autonomy, who speaks for the city as a cultural aspiration? Who is capable of articulating the potential of collective urban forms? In this context, the design disciplines broadly, and the urban arts specifically, share the potential to redress this historic formation through the development of discursive forms and projective potentials.

Charles Waldheim / Office for Urbanization, "Unbuilt Manhattan," 2016

In this discourse on the status of the city as subject and object of design, one potential subject for a rapprochement between the polity and the project might be found in the relationship between solar orientation and urbanism. While this admittedly ancient topic has been available since the earliest regulations on building in the city, it is, once again, a timely question for the design disciplines. This is particularly true as the topic promises to bolster contemporary interest in the relations between ecology and urbanism. While much of the discourse and many practices of ecological urbanism have focused on the adaptation of urban form for contemporary hydrological and ecological conditions, the prospect of heliomorphism affords a new set of relationships between ecological function and urban form. As such, the topic promises to extend contemporary interest in a range of subjects from landscape urbanism and ecological urbanism through thermodynamics and urban metabolism. Rather than a technical question associated with any one specific design discipline, heliomorphism proposes a return to the design of the city as a collective and cultural act. Instead of making a false choice between architecture's cultural autonomy and more interested engagements in ecological parameters in urban form, heliomorphism affords a third term. In this regard, the heliomorphic "turn" shares much with the topic of thermodynamics as an agenda for mobilizing architecture's autonomous cultural production through drivers found in the externalities of climate and carbon, energy and environment.

The twin topics of landscape urbanism and ecological urbanism have focused much attention on the terrestrial topics of hydrologic networks and their ecological performance in relation to urban form. While these preoccupations remain central for many, the topic of heliomorphism proposes a new line of inquiry through which an ecological urbanism might be conceived.

The perennial topic of urban form and its relationship to solar orientation is an ancient one. The earliest texts on architecture and town planning invoke the importance of considering the orientation, layout, and correspondence of the shape of the city to its relationship to the sun. Various versions of ancient laws regarding the "right-to-light" as a fundamental social construct can be found in cultures around the world, irrespective of latitude. Over the past century, this topic was inscribed in a long-standing tension between the right to light as a social contract versus various forms of capital accumulation through urbanization.

Some of the earliest English-language regulations on limits to building were developed in response to this tension between solar access as a human right and the impact of tall buildings in the city. Many protagonists of modern planning proposed projects in which minimum equitable conditions for solar access across time were built into the shape of the modern city through limits to building height, setbacks, and orientations. Some of the most enduring and powerful images of twentieth-century urbanization stem from the extreme conditions of delirious vertical accumulation versus more socially equitable horizontality. British common-law conceptions of a "right-to-light" shaped the earliest Anglo forms of planning; among other precedents, these ideas informed the formation of the earliest planning regulations in the United States. New York's zoning ordinance (1916) is one example of this cultural inheritance in which the social contract on the right to solar access was codified in canonical urban form. This form of collective social contract is also inscribed in our images of the city as cultural form. Hugh Ferris's *Metropolis of Tomorrow* (1929) delineated the cultural ambition of the city as informed by a collective sense of social equity around solar access.

A contemporary return to heliomorphism recommends a rereading of the history of the topic in twentieth-century architecture and urbanism. A number of notable architects and urbanists explored various aspects of the heliomorphic project over the second half of the twentieth century. This would include a reexamination of German planner Ludwig Hilberseimer's *New Regional Pattern* (1949).(1) Hilberseimer's post-war planning was equally informed by a profound sense of social solar equity in relation to the dominant spatial fix of the decentralized industrial economy. The topic recommends a reconsideration of how concepts of solar orientation informed the work of British architects Jane Drew and Maxwell Fry in their two *Tropical Architecture* books (1956, 1964) as well as their republication of *Architecture and the Environment* (1976).(2) The work of American architect Ralph Knowles and his concept of the "solar envelope" as described in *Sun Rhythm Form* (1982)(3) is essential to the rereading of heliomorphism. Knowles developed his conception of the "solar envelope" in response to the energy shocks and economic transformations of the 1970s. This reconsideration of the second half of the twentieth century for antecedents to a "new" heliomorphism would be further reinforced by a rereading of contemporaneous theories, including, among others, Reyner Banham's *Architecture of the Well-Tempered Environment* (1969).(4) These historical cases would be leavened by a reading of more recent commitments to digital paradigms for urbanism and the potentials of relational urban modeling of urban form in relation to solar performance.

In his 1988 publication *Design for Northern Climates*, Canadian urbanist Vladimir Matus referred to the design of "heliomorphic urban spaces." In his formulation, Matus suggested the potential for a biologically informed urban project: "For decades the optimal milieu for a variety of human activities has been achieved mainly through energy input. ... [N]ow a building can be transformed into a quasi-biological system that sensitively responds to environmental variations, opening itself like a blossom, harnessing and absorbing ambient energies."(5)

1. Ludwig Hilberseimer, *New Regional Pattern* (Chicago, IL: Theobald, 1949).

2. Maxwell Fry and Jane Drew, *Tropical Architecture in the Humid Zone* (London: Batsford, 1956); Maxwell Fry and Jane Drew, *Tropical Architecture in the Dry and Humid Zones* (New York, NY: Reinhold, 1964); Maxwell Fry and Jane Drew, *Architecture and the Environment* (London: Allen & Unwin, 1976).

3. Ralph Knowles, *Energy and Form: Ecological Approach to Urban Growth* (Cambridge, MA: MIT Press, 1974); Ralph Knowles, *Sun Rhythm Form* (Cambridge, MA: MIT Press, 1982).

4. Reyner Banham, *The Architecture of the Well-Tempered Environment* (London: Architectural Press, 1969).

5. Vladimir Matus, *Design for Northern Climates: Cold-Climate Planning and Environmental Design* (New York, NY: Von Nostrand Reinhold, 1988), 49.

These examples, and countless others, rehearsed a central tension in the regulation of urban form, pitting capital accumulation through the aggregation of built form against social equity around the right to a minimum standard of solar access. This longstanding tension between vertical accumulation and horizontal regulation has defined the topic of urban form and solar orientation for much of the modern era. More recently, however, architects and urbanists have articulated the potential of a new range of solar economies. Many of these projects propose to transcend longstanding tensions between capital accumulation and equitable access through an expanded field of solar performance, architectonic expression, and urban form. The prospect of a "new" heliomorphic agenda suggests the interrelated articulation of a pair of distinct tensions, each of them endemic to the design of the city. First among these is the longstanding anxiety between the city as a site for social equity versus the city as an engine for capital accumulation. Second is the more recent tension between solar access for ecological processes as opposed to the capture of solar access for renewable energy. Taken together, these terms offer a potential bio-politics of urban form in relation to social, economic, and ecological parameters for urban form. This expanded bio-political urban field is made possible by the intersection of three distinct modes of design research attendant to the heliomorphic agenda: computational geometry and relational urban modeling in service of thermodynamics; energy modeling and performative measures in the service of architectonic and urban form; and the pluralization and politicization of ecologies and ecological thinking through design.

Some examples from recent practice might be helpful to illustrate this expanded field of solar performance. For the sake of symmetry, and given the disproportionate role that the city has played in the history of the topic, three cases are drawn from Manhattan in the past five years. In the context of (perennial) concern over the access to sunlight and the most recent round of tall buildings in Manhattan, there has been a great deal of collective anxiety about new super-tall residential towers designed by leading architects such as SHoP, Viñoly, and others. The Municipal Arts Society (MAS) has returned to its historic role as the venue to convene these concerns, and it has recently published an online tool to help illustrate the dimension of the problem.

Recent debates over the impact of super-tall residential buildings in New York and their shadows across Central Park suggest that this is a timely question. In December 2013, the *New York Times* published an article describing Manhattan apartments plunged into perpetual shadow by new residential development.(6) The article described the tendency toward super-tall, super-skinny residential towers in midtown Manhattan, as well as residential projects of enormous overall volume across the city. These projects were described in the *Times* and other media accounts as casting shadows across longstanding residential viewsheds, across playgrounds and parks, and into Central Park itself. The *Times* article rehearsed a set of longstanding anxieties around tall buildings, density, and access to sunlight in New York that

6. Cara Buckley, "In the Shadow of Rising Towers: Laments of Lost Sunlight in New York," *New York Times*, 20 December 2013, A26, A30.

have persisted over the past century.(7) The MAS of New York, which led the opposition to Moshe Safdie's Columbus Circle project in 1987, returned to the topic with its December 2013 *Accidental Skyline* report and an interactive mapping tool which describes the looming threat of tall buildings casting shadows across the park.(8) That same month, Cornell University received planning permission to begin construction of an enormous net-zero building on its new Roosevelt Island technology campus to be served by enormous arrays of rooftop solar panels. Designed by Thom Mayne / Morphosis, the Bloomberg Center achieved aggressive energy targets by increasing the surface area of the building dedicated to the collection of solar energy.(9) In Morphosis's Bloomberg Center, the provocation of a net-zero-energy building prompted the development of an enormous roofscape attuned to optimizing production and mitigating emissions. In so doing, it also increased the shadows the building casts, and plunged much of the center of the new campus into darkness. More recently, Jeanne Gang / Studio Gang Architects have proposed a Solar Carve Tower adjacent to the High Line at 40 Tenth Avenue on the Lower West Side of Manhattan. This project successfully petitioned the city for a variance to allow a transfer of allowable development volume in order to not cast shadow over the High Line. In this case, the desire for solar access to the ecological function of the elevated promenade below prompted Gang to carve and redistribute available development rights on the site. In contrast to Mayne's concern for energy production, Gang's tower contorts itself to avoid casting shadows on the public park below. This project effectively inverts the logic embedded in the New York Zoning Resolution of 1916.(10) Equally indicative of the new economy of heliomorphism was the recent debate around Jean Nouvel / Nouvel Architects' West 57th Street MoMA Tower. In spite of its attentiveness to the 1916 (and subsequent) zoning ordinances shaping the height and setback of towers up to 1,000 feet, Nouvel's proposed tower was infamously and unceremoniously circumscribed by New York City planning director Amanda Burden.(11) The coincidence of these three seemingly contradictory impulses suggests that the topic of solar orientation and urban form has renewed relevance in contemporary culture. The subject raises a range of questions from social justice and the right to light and air in the city. It also raises equally compelling questions regarding renewable energy production and consumption in relation to urban life. This research will build a body of knowledge on the potential relevance of this topic for contemporary practice and policy.

7. Thomas Lueck, "Hundreds Rally Against Towers at Coliseum Site," *New York Times*, 19 October 1987.

8. Municipal Art Society of New York, *Accidental Skyline* report (December 2013), http://www.mas.org/urbanplanning/accidental-skyline/.

9. Morphosis, Bloomberg Center, Cornell Tech campus, Roosevelt Island (2013), https://www.morphosis.com/architecture/209/.

10. Studio Gang Architects, Solar Carve Tower (40 Tenth Avenue), Manhattan (2015), http://studiogang.com/project/40-tenth-avenue.

11. Nicolai Ouroussoff, "Off With Its Top! City Cuts Tower to Size," *New York Times*, 9 September 2009, http://www.nytimes.com/2009/09/10/arts/design/10building.html.

These recent projects, and a range of others around the world, suggest the complex and contradictory terms of a new economy (not to say a new politics) of solar performance. The inaugural conference of the Harvard Graduate School of Design Office for Urbanization returned to this ancient aspect of urban order in September 2016.(12) The conference explored the potential for a "new" heliomorphic urban project through three discursive frames: plug-ins, commons, and zero-sum.

Ralph Knowles's concept of the "solar envelope" proposed a design tool that anticipated contemporary interests in parametricism and relational modeling. The envelope offered a projective form through which urban morphology was indexed to solar performance. The technological developments of the last decade have enabled an unanticipated degree of precision and feedback, potentially infusing new possibilities into an idea that has a half-century of history. *Plug-ins* revisit the changes, conceptual and projective, that contemporary models of computational geometry have brought to this design model. Independent of location or latitude, access to the sun is considered an ancient and inviolable right in many cultures. Several current politico-economic conceptions, however, protect it for health considerations, while others regulate it for energy reasons. Regardless of these two distinctions, the *commons* reconsiders both types of solar access to be issues of social equity, and it examines, accordingly, the tensions that exist between built form through capital accumulation, on the one hand, and access to sunlight through environmental consensus, on the other. The energy crisis and economic shocks of the 1970s led to experimental and counter-cultural practices of architecture and urbanism. These practices enabled the emergence of domestic applications and DIY methods of implementation in a new political economy of solar energy. The current environmental crisis embraces zero-carbon responses and has pushed the scale of operation to neo-liberal corporate and governmental urbanizations. *Zero-sum* reviews the shifts from the domestic to the urban, from the individual to the conglomerate (political or economical), from the alternative to the new normal. Taken collectively, these three spaces of design research afford the potential for a "new" heliomorphic agenda for the shape of the city.

12. "Heliomorphism," Harvard Graduate School of Design conference, September 15–16, 2016, http://www.gsd.harvard.edu/event/inaugural-conference-of-the-harvard-gsd-office-for-urbanization-heliomorphism/.

Charles Waldheim / Office for Urbanization, "Unbuilt Manhattan," 2016

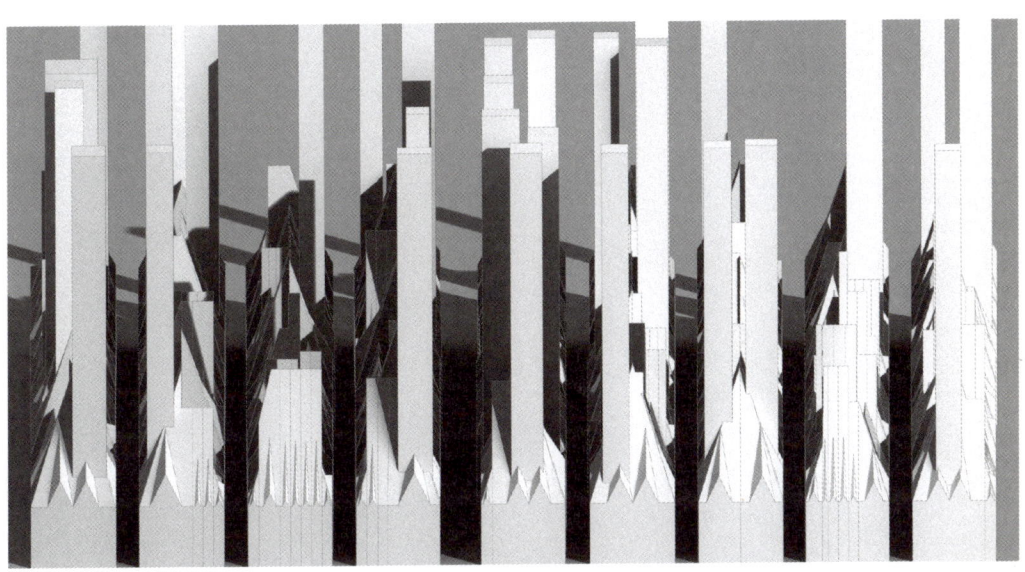

TOWARDS A "NEW" HELIOMORPHISM __ Charles Waldheim

NEW YORK by Mayo Nissen

SENSING

The deployment of artificial sensibilities in cities has a long tradition that is an alternative to the city as an experience, the phenomenological approach of the *City Beautiful*, *Townscapes*, and related architectural approaches to the design of cities. Cities are experienced and sensed, but crucially, cities *sense*. Weathervanes and watchtowers have been part of the traditional urban landscape, allowing citizens to predict weather and navigate increasingly complex urban spaces. Traffic wardens, firefighters, or watchtower vigilantes were sharing their sensorial capacity with citizens in order to regulate urban processes. Weather patterns, security systems, and temporal rhythms have traditionally been part of urban communities.

But these arcane technologies of sensing have now become increasingly artificial, pervasive, and distributed. The proliferation of sensors in urban environments is one of the most defining facts of the imminent urban milieu. Self-driving vehicles and other impending urban technologies will not only provide new forms of mobility but also expand exponentially the population of sensing-agents, documenting every physical feature, traffic delay, and change in air quality, in the city environment. *Lidar point clouds* and computer-vision, high-resolution orthoimagery, or GIS-enabled web applications enable us to visualize—and therefore act upon—urban processes that were previously inaccessible. When these sensors become interconnected, an unprecedented *common*, novel in sensibility, will create a collective *sensorium*. When connected to smartphones, open source sensing data will be instantly accessible to urban populations, enabling constant updates on the urban environment.

The distribution of powered and sensing platforms on the ground and in the air will become one the most significant changes in the imminent urban milieu. This process will significantly increase the resolution of the emerging urban sensorium. There are a number of initiatives and products —*Smart Citizen, Atmotube…*— which promise to increase the resolution of environmental monitoring to the rate of one sensor per person. As air quality in cities like Cairo, Delhi, Beijing, Mexico City has degraded over the last decades, to the development of a public consciousness of the atmosphere may become one of the most powerful tools to address the environmental crisis that many global metropolises have today. Ground vehicles, drones and people may become ideal platforms for sensing on a high-resolution level. Urban populations will be able to make individual decisions increasingly driven by the analysis of these high-resolution sensor networks, connected by growing online data repositories like Pachube (now part of Xively), Umbrellium, and Wolfram's Data Drop. This level of decision making does not need to implicate governmental agencies: it may be down to the choice of cycling routes for commuting, or the decision of investing in one neighborhood or another vis a vis the emerging pictures of environmental toxicity indexes that may quickly produce radical transformations in cities.

Bio-sensing is an interesting emergence in the sensing common. It encompasses a range of technologies to measure the physiological state of a living entity by looking at external indicators. It can use living creatures (such as shells or algae) to measure the pollution of the sea-water, or can also sense human psychological states such as surprise, excitement, calm, fear or stress through external indicators such as pupil dilation, electrical potential on the skin surface, or skin permeability (in galvanic skin responses) which can be measured by body sensors. These entirely new forms of sensibility will open cities to a variety of urban constituencies, such as plants or animals, which were not representable before. Furthermore, they may engage with the constituency of the unconscious by automatically measuring human responses to urban environments. The fast-developing field of Urban Health is one of the most promising application of bio-computation and bio-sensing.[1]

The increasing availability of urban data provided by these technologies will provide opportunities to optimize the collective use of resources. Public transport, freshwater resources, energy consumption and waste collection are some of the sectors where big data analysis is already increasingly effective. Data scientists are now capable to analyze huge amounts of data generated by cities regarding the energy consumption rates over time, the traffic densities, epidemic distributions or the frequency of crime. Big data analytics will produce insights that were previously unavailable, which describe cities as a single collective organism. Big data allows citizens to perceive themselves as part of a collective entity which was not visible before, and therefore not actionable. This new collective sensorium gives us an unprecedented scope to make decisions about the management of urban systems. City authorities can use to improve road and rail transport, reduce crime, improve healthcare, improve public service delivery, and reduce wastage of financial resources, making decisions in real time. The impact of these technologies in urban governance is potentially enormous but it is also plagued with legal and political minefields, still to be properly regulated.

The big question about "smart cities" is that they subcontract urban governance to a number of companies such as Siemens or Cisco, who are obviously interested in monetizing the *Internet-of-Things* and who at some point may start taking advantage of the knowledge they have

1. Daniel Quesada-González and Arben Merkoçi, "Mobile Phone-based Biosensing: An Emerging Diagnostic and Communication Technology," *Biosensors & Bioelectronics* 92 (2016).

to increase their profits. We will not get here into the way in which big data, CCTV and artificial sensing may end up destroying the chaotic and diverse qualities of cities: these sensors are telling us that cities are actually not that chaotic, but rather predictable and uniform when seen from a *Big Data* perspective. We have no nostalgia here for the little corner restaurants and the fortuitous encounters with strangers *a la Jane Jacobs*. We know now that urban processes are not that contingent and our new tools enable us to see the hidden orders which were not visible before, to predict collective behavior and to plan for it. But while these technologies can be used to produce interesting effects of optimization or else, they may also be used for the advantage of those who have access to *Big Data* analysis. Can we trust the government to tell us the indexes of particles in the atmosphere, or the amount of lead in the potable water? Can we trust the government not to invade our privacy? We know now that often we cannot, and this opens a series of approaches which are trying to explore this artificial sensibility. One of the most interesting contemporary developments in this field in the sensing common emerges around the possibilities of DIY sensing where the sensing technologies are assembled by citizens themselves and shared on a peer-to-peer basis, and therefore avoid the risk of being manipulated for anyone's profit. It is not smart cities what we need, but smart citizens, who are properly informed about environmental conditions, shopping opportunities, jobs, contacts etc.

DIY sensing means we can take ownership over our urban life, and use our abilities to sense artificially and to communicate to our peers horizontally to produce an increasingly accurate picture of the processes in our urban habitats. It is often connected to the *makers movement*, and contains an element of aesthetics and a contrarian lifestyle. DIY sensing opens up the issue of who controls, produces and consumes the tools for participation in these new commons. The social imaginaries that are being constructed around DIY sensing imply a certain level of self-reliance of the urban population in terms of resolution of, for example, environmental crisis. The way in which people imagine their social existence through their lifestyle

Switch Data Center, Las Vegas, Nevada

and everyday actions, how they relate to others, and the normative notions and images that underlie these expectations are supposed to almost take over urban governance roles, and resonate also with the devolution of governmental responsibilities, outsourcing and deregulation. David Cameron's "Big Society"[2] and the "Easy Council"[3] models would be ideal implementations of the spirit of self-reliance that we can see in the DIY sensing and the *maker culture*. These imaginaries permit us to understand DIY as a form of urban, *direct action, free speech*. DIYers use technologies as a vehicle to make claims: they create meanings and express ideas not through a political discourse but by physically *doing.* For example, a map made using DIY aerial photography showing the effect of an oil spill conveys the extent of environmental damage.

DIY sensing is grounded in "physical computing," using programmable devices often connected through wireless sensor networks which respond to inputs from the surrounding environment, such as noise, wind, temperature, pollution, radiation, etc. DIY sensing may actually contribute to the democratization of science and technology, bypassing the experts and acting as a mechanism of urban devolution. DIY highlights the power of ordinary people's capacity to act as civic agents.

2. The *Big Society* was a political ideology developed in the early twenty-first century. The idea proposes "integrating the free market with a theory of social solidarity based on hierarchy and voluntarism." Conceptually it "draws on a mix of conservative communitarianism and libertarian paternalism." Its roots "can be traced back to the 1990s, and to early attempts to develop a non-Thatcherite, or post-Thatcherite, brand of UK conservatism" such as David Willets' Civic Conservatism and the revival of Red Toryism. Some commentators have seen the Big Society as invoking Edmund Burke's idea of *civil society*, putting it into the sphere of one-nation conservatism.

The term "Big Society" was originated by Steve Hilton, director of strategy for the Conservative Party, and the idea is particularly associated with the party's leader, David Cameron, who was a strong advocate for it. The idea became the flagship policy of the 2010 UK Conservative Party general election manifesto and formed part of the subsequent legislative program of the Conservative–Liberal Democrat Coalition Agreement. The stated aim was to create a climate that empowered local people and communities, building a Big Society that would take power away from politicians and give it to the people. See "Big Society," *Wikipedia*, https://en.wikipedia.org/wiki/Big_Society, accessed 11 May 2017.

3. Aditya Chakrabortty, "Outsourced and Unaccountable: This Is the Future of Local Government," *The Guardian*, 15 December 2014.

Rhythms are the basic means by which ordered space is marked out from disorder. Deleuze and Guattari talk about rhythm and repetition as the main tool to occupy and inform a territory or a space: "the refrain is essentially territorial, territorializing and reterritorializing."[4] As a territory becomes secured, so the refrain is "picked up" or reiterated by others who come to occupy the same space, much like the bird songs or the frequency of buses. Urban rhythms (such as for example the rhythm of alternation of traffic lights or the frequency of subway trains) are a fundamental component of a city. Since the introduction of SCADA (Supervisory Control and Data Acquisition) systems in the 1950s, urban information technologies have developed to manage and control urban systems in real time, especially with respect to transportation, utilities, and security. In recent years, such dynamic regulation has been widely expanded with the rollout of ubiquitous and pervasive computing. So-called smart city technologies—such as city operating systems, urban control rooms, smart grids, sensor networks, smart parking, smart lighting, city dashboards and real-time information apps—have crucially transformative spatio-temporal possibilities (paces and rhythms, stasis/movement, spacing …) which will crucially alter the experience of future cities. What will happen when those very urban rhythms become controlled by algorithms, which create much more supple and complex rhythms? Cities may have to be designed not just from the human perspective, but according to their ability to interact with this nascent artificial sensibility that is becoming one of the imminent commons to emerge. How we will manage to ensure that this artificial, global sensorium becomes a collective asset instead of being manipulated by certain groups to distort the image we have of ourselves as a collective entity is one of the most daunting challenges facing cities in the years ahead.

4. Giles Deleuze and Felix Guattari, *A Thousand Plateaus: Capitalism and Schizophrenia* (Minneapolis, MN: University of Minnesota Press, 1988), 300.

SENSE AND THE CITY.
TOWARDS A NEW DIGITAL COMMON

Carlo Ratti with Daniele Belleri

INTRODUCTION

The world today is awash with data. In 2016 alone, people produced as much information as was created in all of human history. Every time we send a message, make a call, or complete a transaction, we leave digital traces behind. We are quickly approaching the creation of what Italian writer Italo Calvino omnisciently called the "memory of the world": a complete digital copy of our physical universe.

Such a scenario raises fundamental questions related to both who has access to data, and what data can be used for. As increasing distrust towards political institutions is apparent all over the world, our society finds itself at a turning point: data can become either an instrument exploited for private, adversarial interests or a tool to constitute a new positive "commons." In other terms, to borrow Richard Buckminster Fuller's words, we are at a "utopia or oblivion" crossroads.

To foster a debate on the issues at stake, we should first take a step back from the heated debate on the relationship between democracy and the emerging "dataville." What we want to suggest here is a reflection on the different types of data available today, their taxonomy, and their possible uses. The fundamental premise is that Big Data can also provide us—as planners, engineers, designers, and, above all, citizens—with new tools to understand and transform the spaces we live in. If we take the right steps today, the city of tomorrow could evolve into an open platform to foster civic engagement—a kind of new commons based on the shared knowledge of the city.

As a starting point towards that goal, what we would like to propose here is a classification of data—focusing on its acquisition method and its urban usage. After having described the proposed classification system, we will illustrate them using case studies taken from the present and past work of the MIT Senseable City Lab.

DIFFERENT TYPES OF BIG DATA
There are many different ways we could classify urban Big Data. One could start with its applications—say in fields as diverse as transport, energy, production, etc. Alternatively, one could take a more in-depth approach and look at the structure of the data itself, such as the taxonomy of all the possible fields that it contains. In most urban data, for instance, two commonly recurring fields are time and location, latitude, and longitude coordinates.

Below we propose a classification that starts with the very nature of the data by considering its source. Much of the current research on Big Data is largely agnostic regarding the origin of urban data sets. But data sets do not just appear out of nowhere; the conditions of their generation need to be examined in detail. We think that starting with the "modes of production" is imperative if we want to better understand the politics inherent to Big Data—and work towards a future condition where Big Data can evolve into an open, urban commons.

We could distinguish between three different types of data acquisition. First, we have what can be referred to as "opportunistic data." This is data that is collected by running some kind of system, but that can be "opportunistically" used for something else. Think about data collected by cellphone companies to run their operation. In recent years, thanks also to our research, this very fine-grain recording of human life has become a powerful tool for understanding the city and its dynamics. In general, we can say that "opportunistic data" is a byproduct of some large information infrastructures. To analyze them means taking the generating system as a proxy for another phenomenon of interest. The data sets are uniform, follow a consistent logic, and reflect the properties of the system that generated them. Elaborated data-sharing agreements are often required with the owner of the collection infrastructure. In case of cellphone data, credit card data, and other similar types of data, this process can be rather tedious, governed by detailed data-sharing agreements.

The second type of information acquisition deals with "user-generated data"—such as data produced on social media platforms. Every tweet, Facebook post, or Flickr upload can provide valuable information to better understand cities and society. Access conditions vary: for instance, everyone can access a percentage of all tweets that are produced online—while the possibility to access "all" tweets on a certain subject or geographic area requires ad hoc permissions or payment. However, "user-generated data sets" are generally very large, and even if only partially accessible, can become a valuable input into different types of analytics.

The third and final category of data is "purposely sensed data." Its acquisition is achieved by deploying sensors ad-hoc, in order to better understand a specific phenomenon. If the two previous categories dealt primarily with the "hunter gathering" of data, we could say that the third one refers to the new space of "data farming." With sensors becoming increasingly inexpensive and self-powered—as we enter the new era of "smart dust"—more and more sensors in our cities and buildings will provide an increasing amount of data in real time.

Below we will explore these different categories of data through some of the MIT Senseable City Lab's projects.

CASE STUDIES

I. OPPORTUNISTIC DATA

TREEPEDIA

Increasing a city's tree canopy contributes to lowering urban temperatures by blocking shortwave radiation and increasing water evaporation. In addition to creating a more pleasant microclimate, trees also help mitigate air pollution caused by everyday urban activities. However, how can we measure the tree canopy? Treepedia—a project developed in collaboration with the World Economic Forum's Global Agenda Council on the Future of Cities and the World Economic Forum's Global Shapers community—uses Google Street View (GSV) panoramas. Thanks to artificial intelligence, images are analyzed and canopy obstruction measured. As a result, the Green View Index (GVI) is calculated to evaluate and compare urban areas. The GVI presents human perception of the urban green from the street level (as opposed to other methods based on satellite images) and allows the comparison of canopies among most cities all over the world—virtually all of those scanned by GSV. In 2015, the World Economic Forum's Global Agenda Council on the Future of Cities included increasing green canopy cover on their list of top ten urban initiatives: "Cities will always need large-infrastructure projects, but sometimes small-scale infrastructure—from cycle lanes and bike sharing to the planting of trees for climate change adaptation—can also have a big impact on an urban area." Treepedia shows how to use opportunistically collected data by Google to better understand the green canopy—and to use this information to allow citizens to take action.

HUBCAB

HubCab is an interactive visualization that explores the ways in which over 170 million taxi trips connect the City of New York in a given year. The basis of the HubCab tool is a data set of over 170 million taxi trips by over 13,000 Medallion taxis in New York City: GPS coordinates of all pick-up and drop-off points and corresponding times. The HubCab interface provides a unique insight into the inner workings of the city from the previously invisible perspective of the taxi system. HubCab investigates exactly how and when taxis pick up or drop off individuals and identifies zones of condensed pick-up and drop-off activities. The HubCab tool expands and

Treepedia sources Google Street View (GSV) panoramas, which are analyzed by artificial intelligence to measure "canopy obstruction". This result is the formulation of a "Green View Index (GVI)" to compare human perception of the urban green from the street level in different cities. Image 1: Paris 7 Image 2: Singapore

Screenshot of HubCab, showing pickups and drop offs of all 170 million taxi trips over one year in New York City

Screenshot of HubCab, showing all taxi pickups and drop offs at JFK airport daily between 3AM and 6AM

changes the perception of urban space by using a large-scale data set. Furthermore, the analysis of the data shows the vast potential of taxi sharing. Our mathematical method introduces the novel concept of "shareability networks" that allows for efficient modeling and optimization of trip-sharing opportunities. Such an approach could lead to less traffic congestion, reduced operating costs and split fares, and to a less polluted environment. An interactive map shows the total fare reduction to passengers, the distance saved in miles travelled, and emission savings in kg of CO_2 that come from potentially shared trips. Quantitative results demonstrate how taxi sharing could reduce the number of trips by 40% with only minimal delays for passengers.

URBAN EXPOSURE

Vast digital data sets are also changing how we predict the impacts of the urban environment on human health. In this project we have been looking at this space using a premier example of "opportunistic" data: cellphone information, which is collected for the sake of running a telecommunication infrastructure but at the same time provides invaluable content to better quantify human mobility patterns. Until recently, much of our understanding of the impact of air pollution on population health has been based on the relationship between air quality and mortality and/or morbidity rates in a population which is assumed to be at their home location all the time. Accounting for the movements of people can improve our understanding of this relationship. In this project we quantified human exposure to air pollution at an unprecedented scale thanks to data aggregated from cellphones. We examined 121 days of data from April through July 2013, using many types of wireless devices from a variety of providers, and blending the phone data with pollution information from the New York City Community Air Survey. We mapped the movements of several million people using ubiquitous cellphone data, and intersected this information with neighborhood air pollution measures. Covering the expanse of New York City, the study reveals where and when New Yorkers are most at risk of exposure to air pollution—with major implications for environmental and public health policy. The study broke New York City into 71 districts and found that exposure levels to particulate matter (PM) in 68 of the districts were significantly different when the daily movement of 8.5 million people was accounted for.

II. USER-GENERATED DATA

TWEET BURSTS

Social media has fully pervaded our lives. Thanks to its widespread uptake, it has become possible to study massive data streams in which people express their sentiments, often towards a specific topic. MIT Senseable City Lab, in partnership with Ericsson, has undertaken a visual and scientific exploration of how people express emotions online, and how this information could improve our understanding of human behavior. The study raises a number of important questions: Are people doing this independently, or in response to seeing other short messages? Are people following the herd? Could we use these insights to learn more about financial bubbles by measuring more impulsive, less rational responses? And can we design better communication services?

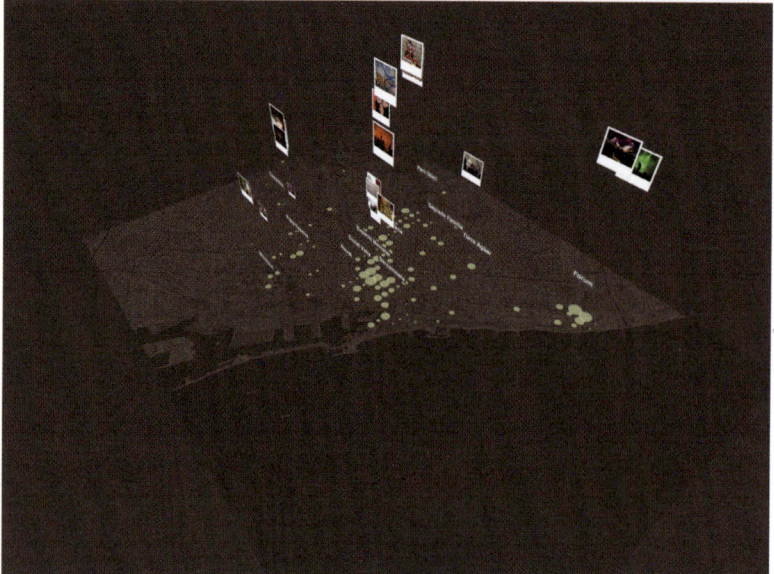

Density and flows of photographers in Spain in 2007

Partying in Barcelona

Los ojos del mundo (the world's eyes) was one of the first projects to employ big data sourced from the web to quantify tourism—and particularly, tourists' paths and choices. Los ojos del mundo provided insights to these issues by mapping digital photos publically shared on the web by people visiting Spain

In this study, researchers used several large data sets of online messages collected from different media sources. Data set 1 contained around 410,000 messages from Twitter during the 2012 Masters Tournament, a major championship in golf, held between April 5 and 8, 2012, in Augusta, Georgia. Data set 2 includes almost 20,000 messages posted in one thread of a popular online forum, the Something Awful (SA) forums (forums.somethingawful.com), during the U.S. presidential election night of November 6, 2012, and a smaller number of messages posted the week before the election night. A third data set includes the well-known Enron email corpus, containing roughly 250,000 emails exchanged between the employees of the Enron Corporation over four years, between October 30, 1998, and July 19, 2002. Data set 4 includes over 200,000 tweets and 40,000 posts on the online social networking service Facebook, with the common topic of the snow storm called "Nemo" which struck the northeastern coasts of the United States and Canada on February 8 and 9, 2013. The last data set contains the entire corpus of almost 3 million posts from the Twitter-like microblogging service app.net over a six-month period.

The results were often unexpected: researchers discovered, for example, that emotional tweets are very short. During the most exciting moments, when Twitter is bursting with short and emotional tweets, the average length drops substantially from 90 characters to 60 characters. The more excited we are, and the more intense the flurry of messages in the collective, the shorter our messages become.

LOS OJOS DEL MUNDO
Los ojos del mundo (*The world's eyes*) illustrates the photos that people visiting Spain leave behind as evidence of contemporary tourism in the country. Tourism in Spain is hardly quantifiable because tourists leave few tangible traces of their stay. As a consequence, citizens and local authorities struggle to identify what tourists see, what tourists enjoy, and where tourists travel to and from. *Los ojos del mundo* provides insights to these question from the digital photos publically shared on the web by people visiting Spain. Through data mining and visualization techniques, the study uncovers the presence and flows of tourists. As photos pop up, they reflect the intensity of tourist activity, thus uncovering where tourists are, where they come from, and what they are interested in capturing and sharing from their visit. The analysis and mapping of this data sheds light on the attractiveness of leisure cities and their hotspots. In contrast, it also reveals the unphotographed regions of Spain, still free from the tourist buzz.

When posting photos online, users of the photo-sharing platform Flickr transmit to the world their perspective of a place or event through the lens of a digital camera. Each digital photo file codes both the time that photo was taken and the location it captures. Analyzing this information allows us to follow each Flickr photographer as they travel through Spain. Also, about 60% of Flickr users disclose information about their home country. Analysis of the time and location data embedded in their digital photo files allows us to examine the Flickr photographers' geographic presence and trails over time, and to differentiate locals from visitors. Researchers, for example, could easily understand that Britons who visited Barcelona in Fall 2007 stayed on the beaten paths delimited by the city's main elements such as Parc Guell and Sagrada Familia, with Passeig de Gracia and the Rambla acting as main arteries. Another possible conclusion that can be deduced from Flickr data is linked to spaces of activity. Photographers often attach descriptions and tags when posting their photos on Flickr. The data mining of these tags allows us to infer what kinds of activities these photos capture. Spaces of activity reveal the regions and cities that host memorable parties in Spain over the course of a year.

III. PURPOSELY SENSED DATA

TRASH TRACK

The Trash Track project investigated the geographic dimension of urban waste systems by following the movement of individual trash items, thus tracing the flows of an urban infrastructure that is often hidden. Over the course of the project, we used ad-hoc sensors to record the trajectories of 3,000 trash items discarded in households, most of them in the metropolitan area around Seattle. We did not want to limit the experiment to assumptions about possible waste destinations; therefore, the project required an active sensing technology that is capable of autonomously reporting back from any location. Active location sensing means that an electronic location sensor is attached to the object, with the sensing device being slightly smaller than a cellphone. Location is acquired and reported by using the cellphone network infrastructure. The deployment of the sensors relied heavily on the involvement of volunteers. Initially, Trash Track was not designed as a participatory project, yet this aspect soon became the most important part. Volunteers eager to learn about the structure of the waste system contacted us, and contributed their ideas, time, and materials to the project. Among the tracked objects were packaging made from metal, glass, paper, or plastic; cellphones, TVs, and computers; books, clothing, furniture, toys, and many other items. After the tagged objects had entered the waste stream, the sensors started reporting their movement at regular intervals via the cellular network. We traced the movement of the discarded objects over a period of six months, until the batteries of most sensors had expired. The aggregated traces conveyed a rich picture of the waste removal chain; facilities including transfer stations, recycling centers, and landfills could clearly be made out as frequented nodes in the network. The project was an initial investigation into better understanding the "removal-chain" in urban areas—a first step towards making it more efficient and promoting behavioral change in society at large.

ART TRAFFIC

From sensors to track waste, to sensors to track people. Museums often suffer from "hyper-congestion," wherein the number of visitors exceeds their capacity. This can potentially be detrimental to the quality of visitors' experiences. Although this situation can be mitigated by managing visitors' flow between spaces, a detailed analysis of visitor movement is required before being able to take action. In this pioneering study, we attempted to analyze visitors' behavior in one of the world's largest museums—the Louvre—from anonymized longitudinal data sets generated by noninvasive Bluetooth sensors. This data enabled us to unveil some features of visitor behavior and spatial impact that shed some light on the mechanisms of museum overcrowding.

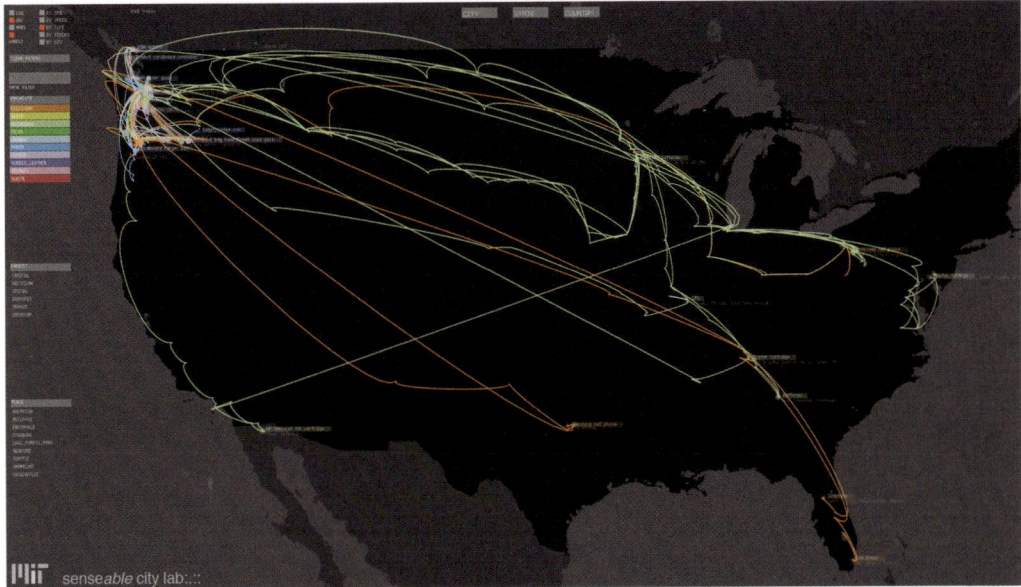

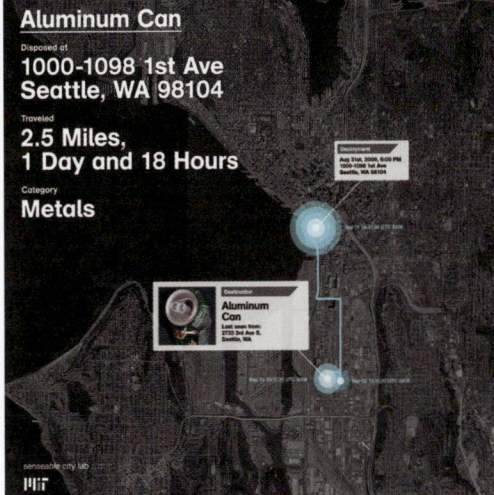

Composite Map of the Recorded Traces

Plastic Container of Liquid Soap in New York

Aluminum Can in Seattle

The Trash | Track project investigated the geographic dimension of urban waste systems by following the movement of individual, sensor-laden trash items, thus tracing the flows of an urban infrastructure that is often hidden

In particular, the research team deployed seven Bluetooth sensors, with sufficient coverage to measure visiting sequences and duration at key representative locations. The sensors recorded a unique encrypted identifier that distinguishes each Bluetooth-enabled mobile device within its range, as well as time stamps for entry and exit times. Assuming that a mobile device belongs to a person, we can relate the movement of the device to that of the visitor. The study was conducted over a twenty-four-day period with a high volume of visitor traffic. During this period, the array of sensors recorded the presence of 24,452 unique devices. The findings increased the understanding of the unpredictable behavior of visitors, which is key to improving the museum environment and experience.

UNDERWORLDS

Sewage contains important health data. Such is the idea behind Underworlds, a cross-disciplinary, open-data platform for monitoring urban health patterns, shaping more inclusive public health strategies, and pushing the boundaries of urban epidemiology. Underworlds consists of a physical sensing infrastructure and biochemical measurement technologies to analyze sewage. The Underworlds project is the first of its kind, and a proof of concept that cities can use their waste water system to do near real-time urban epidemiology and to understand human health and behavior with a fine spatio-temporal resolution. Early warnings of the presence of new flu strains in urban centers could significantly reduce a community's medical costs and even help mitigate outbreaks. In addition, smart sewage could impact the way noncommunicable diseases are studied; for instance, biomarkers for diseases such as obesity and diabetes can be measured at an unprecedented scale and temporal resolution. The implications of this platform extend beyond just disease surveillance to the development of a new type of human population census. Analyzed in tandem with demographic data, this platform can study the aggregate health of a city to the health of a particular neighborhood.

CONCLUSIONS AND NEXT STEPS

The three different categories of data illustrated above each comes with its own set of challenges and particularities. However, looking at these examples, it's easy to understand the importance of combining and aggregating data sets from multiple sources. The aim is an organic and complete perspective on our cities, in order to identifying their patterns.

In doing so, we need to go well beyond our inquiry on accessing data, and must strategize on how to make it accessible to the public. We actually need to intervene between the accumulation of data and releasing it for public usage. Access to information allows the urban public to see hidden patterns that are not otherwise observable. In keeping citizens in the loop, we can improve data volume and quality by expanding its audience. This offers citizens a way to critique the data and its embedded assumptions, leading to better methods for generation, acquisition, and aggregation of data sets. Also, we can instigate a sense of responsibility for the city and its shared public goods—meaning the urban data that allows the decoding of its daily dynamics. Data can promote behavioral change and bottom-up initiative. If managed positively, it can constitute a new and relevant collective voice—a new common among society's more established ones.

A detail of the portable robots used by MIT Senseable City Lab to sample sewage in Boston

Sewage contains important health data. Such is the idea behind Underworlds: a cross-disciplinary, open-data platform for monitoring urban health patterns, shaping more inclusive public health strategies, and pushing the boundaries of urban epidemiology

TELEPATHICALLY URBAN*

Jennifer Gabrys

A medium is a medium is a medium. As the sentence says, there is no difference between occult and technological media. Their truth is fatality, their field the unconscious.
Friedrich Kittler, *Discourse Networks* (1990, 229)

Any sufficiently advanced technology is indistinguishable from magic.
Arthur C. Clarke, *Profiles of the Future* (1962)

CITY OF DUST
The urban ether swims with a multitude of invisible particles: the residue of ash and aerosols, signals and light. Circulating through the city is the dust of industry, a pixelated material history. But dust also circulates through the urban and technological imagination as a potentially "smart" material that shapes wireless sensor communication. In the wireless city, communication technologies have been described as "utility fogs" and "pervasive networks" as well as "smart dust" in order to capture the possibly miniscule yet ubiquitous extent of wireless infrastructures. While smart dust in particular has developed as much as a technology of conjecture as application, the notion of dust that circulates and communicates the details of an electronic urban ecology is pursued in this chapter as a resonant figure for imagining the transmission and sedimentation of signals in an urban context. Smart dust has been envisioned in the form of microscopic and drifting wireless sensors that coordinate radio signals from mote to mote. From clouds of signals to smart particles, the imagined wireless city becomes charged with invisible, instant, and cryptic communication, which primarily occurs among machines. Within the traces of this machinic communication a city emerges that is telepath-

* First printed in *Circulation and the City Book. Essays on Urban Culture*, Alexandra Boutros, Will Straw, eds. McGill-Queen's University Press (2010).

ically urban, where the firing of messages assembles environments into immediate correspondence. Our primary access to this telepathic exchange is through the dust, that nearly imperceptible but electric remainder of technological conjecture.

Particular forms of dust materialize with every industry and era, and distinct cities emerge through the accumulation of debris sloughed off from modes of economic activity (Amato 2000, 8). Dust sediments as well as gives rise to material processes—it is a unit for capturing the transpiration—"the becoming and dissolution" of matter (ibid., 5). Like firing neurons, dust blinks on and off as the minimum recognizable entity of material transformation and circulation. Amassing with the dust of the urban past, smart dust hovers as an imagined residue discharged by the future wireless city. Smart dust has been developed in the form of tiny wireless sensors that could be released en masse, so that countless machines are in constant relay, coordinating information about an environment.[1] Wireless sensors, distributed and embedded in environments, move the "information city" from a zone where digital media is produced and circulated by media workers, to a space where the city itself is a site of information generation—an urban information ecology.

This sensor technology is less concerned with increasing computing power and more attentive to reducing the size of hardware, a technological shift that would allow millions of tiny machines to be deployed in drifts of simultaneous communication. Sensor systems have moved beyond the initial imaginings of smart dust, but both imagined and actual deployments generally are developed with a microprocessor and bi-directional radio and can be installed as distributed networks that can monitor everything from temperature and traffic to humidity and light. Applications ranging from the hypothetical to the mundane have included dropping as many as ten billion motes by airplane into the atmosphere in order to monitor the weather, or simply scattering motes across roadways in order to detect passing traffic (Broad 2005; Estrin et al. 2002).

Once installed, sensors are intended to operate relatively free of human interaction. Constantly transmitting and synchronizing messages in "the same unstoppable conversation" (Johnson 2000), these devices organize and collect environmental data and transmit select information back to databases. The "unstoppable conversation" relayed from machine to machine forms an invisible background of communication in the wireless city. As this exchange among machines transpires remotely, beyond the limits of perceptibility, it gives rise to speculation about the (possibly telepathic) correspondence among machines. Telepathy or, literally, "remote sensation" occurs as invisible and instant communication beyond the channels of sense. This is a process of displaced sensation, of sensing in an extraordinary capacity, or of communicating impressions beyond the reach of usual communicative practices. Wireless sensors—particularly in the more hypothetical form of

---

1. Smart dust was developed by Kris Pisteretal at the University of California at Berkeley between 1997 and 2001, and originally funded by the US Defense Advanced Research Projects Agency (DARPA). Smart dust utilizes microelectromechanical systems, or MEMS. For further technical information, see "Smart Dust: Autonomous Sensing and Communication in a Cubic Millimeter," http://robotics.eecs.berkeley.edu/~pister/SmartDust/; and Brendan I. Koerner, "What is Smart Dust Anyway?," *Wired* 11, no. 6 (June 2003); and Mohammad Ilyas and Imad Mahgoub, eds., *SmartDust: Sensor Network Applications, Architecture and Design* (CRC Press, Taylor & Francis: Boca Raton, Florida, 2006).

smart dust—perform this removal and rerouting of sensation. Urban ecologies are monitored, programmed, and made into transmittable information, but this sensory information transpires through relatively opaque machinic spaces—and the messages circulated may be decoded as much through conjecture as clear communication.

Telepathy is then a form of invisible communication that might describe how a wireless city continually talks to itself, circulating messages and programming urban ecologies. Organized in what Marshall McLuhan would call a "galaxy of machines," our electrical environment of communications—as an extended central nervous system—is at once invisible and pervasive (2003, 150). In fact, McLuhan's central motto revolves around this space of invisibility, as he explains: "The medium is the message' is not a simple remark, and I've always hesitated to explain it. It really means a hidden environment of services created by an innovation, and the hidden environment of services is the thing that changes people" (ibid., 242). The technological medium is a charged electrical environment. It can even put into play a set of automated processes and correspondences that appear fanstastical. This chapter examines how the wireless city shifts—through the circulation of remote sensing and sensation—to become telepathic, and to stimulate uncanny forms of urban communication.

ELECTRIC ATMOSPHERE

From the time of telegraphy and radio, wireless signals have permeated the city. Previously, wireless communication typically involved correspondence from person to machine, yet this transfer of communication now occurs predominantly from machine to machine.

Wireless clouds are suspended over cities, marking the frequency for the relay between microprocessors. Machines speak to machines to facilitate urban surveillance and automation: the operation of CCTV cameras, the monitoring of noise levels, the recording of traffic density, and the updating of local temperatures. In the future wireless city, it is not just multiple forms of urban dust that circulate: urban ecologies also circulate. The environmental attributes of the city become animated by sensors (Gabrys 2007). Above and beyond the circulation of messages moves a flood of material descriptions, not metaphysical claims but hyperphysical documentations. The city circulates as extended phenomena. Traffic moving at 5 mph, noise at 72 decibels, temperature registering 40 degrees Celsius: the air vibrates with local detail that searches for remote modes of assembly.

In his discussion of the "overexposed city," Paul Virilio suggests that electronic telecommunications changed the physical fabric of the city. The surge of communications through the "electronic ether" gave rise to a city "devoid of spatial dimensions, but inscribed in the singular temporality of an instantaneous diffusion." For Virilio, the city is overexposed: it exists all at once and so lacks "here and there" (2003, 272–3). Yet the city of telecommunications, this supposed virtual mirage, does not efface the physical city as much as alter and even intensify its modes of space and time. Electricity, automation, together with multiple modes of communication, rework the ratio and intensity of space and time in the city.[2] With wireless communications, another assemblage of space and time emerges through the operation of invisible frequencies. As an electromagnetic *field*, of the sort that nineteenth-century physicists imagined, the city contains "neighbourhoods" of electricity and magnetism (Luckhurst 2002, 75–88). With the wireless city, communication is more than a process of instantaneity. Electricity exceeds the wires.[3] It is atmospheric, drifting through spaces without edges, pervasive but located with differing intensities. It accumulates as a shifting temporal archive, saturated with ancient static simultaneous with the pulse of the new. Signals do not transmit via a process of conduction but are *induced* across stretches of space.

The relay from mote to mote hovering in this atmospheric surround is suggestive of another era of wireless communications, where the transmission of invisible signals gave rise to fantastic conjecture. At the turn of the nineteenth century, wireless technologies emerged simultaneously with a burgeoning interest in telepathy. Telepathy, and the murky, all-encompassing medium of ether, were figures of technological imagining that at once anticipated and responded to more "applied" technologies. In this sense, these more hypothetical devices performed in direct relation to the qualities of telegraphy. In fact, as Laura Otis points out, Marconi's wireless telegraph suggested new explanations and legitimacy for telepathy (2001, 187). While radio operators were sorting out how to intercept and interpret the transmission of wireless signals, telepathists were similarly exploring modes for communicating through the ether without apparatus. Although both telepathy and the ether have been at turns debated and dismissed as processes of creative interpretation, they have enabled an expanded understanding of the space and operation of wireless communications. There are cases where the practice of "poetic induction," or "pulling signals out of the air," as John Durham Peters writes, initially even surpassed the actual capacities of wireless technology (1999, 106). For this reason, he suggests, "it is misguided to construct a history of radio in which the spiritualism is an excrescence; it was one key to the medium's very development" (ibid.). Through the process of induction, it is possible not to narrowly delimit the scope of technology but rather to expand it beyond the obvious and verifiable into spaces of suggestive possibility. Telepathy and ether, those conjectural leaps into the unknown aspects of wireless transmission, are resuscitated in this chapter as ways to poetically induce signals from the contemporary wireless city.

As an imagined space of conductivity and transmission, the ether was the medium that allowed the envisioning of wireless technologies. The ether was a transducer of signals, a space for the correspondence of obscure communication, a figure of technological imagining. "The mother of all media," ether was the construct that "allowed light, electricity, and magnetism to work at a distance" (ibid., 102). The development of wireless technologies depended on the ether, and it was a critical construct for physicists, including James Clerk Maxwell, who imagined the possibilities of wireless communication through the fantastic medium of the ether. Ultimately, while the ether enables the sense that "the universe seems to be in constant communication with itself" (ibid., 102–3), this idea in many ways was not taken literally, but more speculatively, as a way to imagine new communication capacities. This conjectural aspect of the ether then prompted numerous speculations on wireless communications. Writing on telepathy in the nineteenth century, Roger Luckhurst charac-

2. This argument draws upon and extends McLuhan's notion that new media extend and alter the ratio of the senses (see *Understanding Media*).

3. See Luckhurst (2002) for a discussion of telepathy within a spatial framework and electricity as an emanation, 12 and 89.

terizes the ether as an "expansive matrix with unknown limits" (2002, 90). This imagined but unmapped space of transmissions enabled technological speculation, just as it was eventually rendered obsolete through the development of these same technologies to which it gaverise.

The ether is a space where matter and signals both vanish and appear. The electric transference of communications dissolves into the ether, but the ether is also an infinite reservoir of retrievable particles. In her study of scientific developments that influenced the work of Duchamp, Linda Henderson traces the transformation of matter at the turn of the nineteenth century, where dissipating and dematerializing atoms and electrons eventually found their way back to the ether. Writing on the work of Gustave Le Bon, she notes that he sought a relationship "among ordinary atoms, ions, electrons, x-rays, and energy" and observed that "matter dematerializes little by little; it disincarnates itself, as a spiritist would say. An atom becomes an ion, an ion becomes an electron, then an x-ray, and, finally, energy and ether" (1997). At the limits of matter, the smallest detectable unit of sense—whether speck of dust orelectron—gives way to conjecture about what lies beyond.

Within this zone, the charged particles of smart dust inhabit the world of the miniature, similar to the bit, electron, atom, and chip, another iteration on the miniscule that achieves infinite expanse through absolute reduction. The ether of the nineteenth century, where the sky was imagined to be replete with infinitesimal and "smart" particles, in many ways resembles the clouds of wireless motes that are locked in endless conversation. With smart dust, the ether becomes operational, so that the urban atmosphere assembles quite literally into clouds that could "scan a city and detect traffic patterns or blow through the atmosphere to monitor the weather." With these proposed scenarios, the Internet is inverted to become environmental, an invisible surround that one writer suggests "will be like an ocean, the air, a biological system" (Johnson 2000). Like the weather, this system describes an atmospheric drift of communication that moves through its own accord—a sensory system scanning and spontaneously taking shape.

In the same way that the ether was imagined to be a force guiding the movement of energy and signals, wireless sensors assemble into an intelligent communication ecology. In the furthest imagining of the capabilities of wireless sensors in the form of smart dust, some proposals have suggested that in the future this unknown medium may be completely captured and harnessed, so that "wherever you go, this obedient, intelligent ether will anticipate your needs and await your every command" (Johnson 2000). Such ordering of the electric atmosphere resonates with the declarations of Futurist artist Filippo Marinetti on the triumph of wireless in the early 1900s. He claimed that "wireless telephones" could even be used to plant fields, that vegetables would sprout with the surge of electricity. In this way, "all the atmospheric electricity hanging over us, all the incalculable electricity of the earth, is finally harnessed." Finally, in this totally charged planet, "electricity stimulates assimilation everywhere" (1971 [1917], 105). Wireless electricity enables a sort of planetary intelligence, and gives rise to uncanny correspondences among humans, vegetables, environments and machines.

The force of growth and the means of assemblage are all achieved by tapping into the electric atmosphere that surrounds us. But this assimilation develops as a fantastic pursuit, where the space of the unknown gives rise to strange imaginings. Prior to the parcelling up of the electromagnetic spectrum to control frequencies for commercial purposes, the ether was an operative space for technological speculation and unusual connections. Yet earlier conceptions of ether resurface, as Joe Milutis suggests, "in unstable moments of technological shift" (2003, 72). This other ether "is the idea of a network mind that allows for indiscriminate connections and animistic insight" (ibid.). The imagined correspondence between cosmos and radio sets, or between plants and telephones, is a critical way in which the technologies of communication are fabricated. These are practices of uncanny and telepathic communication, where unusual ideas can be "pulled" from the ether, or seemingly disparate concepts can collide in a space of apparent similarity. Perhaps these practices are even most compelling for how they elicit the curious and latent aspects of communication.

CITY OF COINCIDENCE

With the network of wireless communication and ubiquitous computing proposed in the form of sensors and smart dust, it is not telepathic transference from person to person but rather from machine to machine that presents the possibility for the most unusual connections and correspondences. The atmosphere of wireless sensor communications suggests an even more expanded dimension of machinic telepathy. "The future" has even been characterized as "a world of connecting machines" (Paul Saffo, cited in Johnson 2000). Such autonomous machines would function autonomously, "talking to other machines *on behalf of* people," so that communication among people is projected to be "less than half a percent of the traffic on the Net" (ibid.). Such a degree of automation effectively enables machines to "read and write by themselves" (Kittler 1997, 147). But the feedback loop from machine to machine that plays out in these scenarios for the near future establishes an even more cryptic scenario for communication, where we are immersed in and yet relatively unaware of the surrounding—telepathic—exchange.

Perhaps this is why, when Alan Turing endeavoured to determine whether machines think, he required a "telepathy-proof room." In his well-known essay "Computing Machinery and Intelligence" (1950) Turing modifies his original experiment conducted with a man and woman in one room, and an interrogator (or machine) in another room, to account for the possibility of extra-sensory perception, or ESP. In this modified experiment, the interrogator must tell the difference not between a man and woman, but between a man with telepathic powers and a computer. Yet because telepathy would throw into disarray the entire basis for assessment, Turing concludes, "if telepathy is admitted it will be necessary to tighten our test up. The situation could be regarded as analogous to that which would occur if the interrogator were talking to himself and one of the competitors was listening with his ear to the wall" (1950, 454).

At this point, telepathist and machine, and even interrogator and machine, become conflated. Telepathic chatter is the one constant—and it proves difficult to trace the source or limits of this errant communication. With the prospect of machines talking to machines, one wonders if Turing was finally attempting to limit the possible interference from *machinic* telepathy. What would be the salient difference between a person communicating telepathically and a computer simulating human communication? Perhaps the differences between these—and the possible means for clearing up the interferences between telepathic people and humanoid computers—were too difficult to identify. But the possibility for such telepathic machinic interference is ubiquitous in the wireless city, which is far from an impervious space. The wireless city is full of leaking telepathic signals and the wayward hum of garrulous machines.

The urban atmosphere circulates and sediments with random shadowy particles, so that the process of wireless correspondence is inevitably subject to interference. Telepathy is a similarly imperfect exchange, a process of communication that is riddled with interference and so relies upon considerable acts of induction and conjecture. Studying the possibilities of telepathy in the 1920s, Upton Sinclair and his wife, Mary, performed their own elaborate series of telepathic experiments. Attempting to understand the telepathic exchange, Sinclair asks if it is "some kind of vibration, going out from the brain, like radio broadcasting?" (1930, 4). The resulting study, "Mental Radio," documents the process of thoughts transmitted wirelessly between husband and wife while in separate rooms—much like the Turing experiment, without the third party. They produced a series of comparative drawings, and although their success rate was not astounding (23 per cent successful matches, 24 per cent failed matches, and the remaining 53 per cent a murky mismatch), the Sinclairs were convinced that the matches far exceeded any possibility for random guessing and were evidence of the veracity of telepathic powers.[4]

Regardless of whether their experiments are "proof" of telepathy, the system of correspondence that plays out suggests other dimensions of wireless communication. The Sinclairs' telepathic correspondence matches up an inverted roller skate and a hairy horse, a hanging monkey and a trumpet, a volcano and a beetle with antennae. In the graphic fold of imagined similarity, a shadowy form of communication allows unusual connections to be made, while at the same time rewriting the rules for correspondence.[5] An interpretive leap is often required to match the figures that are sent and received. When the feedback is set sufficiently low, so that a pony and roller skate become one and the same, a system of curious miscorrespondence is put in place. Between input and output, telepathic clarity emerges not in a one-to-one ratio but rather as an expanded space of interpretive resonance. Durham Peters has suggested that the dream of telepathy leans toward a type of "communication without remainder" (1999, 16).[6] But the mental radio experiments demonstrate that telepathy is full of remainder and mis-correspondence. These are sites where interference and residue surface repeatedly in the process of transmission.

---

4. In a subsequent edition of the text, Albert Einstein also wrote the Preface for *Mental Radio*, where he briefly asked the reader to maintain openness to the experiments Sinclair presented.

5. This slipped system of correspondence is also suggestive of the opening discussion in Michel Foucault's *The Order of Things: An Archaeology of the Human Sciences* (New York: Vintage Books, 1994).

6. If for Durham Peters communication is most fully revealed when it breaks down and fails, then telepathy may be the ideal form of communication for just this reason. Noting the successes of telepathy, however, Laura Otis cites British scientist William Barrett, who argues that telepathy, for all its failures, is actually more effective than "the clumsy mechanism of speech." What's more, Otis writes, "in efficiency, telepathy surpassed telegraphy, which had not yet transcended the primitive, organic vehicle of spoken language" (185).

Then as now, the wireless city is infused with these telepathic correspondences, the convergence and timing of machines, the instant transfer of messages, the strange conflation of events, and the lingering remainders. In nineteenth-century Paris, the Eiffel Tower was rigged for wireless transmission and could be tapped into with receiver sets from home balconies. Douglas Kahn has called this structure the "emblematic oracle of simultaneity," even a "wireless landmark" (1999, 53). Today, the ambition to fill the urban skies with such oracular signals continues unabated. Paris has—in turn with many other global cities—been called "the first large wireless city in the world," equipped as it is with contiguous and continuous access to wireless signals (Dembart 2003). Electrical signals enable processes of simultaneity, and the city plays out these synchronized, telepathic possibilities. McLuhan speaks to this process of electricity and instantaneity found in automation, going so far as to suggest that "any process that approaches instant interrelation of a total field tends to raise itself to the level of conscious awareness, so that computers seem to 'think'" (1994, 351). This field of simultaneity, intelligence, and interrelation resonates with Marcel Mauss's definition of "savage telepathy," a scene in which "the whole social body comes alive with the same movement" (2001, 133). The play of instant correspondence suggests an "intelligence" of exchange, where anticipation and event coalesce—in the savage communication of machines. The synchronized sensing and transmissions—the automated stirrings of the city—appear intelligent because of their programmed spontaneity.

The simultaneity, instantaneity, and smartness of wireless communications acquire a "presence," as Sconce would suggest, by virtue of their "liveness" (Sconce 2000, 6). These qualities of presence, moreover, suggest a transition in communications from that of a *channel* to an atmosphere of communication, an "all-enveloping force occupying the ether" (ibid., 11). Like the pervasive presence found in ether-bound communications, a similar presence is located in the ubiquitous computing enabled by smart dust. Replacing what is similarly seen as the "conduit" of the Internet, it is possible to imagine information transformed into landscapes—environments and cities. An atmospheric mode of communication—like the ether, telepathic and electric—delineates a particular type of urban space that is composed not of distance and duration but rather a space of etheric density that gives rise to new forms of presence (Gabrys 2010).

Stephen Graham asks how we can "imagine the 'real-time' city" so that we may account for the ways in which telecommunications reconfigure our notions of urban space and time (1997, 31–2). The atmospheric communication hovering over the city like a sensate cloud moves beyond even the architectures of conduit and screen, not to the virtual but to the imperceptible. This atmosphere is the space in-between: not an idealized representation but a particular mobilization of urban matter through pervasive and automated computation. In fact, with wireless sensors and the proposed applications of smart dust, the virtual collapses. Information is no longer a degree removed but completely embedded. Machinic telepathy reconfigures urban ecologies so that we no longer map the virtual or physical but take inventory of the telepathic *migration* of dust: how does this sensorial information circulate within and transform our urban settings?

DUST OF MACHINES

With autonomous machines connected to autonomous machines, the city is now in telepathic communication. Increasingly instant and automated, urban space circulates through the transitory and monitored circuits of web cameras, surveillance systems, timers, and traffic monitors—all the constitutive parts of a communications city that talks to and watches itself. As a city geared toward infomatic output, this environment is highly coded: at once invisible but thoroughly documented. Smart dust presents the furthest imagined instalment of the programmed city. It enables ways of navigating the city that redirect sense and orientation toward a store of telepathic data. "You want to be able to simply say, 'Take me to the projector in room 515,'" says Hari Balakrishnan, an assistant professor of electrical engineering and a researcher with MIT's Project Oxygen. Or, "Take me to the nearest projector in the building, or in the neighborhood, or find the nearest Chinese restaurant that serves low-sodium food." Cafés, drugstores, post offices, any place you might want to visit—all would be sending out digital beacons to vie for your attention" (cited in Johnson 2000). But the initial—and now even historic—imaginings of this technology have over time reached actual application. It may not yet be possible to telephone your garden, but it is possible to consult mobile phones for low-sodium restaurants. In the smart-dusted wireless city, both landscapes and artifacts are specked with sensors to facilitate wayfinding and consumption. An urban "network mind" can be continually dialled and consulted, revealing not just the circulations of urban messages and information but also informing the pathways of people who are reliant on these systems of navigation.

Locative technologies, wireless sensors, geotagging, and Web 2.0 or Environment 2.0 technologies are now all-pervasive in urban settings. Mobile phones are GPS enabled, and even commodites are tagged with radio frequency identification tags (RFIDs)—a technology that has also been a source of speculation through smart dust, which could similarly be deployed in any number of products. Dust-specked and "smart" commodities circulate in the city to eventually become another type of dust—waste—as the everaccelerating cycle of production, consumption, and obsolescence ensures the rapid decay of objects (Gabrys 2011).[7] The initial "inventor" of smart dust, Kris Pister, elaborates on such a merging of products and information: "Every conceivable object would have a recoverable history, a place in the cybernetic realm: physical space and cyberspace would truly melt into one" (cited in Johnson 2000). This urban space is far from virtual, when the physical world becomes the basis and location for information. This is an attempt not to collapse space and time but to fill it with dense layers of data and dust.

With the project of completely monitoring the physical world and putting the environment "online," there is no limit to the data to be retrieved. The data-gathering task is broken down into the smallest possible scale, so that previously large-scale measurements can be refigured as micro-data. With billions of motes forming detailed sensory networks, an increasing amount of information may be extracted from the urban environment. Smart dust finally offers the possibility of all-encompassing sense technologies that can continually scan, generate data from, and even regulate and modify, our natural-cultural environments.

7. For a discussion on what maybe considered the "dust" of commodities, see Will Straw's "Exhausted Commodities: The Material Culture of Music," *Canadian Journal of Communication* 25, no. 1 (2000).

This database is global in scale, and reflects what McLuhan refers to as an "ecology of media." With the launching of Sputnik, the planet became visible for the first time as an artifact, and as McLuhan writes, "transformed the planet into Spaceship Earth with a program problem" (2003, 242). The environment became programmable, a coherent system. An ecology of media was transposed to this space, and the electric nervous system of communications enshrouded the entire globe (as the subsequent launching of satellites confirms). Such a media surround resonates precisely with the objectives of the purveyors of smart dust, who "have visions of sending billions of these machines into the atmosphere so that the entire planet could be wired. Far-reaching networks of communicating sensors would give the earth a digital nervous system accessible to the web and giant search engines, from which we could instantly access anything about the state of the planet" (Anderson 2003).

With the implementation of micro-data, the question becomes how to make sense of the welter of information. The planet is at once observable as an artifact, such that we can call it an object of data, and yet surrounds us as a space of potentially limitless data production. Wireless sensors are now in place on ocean buoys and in soil matrices, across urban roadways and within the skeletons of buildings. The applications for environmental sensing are inexhaustible. But a critical operation continually emerges from within these extensive data sets. A means of filtering the data is necessary.[8] And so we return to telepathic machines. It is not just the relay from mote to mote that is telepathic; so too is the process of sifting through the static of all possible data to arrive at decipherable communication. In order to read through the haze of information, the machinic radio must be tuned to a legible frequency. Without this capability, smart dust encounters its double: the dust that isnoise.

ENDLESS CITY

Neo-geological, the "Monument Valley" of some pseudo-lithic era, today's metropolis is a phantom landscape, the fossil of past societies whose technologies were intimately aligned with the visible transformation of matter, a project from which the sciences have increasingly turned away.
Virilio, *The Overexposed City* (2003, 297)

By refusing "technological miracles" the artist begins to know the corroded moments, the carboniferous states of thought, the shrinkage of mental mud, in the geologic chaos—in the strata of esthetic consciousness. The refuse between mind and matter is a mine of information.
Smithson, *A Sedimentation of the Mind: Earth Projects* (1996, 107)

The wireless city is a space for the production of dust in all its modalities. The city abounds with compressed and errant signals. Yet instead of dissolving urban space, as so many writers suggest, these communication and sensing technologies fill it with signals. In this space of machines speaking to machines, an inexplicable transference, correspondence, exchange occurs in the noise that irrupts be-

---

8. See also Brendan I. Koerner's "Intel's Tiny Hope for the Future," *Wired* 11, no. 12 (December 2003), where he writes, "Sensors can't become the next big thing until a host of mundane technical issues are resolved: How to get the chipset radios off the crowded 900-mhz spectrum? How to program the networks to not just spew reams of information but be intelligent enough to figure out which measurements are vital and which are junk?"

tween signals. As Friedrich Kittler suggests, the "noise of the real"—another kind of dust—produces an infinitely dense static discharge. "Molecular swarms and whirling electrons" appear in one instance as "dancing sun particles," but "in the real are the noise on all channels" (1999, 51–9). Every medium, and every machinic attempt to access "the real," is saturated with noise—the dust of transmission. The use of the term "smart dust" to describe the possible occupation and ingestion of all the possible data offered by environments—urban and otherwise—then encapsulates this other sense of dust, as it reveals the difficulty of capturing and making operational such a large store of environmental data.

The dissipation and appearance of dust equally describes the formation of cities, as they lapse into wasted zones and residual districts. But as Yves-Alain Bois suggests, dust—particularly the dust of cities—is often not visible until it has settled (1997, 228). Dust is immanent and inescapable, it spreads and multiplies, promising to overwhelm. The modalities of dust offer further insights into the self-organizing, diverse forces of urban systems. Cities, as Nigel Clark writes, "are dynamic and open systems, the multiple forms of matter-energy (including minerals, biomass and genes) which pass through them entering into complex, non-linear relationships whose outcomes tend to exceed the calculations of their human component" (2000, 24). These urban systems—and the devices that would track and circulate information about them—typically surpass our available operating systems. They generate residue—they give rise to remainder that may even be best understood through telepathic modes of correspondence.

While for Bois the city is "pure noise," as it exceeds the limited "transmission of the message" (1997, 230), for McLuhan it is exactly the noise—or dust—that is most characteristic of the medium—as extended environment. The medium, through its side effects and unintended changes, gives rise to this environment of communications, which exceeds the message as sound-bite (Cavell 2002, 153). But in a medium that is noise and extended effect, how does that other kind of "smart" dust filter through the urban background, replete as it is with interference, to extract information? Here the operation of smart dust must be telepathic on another level: in order to sift through the urban environment and coordinate correspondence from mote to mote, a telepathic filter must be in use. Even though wireless sensors are tuned to specific forms of input, a completely accurate reading of the city is impossible (as the Surrealists and Situationists have demonstrated, and exploited). The noise of the environment inevitably impedes the clear transmission of messages.

Sensing, moreover, is not a singular mode of communication. Wireless sensors operate as a multitude of devices that make tentative attempts to assemble a whole. But the matter is not whether they arrive at an accurate assemblage but how they will filter through the noise and dust, and what sensorial arrangements and circulations will be the most compelling and pertinent. This is the telepathic imperative. Data exists everywhere in excess. In the wireless city, it floats and settles in a hazy surround. Sifting through the modalities of dust to sense and communicate through the urban medium will ultimately require a well-tuned telepathic sense.

REFERENCES

Amato, Joseph A. 2000. *Dust: A History of the Small and the Invisible*. Berkeley: University of California Press.

Anderson, Alun. 2003. "The Smart-Dust Revolution." *The Economist* (November 20).

Bois, Yves-Alain, and Rosalind Krauss. 1997. "Zone." In *Formless: A User's Guide*, 224–34. New York: Zone Books.

Broad, William J. (2005). "A Web of Sensors, Taking Earth's Pulse." *The New York Times* (May 10).

Cavell, Richard. 2002. *McLuhan in Space: A Cultural Geography*. Toronto: University of Toronto Press.

Clarke, Arthur C. 1962. *Profiles of the Future: An Inquiry into the Limits of the Possible* London: Victor Gallancz.

Clark, Nigel. 2000. "Botanizing on the Asphalt? The Complex Life of Urban Bodies." *Body & Society* 6, nos. 3-4: 12–33.

Dembart, Lee. 2003. "In the Cards: Unplugged Net Surfing All over Town." *International Herald Tribune*, May 5.

Durham Peters, John. 1999. *Speaking into the Air: A History of the Idea of Communication*. Chicago, Illinois: University of Chicago Press.

Estrin, Deborah, et al (2002). "Connecting the Physical World with Pervasive Networks." *Pervasive Computing, IEEE* 1, issue 1, Jan-Mar: 59 – 69.

Gabrys, Jennifer (2010). "Atmospheres of Communication," in *Sampling the Spectrum: The Politics, Practices and Poetics of Mobile Technologies*, eds. Barbara Crow, Michael Longford and Kim Sawchuk (Toronto: University of Toronto Press).

Gabrys, Jennifer (2007). "Automatic Sensation: Environmental Sensors in the Digital City," *Senses and Society*, Vol. 2, Issue 2, 189-200.

Gabrys, Jennifer (2011). *Digital Rubbish: A Natural History of Electronics* (Ann Arbor: University of Michigan Press).

Graham, Stephen. 1997. "Imaging the Real-Time City." In *Imagining Cities: Scripts, Signs, Memory*, edited by Sallie Westwood and John Williams, 31-49. London: Routledge.

Henderson, Linda Dalrymple. 1997. "Marcel Duchamp's 'The King and Queen Surrounded by Swift Nudes' (1912) and the Invisible World of Electrons." *Weber Studies: An Interdisciplinary Humanities Journal* 14 (winter): 83-101; accessed online as part of special supplement to electronic book review (ebr 5) at http://www.altx.com/ebr/w(ebr)/essays/henderson.html

Johnson, George. 2000. "Only Connect." *Wired* 8, no.1 (January): 148-60.

Kahn, Douglas. 1999. *Noise, Water, Meat: A History of Sound in the Arts*. Cambridge: MIT Press.

Kittler, Friedrich A. 1990. *Discourse Networks, 1800/1900*. Translated by Michael Metteer and Chris Cullens. Stanford: Stanford University Press.

– 1997. "There Is No Software." In *Literature, Media, Information Systems*, edited by John Johnston, 147-55. Amsterdam: OPA.

Luckhurst, Roger. 2002. *The Invention of Telepathy*. Oxford: Oxford University Press.

Marinetti, F.T. 1971. "Electrical War." In *Marinetti: Selected Writings*, edited by R.W. Flint, 104-8. London: Secker and Warburg.

Mauss, Marcel. 2001. *General Theory of Magic*. London: Routledge.

McLuhan, Marshall. 1994. "Automation: Learning a Living." In *Understanding Media: The Extensions of Man*, 346–60. Cambridge, Mass.: MIT Press.

– 2003. *Understanding Me: Lectures and Interviews*. Edited by Stephanie McLuhan and David Staines. Cambridge: MIT Press.

Milutis, Joe. 2003. "Superflux of Sky." *Cabinet Magazine* 10, accessed online at http://www.cabinetmagazine.org/issues/10/superflux.php.

Otis, Laura. 2001. *Communicating with Bodies and Machines in the Nineteenth Century*. Ann Arbor: University of Michigan Press.

Sinclair, Upton. 1930. *Mental Radio*. New York: Albert & Charles Boni.

Sconce, Jeffrey. 2000. *Haunted Media: Electronic Presence from Telegraphy to Television*. Durham: Duke University Press.

Smithson, Robert. 1996. "A Sedimentation of the Mind: Earth Projects." In *The Collected Writings of Robert Smithson*, edited by Jack Flam, 100–113. Berkeley: University of California Press.

Turing, Alan M. 1950. "Computing Machinery and Intelligence." *Mind* 59, no. 236 (October): 433–60.

Virilio, Paul. 2003. "The Overexposed City." In *ROAM: Reader on the Aesthetics of Mobility*, edited by Anthony Hoete, 264-297. London: Black Dog Publishing.

KENYA by Svin Torfinn

COMMUNICATING

One of the more powerful imminent commons has been created by the radical densification of urban communication networks produced by pervasive computation and wireless communications. While cities have always been characterized by dense communication networks—starting with the postal services, the telegraph, and the telephone—their current technological status has intensified exponentially through the combination of ubiquitous, pervasive computing and the development of the World Wide Web to allow users to interact and collaborate with each other in a dialogue as creators of content in a virtual community.

If the mass-media technologies of the 1950s created a global culture of shared values and references, the Internet is enabling users to become content creators who engage specific communities and specific locations. The combination of the Internet and the development of wireless technologies such as GSM (Global System for Mobile Communications), GPRS (General Packet Radio Service), CDMA (Code Division Multiple Access), WiFi (wireless local area networking with IEEE 802.11 standards), and Bluetooth (short-wavelength UHF radio waves in the ISM band from 2.4 to 2.485 GHz) has entirely freed information from physical attachments.

Following the development of these technologies, the emergence of social media is one of the most important processes that humankind has ever gone through, and likely one of the most crucial developments for cities. It is a phenomenon of enormous proportions. If the emerging artificial sensorium will enable us to sense and to get information (and even interpret this information) which is remote and with an unprecedented precision, the social media is creating a global brain. A few years after the emergence of the Internet, social media started roughly at the same time as the twenty-first century, and after a few startups (Friends Reunited, Friendster, and MySpace), Skype (660 million users) appeared in 2003, Facebook (1.6 billion users) was launched in 2004, YouTube (1.3 billion users) in 2005, Twitter (328 million users) in 2006, WhatsApp (800 million users) in 2009, Instagram (400 million users) in October 2010... Social media can allow people to date (Tinder and Grindr), look for jobs (LinkedIn), share images (Instagram, Tumblr, Pinterest), share videos (Vimeo and YouTube), talk (Skype), or send messages (Snapchat and WhatsApp). An estimated 60% of the world's population is already connected to the Internet, and about 3 billion people are engaged in some social media platform, mainly through mobile devices. The connection of mobile devices to GPS (Global Positioning System) infrastructure is opening unprecedented opportunities to experience or navigate urban spaces and to engage with fellow citizens. Recent phenomena like the *Pokémon-Go* craze, Bluetooth dating in Riyadh, or applications like Grindr or Tinder are now beginning to create entirely new urban geographies which would not have been possible without wireless communications. Social media redefines urban space in a physical manner: inside and outside, public and private, work and leisure are now subject to a radical reformulation in light of the intensification of connections, not only between the inhabitants of a city, but between the global populations which are connected to these engines.

Some of the most transformative processes triggered by new communication technologies relate to the possibility of sharing services and goods in time, including short-term residential rentals, bicycle- and car-share schemes, co-working spaces, and other urban processes based on shared economies. Today's city, inherited from modernist planning, is primarily regulated by functional determinations and private property laws, which are being disrupted by shared ownership. Social media and ubiquitous computation hold the key to the development of new urban protocols, institutions, typologies, and experiences. The management of resources and energy through sharing, recycling, or optimization is increasing, and current legislation needs to shift towards the normalization of sharing protocols. The urbanization of these technologies will open new potentials for architecture to engage with these emerging forms of urban culture.

The possibility of communicating with automated devices will also certainly reshape the way in which we relate to our work or domestic infrastructures. The development of unprecedented forms of domesticity, work, and leisure and their impact in urban cultures and politics will disrupt the traditional forms of urban functions. The pervasive deployment of industrial technologies of physical automation to all aspects of our lives and into everyday objects—the so-called *Internet of Things* (IoT)—is likely to transform life in cities beyond recognition. The technology that makes IoT viable is radio-frequency identification (RFID). If all objects and people in daily life were equipped with identifiers, computers could manage and inventory them. Besides using RFID, the *tagging* of things may be achieved through such technologies as near field communication, barcodes, QR codes, and digital watermarking. Short-, medium-, and long-range wireless systems are capable of connecting tagged objects to

Biennale di Venezia, Russia's Pavilion, 2012

the Internet. Connected through SCADA industrial communication protocols,[1] IoT is widely deployed in home automation (smart home devices): the control and automation of lighting, heating, and ventilation systems, and the remote control of appliances such as washer/dryers, ovens, freezers, vacuum cleaners, and air purifiers through WiFi is already transforming our domestic environments. In terms of urban applications, a number of cities have adopted a smart-city policy that aims to wire almost everything, and have connected and turned that into a constant stream of data that can be monitored and analyzed by computers with little human intervention. Traffic control, parking search, and environmental monitoring are some of the functions which are aimed to be automated through IoT technologies: Songdo City in South Korea, Guangzhou Knowledge City in China, San Jose in California, Rio de Janeiro in Brazil, and Santander in Spain have already initiated the introduction of these mechanisms to improve urban performance.

Urban governance is another field where these tools will have a decisive impact. There is growing interest in the use of citizen-based planning, which puts the actual tools of urban planning and architecture in the hands of the community, supported by evidence-based models using data analysis and integrated governance models with impact and quality-based procurement functions.

---

1. Supervisory control and data acquisition (SCADA) is a control system architecture that uses computers, networked data communications, and graphical user interfaces for high-level process supervisory management, but uses other peripheral devices such as programmable logic controllers and discrete PID controllers to interface to the process plant or machinery. The operator interfaces which enable monitoring and the issuing of process commands, such as controller set point changes, are handled through the SCADA supervisory computer system. However, the real-time control logic or controller calculations are performed by networked modules which connect to the field sensors and actuators.

The SCADA concept was developed as a universal means of remote access to a variety of local control modules, which could come from different manufacturers allowing access through standard automation protocols. In practice, large SCADA systems have grown to be very similar to distributed control systems in function, but use multiple means of interfacing with the plant. See "SCADA, *Wikipedia*, https://en.wikipedia.org/wiki/SCADA, accessed 11 May 2017."

The impact of these technologies on economic and political processes may also be important. There are initiatives testing the enhancement of urban governance by engaging citizens in instant decision making through e-voting protocols, which may entirely change the political systems and rhythms by making the political arena a much more concrete and project-driven endeavor, and much less driven by program and ideology. There are also enormous risks in the deployment of these technologies for governance, including the obvious threats to privacy which were demonstrated recently by the revelations by Edward Snowden in 2013 that the U.S. National Security Agency (NSA) was developing numerous mass global surveillance programs; many of these were run by the NSA itself and the Five Eyes Intelligence Alliance, with the cooperation of telecommunication companies and European governments. Phillip N. Howard has also identified a practice he calls "astroturfing," which enables lobbying groups to maximize their presence on the Internet through the deployment of automated protocols mimicking fake "grassroots" movements.[2] These are just two examples of how new technologies of communication are already affecting crucial political processes, even on a global scale, let alone how effective similar technologies may become when operating at a more reduced local scope.

---

2. Philip N. Howard, *New Media Campaigns and the Managed Citizen* (Cambridge: Cambridge University Press, 2006).

CAN CITIES HELP US HACK FORMAL POWER SYSTEMS?

Saskia Sassen

Cities are complex systems. But they are incomplete systems. These features take on urbanized formats that vary enormously across time and place. In this mix of complexity and incompleteness lies the capacity of cities to outlive far more powerful but formal and closed systems: many a city has outlived governments, kings, the leading corporation of an epoch. Herein also lies the possibility of *making*—making the urban, the political, the civic, a history. Thus, much of today's dense built-up terrain, such as a vast stretch of high-rise housing or of office buildings, is not a city; it is simply dense built-up terrain. On the other hand, a working slum can have many of the features of a city, and indeed, some slums are a type of city—poor, but deeply urban.

It is also in this mix of incompleteness and complexity that the possibility exists for the powerless to hack power in the city, in a way that they could not in a plantation, for example, and to hack particular features of the city. They are thereby able to make a history, a politics, even if they do not get empowered. Thus, current conditions in global cities, especially, are creating not only new structurations of power but also operational and rhetorical openings for new types of actors and their projects. In these cities those without power can make themselves present: in the richest neighborhoods where they are the indispensable household support, in the corporate center where they are indispensable service workers, and so on. Thus powerlessness can become complex in the city. And this is, in itself, a transversal type of hacking.

One way of conceiving of some of this is as instances of urban capabilities.[1]

1. I develop this argument in "Does the City Have Speech?," *Public Culture* 25(2) (April 2013): 209–21; see also *Expulsions* (Cambridge, MA: Harvard University Press, 2014; Dutch translation forthcoming with ACCO).

In this essay I am particularly interested in two features of the city. One is that the global city is a strategic frontier zone that enables those who lack power, those who are disadvantaged, outsiders, and minorities who are discriminated against—even though it decimates the modest middle classes. The disadvantaged and excluded can gain *presence* in such cities in a way they cannot in neat, homogenous provincial cities. In the global city, they become present to power and to each other, which may include learning to negotiate their multiple differences. They can hack power and they can hack their differences of origin, religion, phenotype. The second feature is the strategic importance of the city today for shaping new orders—or, if you will, hacking old orders. As a complex space, the city can bring together multiple, very diverse struggles and engender a larger, more encompassing push for a new normative order. It enables people with different passions and obsessions to work together—more precisely, to hack power together.

GLOBAL CITIES ARE TODAY'S FRONTIER ZONES
The large complex city, especially if it's a global city, is a new frontier zone. In frontiers, actors from different worlds meet, but there are no clear rules of engagement. Whereas historically the frontier lay in the far stretches of colonial empires, today's frontier zone is in our large, messy global cities. Cities are now the places where actors from different spheres have an encounter for which there are no established rules. The historic frontier lay at the creeping and expanding edges of empires; but those edges of empires no longer exist today. Today that space of encounter with differences lies deep inside our large, messy cities. Thus, these cities are strategic for both global corporate capital and the powerless.

Much of the work of forcing deregulation, privatization, and new fiscal and monetary policies on governments actually took place in the corporate sector of global cities rather than in legislatures and parliaments. In this sense, then, the corporates hacked the city because that making of new instruments was a way of constructing the equivalent of the old military "fort" of the historic frontier: the corporate zone in our cities is a protected, de facto private space. And corporate actors have been doing this since the late 1980s in city after city worldwide to ensure they have a global operational space that suits their interests.[2] The global city is then also a frontier zone because it is where strategic spaces of power can be hacked— though they rarely are, which has always surprised me.

But global cities are also strategic places for those without power. They signal the possibility of a new type of politics, centered in new types of political actors. That is one instance of what I seek to capture with the concept of urban capabilities. It is not simply a matter of having or not having power. For the powerless, the city is a strategic space because the political goes well beyond routinized voting and having to accept corporate utility logics, or the dominance of narratives that strengthen powerful actors. Urban space in powerful cities provides new hybrid bases from which to act.

2. This is the process I describe at great length in *The Global City*, 2nd updated ed. (1991; Princeton: Princeton University Press, 2001), and in *Cities in a World Economy*, 4th ed. (CITY: Sage, 2012).

One outcome we are seeing in city after city is the making of new kinds of informal politics. For instance, there is a kind of public-making work that can produce disruptive narratives, and make legible the local and the silenced. Political work gets done this way: it becomes the work of making a new kind of contestatory public that uses urban space as a medium, a tool to hack power, even if it does not bring power down. The Occupy movements that rose in countries in very different parts of the world were momentarily disruptive but educational in the long term. They rhetoricized inequality and provided a narrative to large sectors of the impoverished middle classes, usually a rather conservative and prudent sector. It has evolved as a politics that is making headway at the level of political speech and mobilization, but not necessarily system change: Podemos in Spain, Syriza in Greece, the rise of a seventy-year-old long-term socialist in the United States as a presidential candidate appealing to all ages, but especially the young. Deeper have been the changes in Bolivia and Venezuela, encompassing a whole new vocabulary and governmental logic; less radical but still significant are Peru and Quito. All of these, across their differences, and with varying levels of intensity, share a partial or full repudiation of politics as usual.

It also signals the possibility of making a new type of subject, one abundant in cities across time and place, but always somewhat rare: the urban subject that results from hacking ethnicity, religion, phenotype, inequality, physical disability. Old Baghdad and Jerusalem, industrializing Chicago and New York, early-twentieth-century Berlin and Buenos Aires were such cities. This is not to deny the specific histories and geographies that generated what I like to call the "urban subject." The urban subject is at home with enormous differences of religion, ethnicity, etc. A city's sociality can bring out and underline the urbanity of subject and setting, and dilute more essentialist markers. The need for new solidarities (for instance, when cities confront major challenges) is often what can bring about this shift. Urban space, especially a city's center, can hack our essentialisms, as it forces us into joint responses, into crowded public transport, into highly mixed work situations, into public hospitals and universities, and so on. From there it can move us on to the appreciation of an urban subject, rather than more specific individual or group identities that might rule in a neighborhood. The big, messy, slightly anarchic city enables such shifts. The corporatized city or the office park does not.

There is yet another type of hacking of long-time orders that is taking place today. It is the hacking of well-established larger units, notably nation-states, that are beginning to lose their grip on domains where they once had considerable control. This is an important even if partial and not always desirable change. In *Territory, Authority, Rights*, I identified a vast proliferation of such partial disassemblings and reassemblings that arise from the remix of bits of territory, authority, and rights, once all ensconced in *national* institutional frames.[3] In Europe, these

---

3. The emergent landscape I am describing promotes a multiplication of diverse spatiotemporal framings and diverse normative mini-orders, where once the dominant logic was toward producing grand unitary national spatial, temporal, and normative framings. See Saskia Sassen, *Territory, Authority, Rights: From Medieval to Global Assemblages* (Princeton: Princeton University Press, 2008), chaps. 8 and 9.

novel assemblages include those resulting from the formation and ongoing development of the European Union, but also those resulting in a variety of cross-city alliances around protecting the environment, fighting racism, and other important causes. These generate a European subject for whom protecting the local or global environment matters more than nationality. And they also result from subnational struggles and the desire to make new regulations for self-governance at the level of the neighborhood and the city.

Against the background of a partial disassembling of empires and nation-states, the city emerges as a strategic site for making elements of new partial orders.[4] Where in the past national law might have been *the* law, today subsidiarity and the new strategic role of cities make it possible for us to imagine a return to *urban* law. We see a resurgence of urban law-making, a subject I discuss in depth elsewhere (see *Territory, Authority, Rights*, chapters 2 and 6). For instance, in the United States, a growing number of cities have passed local laws (ordinances) that make themselves sanctuaries for undocumented immigrants; other cities have passed environmental laws that only hold for those particular cities because they are far more radical than national law, or have developed currencies for local transactions that only function in those cities.

These are among the features that make cities a space of great complexity and diversity. But today, cities confront major conflicts that can reduce that complexity to mere built-up terrain or a cement jungle. The urban way of confronting extreme racism, governmental wars on terror, and the future crises of climate change is to make these challenges occasions to further expand diverse urban capabilities and to expand the meaning of membership. Yet much national government policy and the "needs" of powerful corporate actors go against this mode.

In the next section, I discuss a range of issues that illustrate how the powerless can hack power in the city.

WHEN CITY RESIDENTS HACK CLOSED INTELLIGENT SYSTEMS
It is important to appreciate the incompleteness of cities—they can constantly be remade, for better or for worse, and they are remade on their own terms in each case, even when the technologies used are similar. Incompleteness and mutability have allowed many of the world's great cities to outlast kingdoms, empires, nation-states, and powerful firms. To take the imagery of incompleteness further: powerful actors can remake cities in their image. But cities talk back. They do not take it sitting down. Sometimes this talking back may take decades, and sometimes it is immediate. A city's backtalk is one element of open-source urbanism: myriad interventions and little changes from the ground up contribute to making a city. Multiple, small, inconspicuous interventions together are evidence of a city's constant evolution.

---

4. One synthesizing image we might use to capture these dynamics is the movement from centripetal nation-state articulation to a centrifugal multiplication of specialized assemblages, where one of many examples might be the transborder networks of specific types of struggles, enactments, art, and so on.

In sharp contrast to the above scenario, so-called intelligent cities seek to mobilize technologies to *eliminate* incompleteness. The intelligent cities model typically misses the opportunity to urbanize technologies, and instead makes them invisible and puts them in command of rather than in dialogue with users.

Further, in their negotiations with global tech companies, city governments often feel at a great disadvantage in terms of understanding the technologies being promoted to solve a city's problems. But I argue that the city leadership need not think it has to bring to the table deep knowledge of the technologies. Most critical is that the city leadership know its city and its diverse needs—too often it does not. If it has detailed and thorough knowledge about all key aspects of its city, the leadership can interrogate the tech firms and ask them to show how diverse city needs can benefit from whatever the intelligent systems representatives are trying to sell. This turns the tables, and rather than the city leadership being put in the situation of audience to the "brilliant" technologists (or, rather, sales people), the tech companies are pushed to figure out how they can help the city. As a result, some of the techies would have to come to these meetings to address the questions and needs of an informed city leadership that knows what its city needs. Sales people alone would not be enough.

Let me briefly describe one form of deployment of impressive intelligent systems that does not quite contribute to the smart city; in the next section I then take the opposite example: an innovation that does not look so very smart but can actually contribute to the collective intelligence of the city.

One familiar instance of the intelligent city is the smart megaproject developed and managed by a private company that takes over a range of public control functions in a city. An example is the infamous IBM security center set up in Rio for the World Cup and for the coming Olympic games. Generally, such projects are inserted in older urban tissue that is increasingly seen as having little value: narrow streets, small squares, rundown small buildings, and modest public offices. And yet, there is a loss here, albeit invisible to the average city resident, regrettably including its functionaries. The price is the loss of urban tissue with its embedded past and present knowledges. In the particular Rio case, the residents knew and objected to the fact that IBM was running that key security and control apparatus. Further, the concept did not work. While it enabled the police promptly to identify a disturbance in the city, by the time the police managed to get to the spot, the guilty troublemakers usually were gone. The system became a joke. Indeed, even leaving aside the fact of multiple diverse worlds in a city, some of the effects or lack thereof in cities must have taken the insiders by surprise as well. As often happens, this innovation did not work out as planned, or barely accomplished what it was meant to do.

Would it not be smarter to enable residents who know their particular corner of the city to be furnished with devices for communicating with local civic associations or central authorities in case of danger or trouble? The intelligence, knowledge, and intuitions of a city's residents should become part of the notion of a safe and smart city. And so should the fact that users can transform the putative aim of a technology as described by an engineer or techie, and make it work on their own terms.[5] One implication for cities is that if residents feel it is *their* city, rather than the city of the rich or of the mafias, they will work at keeping it safe.

These are some of the vectors that can transform residents into a constitutive element in the "smart city." In this way, learning curves become powerful precisely because they have got to factor in the diversity contained in a city. This is the challenge that smart systems need to confront and engage.

OPEN-SOURCING THE NEIGHBORHOOD: HACKING CODIFIED KNOWLEDGE

How can we strengthen that positive scenario of the city's incompleteness invoked early in the prior section? An open-source urbanism is an antidote. It would mean a deployment of open-source technologies in a variety of urban contexts. The question then becomes: Can we urbanize open-source technology? As a technological innovation, open source has not been about cities, but about collaboratively building tools. Yet, the open-source approach resonates with what cities are at ground level, where its users are. To use an analogy, a park is made not only from the hardware of trees and ponds, but also from the software of people's practices.

Elsewhere[6] I have suggested that the notion of open-sourcing neighborhoods could be a key instrument not only for solving problems that are neighborhood-specific, but also as a first step in mobilizing neighborhoods into collective actions of diverse kinds, from urban farming to demanding better services from a city's government.[7] A second, related fact is that every neighborhood is different and tends to confront slightly different problems—such as transport access, flooding, poverty and unemployment, and more. Hence, every neighborhood has different types of knowledge about the city. Further, a diversity of actors—the grandmother, the shopkeeper, the child—spend time in the neighborhood and in turn have diverse knowledges about the same neighborhood.[8]

These locally produced knowledges are different from the codified knowledge at the center—the knowledge of governments, experts, elites. We could connect these diverse neighborhood actors to

---

5. Elsewhere I examine how when confronted with a given technical capacity in an interactive digital domain, those with power may use it differently than those who are needy. Saskia Sassen, "Interactions of the Technical and the Social: Digital Formations of the Powerful and the Powerless," *Information, Communication & Society* (2012), http://www.tandfonline.com/doi/abs/10.1080/1369118X.2012.667912#.VRrndWbx8zA ; DOI:10.1080/1369118X.2012.667912.

6. See "Open Sourcing the Neighborhood," *Forbes*, 10 November 2013, http://www.forbes.com/sites/techonomy/2013/11/10/open-sourcing-the-neighborhood/.

7. In using the term "neighborhood," I refer to modest sections of a city; usually we do not use this term to name the places where the very rich live.

8. A great innovation along these lines is the healthcare project developed by Dr. Manmeet Kaur to assist low-income workers in Harlem, in New York City; see City Healthworks website, www.cityhealthworks.com.

Umbrella-revolution's sit-in, Central Hong Kong by Katie Brinn

open-access networks, or wikis, that circulate these bits of information.[9] The effect would be to open up what are often closed systems of knowledge coming from the center or the top. Government agencies tend to verticalize their work, as do many leading urban civic institutions. We can hack this codified knowledge by bringing these bits of street and neighborhood knowledge into standard knowledge systems; this would unsettle such organizations and open them up. Central city government agencies could learn aspects about the city they simply are not well positioned to access.

Eventually, some neighborhood users are likely to experiment with developing versions, even if simple ones, of open-source technologies aimed at incorporating diverse bits of knowledge and diverse knowledge practices from the locality—via residents, friends, children, homeless people, grandparents.[10] While none of them is an urban expert, each has specific knowledge about their place. All of this in turn might activate additional elements of both knowledge practices and technological practices, generating more engagement by city residents and more cross-neighborhood comparisons. Ultimately, it can scale up to city level, but from the ground up, leading to exchanges and collaborations and on to a fully mobilized neighborhood and city culture.

Then we might see additional layers of tech space with new alignments and communication vectors. Urban space could be decentralized by bringing more action and initiatives to the diverse neighborhoods that constitute the city. New and unexpected intersections might emerge or be developed, with interesting economic, cultural, and political consequences. In this way, open sourcing the city may allow people to feel that the city is more theirs.

Urbanization—the processes that constitute, shape, and dynamize the city—can evolve also from the neighborhoods, not only from the center. The resulting technology may be more akin to an *urban* Wikileaks. In an ironic twist, neighborhoods could begin to leak knowledge, knowledge that has the capacity to unsettle traditional hierarchical institutions. Neighborhood actors that the center might see as marginal—like that child or homeless person or grandmother—can bring their knowledge of place straight into the codified knowledge of the center. This is hacking the center via subjects that are the extreme "other."

This urbanizing of digital technologies contrasts with the standard model of the smart city.

9. The simplest example of an implementation of this sort, albeit elementary, is the pothole application developed by the Boston municipal government: if you hit or see a pothole in the road, you click on the app, and the city government gets the information that there is a pothole and the coordinates of its location. The app saves the municipal government much wasted time trying to find potholes.

10. In a project on low-wage workers and digitization, I found that what would most enable low-wage workers is the extension of digitization to the larger space within which these workers operate: not only the workplace as narrowly understood, but also, and very importantly, their neighborhood. For a list of innovations, see Saskia Sassen, "Digitization and Work: Potentials and Challenges in Low-Wage Labor Markets," https://osf.app.box.com/s/qlnbrl95vm79720kpvuj3iqgs8ldhc00.

One of my key arguments is that if the so-called smart cities do not mobilize the diverse intelligences and situated knowledges of their residents, they are missing out on a key component of the smart city. And they are also missing out on a potential for democratizing the smart city. My emphasis is thus on outsourcing the neighborhood as one key component of this larger "knowledge space" that a smart city should be able to help constitute.

HACKING OFFICIAL CURRENCIES AND MAKING AUTONOMOUS CURRENCIES

My final example concerns the advantages for communities of using alternative local currencies for some of their purchases and other possibilities. I base this a bit on my contribution to the Money project launched by Geert Lovink on the issue of alternative currencies, which gets at some rather deep issues that are mostly invisible, and never explained by politicians.[11]

We need exchange mediums, such as money. But today's versions of money are mostly the official currencies of countries. And these currencies are becoming extremely problematic because they function less and less as an exchange medium and more and more as a tool for governments and corporations to extract household resources for their aims, often overriding the basic needs of a country's people.

The key mechanisms for extracting citizens' resources are taxation without citizens' participation in how to spend those taxes, and, secondly, the corporatizing of economies. When corporations capture most of what consumers spend, they also disproportionately control how that household money is invested and allocated (for instance, extreme increases in corporate salaries rather than investing in developing organic food).

Under these conditions, money is no longer simply an exchange medium. Nor is it a medium for ensuring large-scale investments—by either governments or corporations—into what a locality, a country, needs for its people. Money becomes an instrument for implementing what governments and corporations want.

Yet, not all alternative currencies are necessarily desirable. The key is a decentralized currency to enable the proliferation of noncorporate economies, and to do so at scales and with modalities that go beyond simple barter. Barter is fine for many operations, and it has thrived in certain settings, notably in parts of Latin America. But it is not enough. We need to scale-up if we are going to take back economic terrain now fully captured by large corporations. And we need to do this even if some of the larger needs of a locality, such as transport systems, will have to be built by large corporations.

Digital currencies are clearly one option. Most recently Bitcoin has drawn a lot of attention. It has also become a destination for speculative investment—and for lawsuits! This result has in turn raised

11. Geert Lovink, Nathaniel Tkacz, and Patricia de Vries, eds., *MoneyLab Reader: An Intervention in Digital Economy* (Amsterdam: Institute of Network Cultures, 2015). I thank the editors for letting me use this text here.

some key questions, notably whether Bitcoin is a decentralized currency. The challenge is to avoid the corporatizing of a currency, which is now the situation with more and more official currencies.

Again, by "corporatizing," I mean that a currency serves to transform household resources (as measured by consumption capacity) into corporate profits, which can then be invested without any concern about a locality's demands and needs. Mostly, a modest firm that depends on a locality's choices is going to have to be responsive in a way that the large corporation is not. Further, the power of large corporations to set up franchises, which might have to be a bit more responsive to a locality's needs, mostly winds up eliminating the locally owned businesses so that the franchise can rule uncontested—a take-it-or-leave-it stance vis-à-vis the locality. Finally, and inevitably, the franchise has to pass on some of the locality's consumption capacity to central headquarters. Ideally, a decentralized currency would favor local initiatives and redistribution in localities.[12]

In the last twenty years, this shift towards the corporatizing of household money has accelerated and become increasingly acute in more parts of the world. Up to a certain point we need governments and corporations for some of our needs: vast transport systems, public buildings, airports, harbors, and so on. But much of this far too easily winds up using our money for their profit rather than our needs. One result is growing asymmetries of all sorts, marked by growing concentrations of wealth and expanded impoverishment. There are exceptions here and there, but they are not enough to obliterate these asymmetries.

Further, to some extent our governments have enabled the power of corporations to extract household money not just via consumption but also via their policies. The elegantly named "quantitative-easing" is one such example. In the post-2008 crisis period, the United States has been the most active government in transferring households' money to corporations, especially big banks and major financial firms. Only a small portion of this (U.S.$ 320 billion) has been moved via the proper channel—the legislature, where there is a chance of a public debate in which we citizens can, in principle, voice our opinion. But by far most has been done secretly, and we only found out via Freedom of Information requests how our money was spent: over $7 trillion was secretly transferred from U.S. households to the global banking system. Several trillion more dollars were transferred via quantitative easing, a public event, but incomprehensible to the average household; this is language that does not spell out that it is households' money that is being transferred. Quantitative easing is also what the European Central Bank wants to implement in the European Union.

Yes, we need decentralized currencies that function as genuine exchange mediums to handle a vast range of the needs of households, modest firms, and localities. This would mean avoiding franchises and establishing locally owned operations; the profits then recirculate in the community or city rather than partly being captured by corporate headquarters. At the same time, we need national currencies to engage in the vast infrastructural and servicing projects that a country requires to address the

12. See also my analysis in chap. 3 of *Expulsions*, "Finance and Its Capabilities."

needs of its people; and this may mean contracting with large engineering corporations. But national currencies should not be necessary for buying most of a household's food, furniture, and such.

Decentralized currencies should enable significant components of our modern economies to be brought back into our communities. And if these currencies are digitized, local initiatives and innovations can get replicated across a region or a country's or a continent's localities. This is one way of constructing larger multinodal operational spaces that can cut across diverse types of boundaries without losing their local insertion.

What we do not need is what is happening today in a growing number of countries: the large-scale direct and indirect appropriation of the income of households and of modest firms to finance the profit-seeking aims of corporations.

CONCLUSION

Across time, cities have complicated the straightforward implementation of technologies. Cities are great hackers, though they mostly are so in ways we cannot quite capture in our language—it has its own language. The mix of urban materialities and people's cultures in the city does not always lead to predictable outcomes, and hence can unsettle or disrupt the best designs. This holds at many levels—from advanced transportation systems to "intelligent systems" installed in buildings, to name just a few. The city also is a lens that allows us to understand the diverse interactions between users (whether systems, organizations, or people) and the design and implementation of the technologies used in cities.

The DNA of the city is more akin to open-source technology—the notion of the perpetual beta also comes to mind. An approach that takes open sourcing into account would enable interactions between the technology and the user beyond those already pre-programmed within these systems. This approach would strengthen an understanding of the city as a combination of incompleteness and complexity: it is this mix that has enabled cities to outlive enterprises, kingdoms, nation-states, and, yes, Cisco Systems. These are all rather closed formal systems, which has made them rigid and more susceptible to obsolescence. One implication is that the current practice of installing more and more closed, centrally controlled intelligent systems in cities puts those cities themselves at risk of becoming obsolete when the technologies become obsolete.

The city puts technologies to a test. It is one window into understanding successful technological innovations for urban systems and urban life. Powerful actors can remake cities in their image. But cities talk back—sometimes it may take decades, and sometimes it is immediate. We can think of the multiple ways in which the city talks back as a type of open-source urbanism: the city as partly made through a myriad of interventions and little changes from the ground up. Diverse versions are seen at a local and immediate level—do-it-yourself urbanism, tactical urbanism, urban guerilla tactics, urban acupuncture, urban prototyping. Each of these multiple small interventions may not look like much, but together they give added meaning to the notion of the incompleteness of cities and the fact that this incompleteness gives cities their long lives, thereby outlasting other more powerful entities.

A TALE OF THREE CITIES, OR:
THE SMART CITY AS WILL AND CATEGORY ERROR

Adam Greenfield

Humanity is now, we are so often told, an urban species. Though there are real questions as to what the numbers actually mean, the statistics on planetary urbanization are so often bruited about that they have become something of a cliché. What's more, popular discourse on the subject appears to have internalized the notion that the great cities of Earth aren't merely significant for their concentration of habitation, but for the beneficial effects that habitation gives rise to. Disproportionately generators of economic vitality, technical innovation and cultural dynamism, our cities may even be able to function as lifeboats capable of sustaining us through the ecological reckoning that is now bearing down on our civilization.

If it is an urban age, though, it is also a networked age. Between the comprehensive instrumentation of the built environment, and the smartphones that so many of us now carry through every moment of the waking day—simultaneously sensor platform, aperture onto the global network, and remote control for the connected systems and services all around us—the colonization of everyday urban life by information processing is virtually complete.

And finally, we appear to have entered an age in which the more-or-less stable neoliberal consensus that held global sway for the past four decades has started to erode. Thus far, the most notable and distressing result of this erosion has been a turn toward authoritarian and xenophobic ethnonationalisms of one stripe or another, its traces evident in the Brexit referendum, the 2016 U.S. presidential election, and a long list of autocracies in the ascendant, from Russia to Turkey to the Philippines. But more hopefully, the eclipse of neoliberal hegemony has opened up a space in which some dare to imagine an entirely new way of organizing the productive processes of life: a commons beyond state and market both, in which networked collaboration, distributed material and energetic production, and horizontal forms of governance give rise to striking new possibilities for a just, equitable and fructifying urbanism.

By leveraging the decentralizing tendencies that appear to be implicit in our networked technologies, and the configurations of power they in principle give rise to, we can even begin to imagine what a networked urban commons would look like, and how it might work, at global scale—as a desirable end in itself, an antidote to the anomie and widespread sense of powerlessness that underlie the turn toward xenophobic authoritarianism, and a means of restoring some semblance of ecological balance.

Those of us who are interested in bringing such a state of affairs into being, though, might find that our hopes are dashed at the outset by a lack of clarity about how the technologies involved actually work, naiveté about those parties who currently wield them most effectively, or confusion about what a true commons would require of us. At present, we can see networked technology being layered onto urban place along three basic trajectories: one based largely on the needs of multinational technology vendors; one with roots in the Silicon Valley startup culture; and one—the subtlest yet most promising of all—as yet indistinct. By examining each of them in turn, we can learn more about what is at stake in the advent of networked urbanism, and perhaps chart a course through the Scylla and Charybdis of unwise choices toward a more fruitful future for all.

AVATAR I: SONGDO
In his public appearances, Moon Jae-in, as the president of South Korea, was fond of invoking a comprehensive vision of heavily technologized everyday life that involves "smart house, smart road, smart city"—indeed, an entire "Smart Korea." There may be no place on Earth closer to concrete fulfillment of Moon's objective than New Songdo City, a municipality of 90,000 souls built on some 53 square kilometers of tidal flats recovered from the Yellow Sea. In Songdo, both domestic spaces and the entire built fabric have been instrumented, allowing the city's controllers to monitor and adjust traffic flow and energy utilization in real time.

As ambitious as this sounds, it's an only slightly more elaborate version of a conception of networked urbanism that is common to municipal administrators and technology enthusiasts the world over. In its raw outlines, this conception seeks to harness the CCTV cameras and networked sensors installed throughout the urban milieu, as well as the torrential streams of data flowing off of our personal devices, to realize greater efficiency and enhance that ever-elusive property known as "quality of life." By submitting these flows of data to advanced analytic techniques based on machine learning, all kinds of benefits can be obtained: the nominal "optimization" of material and energetic flows, the streamlined delivery of municipal services, even the preemption of undesirable conditions (whether traffic jams or criminal offenses).

This, anyway, is the theory of smart urbanism. In practice, however, a number of issues conspire to ensure that what gets delivered invariably turns out to be rather less than the sum of its parts. The first is that, in looking to a rising technology sector to achieve this ambition, municipal-scale actors leave themselves at the mercy of powerful vendors—globally, multinationals like Siemens, IBM, Hitachi or Microsoft; in Korea the infrastructure, systems-integration and real estate development arms of the familiar chaebol. Because they generally lack the organic technical competence to determine what kinds of hardware and software might best serve their needs, city governments entering this market are perforce compelled to buy what these vendors have to sell, whether or not the problems those systems are designed to solve bear any particular resemblance to the issues perceived by their constituents. This was certainly the case in Songdo, where the expensive and elaborate Cisco "telepresence" hardware planned for each apartment unit in the city was rendered obsolete even before it was deployed, outmoded instantly by free smartphone- and tablet-based video chat applications like Kakao Talk and FaceTime.

The second problem follows on from this. By its very nature, the municipal procurement process involves one set of centralized, hierarchical actors (i.e. technology vendors) interacting with another (local bureaucracies). As a result, the multispectral awareness that might in principle be derived from large-scale analysis of data is generally retained for the exclusive use of municipal administrators, habitually and instinctively—and not, in other words, made available to the public who generated the data in the first place. What is offered to us wreathed in the glamor of technological futurity, then, is here revealed to be something that's actually rather dowdy and retrograde: old-style technocratic management from the top down. Not by any stretch of the imagination something consonant with the will to collective self-determination, it cannot be reconciled with the commons without contortions that verge on intellectual dishonesty, however well-intentioned they may be.

And there is a final issue: daily life in Songdo, at least, appears to be rather soulless and dull. NPR quotes a young resident who describes it as a nonplace and a "prison," and compares her escape into Seoul and all its nightlife at the end of the workweek to a jailbreak. This is admittedly a single data point, but it hardly makes a compelling argument for quality of life in the well-tuned city.

In its current form, then, the smart city as delivered by vendors is not merely illadvised, nor merely unlikely to support the kind of vivid experiences we associate with big-city life, but actively detrimental to the achievement of an urbanism consistent with the values of the commons. A case in point can be found in the recent Korean experience of mass public demonstrations, which illustrate like relatively few other moments in history the power that an aggrieved citizenry claims for itself when it takes to the streets in protest of an order that has become intolerable. As it happens, the technologies bound together under the banner of the smart city have no way of accounting for this kind of active practice of democracy. Far from recognizing mass demonstrations as the signal of public sentiment they surely are, the smart city can only interpret such protests as a disruption to business as usual: first as an anomaly to be detected, then as an inefficiency to be contained, minimized, neutralized or eliminated.

AVATAR II: SAN FRANCISCO
It's worth unpacking just what business as usual looks like to the architects of the smart city, what conceptions of the normal and the ordinary they may hold in mind when designing the algorithms responsible for detecting imminent departures from normalcy and triggering preemptive action.

And here we need to address the fact that even in software development, there is such a thing as fashion. Once something practiced by a self-consciously professional cohort given to horn-rim glasses, crisp short-sleeve shirts and pocket protectors—call it the Mission Control look—software engineering is, in its Northern Californian and Pacific Northwest fastnesses, dominated by a young, privileged and remarkably homogeneous technical elite. At present, you cannot walk down the streets of San Francisco—a city whose name was once synonymous with the radical, the queer, the experimental and the frankly marginal—without running headfirst into a mostly male scrum of software engineers in their mid-twenties, in their universal uniform of fitted hoodies and $400 sneakers, talking unit tests and code sprints. To a surprisingly great extent, it is their tastes, predilections, priorities and values that urban technology is increasingly designed around.

If the multinational vendor, in all its centralization, conservatism and ponderous lack of agility, represents one of the two predominant modes in which information technology is now applied to the life of cities, the other is typified by the proverbial Bay Area tech startup, with its addiction to venture capital and its imperative to "move fast and break things." Thus the emphasis on convenience and immediate gratification we see in offerings like Airbnb, Tinder, TaskRabbit and above all Uber: services whose socially corrosive effects were self-evident virtually from the outset, though they are only recently becoming matters of widespread controversy.

It is now beyond dispute that Airbnb has undermined the market for affordable rental housing in city after city, just as Uber's massive, outsourced fleet has drastically increased traffic in cities around the world, even as it drained custom and resources from public transit. What these services offer is nothing less than a shared reality platform for everyone wealthy enough, and sufficiently comfortable with technology, to use them fluently—a platform that privatizes benefits and sheds costs on the public so nakedly indeed that we no longer hear much talk of a putative "sharing economy." Though these effects can be noted in every market where these services operate, they're felt particularly acutely in the Bay Area, where life for those who most closely resemble software developers demographically and psychographically often does seem to consist of near-effortless algorithmically-streamlined ease, albeit at the cost of a slowly decaying public realm for everyone else.

It is telling, in this withdrawal from any pretense at convivial urbanity, that we don't even discuss progress anymore, only "innovation." In doing so, we preemptively surrender the terrain of the social imagination to the likes of Elon Musk, Jeff Bezos and Mark Zuckerberg, if not still more impoverished souls like Travis Kalanick or Peter Thiel. If the urban condition that results from their everted imaginings is not quite the brutal reality of first-generation smart cities like Masdar City, in the United Arab Emirates—where Pakistani, Bangladeshi and Filipino guest workers labor long, thanklessly and at great personal risk to keep the city turning over, and end their days in metal shipping containers arrayed behind razor wire under the broiling desert sun—neither does it have much to do with how cities have traditionally generated meaning and value for their inhabitants. Thus far, at least, everyday life in this capsular, app-mediated city appears to be defined by its exclusions.

AVATAR III: SEOUL

By contrast, the Greek architect and activist Stavros Stavrides, in his recent book on practices of spatial commoning, emphasizes the profoundly invitational aspect of any true commons, its quality of radical openness and porosity. If neither the multinational nor the startup way of doing networked cities quite works to produce such conditions on the ground, where can we go looking for a model that might do so?

Perhaps the greatest irony of all, in the present context, is that certain aspects of vernacular Korean urbanism already work quite well in this regard. Without fetishizing them, or sugarcoating their less felicitous aspects, Korean cities even now reliably generate an informality and canniness in the use of space that comes much closer to achieving the vision of a life in common than anything on offer from either wing of the tech industry. Not so much the newly-built, gated apartment complexes, of course, with their Ballardian full-service towerblocks rising in endless numbered ranks, but in older city cores throughout the country. Here the ajeossi play an impromptu game of baduk in a doorway, seated on torn cardboard box covers; there a sudden chicken-and-beer stand has popped up on an unused concrete forecourt; above, tucked into the fifth floor of an otherwise anonymous office building, is the jjimjilbang with beauty salon and restaurant and game parlor attached, pulsing with life and activity through 24 hours of the day.

These things may not read that way to a globalized elite smitten with enticingly glossy corporate visions of the future, but to a certain kind of Western visitor, these feel like signals of the way life in the networked city could be: spontaneous, mobile, flexible, convivial, and above all open.

Could we design networked platforms and systems that generated this kind of urban experience, not merely for a few, but for everyone? The answer is almost certainly yes—but successfully doing so would require that we learn to wield networked technology quite differently than we do at present.

It would be necessary, first, to step back and ask what we are actually trying to achieve by deploying networked systems in the urban frame. We would have to test and iterate and test again, and discard for good that which is seen not to work. This, of course, runs almost directly counter to several aspects of the way we do things now: the headlong pace of technical innovation most obviously, but also its ahistoricity.

It would be necessary to press for specifics, whenever we are offered hype, buzzwords and promises. We would have to ask hard questions about how technologies actually function when used by real people in real environments, and not simply be seduced by lovingly-crafted renderings or animated flythroughs.

It would be necessary to nurture more space outside the market in particular. If "the commons" is to mean anything at all, it can only refer to a milieu where neither the values of the state nor those of the market prevail, leaving room for mutuality, solidarity and positive-sum collaboration—the diametric opposite, in other words, of the condition that broadly obtains in the West now, where the market sets the ground conditions of everyday life, and the state is increasingly figured as something that exists solely to guarantee the operating conditions for private enterprise. It remains to be seen how this model might apply to a place like Korea, where the dynamics of the developmental state retain a powerful hold on the national psyche, but it would clearly be an uphill battle.

Finally, regardless of the particular set of political commitments we hope to see observed in the design of urban technologies, it would be necessary for us to consider with the greatest care what kind of subjectivity our use of these systems give rise to. We would have to ask who we become in their presence and through their use, and be prepared to redesign everything if we don't much care for the answers.

The examples I've offered here ought to make it clear if what we seek to achieve is a life in common, the whole quest for technological "smart" is something akin to a category error, where it isn't simply intellectually bankrupt. We know in any event that any city deserving of the name is always already smart, and that its intelligence resides in the people who live in it and give it life. The task that remains before us is to design technical systems that are respectful of that intelligence, and allow it to speak itself. In the final analysis, this task cannot be outsourced. It cannot be optimized. It cannot be automated. It will require of us profound investments of time, energy and care. But the reward would be considerable: a place, or a meshwork of places, where everyday life is spontaneous and convivial, where the conditions of equity, justice and ecological balance are finally realized, where our quest to be human in full might find at last a natural home and ground.

MOVING

Locomotion is one of the basic functions of animals, and the most important discriminant from the vegetal realm. Human mobility has always been strongly influenced by technology, which has enabled humans to increase their action radius far beyond the natural capacities of the human body. In this technological development, human mobility has become a collective endeavor, often connected to larger concentrations of population. The first paths were created almost automatically, simply through the density of human traffic, and sometimes "designed" by animals and for animals, who became an integral part of the arcane human logistic. The "domestication" of animals enabled the development of the paths, which simplified the traffic of animals and humans in the most populated routes. Animal-drawn wheeled vehicles were developed in the Middle East in 4000 BC and then spread to Europe and India. In 1200 BC they were also extended to China. Both the use of domestic animals—one of the more paradigmatic ancient commons—and the construction of tracks and roads are an essential common which radiates from the early urban populations to the surrounding—and nurturing—land. The origin of cities is inextricably linked to the development of collective forms of mobility and their infrastructures, capable of supplying the resources needed to sustain concentrations of population which are unsustainable without the support of a hinterland.

The first comprehensive system of a wide-ranging mobility infrastructure was developed by the Roman Empire. It became crucial not only as a feeding mechanism but also as a political tool capable of maintaining control over vast expanses of the territory. To extend and maintain their empire, the Romans needed roads, which were built primarily using cobblestone. The Roman roads deterritorialized cities from their hinterland and initiated cities as a commercial network and a military asset.

The radical increase in urban densities caused by industrialization multiplied exponentially the need for mobility. The development of underground systems in London, Paris, Berlin, and New York became a crucial tool of urban development in the early twentieth century. Modern rail transport systems first appeared in England in the 1820s. Steam locomotives became the first practical form of mechanized land transport, and they remained the primary form of mechanized land transport for the next century.

The spread of the automobile in the post—World War II period transformed cities beyond recognition. Transportation became one of the most energy-intensive activities in cities, accounting for a large percentage of the overall carbon emissions and pollution. While the public transport infrastructure remains the primary alternative to the ecological and economical costs of the car-driven city, a set of new transport-related technologies appears to be shaping up as an alternative that is based not on an economy of scale, but on the use of lighter vehicles which are computerized and connected and consume electricity instead of fossil fuels.

In response to these ecological concerns, unipersonal electromobility and self-driven vehicles are likely to change urban traffic substantially. Internal combustion engines have been predominant for private urban mobility, while electrical engines have been favored for forms of collective mobility such as trains, trams, and subways. However, during the last few decades, the environmental impact of fossil-fuel consumption infrastructure, and the rising oil prices have led to a renewed interest in electric transportation. Electric vehicles (EVs), unlike fossil fuel–powered vehicles, consume a form of energy that can be generated from a wide range of sources, including fossil fuels, nuclear power, and renewable sources such as tidal power, solar power, and wind power or any combination of those. The carbon footprint of EVs varies depending on the fuel and technology used for electricity generation. The electricity may then be stored onboard the vehicle using a battery, flywheel, or supercapacitors. EVs also have regenerative braking due to their ability to recover energy normally lost during braking, as electricity is stored in the onboard battery. It is likely that this form of energy will become predominant in urban transportation in the near future, as lithium-ion battery technologies are developing to provide higher autonomy to these vehicles. The reduced use of vehicles in cities is an overall tendency which will increase the autonomy of EVs.

The advantage of EVs is that they are more easily adapted to operate with a computerized control system, and therefore, to communicate with other vehicles. Such advantages will prove to be unbeatable when pervasive computation and the Internet of Things become incorporated into urban transport systems. The incorporation of this type of vehicle into shared fleets is increasing, both in the case of bicycles and four-wheeled vehicles. EVs and sharing schemes are now spreading worldwide, anticipating new forms of decentralized urban transport systems with a minimal carbon footprint. Unlike previous modes of individualized transport, EVs are breaking with traditional models of vehicle ownership and developing more granular forms of sustainable urban transport. How this will be articulated with the classical mass-transport systems remains to be seen. Municipal bike-share schemes, peer-to-peer car rental, and a number of companies are seeking to make a profit from the sharing economy applied to transport: Car2Go, Zipcar, Uber, HubCab, NuTonomy... It is unclear whether the future of urban transport will be resolved with collective transport systems such as those implemented in Curitiba's *BRT* and in Bogota's *Transmilenio* in the last decade, which are based on a top-down collective transport infrastructure, or whether we will attain a mass individualization of urban transport through the use of fleets of shared and interconnected individual vehicles such as electric motorbikes, Segways, or other unipersonal EVs. A range of granular forms of urban transport, such as electric motorbikes, scooters, land-drones, etc., are rapidly developing increasing capacity, often as part of sharing schemes. Whether the *common* transport has to be discussed in traditional forums, and implemented as an infrastructure, or will be resolved in a distributed manner by the new connectivity and collective intelligence of a myriad of unipersonal EVs is one of the questions that the imminent cities will have to resolve. It is unlikely that the solution will be exclusive: most likely a combination between these two systems will have to be found, depending on the density and scale of the population, the climate, and so on. What is quite clear is that the scale of the transport infrastructure in cities will tend to diminish: roads will have to cater no longer to four-wheeled gas guzzlers, but to scooters and bikes, and so parking structures and roads are likely to become overcapacitated.

We are also beginning a new phase of industrial production, named by some theorists *logisticalization*,[1] which is having an important impact on the built environment. Logistics are becoming embedded into the fabric of our cities as well as in our urban cultures. The global rise of online retail, headed by Amazon, is increasingly affecting the protocols of urban life, making deliveries a routine new domestic occurrence.

1. Claire Lyster, *Learning from Logistics: How Networks Change Our Cities* (Basel: Birkhauser, 2016).

The logistics infrastructure that has developed to support this supply chain is enormous. Cities like Memphis, Brussels, or Singapore have become global hubs of logistic distribution and demonstrate the strength of logistic centres as urban development engines. But this development has also generated struggles with urban populations. For example, there have been important struggles in Northern Italy's logistics sector, located around the old city of Bologna, that reveal many aspects of this crisis of the traditional city. Strikes against the main firms that circulate commodities have shown a new logistical urban fabric which dissolves Bologna within a complex geography of interconnections stretched over a huge territory, radically redrawing the old city boundaries. The manpower of these businesses is often migrant, and much of the conflict is triggered between the native population of small-scale merchants and the incoming population of foreign low-cost workers, highlighting tensions in respect to identity and citizenship. Similar problems tend to exist when these global logistic cities clash with a more traditional urban population. Courier-service crowdsourcing is becoming an alternative to traditional delivery companies, although it is also creating huge employment problems.[2]

In terms of urban logistics, the recent proliferation of online shopping, sharing economies, and peer-to-peer rentals and exchanges is giving rise to a new logistic function which is not about movement but about stasis: short-term urban storage. Originally conceived to resolve the problem of what is called "last-mile delivery," which can substantially reduce the cost and increase the speed of a delivery, but also conceived to protect the privacy of buyers, these storage spaces, which can be operated with a password, enable a much faster, much cheaper, and totally anonymous purchase experience.[3] Amazon Lockers are one example, but potentially it could be an entire infrastructure where urban inhabitants exchange goods with others, or perhaps where they keep their properties during the day if they do not want to carry certain items around.

2. Simon Goodley, "Deliveroo Told It Must Pay Workers Minimum Wage," *The Guardian*, 14 August 2016.

3. McKinsey & Company report, *Parcel Delivery: The Future of Last Mile*, September 2016, www.mckinsey.com/~/media/.../parcel_delivery_the_future_of_last_mile.ashx.

Tokyo's railway stations always have an abundance of lockers which have become part of many urban legends: from schoolgirls using the lockers to keep forbidden makeup and high-heel shoes for after-school activities to babies being abandoned in lockers, the railway station lockers are a place of exchange and partial stasis for a commuting population, and a place with a great presence in the popular imagination. Some of the advantages of the shared economy cannot take place without these types of temporary urban storage—hence the current proliferation of these types of urban lockers for many different uses.

Last but not least, drones and self-driven vehicles are an important part of the future of all these urban mobility developments: Amazon Robotics' warehouse systems and drone delivery are some of the new initiatives being tested to make shipping in cities more efficient. The combination of *lidar* scanners and GPS technologies has recently enabled the development of vehicles with the possibility of full reliance in automatic controls. While the regulatory framework of these vehicles is still uncertain, there is little doubt that these vehicles may radically transform urban mobility as we know it, by developing entirely new urban routines and protocols.

ACCESSIBILITY IN CITIES:
TRANSPORT AND URBAN FORM*

Philipp Rode and Graham Floater**

INTRODUCTION

Access to people, goods, services, and information is the basis of economic development in cities. The better and more efficient this access, the greater the economic benefits through economies of scale, agglomeration effects, and networking advantages. Cities with higher levels of agglomeration tend to have higher GDP per capita and higher levels of productivity. The way in which cities facilitate accessibility through their urban forms and transport systems also impacts directly on other measures of human development and well-being. Urban travel currently constitutes more than 60% of all kilometres travelled globally (van Audenhove, Korniychuk et al. 2014) and, as a result, urban transport is currently the largest single source of global transport-related carbon emissions and the largest local source of urban air pollution.

This paper will present evidence first on how accessibility in cities is created through the co-dependence of urban form and transport systems and how this relates to urban carbon emissions.

---

* This essay is a condensed version of the NCE Paper 03, "Accessibility in Cities: Transport and Urban Form," which was an output of the New Climate Economy project of the Global Commission on the Economy and Climate (www.newclimateeconomy.net). The latest version of that paper is available by LSE Cities at https://lsecities.net/publications/reports/the-new-climate-economy-report). It builds on the LSE Cities research and publications, including the Green Cities and Buildings chapters for UNEP's Green Economy Report; P. Rode's research on integrated planning, design, and transport; and research by the LSE's Economics of Green Cities programme led by G. Floater, P. Rode, and D. Zenghelis.

** Contributing Authors: Nikolas Thomopoulos, James Docherty, Peter Schwinger, Anjali Mahendra, Wanli Fang. LSE Cities Research Team: Bruno Friedel, Alexandra Gomes, Catarina Heeckt, Roxana Slavcheva.

This paper is primarily based on an extensive literature review and aims to assist a further reframing of the urban transport debate by emphasizing accessibility as the underlying objective of mobility and transport in cities. Above all, such a reframing implies a far greater recognition of urban form characteristics such as land use, the distribution of densities, and urban design, in addition to more conventional transport characteristics such as related infrastructure, service levels, and travel speeds.

ACCESSIBILITY IN CITIES AND IMPLICATIONS FOR CARBON EMISSIONS

In any city, patterns of urban development are inseparable from the evolution of urban transport and mobility. Likewise, urban transport cannot be considered independently from urban form (Newman and Kenworthy 1989; ECOTEC 1993; Houghton 1995; Newman and Kenworthy 1996; Knoflacher, Rode et al. 2008; Dimitriou and Gakenheimer 2009; UN Habitat 2013). It is a combination of the two that facilitates accessibility[1] within metropolitan regions and thus creates economies of scale, agglomeration effects, and networking advantages. Recognition of this interrelationship between transport and urban form is particularly important at a time of unprecedented urban expansion. Some estimates suggest that globally, the total amount of urbanised land could triple between 2000 and 2030 (Seto, Güneralp et al. 2012) and urban kilometres travelled could increase three-fold by 2050 (van Audenhove, Korniychuk et al. 2014). Such unprecedented change would bring with it enormous risks associated with locking in energy-intense patterns of accessibility and urban form for decades to come (Ang and Marchal 2013).

URBAN ACCESSIBILITY PATHWAYS

Each city has developed its own unique spatial structure and transport system to provide access to people, goods, and information. Nonetheless, different principal development patterns have evolved with respect to the most common combinations of urban spatial structures and transport. Given the strong path dependency of these patterns, we call these "urban accessibility pathways" (Figure 1). A defining characteristic of these pathways is the degree to which accessibility is based on the physical proximity between origins and destinations or on transport solutions which can overcome spatial separation, and the degree to which these solutions involve private or public motorised transport.

---

1. Accessibility is frequently contrasted with mobility-based frameworks that dominate urban transport policy (Litman 2008). It draws attention to the interaction of transport conditions, land-use patterns, and individual attributes in determining how easily residents of a city can access a range of social and economic opportunities. Improving accessibility may well involve an increase of people's levels of mobility through improved transport systems; however, the concept has advantages in opening up a wider range of policy responses for addressing transport problems, including changes to the spatial distribution of opportunities that bring activities closer to residents, rather than requiring increased mobility (Farrington 2007; Litman 2008). Accessibility has been defined as "the extent to which land-use and transport systems enable (groups of) individuals to reach activities or destinations by means of a (combination of) transport mode(s)" (Geurs and van Wee 2004, p. 128).

The first principle of achieving accessibility in cities is based on the physical concentration of people, services, economic activities, and exchange. In that regard, the most defining characteristics include residential and workplace densities; the distribution of functions and degree of mixed use; the level of centralisation; and local-level urban design. More compact and dense cities[2] (also referred to as "smart growth"; see Appendix for key features) are typical examples of facilitating agglomeration economies through greater proximity. Creating accessibility based on physical proximity implies a particular attention to planning, designing, building, and managing the specific local condition at a human scale.

To a certain extent, physical proximity in cities can be substituted by increasing the speed of travel through the use of rapid, motorised modes of public and private transport. It is important to note, however, that even then the overarching objective remains the provision of access to opportunities rather than mobility or movement itself. Infrastructural features that define such "access by velocity" include the surface coverage of roads, the quality of road and rail networks and other public transport infrastructure. In addition, transport operations and service quality determine transport-based access and typically include the service level of public transport and the availability of privately owned vehicles.

Over the last century, the mechanisation of transport and the associated reduction in mobility costs relative to incomes have allowed cities to de-densify and expand horizontally, resulting in the substitution of access by proximity with access by movement. Initially driven by the introduction of streetcars, metro, and regional rail systems (Heinze and Kill 1991; Gayda, Haag et al. 2005; Knoflacher, Rode et al. 2008), this process reached a new and entirely different scale with the onset of mass motorisation and the widespread introduction of privately owned cars (UK Ministry of Transport 1963; Bottles 1987; Cervero 1998).

Previously, transit systems allowed for horizontal expansion that both facilitated and required compact, dense urban development and continued to produce human-scale urban environments. Urban design had to acknowledge the fact that at some point in their journey, all public transport passengers remained pedestrians, navigating through public urban space. By contrast, the introduction of the motor car not only facilitated suburban development at far lower density levels, but also introduced a transport mode that needed significantly more space to operate than any other previous means of transport.

---

2. We define "compact urban growth" (which can be both new urban development and urban retrofitting) as urban development characterised by human-scale built environments with higher density, mixed-use urban form and high-quality urban design. Compact urban development typically focuses on urban regeneration, the revitalisation of urban cores, the promotion of public and non-motorised transport, and high standards of urban management (Floater, Rode et al. 2014b). Related concepts include the European City model, smart growth, and transit-oriented development (TOD).

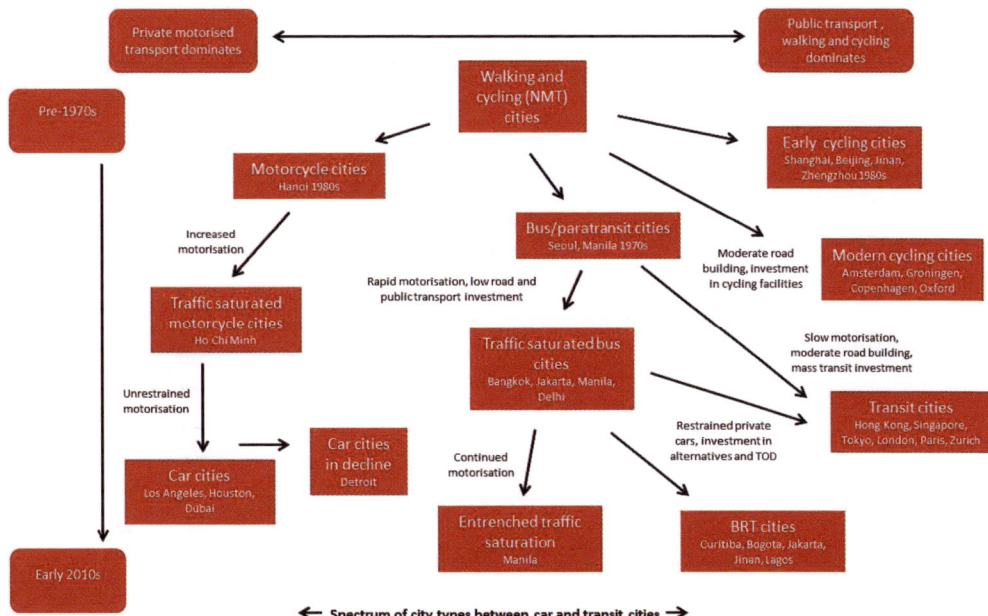

In short, public transport requires urban density, while car use requires space. In most cities, this has led to extraordinary tensions as a result of the inefficient use of scarce urban space by private vehicles. This provides a particular challenge for dense, developing cities where contemporary motorisation far outpaces the provision of road infrastructure or public transit alternatives.

URBAN ACCESSIBILITY PATHWAYS BASED ON BARTER'S CITY TYPOLOGY AND TRANSPORT DEVELOPMENT PATHS

Today, urban agglomerations can be based on many possible combinations of transport and urban form, each providing different levels of access. These combinations can range from walkable, public transport—based compact cities to sprawling car-oriented cities (Glaeser and Kahn 2004), and different types can be found in different parts of the world at different levels of development.

More sprawling cities require rapid modes of transport to reduce journey times and often rely on individualised motorised transport modes as the only viable transport for low-density urban areas. In turn, these car-based transport systems require substantially more space than any other urban transport system. For example, at 50 km/h, cars require more than 160 square meters per person, compared to 4 square meters for buses (assuming typical occupancy levels) (Rode and Gipp 2001).

Urban Accessibility Pathways based on Barter's city typology and transport development paths

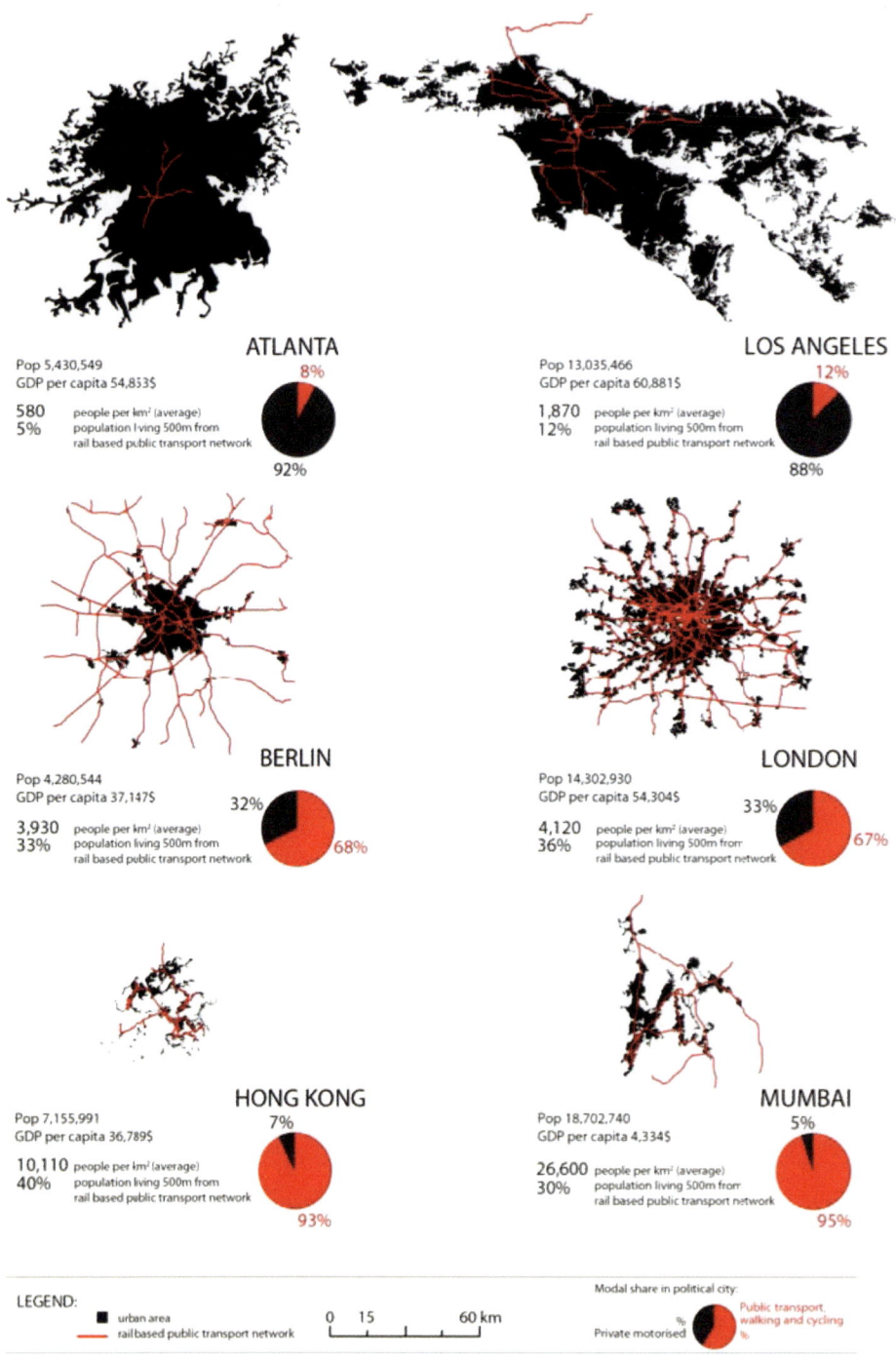

Urban form and modal share (black in pie chart is private motorised) of selected cities

Space for car parking is an additional need, with cars being idle for most of the time. The average car in the United States is parked for 96% of the time (Heck and Rogers 2014), and aggregate parking space in car-oriented Central Business Districts (CBDs) such as in Los Angeles is more than 80% of the CBD land area (Manville and Shoup 2004). Under a business-as-usual scenario, an additional 45,000 to 77,000 km^2 would be required globally for car parking alone by 2050 (Dulac 2013), a land area equivalent to the size of Denmark. As a result, the space requirements of private vehicular traffic not only imply further de-densification of cities, but they are also a major contributor to congestion and parking pressures on public space, as road infrastructure provision is frequently unable to keep up with rising levels of vehicular traffic (Kersys 2011; World Bank 2014b).

Over recent years, compelling evidence has emerged on the degree to which urban form and transport are interrelated (Smith 1984; Holtzclaw 2000). Controlling for other factors, the difference in transport intensity between high- and low-density areas can be more than 40% in vehicle-miles-travelled per capita (Ewing, Bartholomew et al. 2008). The National Research Council in the U.S. estimates that doubling densities within metropolitan regions can reduce vehicle-kilometres-travelled (VKT) by up to 25% when also concentrating employment (National Research Council 2009). Overall, automobile dependence is negatively street design have a significant impact on the likelihood of walking (Ewing and Cervero 2010).[3] Similarly, the impact of transport infrastructure on urban form is increasingly well understood. For U.S. metropolitan regions, empirical estimates show that each new highway constructed through an urban core led to an 18% decline in central city residents (Baum-Snow 2007). Recent research on the expansion of Chinese cities found that the combined effect of radial highways and ring roads was a relocation of around 25% of central city residents to surrounding regions, while regional railways were found to have no such effect (Henderson 2010; Baum-Snow, Brandt et al. 2012).

A particular feature of the transport-urban form relationship is the time lag between spaces and flows: land-use and physical environments change at a far slower pace than activities and related movements (Medley, Wong et al. 2002). A second feature is the long design life of urban form and transport infrastructure, creating significant "lock-in" effects. Some of these lock-in effects could be overcome by innovations in transport systems and technology, as discussed later in this paper. However, where urban form and transport infrastructure is too biased towards sprawling, automobile-dependent patterns of development, it can in turn lead to a change-inhibiting cultural and political equilibrium. For these reasons, dealing with urban transport or land-use planning

---

3. It is important to note that a range of earlier studies were more critical of the potential of reducing travel demand through higher residential densities (see Kagermeier 1997; Crane and Crepeau 1998; Kockelman 1997; Hall 2001; Gomez-Ibanez 1991; Gordon and Richardson 1989). However, these studies also tended to look at density in isolation and independent from related changes such as mixed use or design quality. Studies supporting the land-use transport pattern impacts further include Cervero and Duncan (2006), Limtanakool et al (2006), and Chen et al (2008).

in isolation from their interdependencies can easily lead to adverse effects and unintended consequences. Furthermore, urban transport is more complex than other transport sectors, not just because it involves the integration of different transport systems, but also because it co-produces accessibility jointly with spatial development.

CARBON EMISSIONS FROM THE PROVISION OF ACCESS IN CITIES

The co-dependence of urban transport systems with urban form also plays a central role in the global transition to a low-carbon economy (Hickman and Banister 2014). Around ten billion trips are made every day in urban areas around the world. Of these, a significant and increasing proportion is undertaken using high-carbon and energy-intensive private motorised vehicles. About 80% of the increase in global transport emissions since 1970 has been due to road vehicles (IPCC 2014b).

As a result, transport is one of the major sources of carbon emissions in cities. Overall, the transport sector produced around 23% of global energy-related CO emissions, equivalent to 6.7 gigatonnes of CO in 2010 (IPCC 2014b). While urban car use is the single largest contributor to transport carbon emissions, freight transport—which accounts for up to 20% of urban traffic and up to 50% of urban transport greenhouse gas (GHG) emissions—is often underrepresented (Savy 2012).[4] In addition, life cycle analysis suggests that carbon emissions embedded in transport infrastructures are substantial,[5] typically adding another 63% for on-road and 155% for rail in addition to emissions from vehicle operations (Chester and Horvath 2009). Emissions are growing more rapidly in the transport sector than in any other sector and are projected to increase by 50% by 2035 and almost double by 2050 under a business-as-usual scenario (Dulac 2013; IPCC 2014b).

Part of this growth is due to rapid urbanisation in emerging economies and developing countries. Although transport emissions per capita in developing countries are relatively low on an absolute basis compared to those in OECD countries, around 90% of the increase in global transport-related CO emissions is expected to occur in developing countries, mostly from private vehicles and freight (UNCSD 2012). Growth in embedded carbon emissions is another significant factor. If developing countries expand their infrastructure (transport and others) to current global average levels using currently available technologies, around 470 gigatonnes of cumulated CO emissions would be emitted as a result of infrastructure material manufacturing (IPCC 2014a)—or thirteen times the global emissions in 2012.[6]

4. Urban freight transport accounts for 31% of energy use and CO emissions throughout Europe (Herzog 2010).

5. Embedded emissions are upstream CO_2 emissions from energy used for transport, housing, or the production of goods and services (Druckman and Jackson 2009). These also include emissions that occur as part of constructing or building transport infrastructure or vehicles.

6. Rapid urbanisation in conjunction with population growth in developing countries and maintenance of existing transport and urban infrastructure in developed countries impose high demand for building materials. In 2006, 30 billion tonnes of concrete were consumed in contrast to 2 billion tonnes in 1950 (WBCSD 2009), while cement production accounts for 5% of global anthropogenic CO emissions (WBCSD 2012).

Over the last decade, significant carbon emission growth was registered for emerging economy megacities. A World Bank study showed that urban transport energy use and carbon emissions were growing by between 4% and 6% a year in the 2000s in Beijing, Guangzhou, Shanghai, and Xian (Darido, Torres-Montoya et al. 2009). Between 2005 and 2010, carbon emissions from transport in Shanghai even grew by 15% annually, the highest growth rate of any sector (Li and Cao 2012). But even within the European Union—an already highly urbanised area with ambitious carbon-reduction goals—transport-related CO_2 emissions increased by 36% between 1990 and 2006, while other key sectors achieved modest reductions (European Commission 2007).

While urban transport emissions correlate strongly with income, there are major differences between cities with similar levels of wealth. The carbon intensity of urban accessibility is determined by two main factors: the overall distance of motorised travel required (which is largely informed by urban form characteristics) (Figure 3) and the carbon intensity of these modes (Figure 4). The latter is informed by the energy intensity of different transport modes and the carbon intensity of their fuels.

Figure 3 shows the well-known research findings linking urban form with transport energy use in larger cities across the world, which initially established a strong negative correlation between population density and annual gasoline consumption (Newman and Kenworthy 1989). Overall, more recent research has confirmed this relationship, when controlling for wealth, and they also apply for carbon emissions (OECD 2012a; Qin and Han 2013; UN Habitat 2013; IPCC 2014a).

For example, at similar wealth levels, sprawling Atlanta produced six times more transport-related carbon emissions than relatively compact Barcelona (ATM, 2013; D'Onofrio 2014; LSE Cities 2014). This finding aligns with analysis conducted for thirty cities in China, which showed that compact cities have higher CO efficiency, particularly as a result of supporting non-motorised transport (Liu, Chen et al. 2012).

The IPCC suggests that over the medium to long-term, an urban accessibility pathway consisting of more public transport- oriented compact cities, combined with improved infrastructure for non-motorised transport, could reduce GHG intensities by 20% to 50% compared to 2010 levels (IPCC 2014b).

POPULATION DENSITY AND TRANSPORT ENERGY USE PER CAPITA FOR SELECTED CITIES

The substantial impact on carbon emissions of modal choices in cities is illustrated in Figure 4, which shows the carbon emissions per passenger kilometre for different transport modes. As a result, the share of public transport, walking, and cycling is a strong predictor of transport-related carbon emissions at broadly similar wealth levels (Table 1). While all motorised modes have a substantial technical potential to reduce carbon emissions per passenger kilometre—by between 30% to 50% compared to 2010 levels (IPCC 2014b)—actual reductions remain highly uncertain.

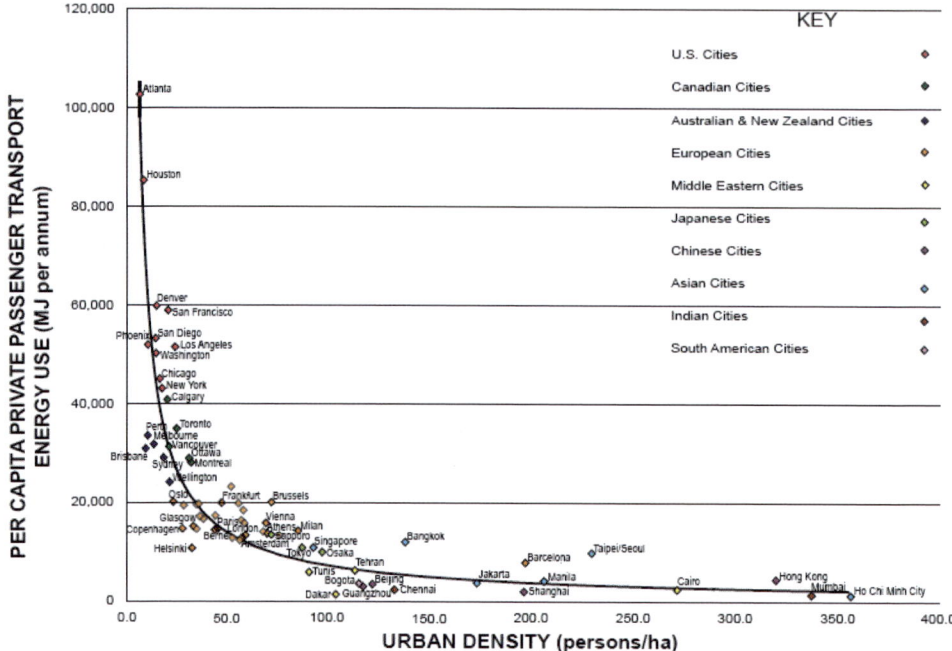

These relationships matter for the developmental choices which rapidly growing cities face today. A scenario study for U.S. metropolitan areas in cities such as Atlanta and Phoenix suggests a reduction of 7% to 10% in carbon emissions as a result of a 20% to 40% reduction in vehicle-miles-travelled due to compact urban development (Ewing, Bartholomew et al. 2008). In the Indian city of Surat, estimates for annual carbon emissions resulting from a projected tenfold increase in the number of trips varies according to the mode choice and trip length—from 1.9 up to 9.5 million tonnes of CO_2. For Mumbai, the same study suggests a range of 10.3 to 49 million tonnes (Rayle and Pai 2010).

The positive correlation between energy or carbon efficiency and urban density can also be observed outside the transport sector and, together with levels of affluence, can have an impact on variations in carbon emissions at the national level (Figure 5). Compact and taller building types can improve heat energy efficiency at the neighbourhood level by a factor of six compared to detached houses (Rode et al 2014). According to the Residential Energy Consumption Survey (RECS) in the U.S., households in suburban areas use more energy on average both in total (22.5%) and per capita (12.7%) compared to those in cities (Estiri 2012), which translates to 36% higher electricity, 19.5% higher natural gas, and 29% higher consumption per household in suburban areas (EIA 2001).

Population density and transport energy use per capita for selected cities

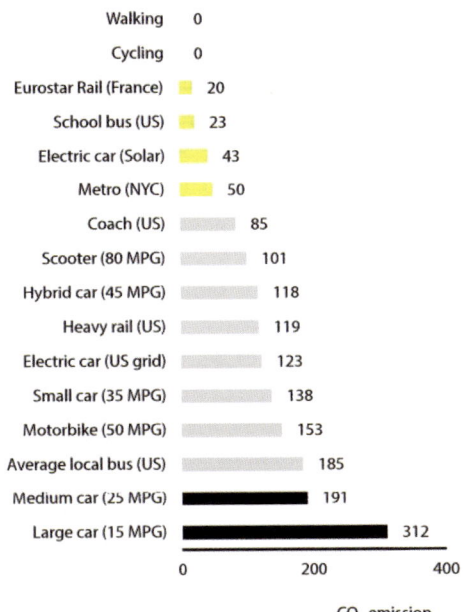

These patterns also indicate similar effects of density at different scales, whether at the level of an entire city or at the intra- urban level of individual neighbourhoods. A study on residential GHG emissions and the impact of urban form in Toronto shows notable variations in total car- and building-related emissions between census tracts, varying between 3.1 and 13.1 tonnes of CO equivalents per year. Comparing all tracts, the ten with the highest GHG emissions are located within the lower-density suburbs, where these high emissions were directly linked with private car use (VandeWeghe and Kennedy 2007). Another study identifies a 2- to 2.5-fold difference in GHG and energy intensity when comparing high-density urban core development (lower intensity) with low-density suburban development (Norman, MacLean et al. 2006). GHG emissions related to car use in London's peri-urban[7] area are more than double compared to those in the core urban area (1.14 tonnes of CO_2 compared to 0.51 tonne per capita of CO), whereas in New York they are four times higher in the peri-urban area compared to the core urban area

7. The urban area in London includes Greater London, whereas the peri-urban area includes the rest of the Southeast of England. The urban area in New York includes urban New York—i.e., New York City (Bronx, Brooklyn, Manhattan, Queens) including the largely built-up Hudson County of New Jersey apart from Richmond County (Staten Island)—whereas the peri-urban area includes the rest of the Tri-State area—i.e., New York state, New Jersey, and Connecticut (Focas, 2014).

Emissions per passenger km by urban transport mode
Share of green transport modes and carbon emissions per capita per cities

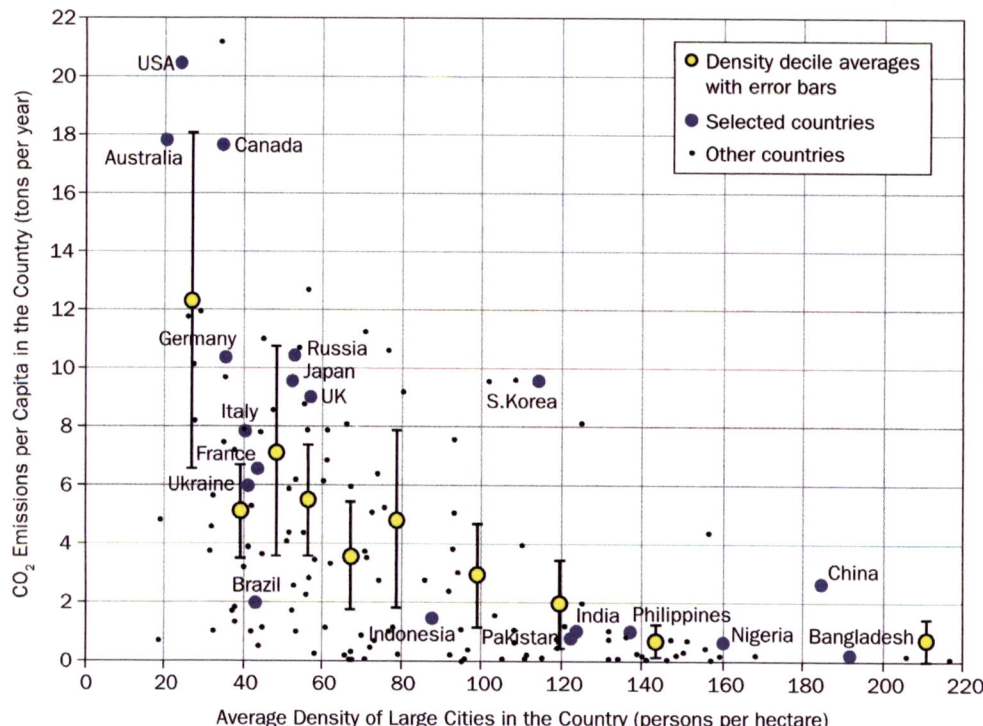

(3.37 tonnes of CO per capita compared to 0.84 tonnes of CO per capita) (Focas 2014). A study of 11,000 households in Germany provides evidence that 50% of the total emissions from private transport and building operations can be attributed to urban and residential design choices, with density and physical concentration being key parameters contributing to greater carbon and fuel efficiency (Schubert, Wolbring et al. 2013).

ENABLING ACCESSIBILITY THROUGH COMPACT CITIES AND SUSTAINABLE TRANSPORT

Promoting efficient urban accessibility pathways based on a compact, public transport–oriented city form must play a central role in global GHG emission reduction strategies. While city-level policy initiatives are not a substitute for concerted carbon-reduction efforts at a national and sectoral level, they can play an important complementary role. For example, evidence suggests that the price elasticity of fuel consumption is low in the absence of viable public transport offers (Avner, Rentschler et al. 2013). Furthermore, policies supporting higher urban densities and congestion charging were found to have lower stabilisation costs compared to carbon taxes and other economy-wide approaches (IPCC 2014a).

Average urban densities in large cities and average carbon emissions per capita

Urban accessibility pathways based on compact and public transport–oriented cities may involve both the retrofitting and re-densification of established urban cores and the promotion of dense, transit-oriented urban expansion (particularly within already high-density, high-growth cities) (Angel 2011). Within urban transport policy, three key principles are commonly recognised—usually summarised as "avoid, shift, improve" (UNEP 2011; Government of India 2014). First, the travel intensity in cities should be reduced through greater physical proximity and co-location of different urban functions; second, there should be a shift from spatially inefficient and energy-intensive private motorised modes of transport to public, shared, and non-motorised transport; and third, the efficiency (in terms of energy and space consumption) of road-based vehicles must be improved.

Above all, to be more effective in the future, urban policies will have to build on the experiences of those cities already registering a shift towards more compact urban development and sustainable transport, and learn from the related tipping points discussed above. In addition, the promotion of these urban accessibility pathways will have to be driven by sound institutional structures and planning processes as presented in the NCE Cities Paper 02, "Steering Urban Growth: Governance, Policy and Finance" (Floater, Rode et al. 2014a). This section presents an overview of some of the key barriers and enabling conditions of particular relevance for urban form and transport.

BARRIERS

Some cities are already working to deliver a paradigm shift in urban transport and accessibility, prompted by socio-demographic shifts, changing public attitudes, and technological innovation. Even pioneering cities, however, continue to face significant barriers to progress, several of which are important to highlight.

First, while the economic, social, and climate-change reasons for limiting car dependency and urban sprawl are strong, there exist potential negative trade-offs in industry sectors that are currently highly dependent on the business-as-usual urbanisation model. In particular, business models (and key business actors) in the automotive, construction, and real estate sectors have proven resistant to change to date. Secondly, strong consumer preferences for car ownership and suburban lifestyles remain, and are often most pronounced in developing cities where car use by higher-income households is driven by status and safety concerns, and a lack of viable alternatives. Third, switching costs in many existing cities are high, particularly in urban areas that have already developed as low-density and car-oriented settlements (which includes most of the wider metropolitan hinterland of even dense and public transport–oriented cities).

And fourthly, a range of institutional and process barriers to a paradigmatic shift in urban and transport planning also exist. Policy integration across urban planning, design, and transport is frequently compromised by sectoral and disciplinary silos. Fragmented governance and the lack of coordination between national and local policy frameworks for urban form and transport are widespread (Ang and Marchal 2013; IPCC 2014a); and the continued use of narrowly defined cost-benefit analysis (CBA) for transport projects (Odgaard, Kelly et al. 2005; Mackie and Worsley 2013; Thomopoulos and Grant-Muller 2013) often obstructs more effective and well-coordinated transport-related investments.

PLANNING AND REGULATION: SHAPING CITIES ACROSS TEMPORAL AND GEOGRAPHIC SCALES
Given the strong interrelationship between urban form and transport, the integration of land-use and transport planning represents a unique policy opportunity. Above all, the provision of strategic infrastructure is one of the most critical public policy instruments informing the long-term shape and character of a city at any stage in its development (Hall 1993; Müller and Siedentop 2004; Zacharias and Tang 2010; UN Habitat 2013; Lecocq and Shalizi 2014). Transport infrastructure and services also play a key role in determining urban mobility patterns, including modal choice (Pucher and Buehler 2006; Andrade, Woods et al. 2011; Dulal, Brodnig et al. 2011; Van Dyck, Cerin et al. 2012). Ideally, infrastructure developments are directly linked to strategic planning policy, which in turn informs local planning and regulation. While this approach to planning is commonly adopted in many developed cities, it is far less effective in the developing world, where there is typically limited institutional capacity and a high degree of informal urban growth. Here, it is primarily the provision of infrastructure and national-level market-based policies that guide development pathways—see also a discussion of infrastructure finance and spatial planning in Paper 02 (Floater, Rode et al. 2014a). Furthermore, in many countries, institutions governing land use may only mature enough over time to effectively regulate land markets and manage land conversions, potentially requiring the adoption of alternative approaches which acknowledge current levels of informality and institutional capacity.

Within spatial planning, the effective management of urban growth is essential to promoting compact, well-planned city forms. Urban growth boundaries and other policies that incentivise the development of brownfield over greenfield land are common compact-city policy instruments (World Bank 2013), and experience has highlighted the importance of working with the appropriate urban scale and shape of development restrictions in order to avoid negative outcomes (DeGrove and Miness 1992; Nelson and Moore 1993; Cheshire and Hilber 2008; Hilber and Vermeulen 2010; Cheshire, Hilber et al. 2011; Cheshire, Leunig et al. 2012). Further instruments include minimum density standards, mixed-use regulation, and a density bonus for developers, in order to support compact city development with a hierarchy of higher density, mixed-use clusters around public transport nodes. For example, Denmark's Planning Act on the "Station Proximity Principle" requires new offices over 1,500m^2 to be located within 600m of a rail station, leading to Copenhagen's efficient, compact urban form (Floater, Rode et al. 2014c).

A further key priority for compact city policy is reforming inappropriate building density limitations (which exist, for example, in many Indian cities) (Glaeser 2011; Suzuki, Cervero et al. 2013).

The World Bank estimates that limitations on building densities in Bangalore has led to urban sprawl which causes welfare losses of 2% to 3% of household income (World Bank 2013).

To be successful, density regulation reform needs to be coordinated with new infrastructure financing schemes.[8] Similarly, shifting from minimum to maximum parking requirements for urban development (ADB 2011; ITDP 2012; Guo and Ren 2013) facilitates urban compaction and lower levels of car use. District-level interventions, including the redistribution of road space away from private vehicles and increasing investment in infrastructure for public and non-motorised transport, have proved successful in reducing motorized traffic in cities (Goodwin, Hass-Klau et al. 1998; Rode 2014). Furthermore, human-scale urban design considerations require a shift away from road capacity–oriented street planning to a focus on finer-grain urban fabric, including smaller block sizes, higher building densities, and mixed use to facilitate micro-accessibility, last-mile connectivity, walkability, and social interaction.

The planning approach implied here involves engagement with the existing urban form and flows of the city in order to identify how best to sequence, coordinate, and integrate various infrastructure investments with land-use development, which in

turn will determine the city's energy efficiency and competitiveness in the long term. Such planning approaches also provide an opportunity to improve social inclusion by actively prioritising housing and infrastructure provision for lower-income households. For example, as part of Ahmedabad's town planning schemes, land along the expanding BRT corridors is banked by the municipal government for later development into affordable housing. The city's "Accessible Ahmedabad" plan also fundamentally embraces accessibility planning beyond simply the provision of transport (Suzuki, Cervero et al. 2013).

Regulatory policy instruments also play a key role in shaping urban transport performance. Measures to manage car use in cities commonly include parking regulations, emissions standards, and driving restrictions. For example, many Chinese cities have started to limit the total number of privately owned vehicles through restrictions on the number of license plates issued per month, with Shanghai beginning to control the growth of private vehicle registrations as early as 1994 (one reason for the city's considerably lower vehicle stock compared to that of Beijing) (Hao, Wang et al. 2011). Reforming urban transport regulation to embrace innovative service provision is also important, for example by moving from a "closed permit system" to an "open permit system" for para-transit and intermediate public transport (Government of India 2014).

8. Building densities in Indian cities were usually kept low as part of formal regulations to ensure that infrastructure systems can still cope with local demand. The World Bank suggests that this argument ignores opportunities of generating revenues from higher land values which can improve local infrastructure as also discussed in the Section Instruments for shaping incentives and mobilizing revenue (World Bank 2013).

INSTRUMENTS FOR SHAPING INCENTIVES AND MOBILISING REVENUE

Effective fiscal policy represents a key tool for delivering equitable and sustainable urban mobility (Floater, Rode et al. 2014a). Within the urban transport sector, fiscal instruments have several purposes, including managing total transport demand, shifting demand to more environmentally and socially beneficial modes, and improving the performance of those modes (Gordon 2005). Fiscal policy can contribute to these objectives by internalising unpriced externalities, positively shaping incentive structures to promote compact urban development and facilitate increased accessibility, and generating revenues for the purpose of investment in urban infrastructure and services.

In relation to private motorised vehicles, fiscal instruments can be applied to vehicle purchase, circulation, and use (Potter 2008). Vehicle purchase taxes and circulation charges such as registration or road tax—typically levied at the national and state levels—can be applied differentially to meet a range of policy objectives, and may be used to influence both aggregate demand for vehicle ownership and vehicle choice (including overall fuel efficiency and emissions standards, and key performance drivers such as vehicle size and weight, engine size, engine technology, and fuel type). In addition to applying purchase and circulation fees, many countries also employ positive fiscal measures (such as tax reductions and subsidies) to actively support and incentivise vehicle purchase. Although these can play a useful role in increasing the adoption of new, less polluting and more fuel-efficient technologies (such as electric vehicles) if correctly designed, they are currently often used to support sales of existing vehicle technologies.

The single most important fiscal instrument related to vehicle use is fuel pricing. Transport fuel taxation has historically been a key part of government fiscal policy due to its characteristics as a stable, dependable revenue source that is easily administered, and typically has progressive characteristics (Ekins and Potter 2010). In addition, it is also now widely recognised as a key mechanism to facilitate the internalisation of external costs imposed by vehicle use, manage total transport demand, influence vehicle and modal choice, and promote urban densification. Despite this recognition, transport fuels in many countries continue to be priced at a level far below their marginal social cost, and in many cases at a level below the cost of production. Figure 6 below highlights the differential in global fuel prices, reflecting the high levels of direct and indirect subsidy in many countries.

In 2011, direct consumer fuel subsidies—the majority of which relate to transport fuels—were estimated by the International Energy Agency (IEA) to amount to at least U.S.$291 billion, and were predominantly concentrated in the Middle East, North Africa, Latin America, and Asia (IEA 2012). Alongside promoting excessive private vehicle use through oil subsidies (Figure 7) and crowding out more productive government expenditure, these distortions can often have highly destabilising macroeconomic consequences, exacerbating fiscal deficits and increasing external-sector vulnerability in major oil-importing countries. Consumer subsidies for transport fuels are also typically highly socially regressive, with the large majority of benefits accruing to higher-income households. Figure 8 outlines the average distribution by consumption quintile of gasoline and diesel subsidies across several countries.

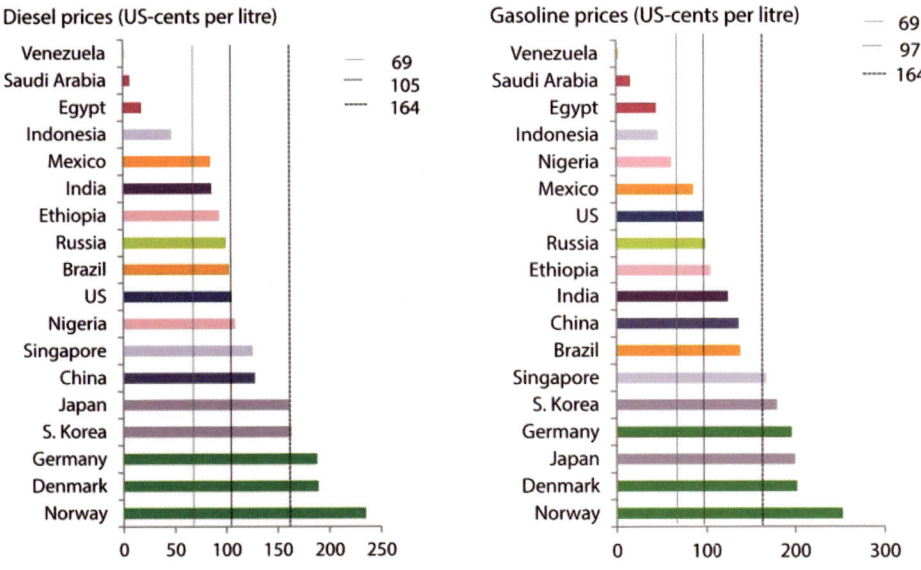

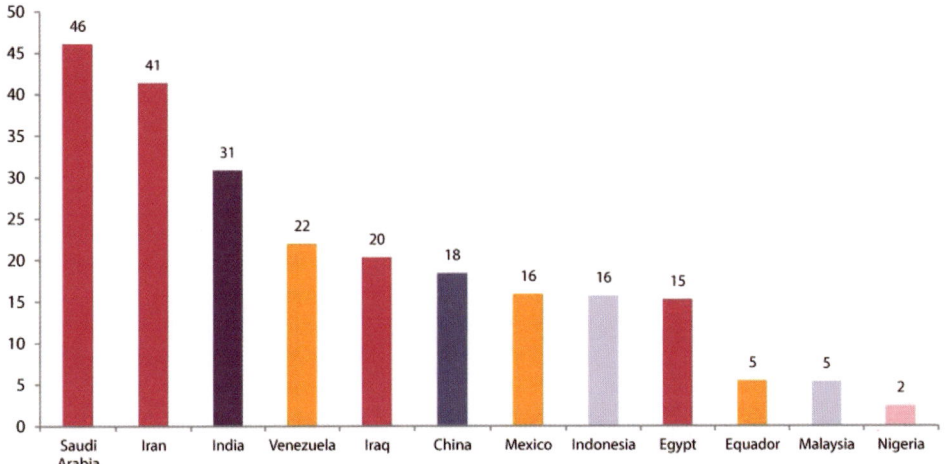

9. Figure 6 (L): 69 – benchmark line (Price of Crude Oil on World Market = 69 U.S.-Cents/Litre); 105 – benchmark (Retail price of Diesel in the United States = 105 U.S.-Cents/Litre); 164 – benchmark (Retail price of Diesel in Luxembourg = 164 U.S.-Cents/Litre). Figure 6 (R): 69 – benchmark line (Price of Crude Oil on World Market = 69 U.S.-Cents/Litre); 97 – benchmark (Retail price of Gasoline in the United States = 97 U.S.-Cents/Litre); 164 – benchmark (Retail price of Gasoline in Luxembourg = 164 U.S.-Cents/Litre).

Global diesel (L) and gasoline (R) prices in U.S.$ (as of November 2012)
Estimates of oil consumption subsidies in U.S.$ billion (2011)

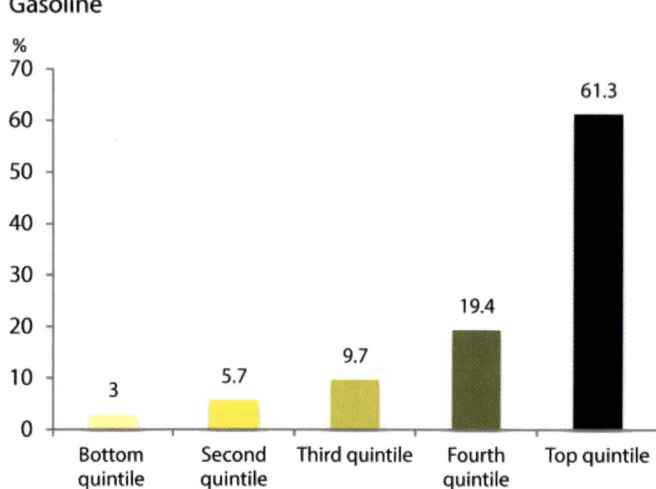

In addition to direct subsidies, transport fuel pricing in many countries frequently fails to fully incorporate externalities, and transport fuels often receive preferential tax treatment relative to taxes on other goods and services. The International Monetary Fund (IMF) has estimated total petroleum product mispricing—predominantly for transport use, and including direct subsidies; consumption externalities such as local pollution, carbon emissions, road traffic accidents, and congestion; and value-added tax—at U.S.$879 billion in 2011, with estimated underpricing in the United States alone accounting for U.S.$364 billion (IMF 2013).

Other fiscal instruments for managing vehicle use (typically delegated to the city level) include road pricing, parking charges, and other user fees. For example, Singapore, London, and Stockholm have successfully implemented congestion charging schemes, leading to a reduction in emissions and congestion while generating increased revenues for transport investment (Börjesson, Eliasson et al. 2012; TfL 2013).

Effective transportation fiscal policy must not only reflect the marginal social costs of a given mode of transport, but also address the relative cost and attractiveness of alternative modal choices. For example, Figure 9 demonstrates the change in the inflation-adjusted cost of various transport modes in the United Kingdom, highlighting the decrease in private vehicle costs relative to public transport costs over the previous decade.

To be most effective, fiscal instruments need to be designed and implemented at a system level, and coordinated with institutional and regulatory measures. For example, simulations of policy

Distribution of gasoline subsidies by consumption quintile

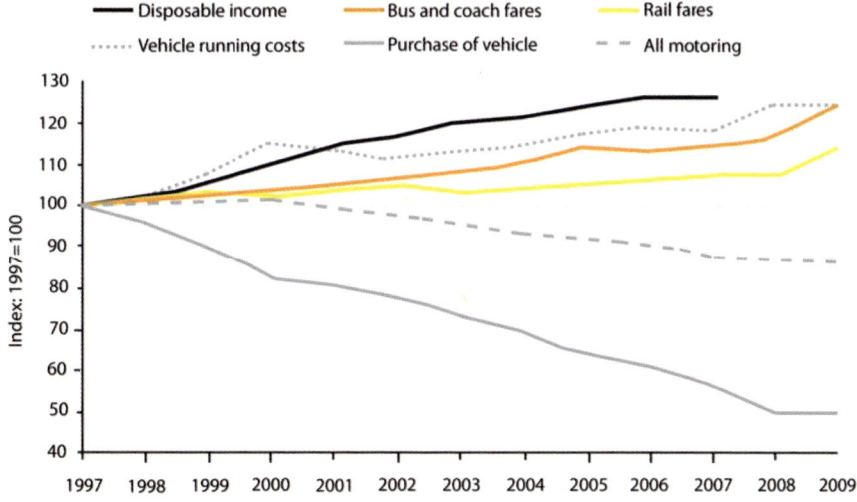

combinations involving increasing car operating costs by 75% and decreasing public transport fares by 50% for seven European cities, supported by improved land-use policies and improvements in public transport functioning, have demonstrated clear synergy effects of coordinating private vehicle and public transport pricing policies (Lautso, Spiekermann et al. 2004).

Shifting cities away from carbon- and resource-intensive accessibility patterns will require substantial funding, particularly for urban infrastructure which can support higher urban densities. As a first principle, this must involve a redirection of existing funding away from business-as-usual urban development, addressing the disparity between current and desired modal use and investment allocations (Dalkmann and Sakamoto 2010; UNEP 2011; ADB 2012). For example, 70% to 80% of federal funding for urban transport in Mexican cities is typically dedicated to car-based transport, while the share of car use rarely exceeds 30% (Arredondo 2013). By contrast, Bogota's pioneering Bus Rapid Transit (BRT) system was partially financed by redirecting funds away from urban motorway programmes.

Many of the compact-city investment projects are within the reach of city governments, who can leverage national or private funds to finance initial capital investments. In addition, private finance can be mobilised through real estate developer charges and fees, property or value capture taxes, loans, green bonds, and carbon finance (Ang and Marchal 2013; Bongardt, Creutzig et al. 2013). This allows monetisation of the positive externalities of public transport investment and can be particularly important in overcoming funding gaps for infrastructure that supports higher levels of urban density. For example, in Hong Kong, the government's "Rail plus Property" model captures

Changes in the real cost of transport and in income, 1997-2009 (United Kingdom)

the uplift in property values along new transit routes, ensuring efficient urban form while at the same time generating U.S.$27 billion in direct financial benefits for the Hong Kong government since its inception in the 1970s (Rode, Floater et al. 2013). Land Value Capture is also applied in several other Asian cities including Delhi and Tokyo (Morichi and Raj Acharya 2013).

POLICY FOR INNOVATION AND TECHNOLOGICAL DISRUPTION

As indicated earlier, a key element of supporting existing urban accessibility pathways that are based on more compact urban development is the application and innovative adaptation of existing technologies, including those for non-motorised transport. Nevertheless, technological innovation and related socio-technical disruption will have to play a significant role in further facilitating the transition to new, more environmentally and socially sustainable urban transport systems. Not only are traditional steel-and-petroleum automobiles highly inefficient in intrinsic spatial and resource intensity and relative capacity utilisation (see Figure 10), their use also generates substantial negative externalities and typically introduces a range of structural rigidities in mobility patterns which reduce economic efficiency by impeding consumer sovereignty (Litman 2014a) and imposing "compulsory consumption" (Soron 2009).

Continuing to ignore the problems intrinsic to conventional car use may no longer just lead to problems of unaccounted externalities, but could also potentially become a liability for the future-proofing of an entire industry sector. The reasons that the automobile sector has had a limited ability to innovate at the scale required are manifold and largely structural in nature. Automobiles have been the ultimate product of twentieth-century industrialisation and have proven to be remarkably resilient. Together with the significant growth rates in car sales seen over the last decade, a certain inertia and lack of desire to innovate and re-invent are inevitable.

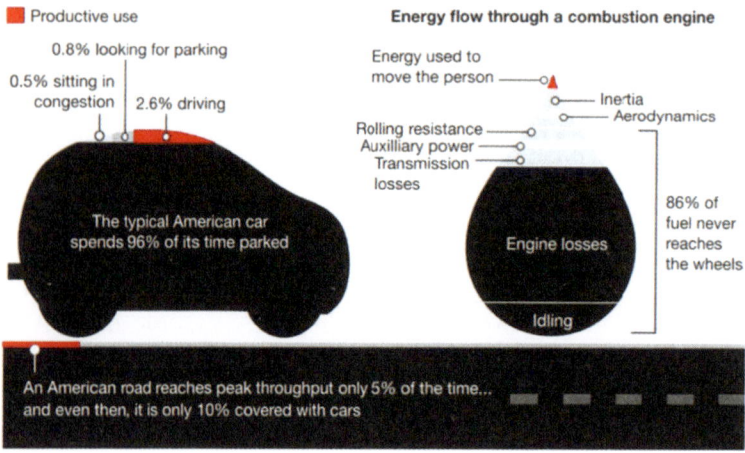

Waste in fuel, cars, and roads caused by automobile transport

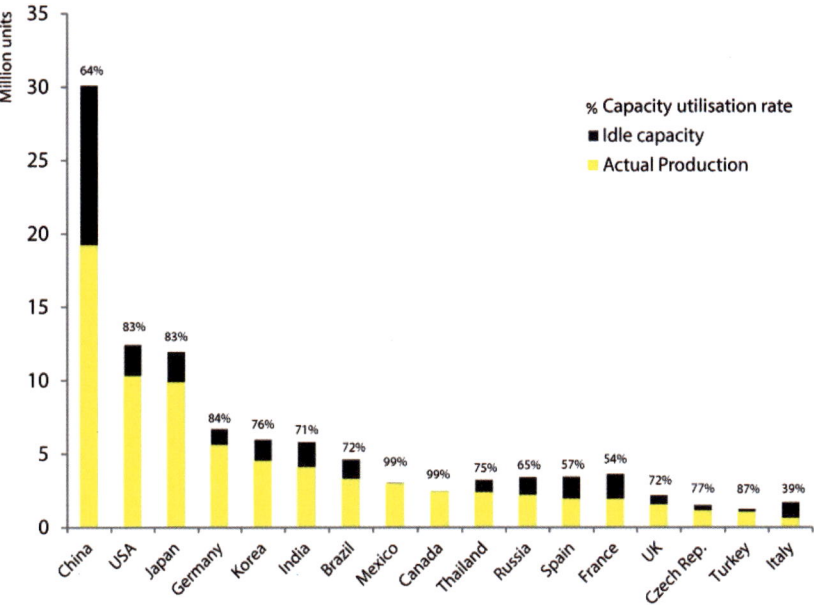

At the same time, considerable misjudgements about the future of the automobile market are becoming increasingly evident. As a result, global automobile manufacturing is now substantially overcapitalised, with underutilised production capacity in most large producer countries. Figure 11 provides an outline of estimated capacity utilisation rates among major producers in 2012, highlighting the scale of the capacity overhang (OECD 2013a). This trend continued in 2013, with capacity utilisation in major developing country producers such as India estimated to be below 60%—the lowest in over a decade (PwC 2013).

At the same time, the potential for system-wide technological innovation in the urban transport sector is considerable. Even within the narrower field of vehicle technology, innovations in engine and fuel technologies, digitisation and materials have the potential to significantly improve the efficiency of motorised vehicles in cities. And these technologies may indeed increasingly shape the scale and nature of mobility, altering living, working, and leisure patterns and potentially affecting both total transport demand and the social and cultural norms related to travel (Denis and Urry 2009). Given the scale of such a socio-technical transformation, the transport industry depends on public policy to provide a framework within which more ground-breaking innovation can take place. Despite this fact, public policy in many countries frequently stalls or actively impedes the emergence of a "post-car system" and the evolution of a more viable and resilient urban transport industry.

Capacity utilisation in selected countries (2012)

Current policy does not even maximise what is already technologically possible and often incentivises irrelevant or counterproductive forms of innovation. National industrial policies in many countries simply continue to actively support and incentivise conventional car manufacturing and use, both directly and indirectly. These sector-specific policies frequently intersect with other economy-wide policy distortions such as the underpricing of transport fuels, introducing a series of negative feedback loops and locking in artificially inflated levels of automobile use. For example, in the wake of the global financial crisis, several of the largest car-producing countries launched economic stimulus packages (such as scrappage schemes) directly targeted at the automobile sector, with Germany, Japan, and the United States alone spending almost U.S.$10 billion subsidising new vehicle purchases (Schweinfurth 2009; OECD 2012b). This support often exists in direct contradiction to competing national and subnational policy goals, including addressing externalities such as carbon emissions (particularly when considering embedded emissions) and congestion, and promoting responsible macroeconomic policy. For example, major car producers such as China and India are now increasingly dependent on oil imports for the majority of their consumption, with transport representing the single largest consuming sector.

Partially as a result of such policy frameworks and despite consistent improvements in the intrinsic performance of established transport technologies such as the internal combustion engine, technological progress has repeatedly failed to feed through to a more substantive improvement in overall vehicle performance for urban mobility and energy efficiency. Ultimately this failure may weaken the long-term competitiveness of established transport industry sectors, artificially extend the contemporary auto-based mobility system, and shift future business opportunities to more innovative digital technology companies that will eventually transform the urban transport sector.

Instead, industrial and innovation policy could recognise the inconsistencies described above and provide a much stronger and coherent policy context within which urban transport technology can evolve. Above all, political leadership coupled to a long-term political commitment will have to set out the principal policy direction and eliminate policy uncertainty as far as possible in order to unlock greater levels of investment in more ground-breaking innovation. Innovation policy would first have to acknowledge that the status quo car system is part of the problem and that future projections of private vehicle use are often linear assumptions, based on the recent past extrapolated into the future. On the basis of correcting existing market distortions—particularly the underpricing of car use—a range of proactive measures can then be applied.

Overall, the optimum policy set is a blend of pricing and regulatory mechanisms, and it needs to be applied at a system level of urban mobility. Furthermore, national and subnational policy need to be congruent and coordinated (Lautso, Spiekermann et al. 2004) in order to capture synergistic effects and to include policies for education and professional training as well as direct research and development. Regulatory interventions such as emission or fuel-consumption standards have repeatedly proved highly effective in triggering substantial technological innovation (Jaffe, Newell et al. 2002; Gerard and Lave 2005; Farrell and Sperling 2007; West 2010; Saikawa and Urpelainen 2014). In many instances, they have also increased the global competitiveness of vehicle manufacturers that were exposed to more stringent regulation (Saikawa and Urpelainen 2014).[10]

As with price distortions, regulatory impediments to the adoption of new urban transport technologies and the innovative use of existing technologies are ubiquitous. For example, the regulation of taxis in most cities has created monopolies which today act as a major barrier to the introduction of more effective, efficient, and affordable mobility services assisted by digital technology. Electric rickshaws in Indian cities have started to operate in a legal vacuum and would immensely profit from supportive regulation, while alternative dealership models for the purchase of electric vehicles have been challenged by several states and countries. Most important for incentivising innovation, the international patenting system has been repeatedly singled out as a potential barrier to innovation (Scotchmer 2004; Jaffe and Lerner 2011).

The policy context in which cities can play a particularly important role in assisting urban mobility innovation relates to the support and establishment of urban test beds. Besides acting as brokers of relevant public-private partnerships and securing the support of the general public, cities can proactively support the establishment of technological experiments in the field by providing legal and technical assistance. Important areas for related experimentation include shared electric mobility, grid-to-vehicle technology, and in the medium term, the testing of autonomous vehicles. In addition, progressive local transport policy in individual cities has again and again proved to be an important factor in the innovation cycle. For example, local parking and congestion charging policies in London have facilitated the rollout of electric vehicles ahead of their appearance in most other European cities.

CONCLUSION

This paper introduces the concept of "urban accessibility pathways" and argues that policy choices leading towards either more sprawling, car-dependent urban development or, alternatively, more compact, public transport–oriented cities have substantial implications, both for the economic and social performance of cities and for their carbon emissions. The paper began with an overview of the role of spatial structures and urban transport systems in determining the level of accessibility in cities, which in turn facilitates the creation of economies of scale, agglomeration

---

10. The current difference between carbon emission standards required by the European Union and the United States will provide important lessons. In Europe, average fleet emission standards need to be met by individual automobile manufacturers (OJEU 2009), whereas in the United States, manufacturers producing vehicles above the average emission target can purchase "emission permits" from vehicle producers significantly outperforming these standards (An et al 2011; Hansjèurgens 2010). As a result, innovation in Europe is internalised and mainstreamed within each manufacturer, whereas in the U.S. innovation is "supercharged" and concentrated within a few more radical producers that have recently entered the market, above all Tesla (Sperling and Nichols 2012).

	Sprawl	Smart Growth
Density	Lower-density, dispersed activities.	Higher-density, clustered activities.
Growth pattern	Urban periphery (greenfield) development.	Infill (brownfield) development.
Land use mix	Single use, segregated	Mixed.
Scale	Large scale. Larger blocks and wide roads. Less detail, since people experience the landscape at a distance, as motorists.	Human scale. Smaller blocks and roads. Attention to detail, since people experience the landscape up close.
Services (shops, schools, parks, etc.)	Regional, consolidated, larger. Requires automobile access.	Local, distributed, smaller. Accommodates walking access.
Transport	Automobile-oriented transportation and land use patterns, poorly suited for walking, cycling and transit.	Multi-modal transport and land use patterns that support walking, cycling and public transit.
Connectivity	Hierarchical road network with many unconnected roads and walkways, and barriers to nonmotorized travel.	Highly connected roads, sidewalks and paths, allowing more direct travel by motorized and nonmotorized modes.
Street design	Streets designed to maximize motor vehicle traffic volume and speed.	Reflects complete streets principles that accommodate diverse modes and activities, with lower traffic speeds in urban areas.
Planning process	Unplanned, with little coordination between jurisdictions and stakeholders.	Planned and coordinated between jurisdictions and stakeholders.
Public space	Emphasis on the private realm (yards, shopping malls, gated communities, private clubs).	Emphasis on the public realm (streetscapes, pedestrian areas, public parks, public facilities).

Comparing smart growth and sprawl land use patterns

effects, and networking advantages. While each city has developed a unique configuration of transport provision and urban form, we argue that some basic differentiating characteristics between urban accessibility pathways can be identified. These are largely determined by the degree of provision for public and non-motorised transport and the level of urban compactness, both of which are affected by substantial degrees of path dependency.

In summary, this paper suggests that more compact urban growth, aligned with the increased provision of public transport infrastructure and services and proactive support for non-motorized transport use, is likely to deliver substantial net economic and social benefits. Overall, cities continue to sprawl excessively, with some estimates suggesting that total urban land area could triple between 2000 and 2030. Similarly, in many key emerging economies (such as China and India), private motorized vehicle use and modal share are expanding rapidly, with a range of negative economic and social implications. At the same time, however, evidence is emerging that cities across different wealth levels are reaching the tipping point towards more sustainable development trajectories.

This paper then discusses the key policy areas (and related instruments) relevant to enabling spatially efficient and energy-efficient urban development. Undertaking strategic spatial planning in relation to key infrastructure developments, managing compact urban growth by identifying areas for intensification rather than simply restricting development, and closely integrating the provision of housing with public transport are among the key planning approaches adopted by leading city governments. In addition, the strategic use of incentives and revenue mobilization instruments is recognized as essential to ensuring the availability of financing for urban infrastructure investment, respecting the "polluter pays" principle, and creating positive feedback mechanisms between infrastructure investments, transport modal choice, and urban form.

And finally, broader policy frameworks may have to be tested further with regards to their impact on innovation and technological disruption. Here, the paper has identified a substantial number of perverse incentives which act as considerable barriers towards the development of more efficient and effective urban transport. Across all these policy instruments, national and city governments can increasingly learn from existing transformative change in a range of cities and also build on potential tipping points that have emerged in recent years.

REFERENCES

ADB. 2012. *Green Cities*. Mandaluyong, Philippines: Asian Development Bank.

An, F., R. Earley, and L. Green-Weiskel. 2011. "Global Overview on Fuel Efficiency and Motor Vehicle Emission Standards: Policy Options and Perspectives for International Cooperation." United Nations Background Paper. New York, UNDESA.

Andrade, K., L. Woods, and S. Kagaya. 2011. "Cycling within Urban Areas: The Cases of England and Japan." European Transport.

Conference 2011, Glasgow.Ang, G., and V. Marchal. 2013. "Mobilising Private Investment in Sustainable Transport: The Case of Land-based Passenger Transport Infrastructure." OECD Environment Working Papers. Paris: OECD Publishing.

Angel, S. 2012. *Planet of Cities*. Cambridge, MA: Lincoln Institute of Land Policy.

Arredondo, J. G. 2013. "Invertir para overnos, prioridad inaplazable: Diagnostico de fondos federales para transporte y accesibilidad urbana en Mexico, 2012." Executive summary, ITDP and British Embassy in Mexico.

Arze del Granado, F. J., D. Coady, and R. Gillingham. 2012. "The Unequal Benefits of Fuel Subsidies: A Review of Evidence for Developing Countries." *World Development* 40(11): 2234–48.

Avner, P., J. Rentschler, and S. Hallegatte. 2013. *Carbon Price Efficiency: Lock In and Path Dependence in Urban Forms and Transport Infrastructure*. Washington, DC: World Bank.

Baum-Snow, N., L. Brandt, J. V. Henderson, M. A. Turner, and Q. Zhang. 2012. "Roads, Railroads and Decentralization of Chinese Cities." Citeseer.

Bereitschaft, B., and K. Debbage. 2013. "Urban Form, Air Pollution, and CO Professional Geographer 65(4): 612–35. Emissions in Large U.S. Metropolitan Areas." *The* Bongardt, D., F. Creutzig, H. Hüging, K. Sakamoto, S. Bakker, S. Gota, and S. Böhler-Baedeker. 2013. *Low-carbon Land Transport: Policy Handbook*. New York and Abingdon: Routledge.

Börjesson, M., J. Eliasson, M. B. Hugosson, and K. Brundell-Freij. 2012. "The Stockholm Congestion Charges—5 Years On. Effects, Acceptability and Lessons Learnt." *Transport Policy* 20: 1–12.

Cheshire, P., C. Hilber, and I. Kaplanis. 2011. "Evaluating the Effects of Planning Policies on the Retail Sector; or, Do Town Centre First Policies Deliver the Goods?" SERC Discussion Paper, London School of Economics 66.

D'Onofrio, D. 2014. *Understanding the Regulatory Environment of Climate and the Impact of Community Design on Greenhouse Gas Emissions*. Atlanta, GA: Atlanta Regional Commission.

Dalkmann, H., and K. Sakamoto. 2010. *UNEP Green Economy Report: Transport Chapter—Full Technical Report*. New York: UNEP.

Dulac, J. 2013. "Global Land Transport Infrastructure Requirements: Estimating Road and Railway Infrastructure Capacity and Costs to 2050." Information paper. Paris: OECD/IEA.

Dulal, H. B., G. Brodnig, C. G. Onoriose. 2011. "Climate Change Mitigation in the Transport Sector through Urban Planning: A Review." *Habitat International* 35(3): 494–500.

Ekins, P., and S. Potter. 2010. "Reducing Carbon Emissions through Transport Taxation." GFC Briefing Paper. London: Green Fiscal Commission.

Estiri, H. 2012. *Residential Energy Use and the City-Suburb Dichotomy*. Seattle: University of Washington.

Ewing, R., and R. Cervero. 2010. "Travel and the Built Environment." *Journal of the American Planning Association* 76(3): 265–94.

Floater, G., P. Rode, B. Friedel, and A. Robert. 2014a. *Steering Urban Growth: Governance, Policy and Finance*. NCE

Cities Paper 02. London: LSE Cities, London School of Economics and Political Science.

Floater, G., P. Rode, A. Robert, C. Kennedy, D. Hoornweg, R. Slavcheva, and N. Godfrey. 2014b. *Cities and the New Climate Economy: the Transformative Role of Global Urban Growth.* NCE Cities Paper 01. London: LSE Cities, London School of Economics and Political Science.

Floater, G., P. Rode, D. Zenghelis, M. Montero Carrero, and D. A.Smith. 2013. *Stockholm: Green Economy Leader Report.* London: LSE Cities, London School of Economics and Political Science.

Floater, G., P. Rode, D. Zenghelis, M. Ulterino, D. Smith, K. Baker, and C. Heeckt. 2014c. *Copenhagen: Green Economy Leader Report.* London: LSE Cities, London School of Economics and Political Science.

Focas, C. 2014. "Cities, Economy and Climate." LSE call for evidence submission, Transport Studies Unit, School of Geography and the Environment, University of Oxford, Oxford, UK.

Government of India. 2014. *India Transport Report: Moving India to 2032.* New Delhi: Planning Commission, Government of India. III.

Guo, Z., and S. Ren. 2013. "From Minimum to Maximum: Impact of the London Parking Reform on Residential Parking Supply from 2004 to 2010?" *Urban Studies* 50(6): 1183–1200.

Hao, H., H. Wang, and M. Ouyang. 2011. "Comparison of Policies on Vehicle Ownership and Use between Beijing and Shanghai and Their Impacts on Fuel Consumption by Passenger Vehicles." *Energy Policy* 39(2): 1016–21.

Heck, S., and M. Rogers. 2014. *Resource Revolution: How to Capture the Biggest Business Opportunity in a Century.* Boston: Houghton Mifflin Harcourt.

Henderson, V. 2010. "Cities and Development." *Journal of Regional Science* 50(1): 515–40.

Herzog, B. 2010. *Urban Freight in Developing Cities.* Eschborn: GTZ.

Hickman, R., and D. Banister. 2014. *Transport, Climate Change and the City.* Abingdon: Routledge.

Hidalgo, D., and H. Zeng. 2013. "On the Move: Pushing Sustainable Transport from Concept to Tipping Point." Retrieved 25 April 2014, from http://thecityfix.com/blog/on-the-move-pushing-sustainable-transport-concept-tipping-point-dario-hidalgo- heshuang-zeng/.

Hilber, C., and W. Vermeulen. 2010. *The Impact of Restricting Housing Supply on House Prices and Affordability.* UK Department for Communities and Local Government. London: HM Stationary Office.

IEA. 2011. *World Energy Outlook 2011.* Paris: OECD/International Energy Agency.

IEA. 2012. *World Energy Outlook 2012.* Paris: OECD / International Energy Agency.

IMF. 2013. *Energy Subsidy Reform: Lessons and Implications.* Washington, D.C.: International Monetary Fund.

IPCC. 2014a. *Climate Change 2014: Mitigation of Climate Change—Human Settlements.* Working Group III: Mitigation of Climate Change. Potsdam: Intergovernmental Panel on Climate Change.

IPCC. 2014b. *Climate Change 2014: Mitigation of Climate Change—Transport.* Working Group III: Mitigation of Climate Change. Potsdam: Intergovernmental Panel on Climate Change.

ITDP. 2012. *Transforming Urban Mobility in Mexico: Towards Accessible Cities Less Reliant on Cars.* Mexico City: Institute for Transportation and Development Policy.

Jaffe, A. B., and J. Lerner. 2011. *Innovation and Its Discontents: How Our Broken Patent System Is Endangering Innovation and Progress, and What to Do about It.* Princeton, NJ: Princeton University Press.

Kersys, A. 2011. "Sustainable Urban Transport System Development Reducing Traffic Congestions Costs." *Engineering Economics* 22(1): 5–13.

Lecocq, F., and Z. Shalizi. 2014. "The Economics of Targeted Mitigation in Infrastructure." *Climate Policy* 14(2): 187–208.

Li, F., and B. Cao. 2012. *Path and Potential of Carbon Emissions Reduction Caused by Urban Energy Use: A Case Study of Shanghai*. Urban China Project Report.

Litman, T. 2014a. *Evaluating Public Transit Benefits and Costs*. Victoria: Victoria Transport Policy Institute 65.

Litman, T. 2014b. *Smart Growth Savings*. Victoria, Canada: Victoria Transport Policy Institute.

Liu, Y., T. Chen, and X. Song. 2012. Relationship between Urban Form and Urban CO Recommendations. Efficiency with Policies and LSE Cities. 2014. "Transport Related Carbon Emissions in Atlanta and Barcelona: Updated Comparative Calculations." Working paper. London: LSE Cities.

Mackie, P., and T. Worsley. 2013. "International Comparison of Transport Appraisal Practice." Institute for Transport Studies for the UK Department for Transport, www.its.leeds.ac.uk.

Morichi, S., and S. Raj Acharya. 2013. *Transport Development in Asian Megacities*. Berlin: Springer.

Newman, P., and J. R. Kenworthy. 2015. "The End of Automobile Dependence: How Cities Are Moving beyond Car-based Planning." Washington, DC: Island Press.

OECD. 2010. *Trends in Urbanisation and Urban Policies in OECD Countries: What Lessons for China?* OECD, China Development Research Foundation.

OECD. 2011. "STAN indicators." Retrieved 22 April 2014 from http://stats.oecd.org/Index.aspx?DataSetCode=STANINDICATORS.

OECD. 2012a. *Compact City Policies: A Comparative Assessment*. OECD Green Growth Studies, OECD.

OECD. 2012b. *Inventory of Estimated Budgetary Support and Tax Expenditures for Fossil Fuels 2013*. Paris: OECD.

OECD. 2013a. *Medium-run Capacity Adjustment in the Automobile Industry*. OECD Economics Department Policy Notes. OECD. 2013b. *Tracking Clean Energy Progress*. Power generation figures, OECD.

OECD. 2014. *The Cost of Air Pollution: Health Impacts of Road Transport*. OECD. OJEU. 2009. Regulation EC 449/2009.

ONS. 2010. *Transport trends: 2009 edition*. Transport Statistics. London: Office of National Statistics.

PwC. 2013. "Technological Breakthroughs: Global Annual Review 2013." http://www.pwc.com/gx/en/annual-review/megatrends/technological-breakthroughs-bob-moritz.jhtml.

Qin, B., and S. S. Han. 2013. "Planning Parameters and Household Carbon Emission: Evidence from High- and Low-carbon Neighborhoods in Beijing." *Habitat International* 37: 52–60.

Rayle, L., and M. Pai. 2010. "Scenarios for Future Urbanization: Carbon Dioxide Emissions from Passenger Travel in Three Indian Cities." *Transportation Research Record: Journal of the Transportation Research Board* 2193(1): 124–31.

Rode, P. 2014. "The Politics and Planning of Urban Compaction: The Case of the London Metropolitan Region." In *The Economy of Sustainable Construction*, ed. Ilka and Andreas Ruby. Berlin: Ruby Press.

Rode, P., G. Floater, J. Kandt, K. Baker, M. M. Carrero, C. Heeckt, D. Smith, and M. Delfs. 2013. *Going Green: How Cities Are Leading the Next Economy*. London: LSE Cities, ICLEI and Global Green Growth Institute.

Rode, P., C. Hoffmann, J. Kandt, A. Graff, and D. Smith. 2014. *New Urban Mobility in London and Berlin*. London: LSE Cities and InnoZ.

Saikawa, E., and J. Urpelainen. 2014. "Environmental Standards as a Strategy of International Technology Transfer." *Environmental Science & Policy* 38: 192–206.

Savy, M. 2012. *Urban Freight: A Comprehensive Approach*. Urban Freight for Livable Cities, Gothenburg, Volvo Research and Education Foundation.

Schubert, J., T. Wolbring, and B. Gill. 2013. "Settlement Structures and Carbon Emissions in Germany: The

Effects of Social and Physical Concentration on Carbon Emissions in Rural and Urban Residential Areas." *Environmental Policy and Governance* 23(1): 13–29.

Seto, K. C., B. Güneralp, and L. R. Hutyra. 2012. "Global Forecasts of Urban Expansion to 2030 and Direct Impacts on Biodiversity and Carbon Pools." *Proceedings of the National Academy of Sciences* 109(40): 16083–88.

Sperling, D., and M. Nichols. 2012. "California's Pioneering Transportation Strategy." *Issues in Science and Technology* 28(2): 59–66.

STF. 2014. "Shrink Your Travel Footprint." Retrieved 12 June 2014 from http://shrinkthatfootprint.com/shrink-your-travel- footprint.

Suzuki, H., R. Cervero, and K. Iuchi. 2013. *Transforming Cities with Transit: Transit and Land-use Integration for Sustainable Urban Development*. Washington, D.C.: World Bank Publications.

TfL. 2013. *Annual Report and Statement of Accounts 2012/13*. London: Transport for London.

Thomopoulos, N., and S. Grant-Muller. 2013. "Incorporating Equity as Part of the Wider Impacts in Transport Infrastructure Assessment: An Application of the SUMINI Approach." *Transportation* 40(2): 315–45.

UN Habitat. 2013. *Planning and Design for Sustainable Urban Mobility: Global Report on Human Settlements 2013*. United Nations Human Settlements Programme. New York: United Nations.

UNCSD. 2012. "Sustainable, Low Carbon Transport in Emerging and Developing Economies." Rio 2012 Issues Briefs, Rio+20 United Nations Conference on Sustainable Development. 13.

UNEP. 2011. *Towards a Green Economy: Pathways to Sustainable Development and Poverty Eradication*. New York: UNEP.

van Audenhove, F.-J., O. Korniychuk, L. Dauby, and J. Pourbaix. 2014. "The Future of Urban Mobility 2.0." Arthur D. Little and UITP.

Van Dyck, D., E. Cerin, T. L. Conway, I. De Bourdeaudhuij, N. Owen, J. Kerr, G. Cardon, L. D. Frank, B. E. Saelens, and J. F. Sallis. 2012. "Perceived Neighborhood Environmental Attributes Associated with Adults' Transport-related Walking and Cycling: Findings from the USA, Australia, and Belgium." *International Journal of Behavioral Nutrition and Physical Activity* 9(1): 70.

Wagner, A. 2013. *GIZ International Fuel Prices 2012/2013*. Data preview April 2013. Eschborn: Gesellschaft fur Internationale Zusammenarbeit (GIZ).

WBCSD. 2012. "About the Cement Industry." Retrieved 27 May 2014, from http://www.wbcsdcement.org/index.php/about-cement.

West, S. E. 2010. "Taxes versus Standards." *21st Century Economics: A Reference Handbook* 1: 247.

World Bank. 2013. *Urbanization beyond Municipal Boundaries: Nurturing Metropolitan Economies and Connecting Peri- Urban Areas in India*. World Bank.

World Bank. 2014a. *Supporting Reports II: Urban China*. World Bank.

World Bank. 2014b. *Urban China: Toward Efficient, Inclusive, and Sustainable Urbanization*. World Bank.

Zacharias, J., and Y. Tang. 2010. "Restructuring and Repositioning Shenzhen, China's New Mega City." *Progress in Planning* 73(4): 209–49.

THE RESTLESSNESS OF OBJECTS*

Jesse LeCavalier

On 25 October 2010, in the atrium of Beijing's Viva Shopping Mall, a group of thirty performers dressed as UPS drivers and customers spontaneously broke into a series of choreographed dance numbers to a modified version of "That's Amore." UPS organized this bit of publicity as part of its "We <3 Logistics" campaign, designed by Ogilvy & Mather and launched in 2010. Lauren Zhao, one of UPS's general managers in Northern China, explained: "Having worked at UPS for more than 10 years, this is the first time I have seen what we do—logistics—represented as a dance routine."[1] In addition to such events, UPS launched a range of TV spots that show their shipping and transport operations traversing a frictionless globe to the delight of their customers, also to the tune of "That's Amore" but with modified lyrics. For example, the original line: "When the world seems to shine / Like you've had too much wine / That's amore" gets updated to: "When technology knows / Right where everything goes / That's logistics."[2] In the commercials, UPS is represented by a large golden arrow tracing its way along recognizable urban infrastructures and by its workers as they glide over omnidirectional warehouse floors and slip through Venetian alleys.

1. Promotional video related to the Beijing performance on UPS's official YouTube channel "Logistics: Live in Beijing (Behind the Scenes)," YouTube, youtu.be/GpDAYWDxiI0, last accessed 15 July 2012.

2. UPS, "We <3 Logistics" commercial, YouTube, youtube.com/watch?v=mRAHa_Po0Kg. {Video not available, but I found a similar UPS commercial at: https://www.youtube.com/watch?v=VCh6HnXHKRc –If you can't use this one, add "last accessed" date}.

* First printed in Cabinet no. 47 (Fall 2012).

As marketing campaigns go, selling logistics is a challenging exercise, and the performance in Beijing was an effort to humanize what is largely a technologically driven field. In fact, the choice of words by UPS and Ogilvy & Mather reveals some of the difficulties that lurk in trying to understand something like logistics. Instead of letting it remain in the domain of technocrats and engineers, UPS tries to animate it and to personalize it, even to make it *loveable*. UPS is not expressly stating that they are good at logistics—that is, they are not making any of the more standard claims of authority. Rather, they present themselves as devotees and are happy to count instead the many ways they love logistics: "We love its precision, its epic scale, its ability to make life better for billions of people. Each day, our customers count on us to choreograph a ballet of infinite complexity played across skies, oceans and borders. And we do. What's not to love?"[3] In addition to framing their concern around love of, affection for, and commitment to logistics, the suggestion that UPS is a choreographer also reveals the need to make sense of an industry that has no fixed form and no real image, and is largely communicated in systems illegible, if not incomprehensible, to humans.

Logistics has roots in the military, as it anchors the management trio that includes strategy and tactics, and it concerns the infrastructure of an operation: the three Ms of materiel, movement, and maintenance. Logistics has also been called "the art of defining and extending the possible" due to its capacity to overcome unexpected challenges or to push at the edges of feasibility.[4] Logistics, in this way, is a world-making enterprise that emphasizes awareness, foresight, and preparedness. At the same time, logistics requires a tactical mindset that accepts that things rarely go according to plan. While the latter is a reality of military operations, for UPS, acknowledging the likelihood of disruption is not an attractive selling point—hence the company's efforts to conjure the image of a choreographer, a figure associated with detailed knowledge of, and power over, the entirety of the operation at hand. Thus, the claim that each day UPS "choreograph[s] a ballet of infinite complexity" is an effort to insist that their logistics is not merely a reactive enterprise but is part of a regime of total awareness and control, a new kind of hyper-management.

In case its claims to be a global choreographer were not broadcast loudly enough, UPS's Beijing performance reiterates the message in the most literal way. Much of the footage from the UPS dance routines in Beijing was filmed from above, allowing viewers to witness the dynamic forms produced by the assemblage of bodies. Such images cannot fail to evoke the more spectacular dance numbers in the musicals of Busby Berkeley, especially his work for Warner Brothers in the early 1930s, including *42nd Street*, *Gold Diggers of 1933*, and *Dames*. Berkeley's work is characterized

3. Official description accompanying select UPS commercials on the company's YouTube channel; for example, youtube.com/watch?v=mRAHa_Po0Kg.

4. James Huston, *The Sinews of War: Army Logistics 1775–1953* (Washington, DC: Office of the Chief of Military History, United States Army, 1960), p. viii. Huston's reference is to a statement attributed to Otto von Bismarck that "politics is the art of the possible."

by the precisely coordinated organization of battalions of showgirls to create dazzling geometric effects. Often shot from above using specially designed armatures, the hordes of dancers are transformed, with the help of elaborate stage mechanisms, into kaleidoscopic displays of bodies. For example, "I'm Young and Healthy" from *42nd Street* uses a patented, segmented turntable stage to transform its performers into efflorescent cogs and whorls, simultaneously mechanical and botanical. Choreography for Berkeley amounted to an exercise in control in which every piece, whether human or nonhuman, is accounted for with exacting measure. For example, in preparation for the film *Waterfall*, Berkeley instilled discipline in his performers by relentlessly mapping out the routines through drawing: "In the first two days of rehearsal, before the Berkeley girls entered the pool, they studiously watched Buzz at the blackboard where, like a football coach, he whitechalked the patterns and movements the girls would undertake in the pool."[5] Choreography here is associated with awareness of the time and the space of each piece, but also with *notation*. In the same way that Berkeley would trace out the paths of his dancers, so too do the arrows of UPS's advertisements inscribe their objects' trajectories on the space of the city. Perhaps not coincidentally, the composer who worked most closely with Berkeley in these years was Harry Warren, one of Hollywood's most prolific and successful songwriters and, as it turns out, the composer of "That's Amore." While the connection may be distant, the links between Berkeley's regimented choreography, Warren's song, and UPS's new campaign trigger a longer story about just what logistics *is*, what it does, and what love has got to do with it, anyway.

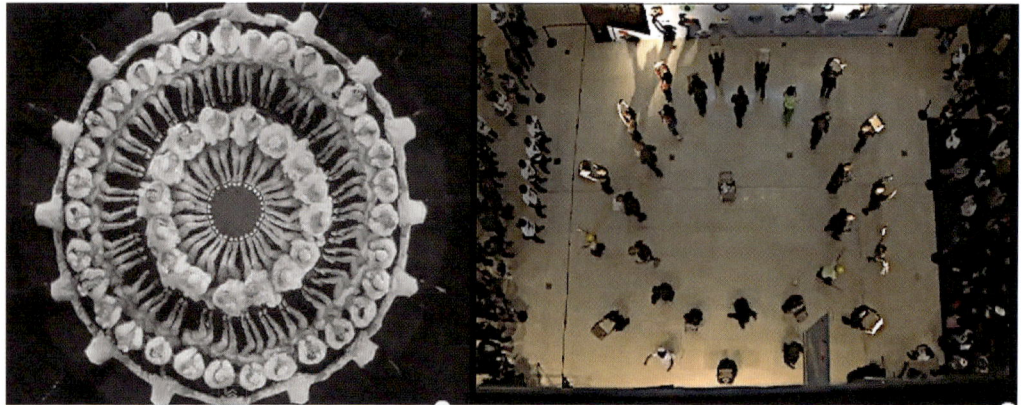

5. Jeffrey Spivak, *Buzz: The Life and Art of Busby Berkeley* (Lexington, KY: The University Press of Kentucky, 2010), 91.

Left: A still from the Harry Warren song "I'm Young and Healthy" from Busby Berkeley's 1934 musical *42nd Street*.
Right: A still from a promotional performance in Beijing in 2011 as part of UPS's "We <3 Logistics" campaign, set to the tune of "That's Amore," also by Harry Warren

In the UPS television ads, amid the strains of "That's Amore" one can discern the chirps of bar codes being scanned as the camera pans over boxes in motion. The bar code symbols themselves are superimposed over the objects, suggesting a new vision that will attend the new logistics promised by UPS. Bar codes are machine-readable symbols that translate a string of numbers legible to humans—in this case, a product code—into a string of bits legible to computers. Different standards govern bar codes, but in retail, at least, the Universal Product Code (UPC) is the most common. The first product ever to be recorded using a bar code and scanner was a ten-pack of Juicy Fruit chewing gum, purchased for $0.67 on 26 June 1974 in Troy, Ohio, at 08:01.[6] The specific information attached to this transaction reflects the bar code's ability to instantly record precise spatio-temporal data. Moreover, the bar code is one of the first symbols designed *for* computers to be read *by* computers. In order to better visualize the structure of the bar code, one can separate it into smaller bundles, each containing one number and eight bits. Each number is composed of a sequence of ones and zeroes, represented as solid or as void. With practice, one might come to more easily recognize the fortified "01111101" of the three or the wispy "10001000" of the eight. But reduced to the size of a postage stamp, the difference between one number and the next becomes harder to parse.

The introduction of the bar code, like many logistical transformations to follow, was intended to increase the speed of the transaction while reducing the likelihood of mistakes. The bar code also has the added benefit of information and inventory coordination. Not only was the clerk suddenly freed of the task of manually inputting price information, so too were the stock keepers relieved of having to physically inspect their inventory. They needed only look at the compiled data generated by the day's bar code scans. So while the bar code sped things up, it also transferred labor to customers. Simply by retrieving desired items and handing them to a cashier to be scanned (and paid for), shoppers became a store's stockists and market analysts. Not only did they help manage and record inventory, they also helped the store better understand which items people were buying. And in the retail context, this is what matters most.

6. This inaugural ten-pack of gum is enshrined in the Smithsonian's National Museum of American History. See, for example, James Surowiecki, "EZ Does It" in the *New Yorker*, 8 September 2003.

Preparing to photograph a sample Universal Product Code

In fact, consumer desire, and the will to capitalize on and manipulate that desire, remains the driving force behind the huge techno-spatial complex that comprises retail logistics systems.

While the bar code is designed to be scanned easily and to reduce errors, it works best if placed in certain locations relative to the shape of the product it represents. This design consideration became acute when the symbol's rapid implementation required it to be folded into the front-end manufacturing processes of all manner of goods. To resolve this difficulty, sets of guidelines were established to help producers figure out the best place on their products for their codes. A telling set of diagrams from a 1975 document about the UPC suggests ideal locations for bar codes on, for example, a six-pack of beer, an eight-pack of hotdogs, or a ten-pack of luncheon meat. In these diagrams, all the imagery relating to brand differentiation, the very stuff that wins the hearts and minds of customers, is conspicuously absent. The only mark on the products is the diminutive bar code. In the eyes of those responsible for circulating these objects, however, this is the only mark that matters for it contains all the necessary information, including the manufacturer, the name of the product, its price, and—once it is scanned—information about its location in time and space.

The bar code for any given product is scanned at significant points along that product's journey. For example, as it leaves a warehouse bound for a retail outlet, as it is received by its destination, as it is purchased at the checkout counter, etc. While the bar code cannot communicate the specific location in space and time of a product at any given moment, it can at least narrow the options down to being either in a certain general location or between two of them.

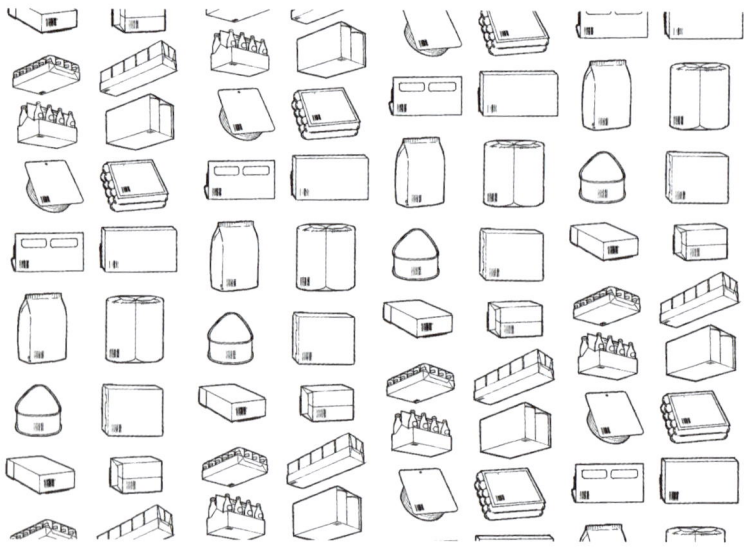

Guide to placement of bar codes on a range of package types

This information allows inventory managers to maintain an awareness of the whereabouts of all their products. If their products have not yet arrived, managers can at least reassure themselves by knowing when they left their former location. Moreover, in the eyes of inventory managers, the physical aspects of these products, numerous as they are, start to matter less than their schedules and locations. Inventory management, once concerned only with the physical handling of material, has increasingly become an exercise in information management as the objects themselves are reduced to and encapsulated by the bar codes on their surfaces. However, this spatio-temporal geography of objects is fleeting because by the time any one thing is scanned, it is already on its way elsewhere.

The obdurate materiality of inventory nonetheless remains, and its stubbornness illuminates the tension between physicality and ephemerality at the heart of logistics. Managers want to move merchandise around as if it were only composed of the bar code's ones and zeroes, but the persistence of its substance requires a huge material apparatus to engineer its handling—replete with its own branch of science. These efforts bring with them new ways of perceiving location and distance, or even of understanding space. The bar code enables an enterprise's tighter control of its merchandise and allows it to further streamline its operations, making it "leaner," in logistics vernacular. When a bar code is scanned, a message is sent to coordinating software that maintains an overview of a given retail location's stock of inventory. Once a certain product's quantities dip below a certain point (a point calculated based on past and anticipated demand), a request is sent to the supporting distribution center (DC) to prepare more of that item for delivery. All of this is done in the hopes of minimizing the amount of time that any product is stationary, be it in the distribution center, on a truck, or on a shelf.

Distribution networks are measured in both miles and minutes. For example, the success of Walmart, one of the retail sector's leaders in logistics, is based on founder Sam Walton's early recognition of the importance of a nimble distribution system that would allow the frequent replenishment of inventory, even in small amounts. Walton and his planning team based the location of their distribution centers on a rule of thumb that stores should fall within a 100-mile radius around a DC but also that any round-trip from a DC to a store could be made in less than a day.[7] This flexibility helped to accommodate the diverse transportation conditions in the rural areas in which Walmart first established itself. Such a mental overlay of time onto space is apparent in a much earlier map from Alfred Chandler Jr.'s book *The Visible Hand*. Using what could be called "isotemporal" contours, the political map of the United States in 1857 shows travel time by rail to the rest of the country from New York City. Without showing any of the

---

7. Sam Walton, Walmart founder and former CEO, describes the process of opening stores: "We figured we had to build our stores so that our distribution centers, or warehouses, could take care of them, but also so those stores could be controlled … each store had to be within a day's drive of a distribution center." Sam Walton with John Huey, *Sam Walton, Made in America: My Story* (New York: Bantam, 1992), 141.

tracks or routes, privileged sites of access are apparent. For example, Chicago can be reached in less than two days, while more proximate but less well-served destinations in Virginia will take upwards of four. More significant with a drawing like this is how it enables a particular way of viewing territory based on time rather than physical distance. Two destinations may be equally distant, but transportation technology might render one of them twice as close.

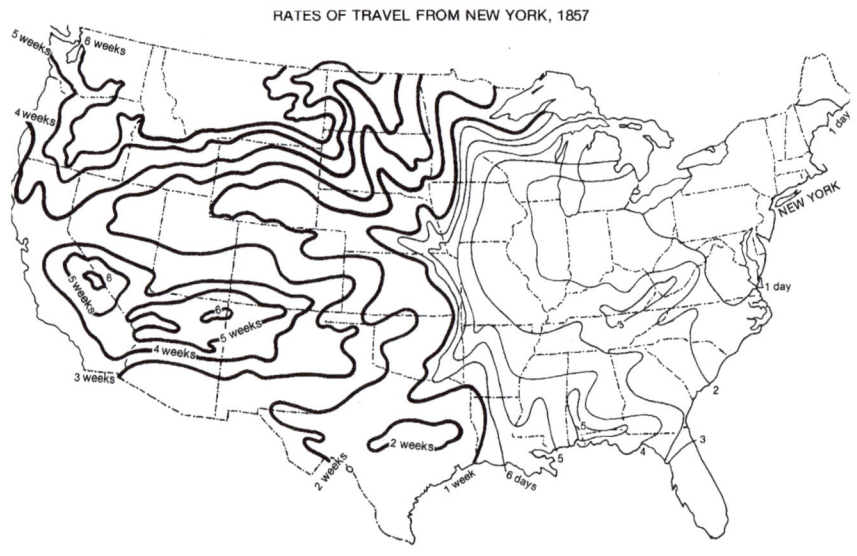

Such an understanding of territory is further enabled by the bar code's capacity to map an object's location range. Based on assumptions about the regularity of travel time, retailers can plan for replenishment runs and calculate the time of delivery with increasing precision. Walmart, for example, spaces its distribution centers at relatively consistent intervals and in close proximity to the interstate highway system, generating, at least in the eastern half of the country, a nearly continuous space of distribution coverage. The company's distribution centers and the stores they support develop in a cyclical manner, with retail outlets being built around a distribution center until its capacity is stressed. As this stress begins to reach a critical threshold, a new center is built. Pressure is relieved, new retail stores can open in adjacent territory, and the cycle continues.

These distribution centers (DCs) demonstrate the effects logistics will have on architecture as it brings with it a shift from buildings defined by prescribed, stable, and discrete envelopes toward a network of configurable, fluid, and connected interiors, tethered to each other through the

Isotemporal map of rates of railroad travel from New York, 1857

constant shuttling of transport vessels. In Walmart's case, merchandise is consistently on the move, and the DCs enable this restlessness of objects. These expansive installations—typically over one million square feet in area—mainly comprise miles of conveyors and row upon row of high-density shelving. It happens that there is a perimeter defined by a thin envelope and a roof, but these elements are incidental to the purposes at hand. Moreover, the layout of each company's distribution center functions like its fingerprint; each one is different, and each reflects the specific character of an organization. The conveyor spine connecting induction risers to feed conveyors of one center suggests a company dealing with varied inventory and rapid turnover. The manifold shelves and small number of docks of another indicates inventory of a more specialized nature. The towers of small containers of a third indicate a company specializing in large objects whose size makes stacking them the most economical storage configuration. In all cases, the distribution center is a highly specialized custom-designed *thing*, ambiguous in its boundaries, behavior, and operation. These hybrid spaces also require a special kind of operator to work them.

In the context of retail logistics (including e-commerce), the task of a worker in one of these distribution centers is to assemble orders of merchandise destined for specific retail outlets. Goods are delivered from suppliers to the DC and stored in specific locations. DC operators are charged with "picking" items on a manifest issued by the DC coordinator. There are different versions of this process, but basically it amounts to taking homogeneous input sent from a supplier (e.g., cases of staplers) and assembling a heterogeneous output to be sent to a store based on its specific product-mix requirement (e.g., one case of staplers, one box of pens, a single office chair, etc.). These lists vary from day to day and depend on a number of factors, including customer demand, sales projects, and even the weather.[8]

8. For example, the company Weather Trends International sells weather analysis forecasts to retailers to help them plan their merchandising efforts accordingly. The company points out that small changes in temperature from year to year can influence consumer spending significantly. According to the website, "+1° HOTTER = +13% more HEDGE TRIMMER products sold each week," while "+1° COLDER = +25% increase in MOUSE TRAP products sold each week." The list is quite extensive. Weather Trends International, wxtrends.com/retailers-suppliers.

Even though this illustration simulates a warehouse environment, its abstract interior in which inventory and architecture merge into a blank surface echoes the experience of the contemporary distribution center

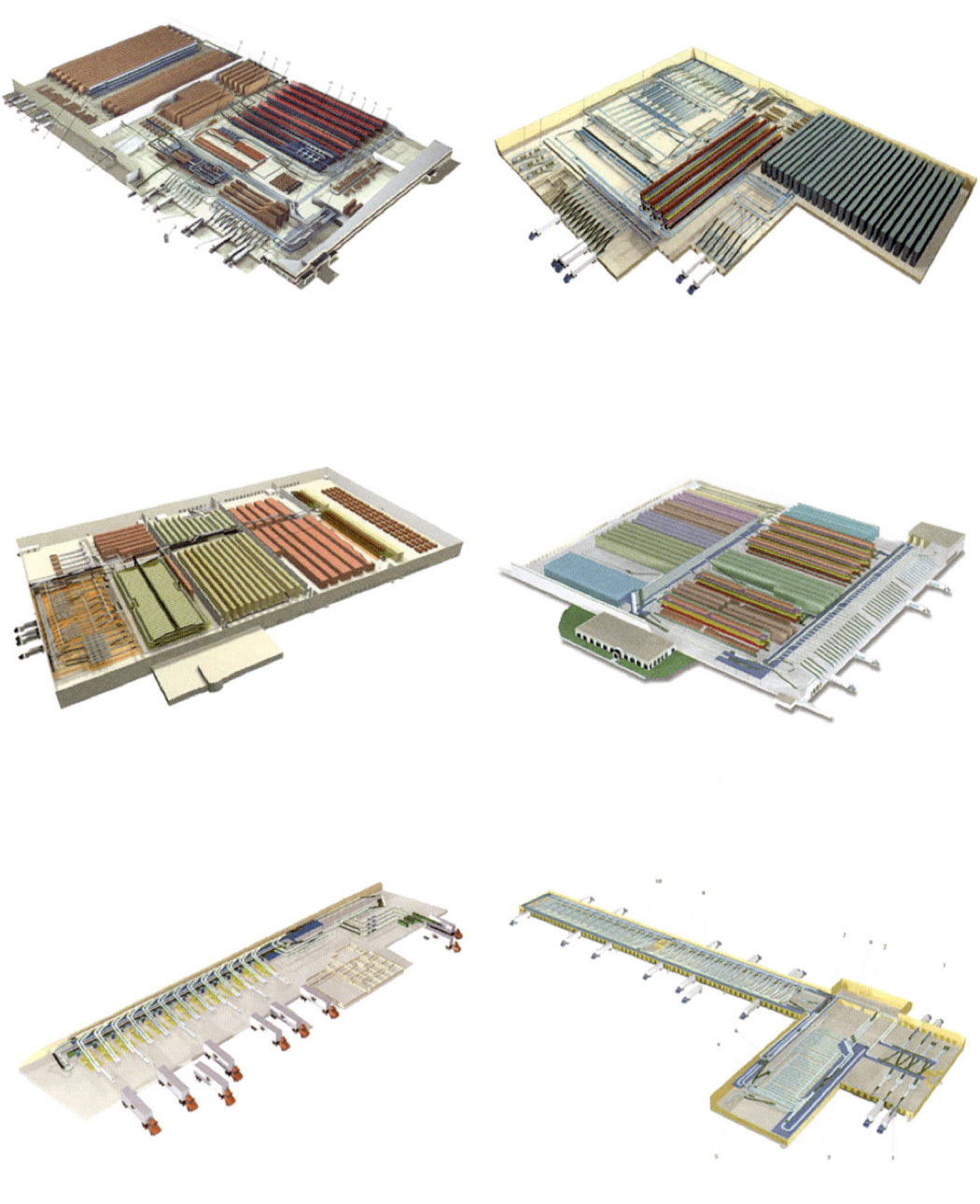

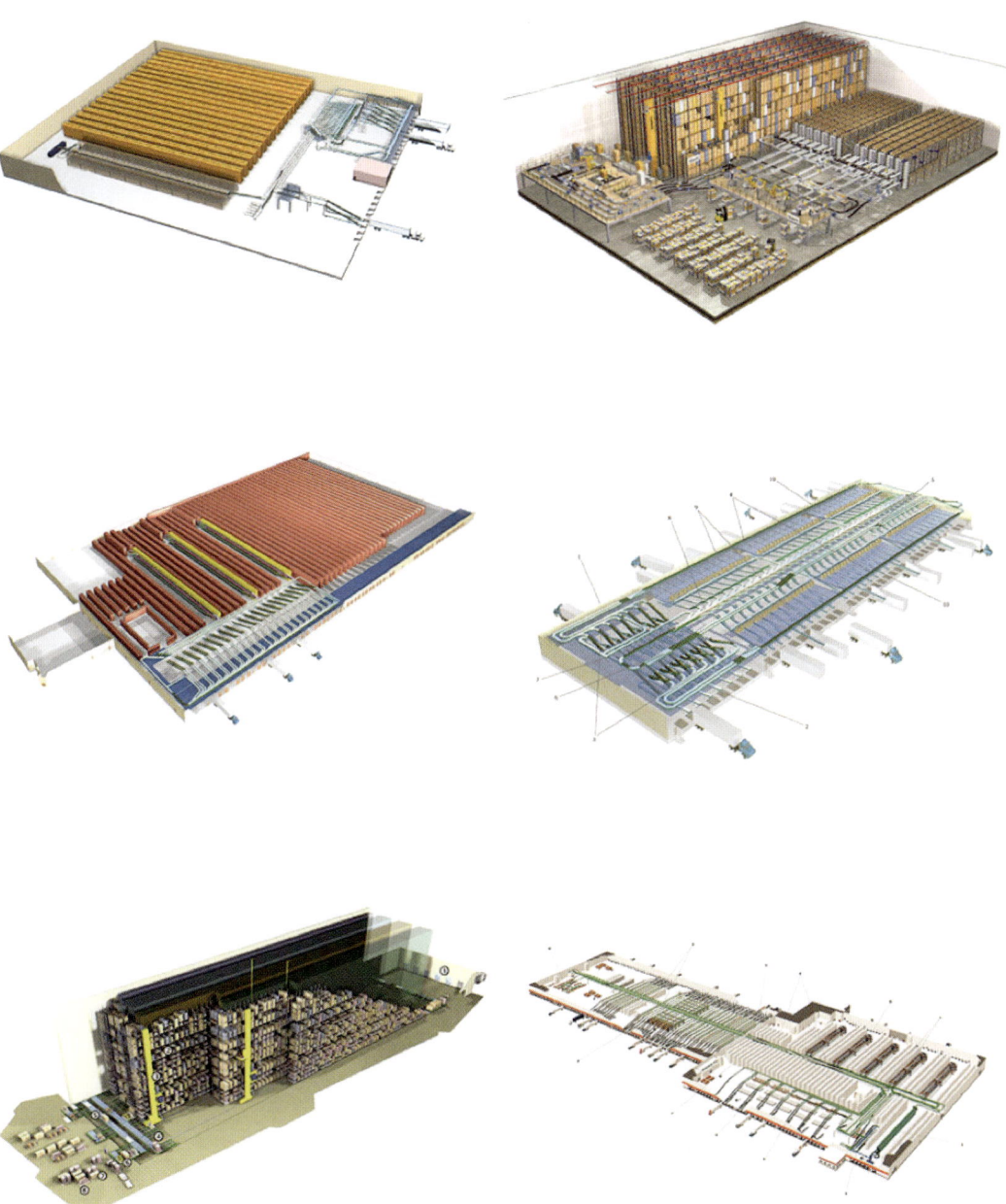

A comparison of distribution center materials-handling systems and interior configurations. Top row, left to right: Access Logistics, American Eagle Outfitters, Children's Place, Distribution Solutions. Middle row, left to right: Ingram Micro, Jo-Ann Stores, Liberty Hardware, National Retail Consolidators. Bottom row, left to right: PFI Crossdocking, Saks, Inc., Art Van Furniture, Supply Chain Management, Inc.

There are different ways to assemble these orders. The simplest way is also the slowest, in which a DC worker gathers a list of items by walking to each one's location. Before the bar code was implemented, workers would enter all their data manually, writing down product names, quantities, etc. The bar code accelerated this process but also shifted power to the control system charged with coordinating the enterprise. The bar code allows things to be easily scanned but, as a result, the nature of the objects is abstracted and mediated through this computer language. Only the scanning technology is capable of reading it, especially at the pace demanded of rapidly accelerating logistics spaces. Increasingly, DC operators use a system often referred to as "hands-free" because the scanning component of a wearable computer system is physically attached to their bodies. On one hand, workers wear a scanning "ring" that records the bar codes, and on the opposite forearm, they wear a digital display that shows the product's information and also prompts the next item on the order. Meanwhile, the items being picked are physically moved on to a conveyor or into an intermediate container, often called a "tote," to be assembled later into a larger order. With this approach, workers' hands are free to handle merchandise more easily, but they are unable to put their scanning tools down. "Hands-free" thus means wired in.

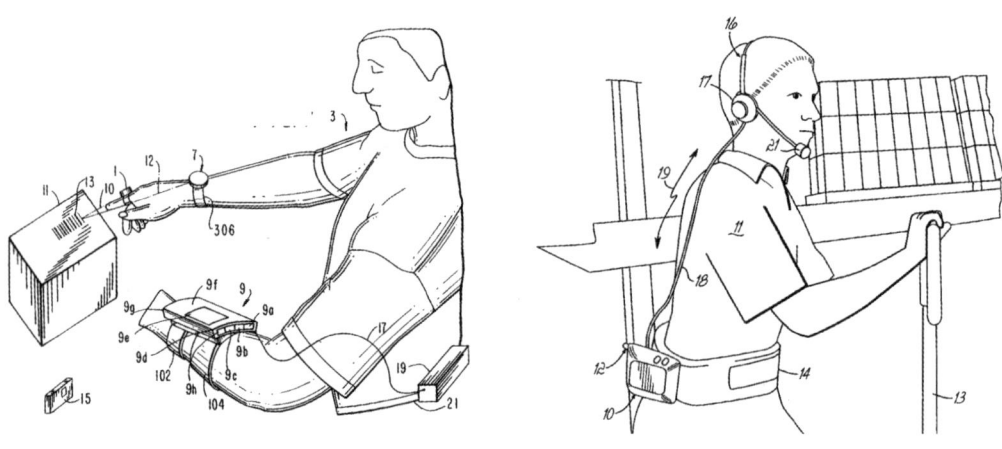

Left: Scanners can also be worn on the body of their users. This patent drawing for Motorola highlights the features of this system, including the ring used to scan bar codes and the readout attached to the forearm. The illustrator's decision to render the operator as a disembodied figure with eyes closed and an amputated hand is puzzling but suggestive of the new capacities for vision and knowledge offered by the embrace of this technology

Right: Lucas Systems uses personal wearable computers like these, developed by the company Vocollect, for their Jennifer™ VoicePlus voice-directed picking system

The next step in the development of such systems is the elimination of the readout altogether. If workers can be freed of the requirement to be constantly checking a screen, the thinking goes, they will be able to do their jobs faster and with fewer errors. The technology that allows this approach, called "voice-directed picking," replaces the visual manifest with an audible one that is broadcast to headsets worn by DC workers. Software translates order requirement data into synthesized human speech that directs the picking, packing, and shipping work. Voice-directed picking is deemed much faster because the pickers can be locating orders while communicating their location and actions via the headset's microphone. Because operators do not need to check their lists constantly, this system is also referred to as "eyes-free."

Some companies are trying to humanize the synthesized verbal commands in voice-directed picking. Lucas Systems, Inc., in partnership with Motorola, has developed a voice-directed picking system they refer to as Jennifer™ VoicePlus. Not only is the system of software, voice synthesizers, receivers, and scanners humanized, it is also gendered. One employee gushes, "You just have to listen to where Jennifer tells you to go, go get the product, and put it in the tote. There's no way of making errors with Jennifer because you give her a number that tells her that you're at the right location."[9] This step in location confirmation is one means of the sustained feedback necessary in a picking system like this. Jennifer's voice has a metallic shimmy as it breathlessly relays strings of numbers, verifications, questions, or commands. As speed remains an obsession, the voice playback is accelerated, almost eliminating the pauses between words. Here is a sample exchange between an employee (E) and Jennifer (J):

J: Sixonethreefour.
E: Nine four three.
J: Pickoneinnerpackofsix.
E: Grab one.
J: Oneinnerpackgrabbed. Pickthreeeach.
E: Grab three.
J: Bravo,putfiveeach.
E: Eight seven, put five.
J: Alfa,puttwoeach.
E: Five eight, put two.

J: India,puttwoeach.
E: Seven zero, put two.
J: Sixonethreeone.
E: Seven six four.
J: Pickoneeach.
E: Jennifer, what is item.
J: Itemonezerozerofivesixeightninesix.
E: Grab one.
J: Bravo,putoneeach.
E: Eight seven, put one.[10]

9. Lucas Systems, "Voice Picking at Do It Best with Jennifer and Motorola MC9000," YouTube, March 16, 2009, youtu.be/t7-Vlf47raA.

10. Lucas Systems, "Voice Picking at The Container Store: B2C Fulfillment," YouTube, March 22, 2012, youtu.be/alsdU0sR8jQ.

This seemingly nonsensical conversation is a precisely encrypted exchange but also a training session, as Jennifer directs the employee to operate in a more machine-like way. Such feedback mechanisms are familiar tools of the disciplined institution, from Robert Owen's experiments in self-assessment to the scientific management of a Taylorist shop floor to the cybernetic entanglements articulated by Norbert Wiener. However, the feedback in this case is not a matter of reciprocal calibration but a unilateral and ceaseless stream of numbers posed as questions and correctives. If the wearable scanners help workers to see like a computer, voice-directed picking helps them to operate like one.

In a further step of amputation, after giving up eyes and hands, workers give mobility itself over to the picking system in what is called a Man-on-Board Automated Storage and Retrieval System (ASRS). Such an approach is particularly well suited to high-density fulfillment centers and consists of small platforms mounted to cranes that move along tracks in two axes. This system allows workers on board to reach the tops of very high shelving units to assemble their orders. The automated dimension to this form of picking is through the movement itself. Workers do not steer the crane but are brought to each location directly in order to grab the right eaches, innerpacks, or cases to fulfill their orders. With Man-on-Board ASRS, a single worker can quickly cover one large, tall aisle, gliding from point to point, just as his or her colleague in the next aisle is doing, and the next, and so on to the end of the racks.

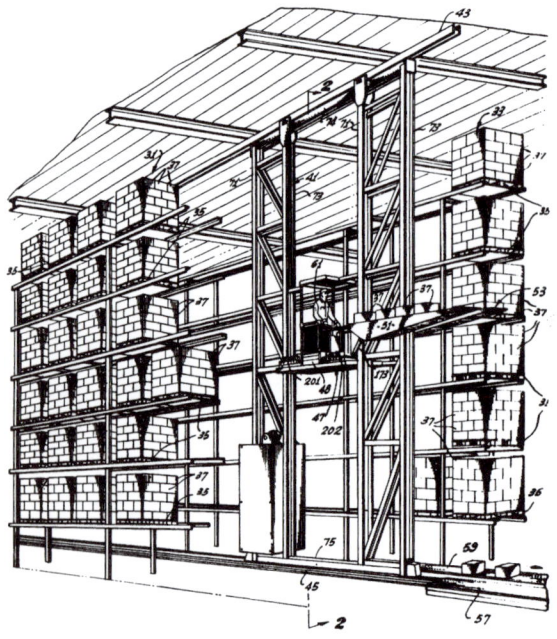

Distribution center employees are charged with, among other things, tasks of "picking" and "putting." To accelerate the picking process, many companies use an Automated Storage and Retrieval System (ASRS). This diagram depicts a Man-on-Board ASRS in which DC employees are automatically transported to the locations of the items on their order fulfillment list

Rather than bringing people to the objects, a company called Kiva has figured out a way to use their system to bring objects to people.[11] Their system replaces conveyors with small robotic drive units (RDUs) that transport "inventory pods" to a picking station, where a worker takes items from one rack and puts them on another, eventually to be packed and shipped. The robots are controlled by a series of inventory algorithms that search for the required inventory pod and direct the nearest robot to it. A grid of two-dimensional bar codes on the floor of the space provides checkpoints for the robots and controls their movements to ensure a smooth flow of traffic to the picking stations. As opposed to the conveyor-based model in which inventory is hierarchically managed and placed in predictable locations, the objects in Kiva's system have *no fixed location*. Because the RDUs can reach any point in the warehouse, and because their movement can be calibrated to eliminate traffic interference, the distribution of goods in the warehouse floor is constantly changing based on what customers have ordered. But neither is the organization of the floor random—to speed up the process, the most desirable inventory is kept close to the picking stations, while the rest is gradually pushed to the edges.

11. The short story "The Machine Stops," written in 1909 by E. M. Forster, addresses a number of themes apparent in contemporary logistics systems. Early in the story, one of characters derisively acknowledges that "of course she had studied the civilization that had immediately preceded her own—the civilization that had mistaken the function of the system, and had used it for bringing people to things, instead of for bringing things to people."

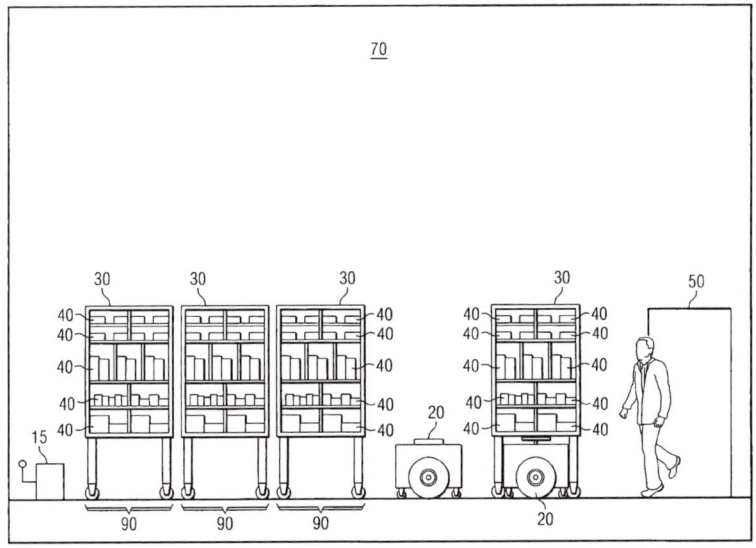

Kiva's order picking system involves automated robotic drive units equipped with threaded supports that rotate to lift inventory shelving units slightly off the ground in order to shuttle them to the correct picking station. Warehouse employees remain stationary in their fulfillment stations as inventory is brought to them

The logistics paradigm of inventory systems based on conveyors and regulated by bar codes like the UPC might be deemed "notational" due to their concern with controlling the exact paths of things through space and time. Notational logistics relies on routine: objects follow the same path over and over again. In this sense, UPS's claim to be a choreographer holds, if they are referring to this kind of logistics. However, while no less concerned with getting inventory from one place to another, the logistics of the two-dimensional bar code could instead be called "algorithmic" because it controls operations through formulae contingent on the specific requirements at any given moment. And, in spite of its claims to be a choreographer, much of UPS's logistics practices are in fact more concerned with establishing the basic performance conditions that ensure an object's arrival from one point to another and have less interest in controlling the specific nature of each journey.

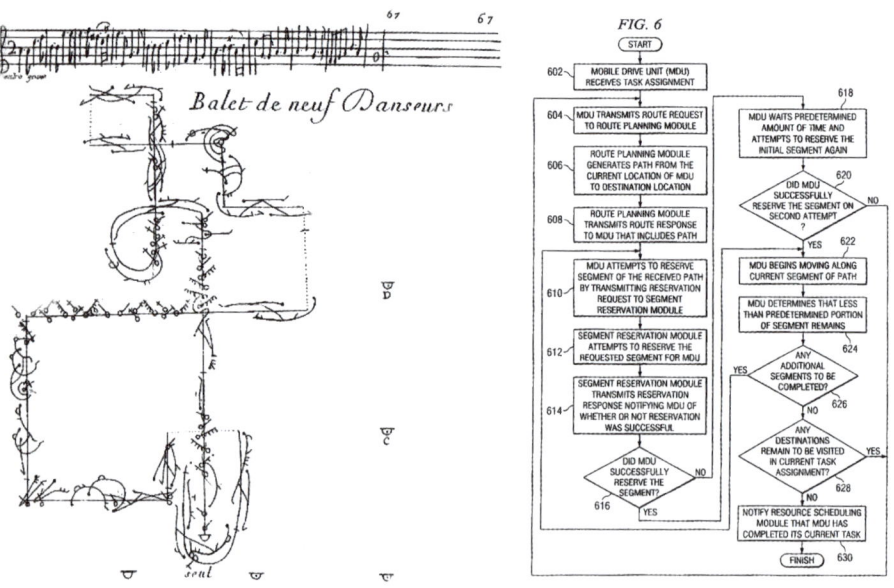

The distinction between these two forms of logistics helps us to puzzle through some issues in the current state of the field. Notational logistics follows a deductive, top-down route in which a plan is designed and executed repeatedly. With an algorithmic logistics, certain constraints are determined, but the process is allowed to unfold in unanticipated ways, perhaps even ways that exceed the intuition of the designers. In a Kiva warehouse, for example, what seems like a chaotic jumble makes total sense to the computer systems organizing it. However, for all the

Left: A page with dance notation from Raoul-Auger Feuillet's *Chorégraphie* from 1701.
Right: A sequencing diagram from one of Kiva Systems' many patent applications that explains how the paths of the robotic drive units are determined

sophistication behind the design of such a responsive system, the form and performance of the distribution center floor is based on one of the most fickle and irrational of principles: love. That is, the fluid constitution and configuration of the inventory is a dynamic index of consumer desire mediated through the bar code and mapped onto space, all fueled by extensive transportation and information networks. Logistics, in other words, underpins this apparent pursuit of happiness.

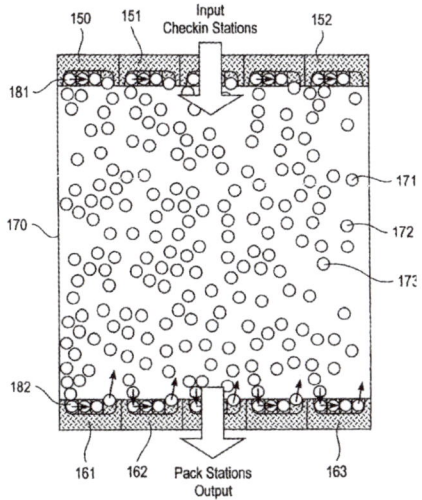

But does the ability to get the things we want faster and easier actually make us happier? In the emerging field of Happiness Studies, measures of happiness can be divided into three basic categories: "momentary feelings of joy and pleasure, … overall contentment with life, … [and] the quality of life achieved by developing and fulfilling one's potential, which has been called *eudaimonia* or 'the good life.'"[12] While conclusions that "individuals tend to make systematic errors when choosing between alternatives"[13] or that "happiness in the sense of subjective well-being doesn't seem to rise systematically with income"[14] might seem obvious, their emergence within institutional discourse is significant. After all, the "pursuit of happiness" is inscribed as an inalienable right in the Declaration of Independence and forms a fundamental feature of economic identity in the United States. Even more, mainstream economics still largely assumes that consumers behave to "maximize utility and that utility increases with the individual's consumption."[15] Such a belief has allowed economic growth to become a major policy imperative—enabled and reinforced by the logistics systems discussed here. However, if the findings from Happiness Studiers were to have some influence, these policies and their attendant logistics networks might change, triggering subsequent transformations in the ways consumable items are bought, sold, marketed, measured, and managed. Contemporary algorithmic logistics orchestrates hedonic landscapes of desire as customers pursue happiness. Could logistics also play a role in the development, instead, of a eudaimonic landscape, a landscape of fulfillment, of love? We might have to change the song, though: "When technology knows / Right where everything goes"—that's not logistics—"that's *ah-MOH-reh!*"

12. Daniel Nettle, quoted in Bruno S. Frey et al., *Happiness: A Revolution in Economics* (Cambridge: MIT Press, 2008), 5.
13. Ibid.
14. Amitava Krishna Dutt and Benjamin Radcliff, eds., *Happiness, Economics, and Politics: Towards a Multi-Disciplinary Approach* (Northampton, MA: Edward Elgar, 2009), 9.
15. Ibid., 8.

The paths of Kiva's mobile drive units are determined by coordinating software. Because the location of the inventory units is always changing, the drive units do not follow fixed paths

MICHIGAN by Chrysler

MAKING

If the late neo-liberal city is characterized by the exile of production from the urban core, the takeover of financial services, and the securitization of real estate as a key component of urban economies, the new technologies of digital fabrication, laser 3D scanning, 3D printing, and robotics are relocating some high-value fabrication activities back to the urban cores. The impact of these technologies on urban economies signals the return of production to the city. These changes will not only affect real estate values and even land uses and infrastructures: the changes may affect the whole structure of work and employment, and even the cultural perception of humankind itself. Some people have pointed to the rebirth of the *Homo Faber*. The *Homo Faber* (or Man the

Maker) departs from the idea that human beings are able to transform their environment through the use of tools, and is customarily opposed to the *Homo Ludens* (the playing man) in anthropological terms. The term arises from Latin writer Appius Claudius Caecus' famous sentence: *Homo faber suae quisque fortunae* (Every man is the artifex of his destiny), and was thoroughly reused by Italian humanists during the Renaissance. From very early times, labor was culturally associated with a humanist culture where humans can better themselves via the fruits of their own labor rather than by destiny or God's grace.

But during the Enlightenment, the *Homo Faber* remained in constant conversation with the machine. Diderot's *Encyclopedia* presents manual labor as the source of human happiness. The Enlightenment's perspective on the making of things coped with the onset of industrial production by not competing against the machine. It was in the mid-nineteenth century with the fast development of industrial mechanized production that social critics denounced the reckless abandon of luxury and the inexcusable promotion of waste. William Morris visited the Great Exhibition of 1851 and immediately felt the loss of craftsmanship as a result of industrial production.

Both under marxist and capitalist ideologies, the purpose of humankind was directed by what we can make or produce: Marx himself certainly thought of his political subjects as *Homo Faber*, referring to Benjamin Franklin's definition of "man as the tool-making animal." For Marx, capitalism is the regime where proletarians are alienated by capitalists from the object they produce and therefore are dehumanized, as they become progressively detached from the process of production, from their own humanity, and from their community of fellows.[1]

Trying to address the Marxist critique, the Arts and Crafts movement, an international movement in the decorative and fine arts that began

---

1. Karl Marx, *Karl Marx: Early Writings*, trans. and ed. T. B. Bottomore (New York: McGraw-Hill, 1964).

in Britain and expanded to Europe, North America, and Japan between 1880 and 1920, sought to retrieve craftsmanship as a central element of the arts. It stood for traditional craftsmanship using simple forms, and often used medieval, romantic, or folk styles of decoration. Unlike the Enlightenment, which avoided pointing at the brewing conflict between humans and machines, it was an essentially an anti-industrial doctrine which advocated economic and social reform through a return to the crafts. Even after being displaced by modernism and industrial capitalism in the 1930s, its influence continued among craft makers, designers, and town planners long afterwards. In fact, the Arts and Crafts movement may be considered to be at the origin of some of the political, social, and technological models that we can find in the *makers movement*, which is enacting contemporary sensing, algorithmic, and communication technologies in order to develop new forms of physically driven technologies, associated with a whole range of ethical and political trends.

Fordism triggered the demise of the Arts and Crafts movement after the industrial era due to reasons first laid out in Adam Smith's *The Wealth of Nations*: the division of labor focused on parts rather than wholes. Smith contrasted the monotonous routines of factory workers focusing on a very narrow action, hour after hour, day after day, with the speed and liveliness of the merchant class. Nevertheless, Smith believed that the industrial system would deliver craftsmanship rather than work done manually in the preindustrial mode. Henry Ford argued that strictly machine-built autos were of superior quality compared to those assembled in small workshops. The rise of microelectronics in manufacturing has provided further support for Fordism: microsensors do a much more rigorous job than humans. In sum, machines are better craftsmen than people.

Further developments of this system, driven through the rise of financial capitalism and automated production has produced a constant depreciation of labor's value *vis a vis* capital which is so acute that economists like Piketty state that there is no solution to inequality other than a politically driven redistribution of wealth.[2],

While contemporary post-Fordist urban culture has often been associated with the knowledge society, where most of the wealth and employment are created by the production of knowledge, the progressive elimination of agricultural and industrial sectors is starting to make the urban economy untenable. Several economists have stated that the cause for the 2008 crash was the neglect of manufacturing and the over-development of the financial sector.[3] After decades of service-driven urban economies and real estate speculation, the emerging fabrication technologies may be able to effectively re-industrialize cities.

Fully autonomous robots did not start to operate until the second half of the twentieth century. They were based on the work of Norbert Wiener, who formulated the principles of cybernetics, the basis of robotics and artificial intelligence, in 1948. *Unimate* was the first industrial robot; it worked on a General Motors assembly line at the Inland Fisher Guide Plant in Ewing Township, New Jersey, in 1961, transporting die castings from an assembly line and welding these parts on auto bodies. This was a dangerous task for workers, who might be poisoned by toxic fumes or lose a limb if they were not careful. In 1973, the first industrial robot with six electromechanically driven axes was developed by the Kuka Robot Group.

Commercial and industrial robots are in widespread use today to perform jobs more cheaply, more accurately, and more reliably than humans. Robots are also employed in some jobs which are too dirty, dangerous, or dull for humans. Robots are widely used in manufacturing, assembly, packing and packaging, transport, earth and space exploration, surgery, weaponry, laboratory research, safety,

2. Piketty, *Capital in the Twenty-First Century*.
3. Ha-Joon Chang, "Making Things Matters: This Is What Britain Forgot," *The Guardian*, 18 May 2016.

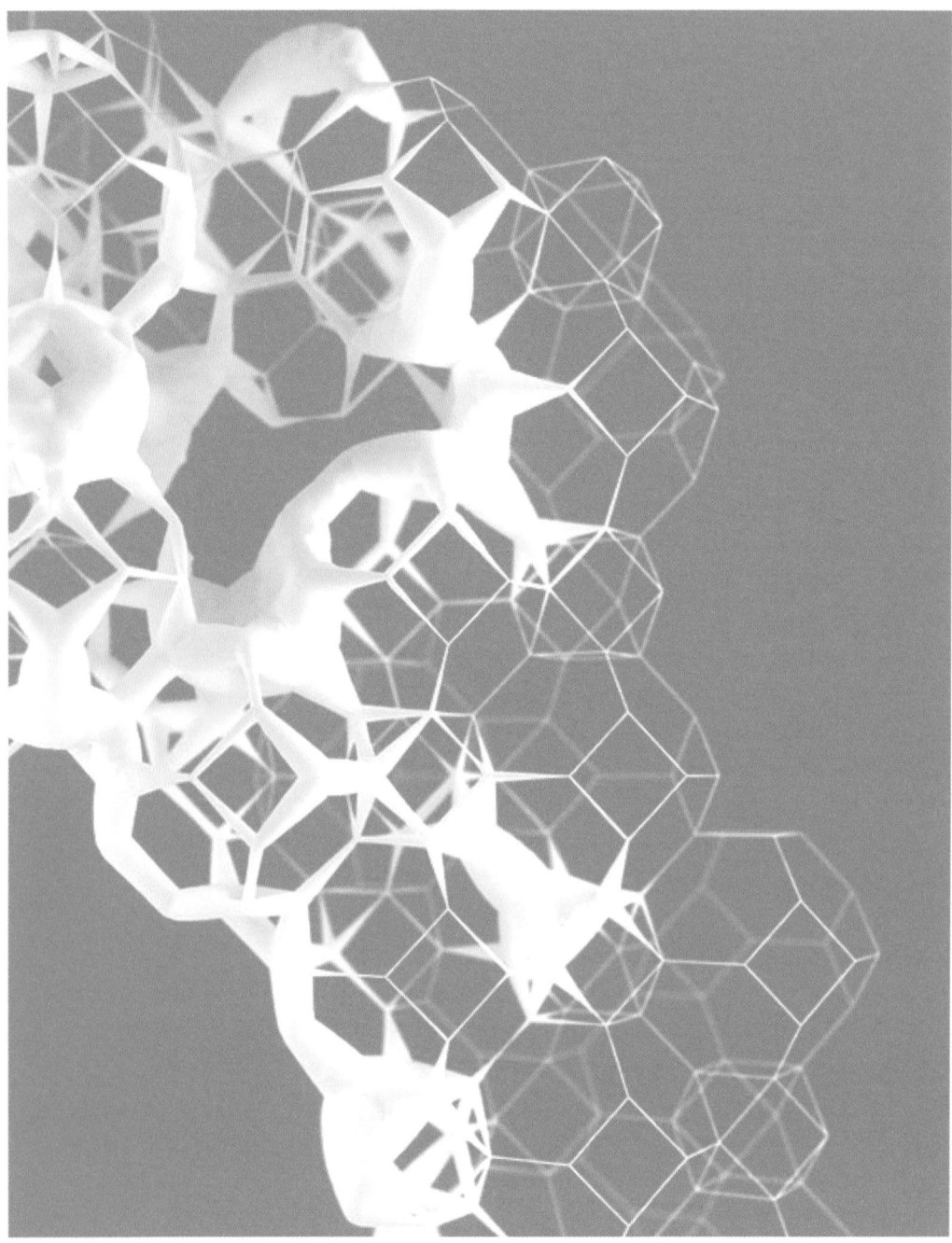

Inflate, Art Project by Domink Raskin

and the mass production of consumer and industrial goods. In the United States, already around one in five manual jobs is already done by a robot, and in twenty years it is expected that one in every three jobs will be performed by a robot in advanced economies: clearly this is a process with vast cultural and political implications.[4] If cities are fundamentally shaped by the capacity to sustain the collective production of goods—first agricultural, then industrial, now perhaps knowledge—the emergence of an entirely new form of production which is largely automatized does not need such a great population as before. If cities grew under capitalism as massive concentrations of human resources, the automatization of production may imply the end of cities as we know them.

"Industry 4.0" is the label that has been coined to describe the current trend of automation and data exchange in manufacturing technologies. It includes cyber-physical systems, the Internet of Things, and cloud computing. Industry 4.0 is aimed at creating what has been called a "smart factory." Within smart factories, *cyber-physical* systems monitor physical processes, create a virtual copy of the physical world, and make decentralized decisions. Over the Internet of Things, industrial cyber-physical systems communicate and cooperate with each other and with humans in real time, and via the *Internet of Services*, both internal and cross-organizational services are offered and used by participants of the value chain.

All of these advances have been labelled generally under the so-called *Fourth Industrial Revolution*, or 4IR, the fourth major industrial era since the Industrial Revolution of the eighteenth century. 4IR is enacted by a range of new technologies that are fusing the physical, digital, and biological worlds, and impacting all disciplines, economies, and industries. Central to this revolution are emerging technology breakthroughs in fields such as artificial intelligence, robotics,

---

4. In "Does the Left Have a Future?," John Harris points at automatized work as the cause of the decline of the left worldwide. (Published in *The Guardian*, 6 September 2016.)

the Internet of Things, autonomous vehicles, 3D printing, bio-computation, and nanotechnology.

If the securitization of urban real estate and the eradication of industrial production of the urban core produced its own cultures and lifestyle, the so-called 4IR is also creating its own cultures: the *makers* are a contemporary urban subculture representing a technology-based extension of DIY activities intersecting with *hacking* activities and revels in the creation of new devices as well as tinkering with existing ones. The maker culture remains committed to the physical, as an extension of the more traditional arts and crafts, or the guilds which once populated the medieval cities, and operate on their own specific moral principles.

Makers emphasize doing as the primary form of knowledge and personal and social development. They emphasize informal, networked, peer-led, and collective making as the vehicle for relating to both the environment and society. Community interaction and knowledge sharing are often mediated through networked technologies, with websites and social media tools forming the basis of knowledge repositories and a central channel for information sharing and exchange of ideas in shared spaces such as *hackspaces*.

The maker movement can be seen as a reaction to the growing sense of disconnection with the physical world in modern cities. Charles Jencks and Nathan Silver examined a sort of early Utopian vision of maker culture back in 1973, around the time when the modern mythology of industrial production of the post–World War II era was crumbling as a result of the 1968 revolt against the post-war Pax Americana and the 1973 oil crisis. In their book *Adhocism: The Case for Improvisation*, Charles Jencks and Nathan Silver outline many of the subjects that have been part of the more contemporary discourse on the rise of the maker culture; they link the culture to the myth of rugged individualism, the possibility of developing a libertarian counterculture based on the transgression of the post-war techno-corporate industrial complex through a return to matter, and, funnily enough, a reintroduction of the *Homo Ludens* into the new *Homo Faber*.[5] In the lineage of William Morris, the emergence of a popular culture of design and making was being presented as a mechanism for social and political liberation. That element of play, as opposed to mechanically organized work, is an interesting ancestor of contemporary versions of *Adhocism* in the form of today's maker cultures.[6]

Published a few years later, *Collage City* by Colin Rowe and Fred Koetter used the term *Bricolage* to address the jumbled effect produced by the close proximity of buildings from different architectural styles, in opposition to the work of Mies Van der Rohe, whom they called a "hedgehog", for being overly focused on a narrow concept. *Bricolage* was the term coined by Claude Levi-Strauss in *The Savage Mind*, to describe the characteristic patterns of mythological thought. *Bricolage* is the skill of using whatever is at hand and recombining things to create new entities. Levi-Strauss compared the *bricoleur* with the engineer as two alternative modes of *making* reality. As opposed to the *bricoleur*, the engineer, who is the enlightened "scientific mind", deals with projects holistically, taking into account the availability of materials, and the creation of new tools. Not unlike the *makers*, Levi Strauss' *Homo Faber* is also working *ad-hoc*, in a space where the maker and the designer, the individual and the collective, and the material and the craft coalesce in the act of doing, of making rather than in the abstraction of the real. And the image of the city they inhabit is also radically different from the modernist city.

In a remarkable parallelism to their Arts and Crafts ancestors, the maker communities also have a focus on health (food), sustainable development, environmentalism, vernacular culture ... and can, from that point of view, also be seen as a negative response to a

---

5. Charles Jencks and Nathan Silver, *Adhocism: The Case for Improvisation* (New York: Doubleday & Company, 1973).

6. In the aftermath of neo-liberalism, Joseph Grima's show "Maker Culture" at the 2012 Istanbul Biennale was a proof of the spiritual continuity of rather similar ideas about making.

globalized, mass-produced, disposables culture, the power of chain stores and multinationals, and consumerism. Except, this time, this approach has gained widespread acceptance, at the highest political levels. On 18 June 2014, President Barack Obama told participants in the first White House Maker Faire: "Your projects are examples of a revolution that's taking place in American manufacturing—a revolution that can help us create new jobs and industries for decades to come." "Today's DIY is tomorrow's 'Made in America.'" Obama pledged to open several national research and development facilities to the public. Moreover, the U.S. federal government renamed one of their national centers «America Makes."

The maker movement is thus a social movement with an artisan spirit in which the methods of digital fabrication—previously the exclusive domain of institutions—have become accessible at a personal scale, following a logical and economic progression similar to the transition from minicomputers to personal computers in the microcomputer revolution of the 1970s. Work has therefore abandoned its productivist connotations and become infused with a playful and material spirit. In 2005, Dale Dougherty launched *Make* magazine to serve this growing community, followed by the 2006 launch of a Maker Fair. The term, coined by Dougherty, grew into a full-fledged industry based on the growing number of DIYers who wanted to build something rather than buy it. Spurred primarily by the advent of *RepRap 3D* printing for the fabrication of prototypes, declining cost and broad adoption have opened up new areas of production. As it has become cost effective to make just one item for prototyping (or a small number of household items), this approach can be depicted as personal fabrication for "a market of one person."

But if the Arts and Crafts movement was associated with the Garden City and a nostalgic return to nature as an escape from the city of industrial capitalism, the makers movement is more closely associated with the recycling of former industrial quarters of metropolises, like Brooklyn in New York or 22@ in Barcelona. The makers are an essentially urban culture which is starting to challenge the humanistic precepts of the fully employed society and the perfect correspondence between urban populations and work availability, connected with the naïve ideologies of personal realization which formed the modernist idea of work. Quite clearly, those correspondences will not be possible with the progressive automation of work, and it is important that the reintroduction of play that was explored in the 1970s is considered when reintroducing new forms of making into the city.

If cities contain a full range of human activities, the city itself is also a manufacture. Urban planning techniques are obviously not entirely alien to industrial planning and many of the political intricacies that emerged throughout the twentieth century and the association between making and planning have to do with the unfolding of these relations. If the post-war industrial complexes in the United States and in the URSS were extremely effective at both generating mighty industrial infrastructures for mass-production, they were equally effective at designing all-encompassing life-style urban systems such as Levittown or the *khrushchoby*, linking in a very direct way the making of things and of cities under comprehensive political systems.

Likewise, the emerging cultures of urban makers are producing very distinctive forms of association and occupation of urban spaces. Sharing spaces of production and fabrication equipment and processing recycled or reclaimed materials are key aspects of these emerging ethics of urban production, often implemented through small-scale urban operations. A revision of new urban production technologies and how they may be reinserted in the urban fabric is now an important field of consideration and research for the making common.

REALITY MATTERS.
THE ROBOTIC TOUCH*

Fabio Gramazio, Matthias Kohler, and Jan Willmann

REALITY MATTERS

With the robot we turn our attention to the physical nature of architecture. In so doing, we open up new aesthetic and functional perspectives and address the digital in architecture as a radically contemporary building culture. Through not only digitally designed but also digitally materialised architectures, it becomes possible to engage with both the fundamental issues of our digital age and the raison d'être of architecture itself—that is, its concrete physical realisation.

Digital technologies have handed architecture a very powerful tool, which has led to an explosion of experimentation in the last two decades. This technology has shaped an entire generation of architects and has had a long-lasting effect on the expression and understanding of contemporary architecture. The capacity to algorithmically manipulate large amounts of data in the virtual space of the computer has made it possible to overcome not only the design principles of modernism but also their standardised industrial forms of production.[1] Paradoxically, the dematerialisation of architecture, often invoked during the 1990s, is no longer an issue today. On the contrary,

---

1. Clearly, modernist standardisation cannot be traced back to the pure rationalisation of production. Rather as Mario Carpo states in his article Non Standard Morality: "Digital Technology and its Discontents, an enormous range of participation," distribution, and complexity was opened up through the perpetual combination and adaptation of standardised processes, notations, and building components. The result is therefore both a new technological and a new cultural dimension of architectural production. Cf. M. Carpo, "Non Standard Morality : Digital Technology and Its Discontents," in *Architecture Between Spectacle and Use*, ed. A. Vidler, (New Haven: Yale University Press for the Clark Institute, 2008).

* This essay was first published in the book *The Robotic Touch–How Robots Change Architecture*, edited by Fabio Gramazio, Matthias Kohler und Jan Willmann, Zurich: Park Books, 2014.

we are now dealing with a "materialisation of the digital" that goes far beyond purely formally motivated architectures. Indeed, today all indications are that the digital is set for a victory march. Interpreting this positively, one can speak of a long-aspired-to technological liberation of architectural production through digital fabrication. One could also speak of the newly won autonomy of architecture. The broad scope and the consequences of this paradigm shift put into perspective a certain scepticism sometimes evinced towards the use of digital technologies in architecture. The central question is how these technologies change architectural production at large and how the digital age can therefore find its most pertinent architectural expression. This question fundamentally shapes our work with the robot and crystallises in the following assertion: Only if digital architecture becomes more radical, more material, only if it begins to understand itself as both aesthetic *and* material practice will architecture finally come into the digital era.[2]

RADICAL TECHNOLOGICAL INTENSIFICATION
It should not escape our attention that the impact of new technologies in architecture follows no predictable order or predetermined pattern ; rather they obtain their own cultural significance through custom, use, and transformation. As history has shown, technology does not develop in isolation from its cultural context ; it emerges out of a process of differentiation from all the associated social, political, and economic interactions. And, as Walter Benjamin points out, the architectural significance of new technologies is not ready-made; it is always being fulfilled through "making use of" its possibilities, which are derived from the perspective of the present.[3] The technology of the robot cannot be exempted from this cultural mechanism.

Whereas eight years ago, when we introduced the robot into the architectural context, it was considered a quasi "exotic" machine and may have been understood as a passing fashion, today robot-based architectural fabrication is starting to permeate the discipline. The accompanying "demystification" of the robot has led to a functional and pragmatic but in no way disenchanted point of view. The architectural double meaning of the robot consists of, on the one hand, digitally connecting to the constructive canon of architecture, and on the other, proposing an alternative to prevailing paradigms of digital architecture. In our perspective, the true significance of robots in architecture is not primarily about being technologically up to date nor about obeying economic pressure to exploit such technologies. On the contrary, the aim is an unbiased and therefore liberated use of technology in order to explore its true conceptual potential and architectural relevance.

2. This is all the more important if one considers that the fabrication technologies that emerged in the machine age changed the design process itself only insignificantly. As the modernist avant-garde shows, the buildings are still characterised by the already existing categories of tectonic elements (column, supporting beam and wall, etc.) and also by their very design logic (draft, grid, and cross section, etc.). Cf. J. H. Gleiter, "Kampfplatz der Theorie : Das Ornament im digitalen Zeitalter," public lecture, University of Innsbruck, 20 November.

3. W. Benjamin, "Das Kunstwerk im Zeitalter seiner technischen Reproduzier- barkeit," W. Benjamin, in *Gesammelte Schriften*, volumes 1 and 2, ed. R. Tiedemann and H. Schweppenhäuser, (Frankfurt: Suhrkamp, 1974), 477.

This becomes clear in the most radical way in the project *Flight Assembled Architecture*.[4] The project represents the first architectural installation to be built autonomously by flying robots: several "Quadrocopters" assembled over 1,500 elements to create a porous, tower-like aggregation. What unfolds is a 1:100 scale model of an architectural vision for a 600 metre high *Vertical Village*. With a total of 180 floors, the urban structure provides living space for 30,000 inhabitants. The structure makes use of a grid-like organisation that allows for a great degree of freedom in the variable arrangement of multi-functional modules. However, the grid does not run horizontally as in a conventional urban organisation; rather, it is turned vertically. Finally, both ends of the grid close to create a circular whole. Thereby the resulting cylindrical structure is not only self-stabilising but also embodies a new type of spatially differentiated and programmatically diverse, dense urban organisation.[5]

4. Cf. F. Gramazio, M. Kohler, and J. Willmann, "The Vertical Village," in *Flight Assembled Architecture*, eds. F. Gramazio, M. Kohler, and R. D'Andrea, Eds. (Orléans: Editions HYX), 13-23, 2013.

5. Here, the Vertical Village almost provides a complementary (although physical) description of that which William J. Mitchell describes in his article, *Space, Place and the Infobahn*. Cf. W. J. Mitchell, "Space, Place and the Infobahn," (Cambridge/ MA: MIT Press, 1995), 163–174.

Flight Assembled Architecture Research and exhibition project FRAC Ventre, Orleans, France 2011-2012

Flight Assembled Architecture represents, above all, a technological intensification that introduces a radically expanded scope of digital fabrication. This results from the swarm-like deployment of the flying robots, in which they reciprocally adjust their operations and cooperatively build the *Vertical Village*.[6] Correspondingly, the "Quadrocopter" is used as an enabling technology and also serves as a "conceptual door opener" in order to make possible a radical architectural utopia that does not need to exclude its concrete material implementation. Here, the air- space not only corresponds to a constructive environment but also becomes a comprehensive design paradigm.

A type of "suspense" results between a physical architectural installation, which is being built almost over the visitor's head, and its manifestation as a future utopia in the tradition of ideal cities.[7] *Flight Assembled Architecture* therefore fosters a revision of the city as a robot-built urbanity.[8] At a scale one hundred times smaller than the vision, the installation calls into question the supposedly clear line between utopia and reality. At the same, time the boundaries between architecture and robotics become less distinct here, so that the "border between the thinkable and the feasible" is newly explored. *Flight Assembled Architecture* thereby expands the conceptual scope and constructive scale of robotic fabrication and promises a productivist reconceptualisation of digital architecture. Only by exploring the physical possibilities and the specific limitations of this technology will the architectural capacities of future robotic fabrication unfold.

MAKE FROM LESS

Key to robotic fabrication is its fundamental affinity for additive construction principles, which are inscribed in the tradition of architecture. The robot's capabilities to digitally inform the material and therefore to make the best possible use of the given material resources directly relates to the contemporary discussion about sustainability.[9] Projects such as *Mesh Mould* clearly demonstrate the ability of the robot to build up architectural material exactly where it is actually needed. Here, an industrial robot extrudes filaments freely in space, and produces digitally controlled three-dimensional mesh structures, which in turn can be used in situ as leaking formwork for free-form concrete construction. Apart from the form-defining aspect, the project investigates the reinforcing capacity of these meshes. In this way, two separate requirements, reinforcement and formwork, are folded into one single robotic fabrication process.

6. Cf. F. Augugliaro, S. Lupashin, M. Hamer, C. Male, M. Hehn, M. W. Mueller, J. Willmann, F. Gramazio, M. Kohler, and R. D'Andrea, "The Flight Assembled Architecture Installation : Flying Machines Cooperatively Constructing Structures," in *IEEE Control Systems Magazine*, 2014.

7. Cf. A. Tönnesmann, *Monopoly. Das Spiel, die Stadt und das Glück*, (Berlin: Verlag Klaus Wagenbach 2011), 85–126.

8. M. Kohler, "Aerial Architecture," in *LOG 25*, (2012): 23–30.

9. This seems all the more important when one considers that "grey energy" is particularly relevant for newly built structures because it can amount to 50 % of the entire energy expenditure when projecting a hundred years of use for a building. Cf. Graue Energie von Gebäuden, Merkblatt 2032 SIA, Zurich, 2010.

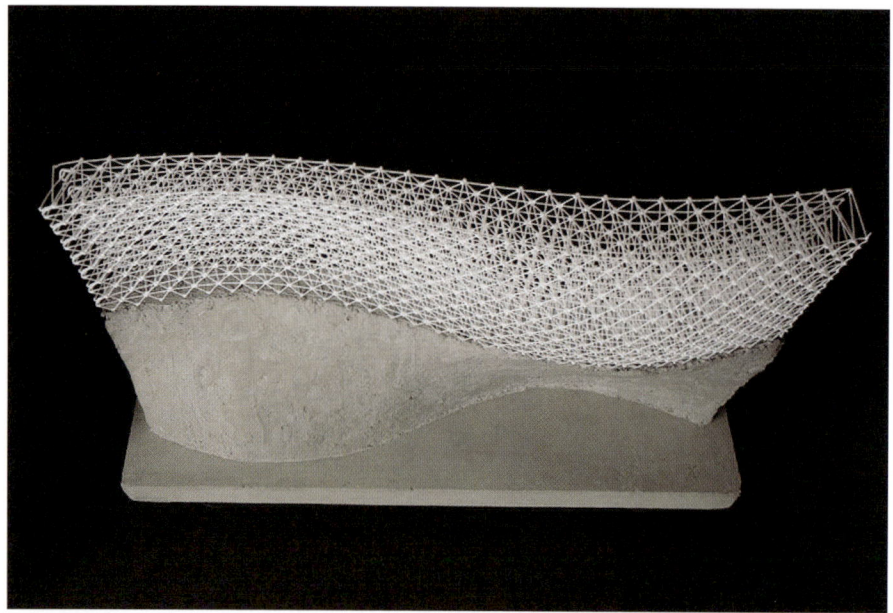

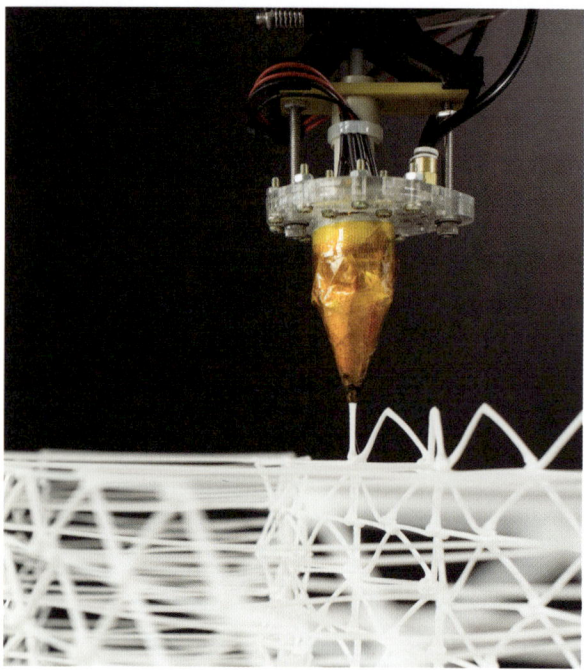

Mesh Mould Research project, Singapore-ETH Centre, Future Cities Labratory, Singapore, ETH Zurich, Switzerland, 2012

The liberty afforded by free spatial extrusion provides the opportunity to fabricate three-dimensional meshes well-adapted to the forces that act upon them.[10] Such an approach yields a high potential for resource efficiency, first because it enables the digitally controlled fabrication of geometrically complex building forms to conform with their required structural performance, and second because these can be produced additively without any formwork or other construction aids. The amount of waste material is reduced to a minimum. From this perspective, what is sustainable is that which can be efficiently built and at the same time individually adapted to specific architectural requirements.

Furthermore, the future prospect of environmentally sound digital fabrication even extends to include building systems that leverage real-time robotic control with the deliberate use of low-grade, locally available building materials. In *Rubble Aggregations*, the robot aggregates building structures from arbitrary "as found" concrete waste on the construction site. The robot grasps individual rubble fragments, scans them, calculates their specific positioning, and intelligently assembles them into architectural structures. Such examples indicate the great promise of future sustainable digital fabrication processes: With the robot, high-performing and very specific building parts can be made out of relatively simple—even unpredictable—raw materials, ranging from filaments to concrete rubble, so that the greatest possible aesthetic and functional value can be extracted from each of the used materials. If materially efficient building processes are key factors for a sustainable development of the built environment, then robots with their unique constructive capacities must necessarily play a central role.

THE "INTERACTIVE" CONNECTION OF HUMAN AND MACHINE

Again and again the question arises of why all these manufacturing processes cannot be managed through traditional, that is to say, manual means and methods. And indeed, it is true that a person might be able to build a simple brick wall more easily and quickly than an industrial robot can. But what might be described as the "operationability of the robot"[11] becomes valid as soon as a certain complexity is reached: that is, where manifold design and constructive relationships exceed the human capacity to oversee and act deliberately upon them.

This in no way implies a dichotomy of human and machine, however. Rather, we should think in terms of a complementarity in which humans and machines are equivalent partners in a collaborative process. This partnership is demonstrated in the project *Spatial Aggregations*. Here, the robot-assisted assembly enables the buildup of complex spatial structures from simple rod elements without any auxiliary support. What is essential here is the direct intervention of the human in the machinic process. The robot grasps an element, cuts it, marks the connecting points, and positions it freely in space in relation to the already built structure.

10. Cf. N. Hack and W. Lauer, "Mesh Mould," in *Architectural Design, Made by Robots Challenging Architecture at the Large Scale*, ed. F. Gramazio and M. Kohler, (Chichester: John Wiley & Sons, 2014).

11. M. Kohler, F. Gramazio, and J. Willmann, "Die Operationalität von Daten und Material im Digitalen Zeitalter," in *Die Zukunft des Bauens*, (Munich : DETAIL, 2011), 8–17.

A person adds elements that connect the rod held in space by the robot and the already built structure. The slight imprecisions brought in through human intervention are compensated for by each element that the robot puts into its absolute position. In contrast to completely automated manufacturing routines, *Spatial Aggregations* is an architectural process in which the unique ability of the robot to place a component effortlessly in space is combined with human dexterity in a seamless cooperation.

In our view, the robotic capacity to manufacture complexity does not necessarily correspond to a devaluation of the manifold abilities of human beings. On the contrary, human and robot complement one another ideally, whereby machine-enabled speed and inexhaustible productivity can be connected with human ingenuity, intuition, and creativity. This coupling should not be geared towards compensating for the deficits of humans. Instead, it should be about the appreciation and valuing of unique human qualities: that is, allowing humans to interface with robots wherever this can enhance architectural quality.

A NEW DIGITAL CULTURE OF BUILDING

Although the digital paradigm has deeply changed the entire world as well as our perceptions of it, its impact on architecture has up to now been marginal. This point has been taken up in the criticism voiced by Antoine Picon : In architecture, the poetics of computation have not yet fully developed. Heretofore, asserts Picon, digital architecture has exhausted itself, intoxicated by the possibilities of generating complex geometries.[12] Thus he concludes that the current digital architecture has not yet managed to develop a profound cultural and aesthetic meaning and so far has not succeeded in using the digital technologies to convey a social dimension.

With our projects and research we mean to convey that the robot can act as a catalyst to impart cultural significance to digital architecture. The robot characterises a seminal change in the production conditions of architecture. It places digital architecture in a close (creative) dialogue with reality. The robot can thus play a decisive role specifically because through it, the digitalisation of architecture becomes physical and tangible. This takes away the abstract and forced artificial character from the digital in architecture and imbues it with a distinct aesthetic significance and identity. The result is an increased sensuousness that originates no longer from outside, through the favouring of formal complexity, but rather arises from inside through the intensification of the creative, material, and cultural expressive content of digitally fabricated architecture. And out of this grows a new contemporary digital building culture.

This essay was first published in the book *The Robotic Touch – How Robots Change Architecture*, edited by Fabio Gramazio, Matthias Kohler und Jan Willmann, Zurich: Park Books, 2014.

12. Cf. A. Picon, "Digital Architecture and the Poetics of Computation," in *Metamorph Focus : Katalog zur 9. Architektur Biennale von Venedig* (2004), 58–69.

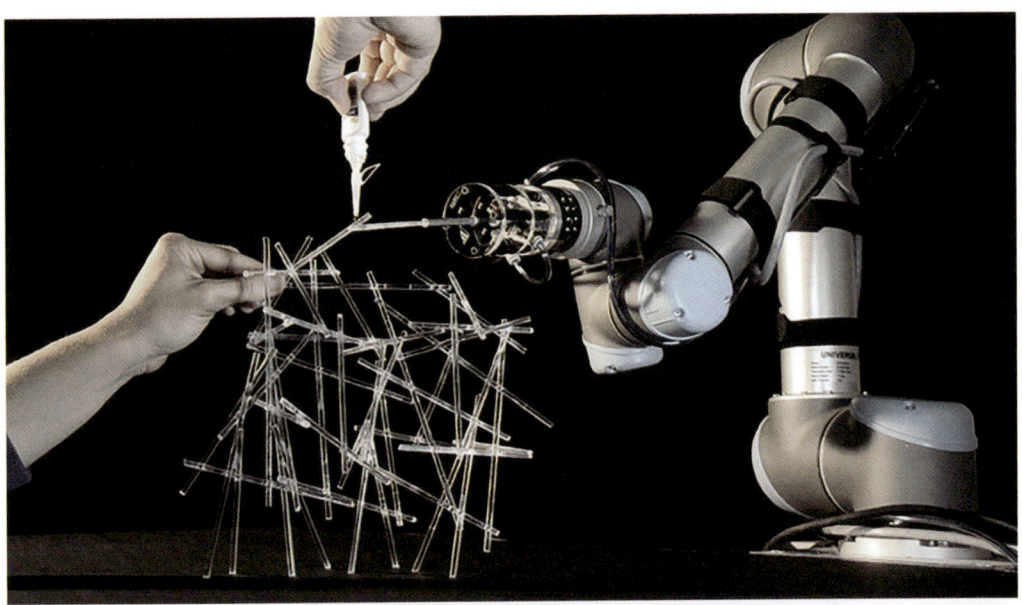
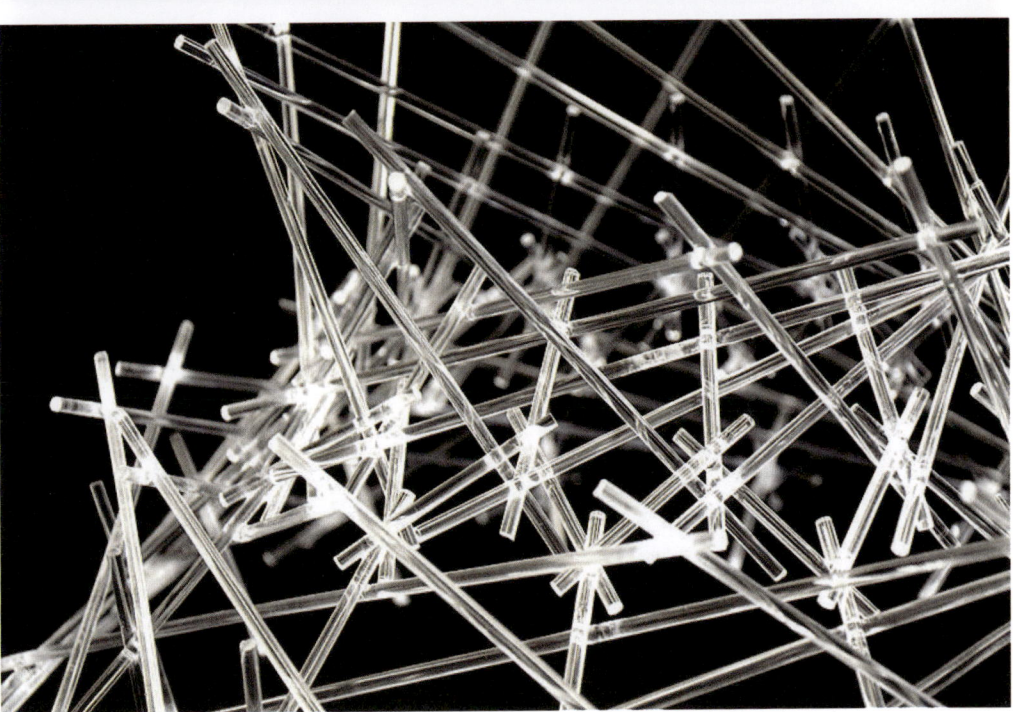

Spatial Aggregations Teaching Project, ETH Zurich, Switzerland, 2012

REPUBLICS OF MAKERS
Mario Carpo

Computers are machines: so we tend to think they work like all the other machines we know. They don't. Computers are a new kind of machine. They do not work like any other machine we have ever seen during the modern age and the industrial revolution. Computers are post-industrial, post-modern, post-scientific machines. If we use computers to make physical stuff, computers follow a technical logic that is the opposite of that of the industrial age. And if we use computers to process information, computers follow a scientific logic that is the opposite of that of modern science. Computers make things the way a good artisan workshop could, not the way any modern industrial factory would. And computers calculate and design objects the way a very smart artisan could, not the way any modern engineer or scientist would. In short, both as tools to *make* and as tools to *think*, computers are closer to the traditional, pre-industrial way of doing things than to the modern, scientific, industrial world as we know it, or knew it—a world that is already falling apart, all around us, precisely because digital tools have started to destroy all of its technical, social, and economic foundations.

Artificial Intelligence is one of the most disruptive, revolutionary innovations of all times. The new science of computation is, simply, the reverse and nemesis of the scientific revolution that started with Galileo and Newton, and indeed of all Western science derived from Aristotelian, Euclidian, and Scholastic premises: a vast and controversial subject that demands a separate discussion.[1] To the contrary, the economic principles underpinning a digital design-to-production

---

1. That is the topic of my forthcoming book, *The Second Digital Turn: Design Beyond Intelligence* (Cambridge, MA: MIT Press, 2017). I discussed the technical logic of digital mass-customization and its implications for design and manufacturing in *The Alphabet and the Algorithm* (Cambridge, MA: MIT Press, 2011): see in particular chapter 3, 81–106.

workflow have been known for almost thirty years, and the reasons why digital manufacturing and industrial production follow opposite technical logics are now largely understood. The technical logic of the industrial world is based on mass-production and economies of scale. Most tools of industrial mass-production use casts, molds, dies, or other forms of mechanical matrixes. Think of a traditional printing press: any matrix used to stamp a copy (an engraving, a woodcut, or a metal plate, for example) costs money, hence once a matrix is made, it makes sense to keep using it to print as many copies as possible, and amortize its cost. This is the logic of industrial standardization: *the more identical copies we make, the cheaper each copy will be.*

Digital fabrication, however, doesn't work that way. In its pure, archetypal form, digital fabrication—either subtractive or additive—does not use mechanical matrixes, casts, or molds. Without mechanical matrixes, there is no need to repeat the same form in order to amortize the cost of the production set-up, hence every piece, when digitally made (milled or 3D printed, for example), is a one-off: making more identical copies of the same item will not make any of them cheaper; making all of them different will not make any of them more expensive. Standardization no longer saves money, and individual variations no longer cost money: just as thirty years ago we learned that, using a digital laser printer, we could print 100 identical copies of the same page, or 100 different pages, at the same unit cost, today we know that we can 3D print 100 identical copies of the same chair, or 100 different chairs (albeit different within given limits) at the same unit cost. An economist would say that in a fully digital production workflow the marginal cost of production is always the same. Economies of scale do not apply to digital manufacturing: using a digital design-to-production workflow, the production cost per unit in the most humongous factory, designed to churn out one billion identical pieces per day, and in a digital workshop at the corner of the street, meant to make a few different pieces every now and then, is theoretically the same; as a result, standardized, centralized production is no longer either needed or warranted.[2] Digital mass-customization, or the mass-production of different pieces at the same unit cost, is the universal technical and economic logic of digital manufacturing—the default mode of use of all digital tools.

Additionally, as the costs of electronic computation have been steadily decreasing for at least the last forty years, many have recently come to the conclusion that, for most practical purposes, the cost of computation is asymptotically tending to zero. Indeed, the current notion of Big Data is based on the assumption that an almost unlimited amount of digital data will soon be available at almost no cost, and similar premises have further fueled the expectation of a forthcoming "zero marginal costs society": a society where, exception made for some upfront and overhead costs

---

2. Alongside the scaleless technical logic of digital mass-customization, as discussed here, other logistical factors speak against the centralization of a digital design and fabrication workflow: a small digital workshop can use local materials and locally sourced electricity, but can profit from data, design, intelligence, and expertise drawn from any remote source at zero cost. Additionally, today's robotic manufacturing is increasingly versatile: robots can be given different tasks to be kept busy around the clock—unlike traditional industrial machines, which must repeat the same operation many times over, or be kept idle. A robotic fabrication set-up can be easily reconfigured to carry out a variety of different operations, further abating the fixed costs of the installation without any need for scale.

(the costs of building and maintaining some facilities), many goods and services will be free for all.³ And indeed, against all odds, an almost zero marginal cost society is already a reality in the case of many services based on the production and delivery of electricity: from the recording, transmission, and processing of electrically encoded digital information (bits) to the production and consumption of electrical power itself. Using renewable energies (solar, wind, hydro), the generation of electrical power is free, except for the cost of building and maintaining installations and infrastructure; and given the recent progress in the micro-management of intelligent electrical grids, it is easy to imagine that in the near future the cost of servicing a network of very small, local hydro-electric generators, for example, could easily be devolved to local communities of prosumers who would take care of those installations as they tend to their living environment, on an almost voluntary, communal basis.⁴ This was already often the case during the early stages of electrification, before the rise of AC (alternate current, which, unlike DC, or direct current, could be carried over long distances): AC became the industry's choice only after the inventions of Galileo Ferraris and others in the 1880s.⁵

Likewise, at the micro-scale of the electronic production and processing of bits and bytes of information, the Open Source movement and the phenomenal surge of some crowd-sourced digital media (including some so-called social media) in in the first decade of the twenty-first century have already proven that a collaborative, zero cost business model can effectively compete with products priced for profit on a traditional marketplace: as the success of *Wikipedia*, Linux, or Firefox proves, many are happy to volunteer their time and labor for free when all can profit from the collective work of an entire community without having to pay for it.⁶ This is now technically possible precisely because the fixed costs of building, maintaining, and delivering these service are very small; hence, from the point of view of the end-user, negligible.

Yet, regardless of the fixed costs of the infrastructure, content—even user-generated content—has costs, albeit for the time being these are mostly hidden, voluntarily borne, or inadvertently absorbed by the prosumers themselves. For example, the wisdom of *Wikipedia* is not really a wisdom of crowds: most *Wikipedia* entries are de facto curated by fairly traditional scholar

---

3. See in particular Jeremy Rifkin, *The Zero Marginal Cost Society: The Internet of Things, the Collaborative Commons, and the Eclipse of Capitalism* (New York: Palgrave Macmillan, 2014).

4. Ibid., 97–106.

5. Due to the availability of AC transformers by the mid-1880s, AC (unlike DC) could be converted into high voltage to be carried over long distances, then reconverted into low voltage for local distribution. Electricity could then be mass-produced, even far from cities or factories, in the pursuit of economies of scale or of available resources (hydro power).

6. See Eric S. Raymond, *The Cathedral and the Bazaar: Musings on Linux and Open Source by an Accidental Revolutionary* (Beijing: O'Reilly Media, 1999); Howard Rheingold, *Smart Mobs: The Next Social Revolution* (Cambridge, MA: Perseus Publishing, 2002), cf. in particular ch. 2, "Technologies of Cooperation," 29–62; Rifkin, *The Zero Marginal Cost Society*, 210–15.

communities, and these communities can contribute their expertise for free only because their work has already been paid for by others—often by universities. In this sense, *Wikipedia* is only piggybacking on someone else's research investments (but multiplying their outreach, which is one reason for its success). Ditto for most Open Source software, as training a software engineer, coder, or hacker takes time and money—an investment for future returns that in many countries around the world is still borne, at least in part, by public institutions.

At the same time, the asymptotic abatement of the costs of computation has another major consequence, mostly undetected and unaccounted for to date, which goes in quite a different direction. Any operation of buying and selling has its own costs—transaction costs. These costs are mostly fixed, i.e. the cost of processing any given transaction is not much affected by the size of the transaction itself: the paperwork required to sell a batch of identical bottles, or to export them to another country, is more or less the same if the bottles being sold are 10, 100, or 100,000. Therefore, in order to amortize these fixed costs, once again it makes sense to aggregate supply and demand and to buy or sell in bulk as many items as possible. This logic however does not apply if the transactions are processed electronically, automatically, or algorithmically, and the cost of each transaction tends to zero. If each transaction costs nothing, the number of transactions we process to purchase any given number of items is irrelevant. In such an environment, we could buy one million identical bottles at the same time, or one bottle at a time one million times, at the same cost per bottle. Or, in other terms, buying one bottle, or ten, or one million in bulk would not make any of them cheaper. Couple this with the normal state of affairs resulting from the digital mass-customization of a design-to-production workflow: the result is an economic environment where both production and commerce are equally unaffected by size—a *flat marginal cost society*, a *society without scale*.

Add to this another consideration: if the fixed cost of a transaction is nothing, monetized transactions bearing on items that are worth very little, or almost nothing, become economically viable. This means that transactions that until now could only exist as gifts, without any monetary string attached, can now be effectively monetized: marketed, bought and sold at a price. When the paperwork to rent a car could take one hour—as it did until not long ago, with a new pile of documents to read and sign each time, often showing up in person in the office of a rental car company—no one dreamt of renting a car for less than one day. Today, when one has an account with a company like Zipcar, for example, the reservation and payment of the rental takes seconds—online. Hence, renting ten different cars for ten nonconsecutive hours on Zipcar already costs more or less the same as renting the same car for ten consecutive hours—a pricing policy that ten years ago any salesman would have flagged as a rookie mistake. Today we can pay to rent a bike for twenty minutes—the typical transaction that until recently could only have occurred as a mutual favor among friends ("Can I take your bike? I'll be right back.") And the same logic equally applies to micro-rentals of all sorts, which can now be managed at a level of granularity that until recently would not have made any economic sense—as each of these micro-transactions is worth, individually, so little. Plenty of such minute transactions can now be brought to market, which sure enough is already disrupting many long-established traditional markets and their respective business models: that of the hospitality industry, for example; and the financial industry may be next in line.[7]

In short, all such instances point to a *flat marginal cost society* which is quite unlike the zero marginal cost society that some are predicting: due to the asymptotic abatement of the costs of computation, we are heading towards a *society without scale*, not towards a *society without costs*. This will come as no surprise to the design professions: while we know that the costs of computation are declining, and possibly tending to zero, we are also well aware that the same is not happening to the materials we need for building: steel or concrete cannot be pulled out of thin air, the way solar power can, and no matter how much we recycle, building materials will always be in limited supply, hence expensive. Designers must hence learn to cope with a *flat marginal cost society*—a society where economies of scale have disappeared from production and commerce. This is a daunting task, because this scaleless logic upends all economic and social foundations of the world in which we live. On the contrary, the zero cost model (where all is free because all is plenty) may apply to the way we produce and deliver streams of electrons, either as carriers of data or of energy, but it is irrelevant to the production and delivery of physical stuff.

None of the above is unprecedented. Civilizations existed and thrived before the rise of industrial mass-production, before the rise of free markets, and before the rise of monetary economies. Digital libertarians and hacker communities have long taken inspiration from the economic and social model of the feudal commons—collectively managed patches of rural land where medieval peasants (commoners) worked not for pay but for benefits, based on covenants, agreements, and obligations. Indeed, the expression "digital commons" has been current for some time to refer to some of today's digitally driven collaborative work environments, which are now increasingly viable due to the declining costs of electronic computation (and, soon, of self-generated electrical power).[8] But while the feudal commons can be a precedent, or even a model,

7. Carpo, *The Second Digital Turn*, ch. 5; Carpo, "Micro-managing Messiness: Pricing, and the Costs of a Digital Non-Standard Society," in James Andrachuk, Christos C. Bolos, Avi Forman, and Marcus A. Hooks, eds., "Money," special issue, *Perspecta* 47 (2014): 219–226.

8. It is not known who started to invoke the medieval commons as a precedent and an inspiration for the collaborative spirit of the Free Software and Open Source movements, or when the comparison was first made. Eric Raymond's seminal *The Cathedral and the Bazaar* (printed in 1999 but circulated on the Internet since 1997) refers to the medieval cathedral as an example of closed design—the opposite of the bazaar, which Raymond sees as a model for digital hackerdom. Raymond also relates the future of intellectual property on the Internet to the legal precedent of homesteading (the appropriation of a common natural resource by an act of labor, which leads to enclosure; i.e., the exact opposite of what today's "digital commons" are meant to stand for: *The Cathedral and the Bazaar*, 76–77). Jeremy Rifkin traces the contemporary, libertarian rediscovery of the medieval commons to his book *Biosphere Politics* (New York: Crown, 1991), which however referred to the common ownership of natural resources, not to the IP issues brought about by the development of digital technologies, barely nascent back then (cited in *The Zero Marginal Cost Society*, 189–200, 202). Howard Rheingold may have been the first to claim, verbatim, that "The Internet was built to function as a commons," and to relate the medieval commons to "the hacker ethic" and to "tomorrow's technologies of cooperation" (*Smart Mobs*, 48).

for a new economy without costs, it hardly relates to an economy of makers where artifacts are produced at nonscalable costs. In fact, more or less at the same time as the commons flourished in the feudal countryside, such an economy of artisan making was taking shape within the fortified walls of late medieval cities, where a new breed of free craftsmen invented ex nihilo the rules of a new society based on manufacturing, and found new ways to manage and organize manual production in the absence of slave labor.

At a time when feudal land could be neither bought nor sold, but only inherited, cities fought for and won privileges and franchises from their feudal lords, and on that basis established a new system of political and economic freedoms inside their walls: first and foremost, the freedom to choose an art or craft and learn it, then to practice it as a free craftsman incorporated in one of the city guilds; manufactured goods could be independently bought and sold, but all aspects of production and commerce, including prices, were strictly regulated by the guilds, which also wielded most of the political power in town. The late medieval city-states, or communes, were republics of makers, where citizenship itself (or the medieval equivalent of it) was the privilege of guild members—i.e., of citizens who could practice an art or craft. Starting in Italy and Germany, late medieval communes invented many economic and even spiritual building blocks of modernity: from the morality of profit under corporate rules (based on frugality, operosity, and the ethics of hard work) to the democratic checks and balances of corporate (i.e., guild-based) governance in republican city-states still nominally under feudal banners. Following the seminal work of Simonde de Sismondi, a Romantic Calvinist and member of Madame de Staël's Coppet circle,[9] this view of the fortified city-states of the late Middle Ages (*burgi*, in Medieval Latin) as citadels and beacons of an artisan economy still untainted by the evils of liberalism and capitalism was famously reinterpreted by Karl Marx, but the same original vision of the virtues and values of an auroral, pre-industrial and pre-mechanical culture of making was equally influential for thinkers like John Ruskin or Lewis Mumford,[10] or for movements as diverse as the English Arts and Crafts or the reenactment of the medieval guild system in Fascist Italy in the 1920s and 1930s. The term "commune" itself has had vast resonance in modern political thought, from Marxists (communists) and anarchists to twentieth-century hippies.

The power of city-states started to wither with the rise of the centralized neo-feudal states of early modern Europe, and the medieval walls and gates that bounded the jurisdiction of urban guilds were often the first victims of the new baroque order: baroque fortifications were made for territorial wars, not to protect cities. A bit later liberal thinkers, notably Adam Smith, argued that everyone, outside of a town or inside of it, should be allowed to make and sell anything at any price freely agreed upon between buyer and seller—in short, that markets should be freed

---

9. Jean-Charles Léonard Simonde de Sismondi, *Histoire des républiques italiennes du moyen âge* (Paris: H. Nicolle, then Treuttel et Würtz, 16 vols., 1809–1818).

10. See for John Ruskin, first and foremost *The Stones of Venice* (1851–53), on the economic and spiritual decline of a mercantile republic when it abandons its pristine, Christian ethic of work to turn into a hereditary aristocracy; for Lewis Mumford, see in particular *The City in History* (1961), chapters 10–12, on the invention of corporate liberties in medieval cities and their eradication by baroque absolutism and neo-feudal regional states.

from guild regulations. Then the industrial revolution came. Medieval guilds already aimed at, and catered for, global markets: at the end of the Middle Ages goods and manufactured products of all kinds traveled far and wide, and were sold across Europe. But, unlike commerce, the logic of artisan production always was, as it still is, alien to economies of scale: an artisan workshop will make one bottle, ten, or one hundred, at the same unit cost. Consequently, artisanal production is mostly made to order and to specifications, and the size of the real or virtual marketplace where these products are sold is irrelevant. On the contrary, any industrial outfit has a calculable break-even point: the upfront cost of the installation must be paid back by making and selling at least a certain number of products. Hence, any factory requires a market of a certain size, and the bigger the factory, the bigger the economies of scale it can generate, so long as its market grows in the same proportion. The geopolitical flip side of the technical history of the industrial revolution is the permanent fight for size of all industrial marketplaces: *bigger markets for cheaper products.*

European nation states fulfilled and in some cases preempted this quest for size by expanding custom unions, and by enforcing the same technical standards across regions: an electric appliance made in Berlin must be usable in Bavaria, and must be allowed to ship from Bremen to Constance without having to pay excise duties every time the train crosses a city border. For some goods and products, colonies could be put to task in similar ways. The modern nation state rose in sync with some powerful cultural and ideological aspirations of the Romantic age, but its establishment and consolidation also aimed at balancing the costs and benefits of industrial mass-production: industrialization required markets of a certain size, and the right size for a nation state was that maximizing economies of scale for each class of industrial products. As artisan making cannot deliver economies of scale, artisan products were priced out of bigger and bigger markets; all technical premises and socio-political expressions of urban manufacturing then just ceased to be, and artisan cities were replaced by industrial nations.

We can understand how this story played out over time precisely because this centuries-old trend is now reversed by digital technologies. Just like artisan making, digital production is alien to economies of scale; moreover, as mentioned, the same scaleless logic now also applies to commerce. Industrial mass-production needed regulations, and a regulator, to create markets big enough to break even; digital mass-customization doesn't need that, hence can also do away with the regulators that were traditionally tasked to provide regulations and scale—first and foremost, the nation state.

A flat marginal cost, scaleless digital society has no technical need for scale at any size: the size of the market where the goods are sold is as irrelevant to digital commerce as the size of the factory where the goods are made is irrelevant to digital production. In fact, as the need to concentrate production facilities in dedicated, often remote locations will decline, and smaller, nimbler technologies may more easily fit into existing communities and their physical environments, towns and villages may become sites of production again, and sooner or later revitalized cities will also find adequate political means to wield their resurgent economic and productive clout.

With the elimination of all technical and economic justification for the existence of a state in the size of a nation, some political associations and institutions will have to be reconfigured at different scales, better suited for new techno-social purposes: some likely much smaller than the nation state, some larger. But national markets made to size for the cost structure of industrial mass-production are gone forever: they are gone with industrial mass-production itself. They belong with the assembly line, the coal mine, and the steam engine; and they will not come back. The prospect of a political and economic revival of city-states as independent powerhouses of digital manufacturing may appear remote. Yet, the few city-states of medieval lineage that are still extant all seem to be doing well—even if for reasons often unrelated to those under consideration here: think of the Corporation of the City of London (a still-functioning corporate commune); of the Swiss Confederation, to this day an alliance of independent corporate cities and rural communities ruled by direct democracy; or of some newly founded city-states, some post-colonial, such as Hong Kong or Singapore, some created on purpose as extra-territorial, deregulated enclaves (i.e., exempt from state regulations).[11] At the same time, the implosion of the nation state we inherited from the industrial age is all but remote. At the time of writing, in February 2017, the governments of the United States and of the United Kingdom have announced draconian plans to revive industrial production and to uphold national identity, based on unprecedented measures of economic protectionism and social xenophobia.[12] But the level of human suffering and collective violence envisaged by the pursuit of such policies is not manageable within the normal framework of modern democracies, and it requires instead, and likely presupposes, the suppression of the rule of law, hence war—both civil wars within nation states and all—out wars against other nation states. After all, the establishment of the modern industrial world order took two world wars. It is unreasonable to expect that the demise of that same world order will be peaceful: industrial technologies of mass-production are being phased out because they are no longer cost-effective, due to technological change; but the nation state that rose with them will not go without a fight. Let's hope that someone will survive to build upon its ruins, as medieval cities did after the destruction of the classical world.

11. See Keller Easterling, *Extrastatecraft: The Power of Infrastructure Space* (London: Verso, 2014), 25–69.

12. As epitomized in U.S. President Donald Trump's inaugural speech on January 20, 2017: "Buy American, hire American." At the time of writing (February 12, 2017), the UK government, with the approval of the Parliament, is planning the deportation of up to 3.3 million legal residents of the United Kingdom because they were born in certain European countries.

MANILA by Noel Celis

RECYCLING

Metropolitan governments have been paying increasing attention to the collection, sorting and recycling of urban solid waste and biosolids. These processes have reached a geopolitical dimension, with regional and even transcontinental impact. For example, garbage was for some time the biggest American export to China, until the Chinese government decided to intervene to stop that process. This, in turn, caused the development of new policies for recycling solid waste in the United States. While these processes have truly global implications, solid waste makes ecology an essentially urban concern. The environment is not merely the framework in which cities occur: it is truly framed by the city and its architectures as a metabolic activity. It is defined on every level at which architecture operates on a metropolitan and regional scale, but also on a spatial, structural, and surficial scale. The production of waste plays a key role in that metabolism as the counterpart to the city as a production mechanism.

The treatment of our undesired matters of waste and their associated logistics, economics, and ecologies is one of the most relevant contemporary ecological processes. Solid waste management is a regular and central municipal service. While service levels, environmental impacts, and costs may vary dramatically, solid waste management is a prerequisite for other municipal action. As the world moves quickly towards an urban future, the amount of municipal solid waste (MSW), one of the most important by-products of an urban lifestyle, is growing even faster than the rate of urbanization. In the year 2000 there were about 3 billion urban residents who generated about 0.64 kg of MSW per person per day (0.68 billion tonnes per year). According to a 2012 report from the World Bank,[1] by 2025 this will likely increase to 4.3 billion urban residents generating about 1.42 kg/capita/day of municipal solid waste (2.2 billion tonnes per year). The global cost of dealing with trash is rising: from $205 billion a year in 2010 to $375 billion by 2025, with the sharpest cost increases in developing countries. The average American produces already nearly 2Kg of waste per day, and growing. Approximately 55% of this waste ends up in one of the over 3,500 landfills in the country. Landfills not only poison substantial areas of urban land, which become sterilized for development, but also emit greenhouse gasses: U.S. municipal landfills are the second largest cause of human-driven methane emissions (around 22% of these emissions, according to the EPA's waste report in 2011).

1. World Bank, *What a Waste: A Global Review of Solid Waste Management*, 2012, https://openknowledge.worldbank.org/handle/10986/17388, accessed 11 May 2017.

In a world without an "environmental outside," understanding the material, political, and economic geographies of waste and its regulation changes, the emergence of recycling systems, the delimitation of waste streams, and the emergence of waste-to-energy processes creates an incredibly important image of how cities work, through the analysis of their metabolism. "Waste control" is the term used to capture the systems that currently resolve urban waste. It includes collection, conveyance, and clearance of refuse, sewage, and other discarded yields, including diverse industries offering various methods for reprocessing elements that can be separated out from trash. It turns refuse into a valuable resource. Waste control is the shared responsibility of resident, user, or institution in the city, and therefore, a crucial common which has many different cultural approaches. For example, in Japan, multiple-track waste recycling is made possible by cultural habits. Other cultures have been less capable to engage with waste as a true common as the Japanese do. Now that carbon emissions are found to produce serious ecological damage, using incineration as a replacement for landfills is becoming suspect.

The cultural dimension of recycling protocols is substantial and directly impacts on citizens and their perceptions of the identity of the city. For decades, Japan, for example, has been at the forefront of incubating a collective consciousness about recycling and installing infrastructure to optimize urban metabolism. Many cities have attempted to follow the Japanese example, only to realize the cultural difficulty of implementing such programs. The cultural difficulties of installing multiple-track recycling protocols in cities appears to be an insurmountable problem, and yet, robotic sorting of solid waste or e-waste is becoming a real alternative which will not have to rely on a cultural background like Japan's, as a single-track refuse system can be effectively sorted using a variety of robotic techniques.

Solid waste management has also been the object of privatization and government regulation policies. Different political approaches are taken towards this issue, which embodies the social ideal of the commons, where each individual is a steward, able to contribute "from each according to his abilities, and to each according to his needs," to the common good.

Waste management issues are deeply intertwined with land management and pollution, as landfills and CO_2 emissions are consubstantial with the processing of waste. Whereas the urban solid waste in the 1970s was likely to end in a landfill, countries like Japan and Germany have for decades been promoting a policy of incineration in order to eliminate landfills while producing urban energy. Despite the elevated cost of urban landfills, given the current concerns with greenhouse emissions and air pollution, the advantages of incineration are becoming less evident and cities are looking for alternative modes of recycling, putting pressure on municipalities to find alternative modes of treating solid waste.

At the urban scale, the complexity of recycling and remediation processes is substantial, because it involves an ecology of multiple industries and multiple waste streams. The physical structure of the city itself is a subject of recycling activities, with an increasing rate of preservation and retrofitting of existing urban infrastructures in most developed economies. In order to structure adequate recycling processes, it is necessary to map the geography and flow of industrial processes (material inputs, energy requirements, emissions, effluents, waste fluids) in parallel with the mapping of urban processes (water courses, surface runoff, sewer outflows, domestic wastes). Only then can we design chemical, biological, and logistic processes able to turn waste from one industry into fodder for another, so that an ecology of waste transactions can be engineered and a network of industrial exchanges constructed. The design, planning and long-term management of the environment as a single, collective, multilayered and complex urban public concern will have to eliminate conventional *end-of-pipe* treatment technologies in favor of the design of upstream waste reclamation strategies. Industrial flows will have to be redesigned to produce a new waste-handling hierarchy: energy recovery first, material recycling second, incineration third, and landfilling last.

Human waste is also becoming a subject of increasing attention for municipalities. During the nineteenth century, when urban populations exploded as a result of industrialization, cities like London or Paris developed profitable sewage farms, as discussed earlier. Profiting from human waste, sewage farms used to collect Paris waste and turn it into fertilizers for the farmers feeding Paris itself, at a profit.[2] The construction of large sewers ended the recycling of human waste for fertilizer, and new fertilizers were in turn produced at great expense through the Haber-Bosch method to synthesize ammonia, one of the most ecologically damaging processes. A more sophisticated approach to the recycling of human waste could have enormous ecological impact in cities worldwide. In light of the recent interest in promoting urban farming to generate food security, CO_2 absorption, and so on., the recycling of human waste obviously has great potential. Waste composting for urban farms on roof gardens, private courtyards, and bioswales appear to be the natural destination of human waste on a local, granular scale. As Pierre Belanger has written, "waste is the twenty-first century food."[3]

---

2. See Sedlak, *Water 4.0: The Past, Present, and Future of the World's Most Vital Resource*.

3. Pierre Belanger, "Landscape of Disassembly," *Topos* Magazine (Munich) 60 (2007): 83–91.

Nairobi by Filippo Romano

THE END OF WASTE?
TOWARDS A SOCIO-ECOLOGICAL COMMONS

Mitchell Joachim and Christian Hubert

In the U.S.A. alone, McDonald's creates 1/2 million tons of garbage each year.
– National Pollution Prevention Center for Higher Education

By 2025 there will be 1.4 billion more people living in cities worldwide, with each person producing an average of 1.42kg of municipal solid waste per day—more than double the current average of 0.64kg per day. Annual worldwide urban waste is estimated to more than triple, from 0.68 to 2.2 billion tonnes per year.
– World Economic Forum, 2017

Prevailing techniques in architecture are intrinsically structured to combat waste in all its iterative forms—or at least they claim to be. In the light of humankind's sweeping transformation of the earth, many scientists have come to call the current epoch the "Anthropocene," in recognition of the driving role of humans as a geophysical force. A narrower term has also been proposed: the "Capitalocene"—an expression intended to indicate that the biosphere is inseparably conflated with the economic realm fabricated by humanity, and with capitalism's failure to accept any limits to growth (also see Lewis Mumford's concept of "the machine"). These new period-based terms recognize not only that the effects of human action have extended to a point at which they have the capability to essentially modify the geophysical activities of the globe, but also that the ecosystem itself is a synthetic structure rather than an *a priori* circumstance. Terms such as these are each "an argument wrapped in a word" (to use Paul Voosen's phrase)—the argument being that the technics of homo sapiens have become a geo-historical force. Consensus on the defining scientific criteria and markers is still in flux, but unlike previous geo-stratigraphic units, these terms create frameworks for recognizing the new socio-ecological drivers of anthropogenic change—and perhaps inflecting their course.

Within the Capitalocene, the reactive protagonist becomes our natural world. Here, nature is carefully demarcated through a particularly alarming relationship to many human technologies. With commanding outlines in the procedures of connecting and encircling, nature is both a physical area and a symbol: it positions humans within a domain, and defines the method in which that domain is comprehended, qualified, and occupied. This makes ecology an essentially architectural concern—or at very least, it makes architecture an essentially ecological concern. The environment is not merely the framework in which architecture occurs. It is truly *demarcated* by architecture as a metabolic activity. It is both materially practiced and symbolically enabled by architecture. And, like architecture, the environment has been and remains expressed in various manifestations with compound significances and consequences. These diverse surroundings are defined at all the scales at which architecture functions, such as a space, a structure, a surface, a metropolis, and a connective regional pattern. The production of waste plays a key role in that metabolism—as the constant counterpart to the production and consumption of "stuff."

The United States alone is responsible for generating 224 million tons of trash a year. The average American produces 4.3 pounds of waste per day. This is 1.6 pounds more than was generated just over fifty-five years ago, in 1960. Where does this garbage end up? Approximately 55% of waste created each year is moved to one of the over 3,500 landfills. Municipally operated landfills are the second-largest cause of human-centered methane emissions in the United States, accounting for roughly 22% of these emissions (EPA 2011).

This quantity of waste and its by-products is far more than that produced by any other country on earth. Because of this circumstance, both the U.S. government and relevant environmental associations have developed numerous methods of dealing with the problem. "Waste control" is the catchall phrase for its current resolution. It includes the collection, conveyance, and clearance of refuse, sewage, and other discarded yields. This intricate issue embraces more than a dozen diverse industries. Waste control is the system of managing solid wastes, and offers an assortment of methods for reprocessing elements that can be separated out from trash. Moreover, it enables refuse to be re-evaluated as a valuable resource. Waste control is the shared responsibility of each and every residential, institutional, or commercial space owner. The waste control system seeks to dispose of commodities and materials that have been expended in a benign and effective manner.

At this critical juncture, (400 ppm of permanent carbon dioxide in the atmosphere as of 2016) when ever-increasing levels of greenhouse gases in the atmosphere threaten the future of many ecosystems and of Homo Sapiens as well. There are a multitude of approaches to mitigating waste, and each of these is further broken down into numerous subcategories. Those sets include source reduction, reuse, recycling, composting, fermentation, landfills, incineration, and energy conversion. Following is an explicatory survey of the most universally used processes in waste management and control.

1. LANDFILL/ OCEANFILL

Dumping daily waste/garbage into landfills is currently the most widely employed method of waste disposal. This detrimental process of waste disposal largely concentrates on burying the waste in the countryside. A precursor process eliminates the odors and dangers of waste before it is placed into the ground. Landfills are most commonly found in developing nations. While this is the most popular form of waste disposal, it is certainly far from the only satisfactory procedure, and it may bring with it a colossal degradation of space, especially where environmental protection is not effectively enforced.

This unfavorable method is becoming less pervasive, mostly due to the absence of available space and the continuous emission of methane and other landfill gases, both of which can pose frequent contamination issues. Landfills give rise to airborne and aquatic pollutants, which relentlessly disturb the environment and can result in properties that are fatal to humans and mammals. Numerous regions are reexamining their chronic exploitation of dedicated land for refuse purposes.

ARCHETYPAL EXAMPLES:

Sudokwon, Incheon, South Korea: Opened in 1992, this 4,000+ acre landfill receives 20,000 tons of waste daily from the capital city of Seoul, with a population of 25 million citizens. Regrettably, it is the nation's largest waste dump. Based on calculations by South Korea's Ministry of Environment, methane gas is tapped to yield 50 megawatts of electric energy. Additionally, the landfill has water recycling and desalination capability, and the cleaned water is used for agricultural and other purposes. According to South Pole Carbon Asset Management Limited, a surprising number of deciduous trees—700,000—have been planted on the Sudokwon site. The vast industrial undertakings on the site have produced 200 jobs, and 50,000 students tour the landfill yearly to gather information about sustainable waste-control practices and climate dynamics. Moreover, a comprehensive waste museum is located on the landfill. The Sudokwon landfill thus acts as a rare prototype of how waste supplies can best be monitored and harvested to attain a net positive impact.

Bordo Poniente Landfill, Nezahualcoyotl, Mexico: This landfill accommodated 12,000 tons of garbage a day before it closed at the end of 2011. Trash is still being discarded there, however, because no plans were made for a substitute area as a dumping site. Mexican officials are still looking for alternative solutions.

Fresh Kills Landfill, New York: Begun in 1947 as a short-term landfill, Fresh Kills was previously the planet's largest manmade artifact. With over 150 million tons of waste, it was finally closed in 2001 after receiving an unforeseen deposit—debris from the World Trade Center.

Lagos Dump, Nigeria: This scrapheap in Africa takes in almost *10,000 tons* of solid waste every day in addition to a sizeable amount of e-waste from the 500 container vessels that unload on its grounds once a month. The e-waste is chemically stripped for rare metals, creating toxic fumes that spread through the area.

Great Pacific Garbage Patch, Pacific Ocean: Extending for hundreds of miles, and feasibly the size of Texas, this unintended migrating mass of pollution, also known as the Pacific Trash Vortex, is visible as patches of plastic floating on the surface of the ocean. This gyre is not purely human design, but rather a counter-example of social and ecological interaction. A symbiotic process of accumulation between humans and ocean currents forms it. Here, fragments of plastic break into smaller pieces but never break down completely. They are ingested by marine life and are working their way up the food chain.

Columbia Ridge Recycling and Landfill, with Wind Turbines

Sudokwon Landfill in South Korea, 20 million square meters in size, it has processed 18,000 tons of waste daily from Seoul

2. INCINERATION/COMBUSTION

This category of waste management is known as thermal treatment, where incinerators convert solid waste materials into heat, gas, steam, and ash. Incineration or combustion is a high-embodied-energy method of disposal, in which municipal solid wastes are burned at elevated temperatures and converted into residue and gaseous by-products. The principal advantage of this technique is that it can condense the heavy volume of solid waste to approximately 30% of the existing volume, decreasing the required area and diminishing the pressure on landfills. For that reason, incineration is a dominant preference in nations where landfill area is nonexistent due to geography and policies. All new plants must tolerate stricter emission regulations, including those with nitrogen oxides (NOx), sulphur dioxide (SO2), heavy metals, and dioxins.

ARCHETYPAL EXAMPLES:

Maishima Incineration Plant, Japan: Exceptional exterior ornamentation designed by Friedensreich Hundertwasser.

SYSAV Incineration Plant, Malmö, Sweden: This plant is capable of handling 25 metric tons of household waste per hour.

3. WASTE TO ENERGY

Waste to energy encompasses converting non-recyclable discarded items into useable heat, power, or fuel through a range of processes. Methods of this kind provide renewable sources of energy, as nonrecyclable trash can be expended repeatedly to recreate energy. It can also fundamentally aid in the reduction of carbon emissions by offsetting the requirements for power from fossil systems.

Waste-to-Energy Plant in Herstal, Belgium

ARCHETYPAL EXAMPLES:

Amager Bakke Waste-to-Energy Plant, Denmark: Currently known as the cleanest waste-to-energy plant globally. As the tallest edifice in Copenhagen, it has a rooftop ski-slope. It discharges its CO_2 emissions in the form of bursting smoke rings.

Shenzhen East Waste-to-Energy Plant, China: The immense circular roof of this plant is calculated to be covered in 44,000m² of photovoltaic discs that provide not only a clean-tech way to remove urban waste but also a method for generating a profusion of renewable energy.

4. PLASMA GASIFICATION

Plasma gasification is an alternative form of waste management. Plasma is an electrically charged or a highly ionized gas. For instance, lighting is one form of plasma, and yields temperatures that surpass 12,600 °F. In this method of waste clearance, a receptacle uses characteristic plasma torches operating at +10,000 °F, generating a gasification zone for the transformation of solid or liquid wastes into a syngas used to create power.

Throughout the treatment of solid waste by plasma gasification, the content's molecular bonds are reduced as a consequence of the intense temperature in the vessels and the elemental components. It is possible to obliterate discarded materials and hazardous substances. This form of waste disposal delivers renewable energy and a mixture of other benefits. However, certain waste categories are considered hazardous and cannot be disposed of without special handling to prevent contamination. One example of hazardous waste is biomedical refuse from healthcare facilities and similar institutions. Specific waste-disposal systems are necessary for a plasma gasification unit to dispose of this type of refuse.

Westinghouse Plasma Gasification Reactor

ARCHETYPAL EXAMPLES:

USS Gerald R. Ford (CVN 78) Supercarrier, US Navy: A Plasma Arc Waste Destruction System (PAWDS) was installed onboard the Navy's next-generation aircraft carrier. The compact system treats 200 kg/h of combustible solid waste on the ship.

Wuhan Kaidi / Alter NRG, Demonstration Plant, China: This Westinghouse plasma gasification unit was designed to process approximately 100 tons per day of biomass waste and convert it to clean syngas. The clean syngas is then to be converted into diesel fuel and other transportation fuels.

5. RECOVERY AND RECYCLING

While the previous techniques are primarily methods for disposing of waste, resource recovery is a method of obtaining useful discarded articles for a specific next use. These discarded substances are then processed to extract or recover materials and/or transform them to energy in the form of useable heat, electricity, or fuel. Common elements that are recovered include aluminum beverage cans, copper electric wiring, steel foodstuff, aerosol containers, glass vessels, corrugated fiberboard cartons, paperboard boxes, newspapers and magazines, polyethylene and PET receptacles, and worn-out metal equipment or paraphernalia. The prime advantage to this approach is that it extracts the maximum benefits from used commodities, delays the depletion of virgin resources, and moderates the quantity of waste generated. Unlike landfill and incineration, resource recovery incorporates life-cycle analysis (LCA) practices to offer logical alternatives to the mass disposal of discarded materials.

Recycling is the third component of the Reduce, Reuse, and Recycle waste hierarchy. It consists of converting discarded yields into new products to reduce the need for further energy use and the consumption of additional raw materials. In addition to reducing energy usage, the overarching idea behind recycling is to reduce the volume of landfills, reduce air and water pollution, reduce greenhouse gas emissions, and preserve natural resources for future use. Recycling is extensively used globally, with plastic, paper, and metal leading the catalog of the maximum recyclable substances. In most cases, the material recycled is reused for its original purpose.

ARCHETYPAL EXAMPLES:

Sunset Park Materials Recycling Facility, Brooklyn, NY: This facility, which opened in 2013, processes a majority of New York City's commingled curbside material. A Recyclarium serves to educate public visitors via interactive exhibits and labs.

Newby Island Resource Recovery Park, San Jose, CA: This is the largest multistream system, capable of processing 110 tons of waste in just one hour. The extremely efficient facility is able to recover 80% of all the material that passes through it.

6. COMPOSTING

Composting is an easy and natural bio-degradation process that takes organic waste, i.e. the remains of plants and garden and kitchen waste, and turns them into nutrient-rich food for plants. Customarily used for organic agriculture, composting occurs by permitting organic provisions to remain in one place for months until microbes decompose them. Composting is one of the preeminent methods of food-waste removal, as it can transform otherwise unsafe organic products into nourishing fertilizer. On the negative side, it is a sluggish procedure and requires a significant amount of space and volume. Nevertheless, recycling and composting are the best methods of waste control. So far, however, composting is feasible only on a lesser scale, either by private individuals or in specialized zones where waste can be mixed with farming soil or expended for landscaping purposes.

ARCHETYPAL EXAMPLES:

Inland Empire Regional Composting Facility (IERCF), Rancho Cucamonga, CA: Enclosed to control odors and to meet stringent air-quality regulations, this is a bio-solids composting facility. It uses the Aerated Static Pile composting process to recycle approximately 150,000 wet tons per year of dewatered and stabilized bio-solids. Ultimately, the facility produces high-quality compost for local landscaping and horticultural use.

Newtown Creek Digester Eggs Wastewater Treatment Facility, NY

7. AVOIDANCE / WASTE MINIMIZATION

The cleanest method of waste management is to minimize the creation or designation of waste materials by reducing the amount of waste before attempting to dispose of it. Of principal concern are objects engineered for planned obsolescence or perceived obsolesce (items that still function but are no longer representative of the latest trend). This destructive practice is undertaken to keep people in a nonstop state of consumption. Waste reduction can be achieved by reusing timeworn materials like jars or bags, repairing inoperative items instead of buying new ones, avoiding the use of disposable products like plastic bags and plastic razors, using second-hand objects, and purchasing items that use less or zero packaging.

8. DESIGN FOR THE CAPITALOCENE

The most suitable approach to waste materials would be to emulate nature's waste and nutrient cycles in their specified environmental context, relative to both organic and inorganic substances—with the supplementary objective of global eco-social security. The design disciplines, including architecture, need to advance effective practices for eradicating waste altogether, echoing the closed-loop nutrient sequences of the planetary biota, in which there is zero garbage—because all things are a resource for something else. In the biological world, one organism's discarded elements are nourishment for another. Substances that provide nourishment essential for growth and the maintenance of life flow continuously in closed-loop cycles of evolution, decline, and renewal—a procedure of design that William McDonough has referred to as "Waste equals food." Constructions must be planned to be disassembled for a benign return to the land (as biological nutrients), or reutilized as valuable elements for new commodities and edifices (as technical nutrients).

McDonough further emphasizes: "One guiding principle for closed-loop design cycles has been called cradle to cradle design—as opposed to the one-way cradle to grave system." Rather than considering junk as a surplus control difficulty, "cradle-to-cradle" design projects positive future uses right in the beginning, in order to invent substances, constructions, communities, and systems that generate entirely positive results on human and ecological well-being. Rather than just creating less trash and fewer damaging effects, this approach produces more of the constructive effects of regeneration—seeds, growth, plants, new products, etc. Closed-loop design doesn't merely recycle, but "upcycles"—moving up the food chain or the production chain, to enhance planetary health. These benevolent goals can be expressed through a small number of catchphrases and globally shared systems, which are described in the following sections.

• USE RENEWABLE ENERGY

Energy derived from fossil fuels is an expenditure of natural capital. Living things thrive on the energy of current solar income. Similarly, human constructs can utilize renewable energy in many forms—such as wind, geothermal, and gravitational energy—thereby capitalizing on these abundant resources while supporting human and environmental health.

- CELEBRATE DIVERSITY

Around the world, geology, hydrology, photosynthesis, and nutrient cycling, adapted to each locale, yield an astonishing diversity of natural and cultural life. Designs that respond to the unique challenges and opportunities offered by each place fit elegantly and effectively into their own niches. Ecology functions at every scale, and design should as well.

9. NEW COMMONS

Addressing human waste and trash is not simply a technical problem. It requires efforts of world-ecological imagination and action at every level of human agency. The Capitalocene system of "cheap nature," with its theories and practices of "externalizing" environmental costs—to the point of "doubting" and denying them—has actively limited the search for remedies. Perhaps the greatest contribution of homo sapiens in the modern era has been its production of waste. We have to share and develop the view of trash as having value.

What sense does it make to think of trash as a form of "commons"? The notion of the commons has enjoyed a revival recently, primarily as an alternative to both privatization and government regulation. As an approach for managing shared resources, the commons embodies a social ideal in which each individual is a steward, where it is possible to expect the common good "from each according to his abilities, and to each according to his needs"—be it on land, sea, or air.

Yet, economists, political scientists, and even some ecologists want little to do with this concept. If the market supposedly harmonizes self-interest and the common good in their estimation, the commons is dismissed as inevitably leading to "tragedy," according to Garrett Hardin's dark vision in which self-interest always trumps the common good. Economists have said that the weakness of the commons is the "free rider" problem: What is to stop someone from taking unfair advantage of the commons and leading to its collapse? If a resource is limited, this kind of problem faces fishermen and herdsmen, along with people who drink water or breathe air.

10. THE "FREE RIDER" PROBLEM?

Examples of common shared resources—such as grazing lands, fish populations, and clean air and water—can be thought of as social "goods." Whether or not we can assign them monetary value, we understand that they are desirable for societies and their populations. Social justice is one of the issues related to shared resources—are there human "rights" to these resources? How can they be equitably shared? How can they be protected? Except for the destitute and some commercial recyclers, most people find trash undesirable—the evil twin of consumerism. Why should we consider it a shared common resource?

The fate of the English commons—eliminated through the expansion of capitalism and industry at the expense of the yeomanry, but with the support and collusion of government—serves as a warning to those who want to protect shared resources such as air and water, and to limit the degradation of the environment. If a commons needs a community to manage and protect it, can this model be effectively sustained in a globalized world—where so little is perceived to be "in common"?

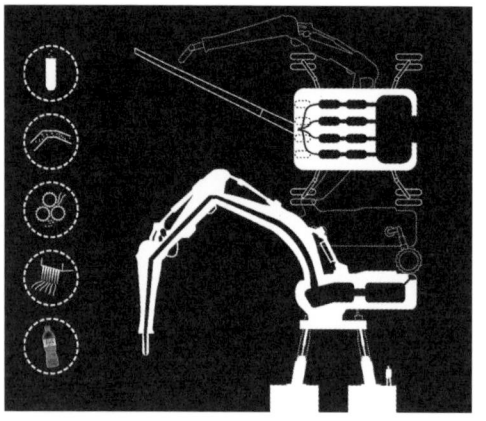

11. SMART REFUSE CULTIVATION

Rapid Re(f)use is an endeavor by Terreform ONE to drastically rethink industrialized waste streams in cities. One aspect of the all-pervasive scheme contains a monumental folly that transforms the refuse produced by New York City every hour on a usual day. This "One Hour Tower" is represented at scale with the charged void of a missing Statue of Liberty foregrounded. The strategy of the monument features the celebrated New York statue in an iconographic negative silhouette. It's intended to communicate an ominous message of wastefulness to all NYC residents. The monument is a part of an expansive project, which envisions a detailed scenario of reusing all the urban refuse to build upcycled infrastructure. In this paradigm, fully automated A.I. driven robotic 3d printers are tailored to reprocess waste and complete the undertaking within decades. Diverse materials serve stipulated purposes; flexible transparent plastics for fenestration, organic composites for momentary scaffolds, metals for primary structural systems, etc. ultimately, the prospective city makes no distinction between waste and supply.

CONCLUSION

Designers, scientists, and activists should stress the "creative" dimensions of waste production. The negative value of trash can be inverted, for example, by considering "trash as food"—following the cycles of nature—as expressed in the ideas of "cradle to cradle" design. Does it also make sense to think of trash not in terms of cost, but in terms of value? It is sobering to think that America's single greatest export to China is trash, and it should serve as both a rebuke and a challenge to us all to consider this example of "trash as food." In this time of reactive nationalism and secession from supranational structures and agreements, it remains essential to assert our common interest in one of the defining features of the Capitalocene: the global impact of human waste. The "commons" is not a panacea, far from it. The global commons requires shared values and effective governance through every form of agency. It requires a common will. The Capitalocene cannot be allowed to mark the end of the Anthropocene.

Rapid Re(f)use Detail of 3D Prototyping Waste Bot, uses organic materials for temporary scaffolds and inorganic for structure

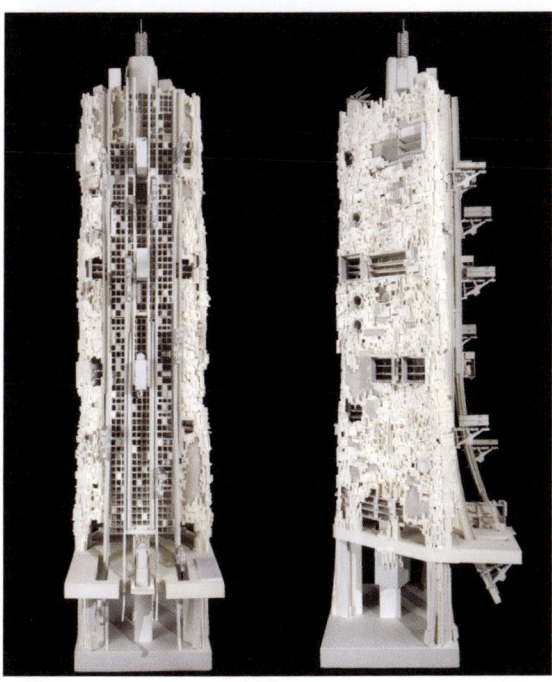

36,000 Tons of Trash Generated Every Day in NYC

A Vertical Landfill Tower of Compacted Discarded Materials

The Statue of Liberty Folly, Made of Compacted Waste Produced in One Hour in NYC

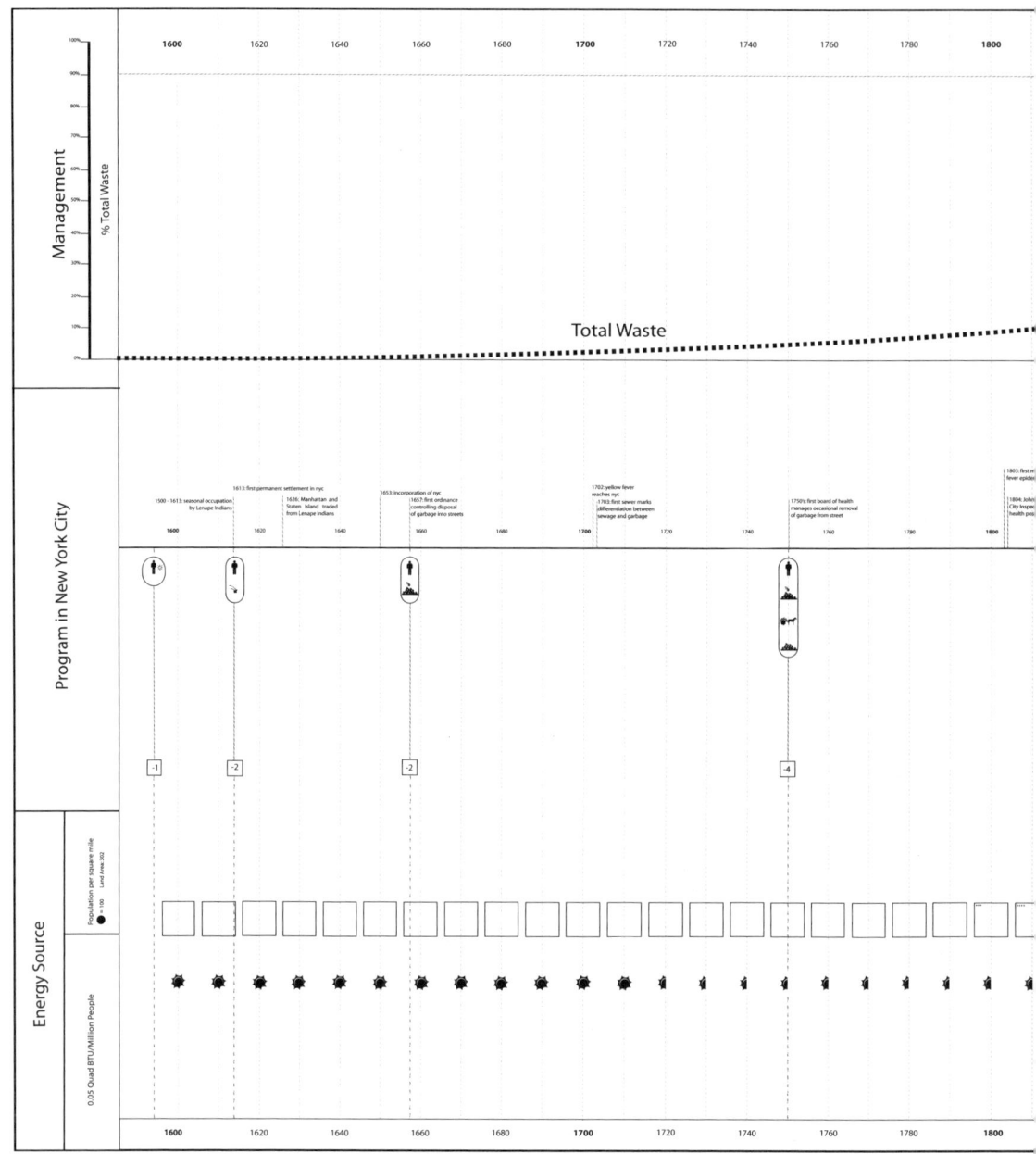

History of Waste Control in NYC From 1600 to Present

RECYCLING

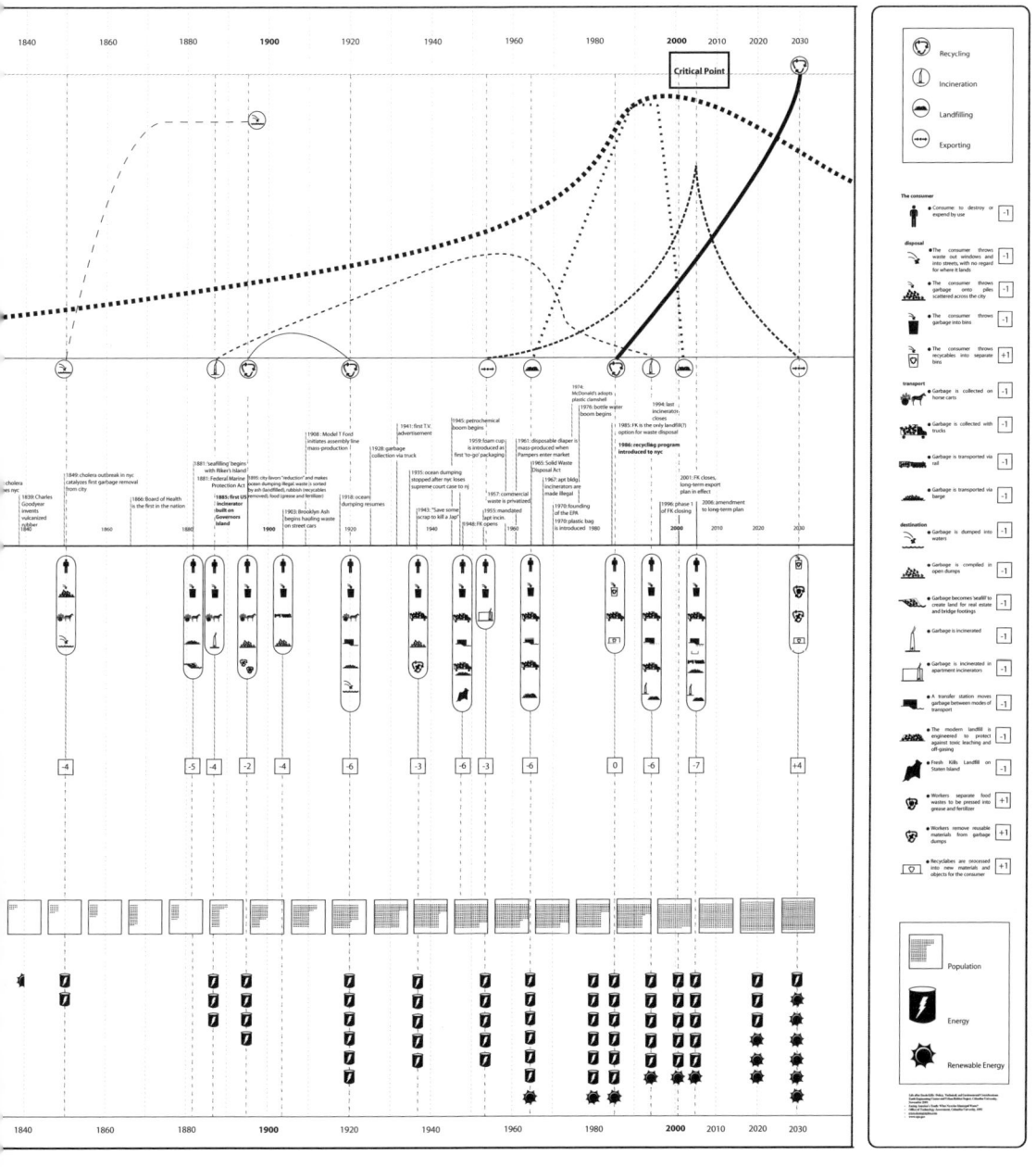

THE END OF WASTE? TOWARDS A SOCIO-ECOLOGICAL COMMONS _ Mitchell Joachim and Christian Hubert

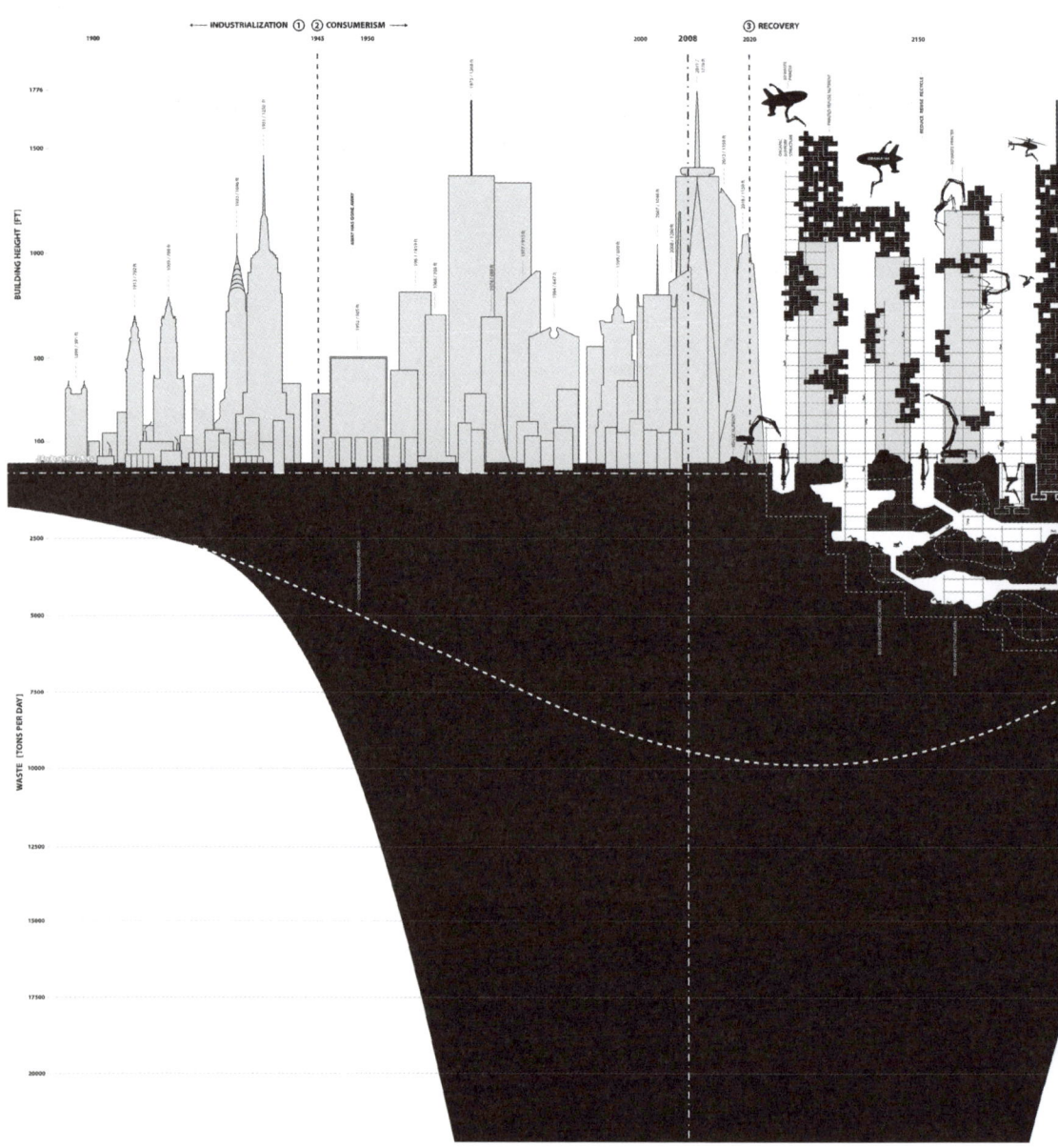

The Rapid Re(f)use project envisions an extended New York reconstituted from its own landfill material. Our concept remakes the city by utilizing the trash at Fresh Kills. With our 3D trash printer bots, we can remake seven entirely new Manhattan islands at full scale

RECYCLING

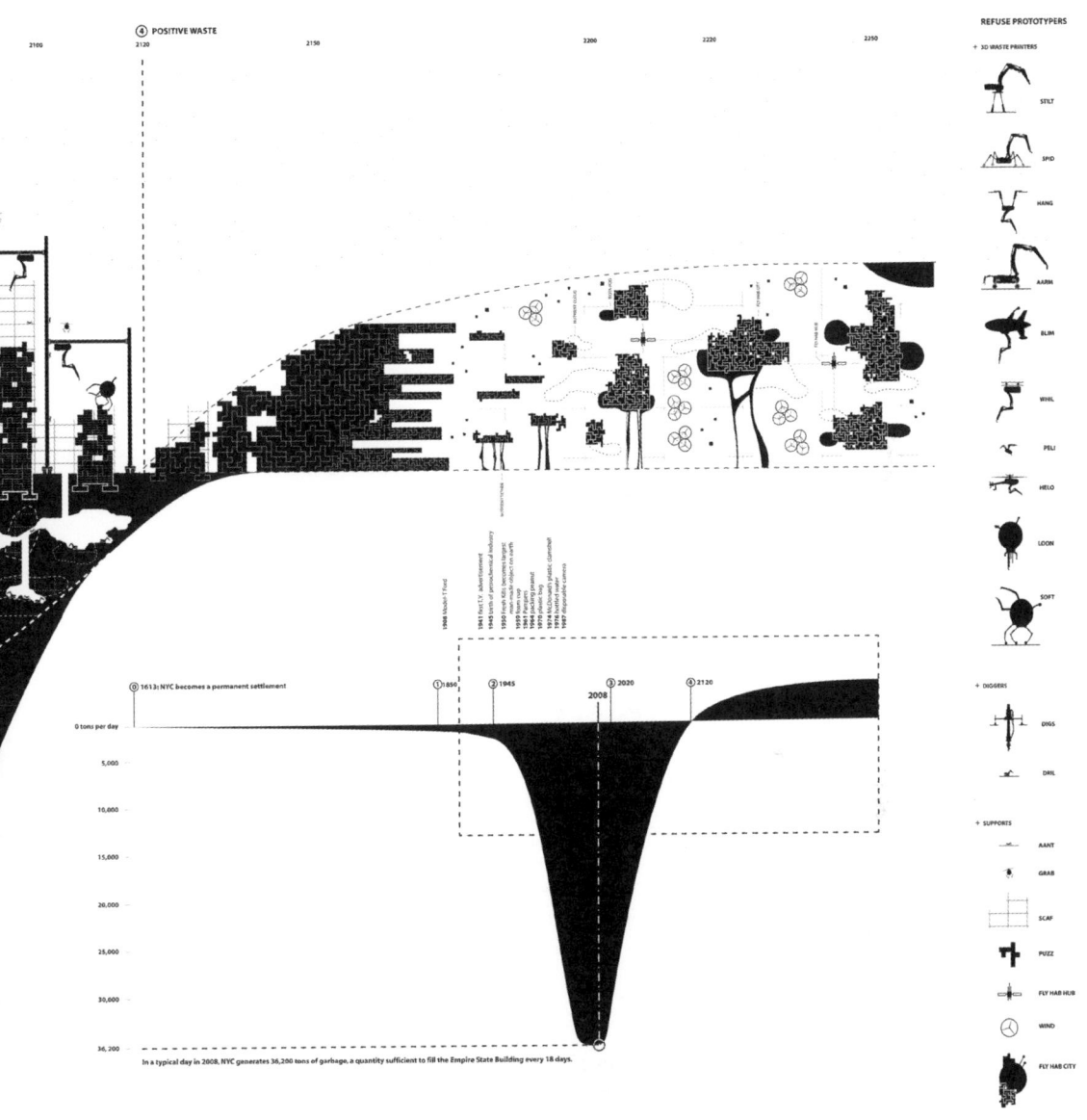

THE END OF WASTE? TOWARDS A SOCIO-ECOLOGICAL COMMONS __ Mitchell Joachim and Christian Hubert

BUILDING FROM WASTE:
THE WASTE VAULT[1]

Dirk E. Hebel, Felix Heisel and Marta H. Wisniewska

Our economic system is based on the principle of the exhaustion of natural resources for the purpose of production, entailing the fabrication of waste. This system functions at the expense of our social integrity and environmental sustainability. Images of the urban poor searching steaming landfills for valuable items are iconic representations of our modern lifestyle. In a dramatic way, the garbage sites show the entanglement of economic success and rapid urbanisation with social segregation into "haves" and "have-nots." It is also telling that this image is almost exclusively to be found in urban agglomerations, where by far the majority of non-organic waste is produced. Instead of being included in a metabolic cycle and flow model of goods and resources, waste is considered within a dead-end scenario of a linear process; to be literally buried from view—out of sight, out of mind—as a formless and value-free substance covered by thick layers of earth, or burned to ashes.

Looking, by contrast, at the waste products reveals a completely different story. It is the story of a resource that has been wasted until now. Every year, 1.3 billion tons of municipal solid waste are generated by cities worldwide. This amount is expected to grow to 2.2 million tons by 2025. Unsurprisingly, the 34 OECD countries (members of the Organization for Economic Cooperation and Development) produce more solid waste than the other 164 nations together. China is on a fast track to break this record; the World Bank estimates that China will produce more than half of the

---

1. Originally published in Dirk E. Hebel, Marta H. Wisniewska, and Felix Heisel, *Building from Waste: Recovered Materials in Architecture and Construction* (Berlin and Basel: Birkhäuser, 2014).

total of solid waste worldwide by 2025.[2] Looking at the map of the most waste-generating nations in the world, two readings are possible: either we can see them as the biggest polluters, following the traditional understanding of waste; or we can see them as countries with an enormous richness of resources. The latter perspective requires a different view of garbage production.

The call to understand waste as societies' wealth also follows, in fact, an economic principal: waste production is an investment, which needs to be returned. So far, this investment is deadlocked and we seem to have lost the key on how to open its potential and benefit from it as a lifelong revenue. Once the waste is produced—i.e. when a natural resource is transformed into a product with a limited lifespan—society should be able to make a profit of its constant reformulation. Instead, today the beneficiaries of the way we treat waste as a result of the exploitation of natural resources are to be found in a black spot of our economic system; they are another by-product, so to say.

SHADOW ECONOMY

Strangely enough, criminal organizations have had a strong interest in garbage for a very long time. It seems that our way of suppressing waste and enclosing it in our subconsciousness generates a legal vacuum where the space can be claimed by outlaws. In addition, the largest export good of the United States of America to China is trash.[3] This has to do with the growing problem in the United States, among other nations, of finding landfill spaces or new locations for incineration plants. Some countries happily accept the trash from other societies, especially when they are paid for taking it. Their understanding of environmental protection or human health is less distinct. In the case of Ghana, one of the main recipients of electronic waste from all over the world, people move from the rural areas to scrap sites next to harbour areas to strip and burn e-wastes in order to collect the valuable metals such as aluminium and copper inside. In the process, the plastic casings are burned, uncontrolled, on open sites, creating thick, black, and toxic fumes containing ingredients known as carcinogens. According to Al Jazeera, people working in the business make between two and three U.S. dollars a day, just enough to survive.[4] The Basel Convention E-Waste Africa Programme estimates that approximately 40,000 tons of e-waste entered Ghana in 2010.[5] This prosperity trash of Western societies will continue to be shipped to Western Africa, as long as the northern nations do not conceive of it as a rich resource.

2. "Daily Chart: A Rubbish Map," *The Economist* online, 7 June 2012, http://www.economist.com/blogs/graphicdetail/2012/06/daily-chart-3.

3. "Garbology: Difference Engine: Talking Trash," *The Economist* online, 27 April 2012, http://www.economist.com/blogs/babbage/2012/04/garbology-0.

4. Chris Stein, "Inside Ghana's Electronic Wasteland," Aljazeera, 2 November 2013, http://www.aljazeera.com/indepth/features/2013/10/inside-ghana-electronic-wasteland-2013103012852580288.html.

5. Matthias Schluep, Andreas Manhart, Oladele Osibanjo, David Rochat, Nancy Isarin, and Esther Mueller, *Where Are WEee in Africa? Findings from The Basel Convention E-Waste Africa Programme* (Châtelaine, Switzerland: Secretariat of the Basel Convention, 2011), http://www.oeko.de/oekodoc/1372/2011-008-en.pdf.

Why is our society accepting these circumstances? The answer is very complex. Waste is banned from our awareness, along with its potential of being a substance of value or even a resource for our economy. Therefore, we usually do not ask what happens to it after it leaves our home. Also, illegally treated waste became a very powerful global economic player, as has been shown in Italy. The environmental organization Legambiente claims that the business of black waste earned over 16 billion euros in Italy alone in 2012, from more than 11.6 million tons of illegally disposed waste substances.[6] Compared to the nation's Gross Domestic Product of the same year, this represents almost 1% of Italy's economic power.

LINEAR ECONOMY

The dominant economic model for our current waste management was phrased by Annie Leonard, the author of the film and book *The Story of Stuff*, as "Take, Make, Waste."[7] This is not per se an unsustainable principle, as it permits that the resource for "taking" could be the outcome of "wasting." But this is not the case. In fact, we are following a linear process where the outcome of our consumption is not valued as a resource, but seen as a kind of product excluded from the cycle of our environmental system—belonging neither to the natural resources nor to the desired products.

Absurdly enough, we pay our local authorities to collect our trash, confirming that it has no value to us nor is seen as a resource. Today, of the approximately 251 million tons of municipal solid waste generated in the United States per year, only around 87 million tons are recycled. The rest, roughly 164 million tons, ends up in incineration plants and landfills.[8] This waste of waste is at the same time a waste of natural resources, if we think only of the energy, water, and other materials which were needed (and wasted) to produce the discarded items from virgin resources. The production of a plastic bag, for example, not only requires crude oil as the raw material but requires the same quantity of oil to produce the energy needed for the production of the bag. In total, one kilogram of CO_2 is emitted for the production of five average-sized plastic bags.[9] Almost half of this amount could be saved if we were to start recycling our plastic waste materials instead of locking them away or burning them to ashes, emitting even more carbon dioxide and toxic fumes. Numbers are even higher in other industries. Recycling steel saves 75% of energy

---

6. See Walter Mayr, "The Mafia's Deadly Garbage: Italy's Growing Toxic Waste Scandal," *Spiegel* online, 16 January 2014, http://www.spiegel.de/international/europe/anger-rises-in-italy-over-toxic-waste-dumps-from-the-mafia-a-943630.html.

7. Annie Leonard, *The Story of Stuff: The Impact of Overconsumption on the Planet, Our Communities, and Our Health—And How We Can Make It Better* (New York, NY: Free Press, 2010).

8. United States Environmental Protection Agency, *Municipal Solid Waste Generation, Recycling, and Disposal in the United States: Facts and Figures for 2012* (2014), accessed online 23 March 2014, http://www.epa.gov/osw/nonhaz/municipal/pubs/2012_msw_fs.pdf.

9. Timeforchange.org, "Plastic Bags and Plastic Bottles: CO2 Emissions during Their Lifetime" (2009), http://timeforchange.org/plastic-bags-and-plastic-bottles-CO2-emissions.

compared to the process of generating it from scratch. And to produce one ton of paper, 98 tons of natural resources are needed. Yet, high amounts of paper waste still end up as trash, even though the recycling of that material is one of the easiest processes we know and could be part of a circular understanding of the stock and flow of materials.[10]

CIRCULAR ECONOMY

What we describe today as a circular or metabolic economy has been rooted for decades in the thinking of economists and, surprisingly enough, architects as well. In the United States, landscape architect John T. Lyle developed a theoretical concept in the late 1970s in which communities were envisioned to base their daily activities on living within the limits of available renewable resources without causing environmental degradation. His work and visions, developed together with his students at California State Polytechnic University, Pomona, found widespread interest due to the work of Walter R. Stahel, cofounder of the Product-Life Institute in Geneva (and graduate of the department of architecture of the Federal Institute of Technology [ETH] in Zurich in 1971). Stahel was a pioneer in the field of sustainable thinking by promoting the "service-life extension of goods" and was one of the first to introduce the three Rs to product life cycles: Reuse, Repair, and Remanufacture.

Stahel is also credited as having coined the term "cradle to cradle," an expression later turned into a well-known principle by Lyle's former student, American architect William McDonough. McDonough, along with German chemist Michael Braungart, developed the Cradle to Cradle[11] framework to introduce the idea that all materials used in the industrial and commercial production process should be acknowledged as constituents of a continual, circular growing process. Imitating a natural metabolic life cycle, the model the authors developed was a technical metabolism of the flow of industrially produced materials. The key idea is very obvious: products should be designed in such a way that they can become part of a continuous recovery and reutilisation process. They act as nutrients in a global metabolism, without ever being discarded as useless and value-free substances. Following McDonough and Braungart's argument, systems need to be installed that constantly recover the stored economic value, and there ought to be a social responsibility to do so. Taking natural processes as a model positions the Cradle to Cradle concept in the vicinity of the principles of biomimicry. Here, nature is used as an ecological standard to measure the sustainability of our doing, in a concept that asks not what we can extract from our natural surroundings but how we can learn from nature to turn the abundance of renewable energies into a circular metabolism of growth and economic surplus—without wasting or polluting a single element inside this system.

10. Heather Sarantis, *Business Guide to Paper Reduction* (San Francisco, CA, and Bellingham, WA: ForestEthics, 2002), citing C. Liedtke, "Material Intensity of Paper and Board Production in Western Europe," *Fresenius Environmental Bulletin*, Freising, Germany, 1993.

11. McDonough, William and Michael Braungart (2002). *Cradle to Cradle: Remaking the Way We Make Things*. New York: North Point Press.

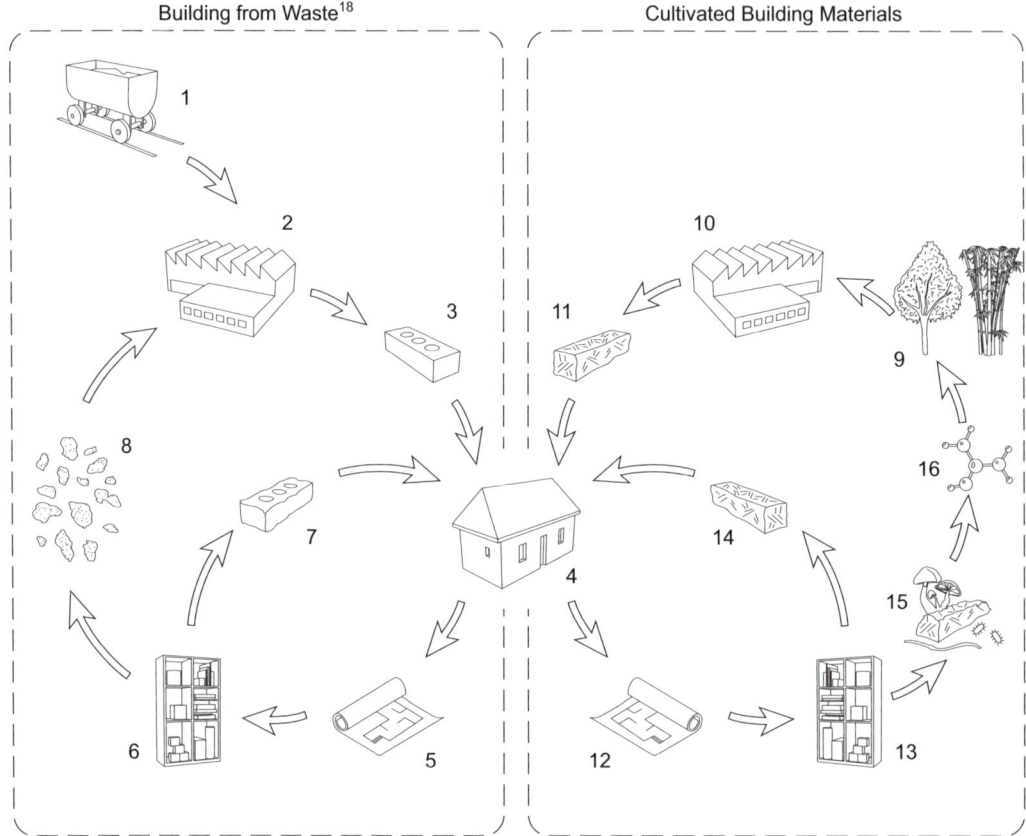

1 Resource mining
2 Manufacture
3 Mined building element
4 Product
5 Design for disassembly
6 Material storage
7 Mined material recycling
8 Technical nutrients
9 Resource cultivation
10 Manufacture
11 Cultivated building element
12 Design for disassembly
13 Material storage
14 Cultivated material recycling
15 Biological decomposition
16 Biological nutrients

The biological and technical cycle of a closed-loop building industry

WHAT A WASTE?

Waste, as we see it, can be defined as unwanted or undesired materials. These materials include human-made matter as well as natural ones. In general, when we use the term "waste," we refer to so-called solid waste in contrast to waste that is produced in the form of energy or radiation being emitted into the atmosphere or the ground. We include in our argument air-borne particles as well as waste discharged in sewage systems, which could be transformed into new building substances. Yet, what is waste to one person is not waste to another, which makes the definition of the term highly complex. It requires a careful and differentiated recognition of the enormous differences in various cultures and social perceptions. Victor Papanek, in his book *Design for the Real World*,[12] quotes Frances Fitzgerald, who wrote about the different views of waste held by American troops and the native population in Southeast Asia during the Vietnam War: "while they [the Americans] saw themselves as building world order, many Vietnamese saw them merely as the producers of garbage from which they could build houses."[13]

"Desire," contrariwise, describes a sense of longing for something, which apparently is absent when we think of items that we do not want around us anymore or that are useless or even nauseous to us. The definition of waste, therefore, includes emotions and feelings, which are not to be measured in objective terms. Aesthetics and other senses play an important role, and the sheer thought that something is made out of waste might trigger negative emotions in various cultural groups. This fact makes it hard to think of waste as a future building material. But in our view, waste should count among the prospective renewable resources of our planet.

WASTE AND SOCIETY

The science that studies the question of trash composition is called "garbology." In many instances it overlaps with the discipline of archaeology, as in the determination of societal developments, the use of different materials and techniques, spiritual preferences, and nutrition compositions, which can all be traced through an analysis of the waste that any civilization produced at a certain moment in time. Today, the rather young discipline of garbology is used to assess solid waste and to figure out new ideas for waste management, since the formation of waste is changing radically. Urbanization and the financial status of diverse societies tend to determine the type of waste generated. As people grow wealthier and move towards urban conglomerates, the percentage of inorganic substances in their waste increases, while organic substances account for only a decreasing share. In rural areas, by contrast, this biological and compostable component still reaches up to 85%, according to the Worldwatch Institute.[14]

12. Victor Papanek, *Design for the Real World* (New York, NY: Pantheon Books, 1971).

13. Frances Fitzgerald, *Fire in the Lake: The Vietnamese and the Americans in Vietnam* (London: Macmillan, 1973).

14. Supriya Kumar, *Global Municipal Solid Waste Continues to Grow*, Worldwatch Institute, 24 July 2012, http://www.worldwatch.org/global-municipal-solid-waste-continues-grow.

The challenge for our society is more and more how to minimize our waste production of inorganic substances and how to convert the remaining—maybe unavoidable—waste into a resource. This is the essence of the idea of a minimum- or even zero-waste society, following the four Rs: Reduce, Reuse, Recycle, and Recover. This hierarchy of waste management, as it is often called, aims for a total circular metabolism in order to avoid any disposal. In the past two decades, this thinking has altered the behaviour of younger generations in our society. For example, it became fashionable to buy accessories made out of reused truck canvases or other discardables. While this trend aims mostly at the reuse of materials and products, it could easily be upscaled to apply also to the other three Rs, leading to a society without waste production. A definition of such a zero-waste philosophy was developed by the Zero Waste International Alliance in 2004: "Zero Waste is a goal that is ethical, economical, efficient and visionary, to guide people in changing their lifestyles and practices to emulate sustainable natural cycles, where all discarded materials are designed to become resources for others to use. Zero Waste means designing and managing products and processes to systematically avoid and eliminate the volume and toxicity of waste and materials, conserve and recover all resources, and not burn or bury them. Implementing Zero Waste will eliminate all discharges to land, water or air that are a threat to planetary, human, animal or plant health."[15]

This definition introduces a socially responsible alternative to the present take-make-throw model. It puts not only the producer but also the consumer into an ethically active role to reuse waste products as a resource and also to avoid producing waste through an unsustainable lifestyle.

URBAN MINING
Urban Mining is a rather young phenomenon, embracing the process of reclaiming compounds and elements from wasted or at least undesired products or buildings, which contain high levels of valuable materials. In their text "Mine the City," Ilka and Andreas Ruby describe the contemporary shift in awareness that raw materials are not to be found anymore in a "natural" realm, but more and more can be found in the "cultural" domain of buildings. They write: "The material resources of construction are becoming increasingly exhausted at the place of their natural origins, while inversely accumulating within buildings. For example, today there is more copper to be found in buildings than in earth. As mines become increasingly empty, our buildings become mines in themselves."[16] In their view, the city is to be seen as a container of buildings and mines at the same time, much needed for its own reproduction.

15. "ZW Definition," Zero Waste International Alliance, last updated 2009, http://zwia.org/standards/zw-definition.

16. Ilka Ruby and Andreas Ruby, "Mine the City," in Ilka and Andreas Ruby, eds., *Re-Inventing Construction* (Berlin: Ruby Press, 2010), 243–47.

Thomas Graedel of the Yale School of Forestry and Environmental Science combines his analysis of Urban Mining with the question of how much energy can be saved by recycling the wasted materials found in landfills or buildings. For him, buildings not only store the materials to be recycled, but together with them store a large amount of energy, which could be reactivated. He argues that the reuse of aluminium that could be recycled from buildings needs only 5% of the originally used energy for its production: "Aluminium is extensively employed in buildings, but it does not remain permanently in place. Buildings are remodelled periodically, and even deconstructed, thereby freeing the aluminium for recycling. Therefore, it is not inaccurate to regard this aluminium as 'urban ore' and cities as 'urban mines.'"[17]

Urban Mining demonstrates how waste products can potentially be resourced at the end of their first lifespan, when entering a second or third lifespan by being transformed, reshaped, remodelled, or reconfigured. But it also opens up questions of whether consideration of the waste state of a product should not become the starting point of its design proper.

BUILDING FROM WASTE
The title of this research combines two terms which so far were understood as separated entities, one—the waste—usually being produced by the other—the building—whether through the act of production, construction, application, inhabitation, transformation, adaptation, or demolition. Following this logic, waste is a result of any human action and interaction that brings raw natural materials—understood so far as our sole form of resources—from one stage of being into another, by applying various forms of skills and energy. In this sense, waste was seen for centuries as something specific which neither belonged to the family of natural resources nor to the one of finished products. Waste was a by-product, unable to be categorized in our dialectic understanding of raw vs. configured.

Our research tries to unfold the possibility of understanding waste as an integral part of what we define as a resource. We would thereby acknowledge its capacity to figure as the required substance or matter from which to construct or configure a new product. And at the same time, the product could be seen as the supply source for other artefacts, after its first lifespan. This metabolic thinking understands our built environment as an interim stage of material storage, or to use the words of Mitchell Joachim: "The future city makes no distinction between waste and supply."[18]

17. Thomas Graedel, "Urban Mining, Recycling Embodied Energy," accessed online 22 January 2014, http://greenbuilding.world-aluminium.org/facts/recycling/?no_cache=1&sword_list%5B%5D=Energy.

18. Mitchell Joachim, "Turning Waste into Building Blocks of the Future City," BBC Online News, 28 May 2013, http://www.bbc.com/future/story/20130524-creating-our-cities-from-waste.

The surface reveals the source material through speckles, which stem from the coloured printing and shiny foil

The expressive pavilion is designed to appear to float in the narrow slot between the buildings of the First Street Garden, allowing and visualizing the use of a nonstandard, weak material in construction; picture during construction

The ETH Zurich Pavilion hosted seminars, lectures, and exhibitions during the IDEAS CITY Festival in New York in May 2015

The pavilion activated the First Street Garden as an event location for the festival, especially in the evenings

All 400 industrial pallets were returned into their regular cycle after the exhibition

WASTE VAULT: THE ETH ZURICH PAVILION

Invited by the New Museum in New York City, professors Dirk E. Hebel and Philippe Block were asked to put their research into practice and to construct a temporary exhibition pavilion for the IDEAS CITY Festival in May 2015 as an event location for seminars, lectures, and exhibitions. Taking this opportunity to test and validate the research described here, the team constructed a 90 m² pavilion made from recycled beverage packaging, aiming to show the immense potential of waste for the construction sector. The pavilion highlights various ways in which waste material—obtained here in the form of discarded beverage cartons—can be used to build even wide-spanning and load-bearing structures, without producing any new waste in the process.

SHREDDED AND PRESSED

In 2013, an estimated 178 billion beverage cartons were consumed worldwide.[19] In theory, the materials (paper 74%, polyethylene 22%, and aluminium 4%) can be reseparated relatively well. But this task requires a special machine and uses large amounts of water and energy. Recycling rates have climbed substantially in recent years. Nevertheless, some 430,000 tons of beverage cartons were thrown away in 2010 in the United States alone.[20] With the cooperation of the U.S. company ReWall, the beverage cartons for ETH Zurich's pavilion first were chopped up with a shredding machine. Subsequently, they were pressed into panels on a conveyor belt using heat and pressure. Neither water, glue, nor other additives are required, as the mixed material made up of aluminium, paper, and polyethylene combines to form a waterproof entity. The surface reveals the source material through speckles, which stem from the coloured printing and shiny foil.[21]
A crucial factor in the choice of materials was the fact that the three substances used by the food packaging industry do not contain any harmful substances. Following their use in the pavilion structure, they can be fully reintegrated into the firm's regular recycling process, as happened a couple of days after the dismantling of the pavilion. Although the initial transformation from a drinking carton to a building panel can be considered as down-cycling, the subsequent recycling of the panels can be done as often as required with no diminishing of its mechanical quality.

MATERIAL TO DESIGN

Until now, the material ReWall was produced for interior panelling and used as a substitute for plasterboard in drywall construction. The ETH Zurich Pavilion, however, deployed ReWall for the first time as a load-bearing construction material in exterior use. As the sheets can warp and

---

19. Tetra Laval, "The Tetra Laval Annual Report: Ensuring Food Protection, No. 2013/2014," Tetra Laval, Pully, Switzerland, 2014.

20. Chaz Miller, "Profiles in Garbage: Aseptic Boxes, Milk Cartons," Waste 360 website, 1 August 2001, http://waste360.com/mag/waste_profiles_garbage_aseptic.

21. The ReWall Company, LLC, "ReWallution," The ReWall Company website, accessed 27 April 2015, http://www.rewallsolutions.com/rewallution/.

possess weak properties in terms of tension and bending, the team optimised the structure's form to account for compression forces only. The 90 m² compression-only shell is composed of 34 single, pre-stressed catenary arches, which follow the flow of forces. Assembled from 2,000 unique, single sheets, the discrete, triangular building blocks enlarge the static height, reduce the structure's weight, and make prefabrication possible. Respecting these structural constraints, the expressive pavilion was designed to appear to float in the narrow slot between the buildings of the First Street Garden, allowing and visualizing the use of a nonstandard, weak material in construction.

The dry-assembled pavilion utilized industrial packaging straps to keep the thin, CNC cut sheets together in triangular blocks. Being extremely lightweight, the arches were tied down using straps. This strap-only construction process also enabled efficient disassembly. Without the need to remove or dispose of metal fixings, glue, or non-recyclable materials, the structure's components could subsequently be fully returned to the recycling process in a straightforward manner. The pavilion's arches touched down on temporary support structures made of industrial pallets. The weight of these modules additionally anchored the shell to the ground without leaving invasive marks on the site after the pavilion's removal. Finally, these support structures were elements of the spatial layout, forming the bar and exhibition areas, providing seating, and creating divisions or wall spaces.

For prefabrication of the elements, ETH Zurich opened a pop-up storefront workshop across the street from the festival's site. During the month of May, this gallery was used to assemble all bricks for construction and build the bases for the arches. The final assembly on First Street Garden lasted for the five days leading up to the pavilion's opening and was executed by the ETH design team in collaboration with local contractors. Underneath and within this structure, ETH Zurich curated a program following the theme of the pavilion. The exhibition *Building from Waste* displayed over twenty-five construction materials derived from waste, activating resources within our cities that have remained invisible until now. A covered area for about thirty to forty people provided space for invited guests from ETH Zurich and its partners to organize lectures and seminars for the general public. Finally, the pavilion was dismantled in only two days, leaving no waste material on the site, as all substances were only "borrowed" for a short period of time before they went back to their regular recycling loops afterward.

Project Credits:
Felix Heisel (Project Lead), Dr. Tomás Méndez Echenagucia, Samuel P. Smith, Nicholas Ashby, Ruben Bernegger, Jean-Marc Stadelmann, Edyta Augustynowicz, Diederik Veenendaal, Skyler Silverman, Chinnaya Nwosu, Michael Stirnemann, Marta H. Wisniewska, Prof. Dirk E. Hebel, and Prof. Philippe Block

BEIJING by Kentaro Iemoto

MUMBAI by Ibay Rigby

CALIFORNIA

ILLINOIS by Chris Bennet

LAGOS by Edgar Cleijne

LEVITTOWN by Meyer Leibowitz

AIR — "The Earth is a very small stage in a vast cosmic arena. Think of the endless cruelties visited by the inhabitants of one corner of this pixel on the scarcely distinguishable inhabitants of some other corner, how frequent their misunderstandings, how eager they are to kill one another, how fervent their hatreds. Think of the rivers of blood spilled by all those generals and emperors so that, in glory and triumph, they could become the momentary masters of a fraction of a dot."

CARL SAGAN
Pale blue dot: a vision of the human future in space.
New York: Random House, 1994.

WATER — "With respect to water and cities, ecosystem services such as flood mitigation, erosion control, and the protection of property and human life, as well as water quality improvement and conservation, wastewater treatment, the creation of habitat, and provision of education, recreation, and aesthetic value, can all be derived from urban aquatic ecosystems."

AZIZA CHAOUNI
HERBERT DREISETL
Out of water design solutions for arid regions.
Birkhäuser, Basel, 2015.

AIR — "Forms of nature become subnatural when they are envisioned as threatening to inhabitants or to the material formations and ideas that constitute architecture. Subnatures are those forms of nature deemed primitive (mud and dankness), filthy (smoke, dust and exhaust), fearsome (gas or debris) or uncontrollable (weeds, insects and pigeons). [...] I argue that any approach relating architecture to nature must acknowledge this 'other' nature embedded within the history of architectural thought, appearing in aggressive ways throughout the most progressive contemporary practices."

DAVID GISSEN
Subnature: Architecture's Other Environments. Princeton Architectural Press, 2009.

AIR — "While some aspects of nature are hard to enclose (such as the air we breathe and the oceans we fish in), a variety of surrogate ways can be devised (usually with the help of the state) to monetise and make tradable all aspects of the commons of the natural world. State interventions are also often developed to correct for market failures.

While these interventions may seem progressive, their effect is to further promote the penetration of market processes and market valuations into all aspects of our lifeworld. This is the case with carbon trading and the growing market in pollution rights and ecological offsets. When the natural commons are privatised, then all things, objects and processes therein are assigned a value (sometimes arbitrarily by bureaucratic fiat) no matter whether any social labour has been expended on them or not. This is how capital creates its own distinctive ecosystem."

DAVID HARVEY
Seventeen contradictions and the end of capitalism. Oxford: Oxford university press, 2015.

| AIR | "Air has been treated in architecture and its historiography as an element that is recognized, which can only be spoken about metaphorically, poetically or phenomenologically." | **IÑAKI ABALOS, RENATA SENTKIEWICZ** *Essays on thermodynamics.* New York: Actar Publishers, 2015. |

| RECYCLING | "Nobody wonders where, each day, they carry their load of refuse. Outside the city, surely; but each year the city expands, and the street cleaners have to fall farther back. The bulk of the outflow increases and the piles rise higher, become stratified, extend over a wider perimeter." | **ITALO CALVINO** *Invisible cities.* London: Vintage, 2009. |

| EARTH | "The Gulf's biotic integrity —that of its waters, estuaries, marshes, depths, and flows, ever at hazard from intensive harvests— is an essential element of the biosphere, a piece of its functional anatomy, integral to the land and sea of the Western Hemisphere. There is no circumstance in which human welfare can be advanced by a sacrifice of the Gulf to corporate purpose. The fossil fuel industry may be large and powerful, but its business success is a double-edged sword. It profits with one swing of the sword, which severs the life support of millions dependent on the biotic integrity of an unpolluted Gulf along with its affiliated dependencies of land, sea, and air. In recovering for another swing, it sells the oil and poisons the planet with its gaseous wastes while collecting public subsidies for the privilege. It is hard to envision such corporate activities in devouring common property at public expense as anything but crude, rapacious, and ultimately suicidal." | **GEORGE M. WOODWELL** *A world to live in: an ecologist's vision for a plundered planet.* Cambridge, MA: MIT Press, 2016. |

| FIRE | "Modern civilization is thus a material and intellectual embodiment of converting fossil fuels into the useful energies of heat, electricity, motion, and chemical potential. While photosynthesis remains the planet's most important energy conversion, as it powers all life (with the exception of deep-sea organisms aggregating near hot thermal vents), our relative reliance on phytomass fuels has been steadily declining. [...] Two arguments are advanced in favor of an accelerated shift away from fossil fuels: concerns about their future supply and worries about the long term environmental consequences of their combustion." | **VACLAV SMIL** *Power Density: A Key to Understanding Energy Sources and Uses.* Cambridge, MA: MIT Press, 2016. |

| WATER | "Water and Air hinge between life and death. Their presence, constitution and control are critical to maintain the minimal conditions of life precisely. Because their absence or transmutation may convey the termination thereof. Water and air are not just another natural entity, but elemental forces upon which the bios rests: without water or air animal and vegetal existence on earth would cease." | **NEREA CALVILLO** *Urban cosmopolitics: agencements, assemblies, atmospheres.* Blok, Anders, and Ignacio Farias. Abingdon, Oxon: Routledge, 2016. |

AIR

"The antifracking movement had coalesced first around the concerns about fracking liquids contaminating local aquifers and about drinking water laden with pollutants that could be set on fire when it comes out of a faucet (this became an iconic image of fracking gone awry). Only later came concerns about longer-term effects of air pollution from escaping gases and the increased potential for localized earthquakes. As with all similar movements, antifracking activists form a heterogeneous group whose members range from professional environmental protesters opposed to virtually any resource developments to people genuinely concerned about fracking wells few hundred meters upwind from their backyards, schools, or playfields."

VACLAV SMIL
Natural Gas: Fuel for the 21st Century. Chichester: John Wiley & Sons, 2015.

RECYCLING

"Solid wastes are the discarded leftovers of our advanced consumer society. This growing mountain of 'Use it up, wear it out, make it do, or do without.' New England Proverb garbage and trash represents not only an attitude of indifference toward valuable natural resources, but also a serious economic and public health problem."

JIMMY CARTER
The Environment Message to the Congress. May 23, 1977.

AIR

"For a long time, environmentalists spoke of climate change as a great equalizer, the one issue that affected everyone, rich or poor. It was supposed to bring us together. Yet all signs are that it is doing precisely the opposite, stratifying us further into a society of haves and have-nots, divided between those whose wealth offers them a not insignificant measure of protection from ferocious weather, at least for now, and those left to the mercy of increasingly dysfunctional states."

NAOMI KLEIN
This Changes Everything: Capitalism vs. the Climate. London: Penguin, 2015.

SENSING

"Environmental issues are always on the policy making agenda and industries have to manage their environmental impact. Developing environmental sensing and monitoring technologies become essential especially for industries that may cause severe contamination to the eco-systems. According to industrial analysts, the market for environmental sensing and monitoring technologies is projected to reach U.S.$17 billion by 2020. Currently there are three main approaches to improve environmental sensing: developing novel environmental sensors, designing more effective sensing algorithms to enhance detection performance and using multiple sensors to form environmental sensor networks. These three approaches are not exclusive but complimentary for an improved environmental monitoring."

ZHONGLIANG JING, HAN PANG, GANG XIAO
Intelligent Environmental Sensing. Lung, Henry, Subhas Chandra Mukhopadhyay. ed., Springer International PU, 2016.

EARTH

RICHARD INGERSOLL TALK
How to Enjoy Climate Change
urbanNext.net

FIRE "Population shifts, increasing scarcity and the wanton consumption of fertile land and natural —renewable and non-renewable— resources could turn out to be a significant global problem, a dilemma of disastrous proportions. We can only hope that global awareness of the fragility of our planet will grow. We appear to have reached a critical and sobering point in history. Despite setbacks and mistakes all is not lost. There is still time left for corrective steps. We as individuals in a 'glocalised' society must heed the warning signs and we will thus be able to avoid falling into a downward spiral. How our future looks, and in whichever built environment we and future generations experience it, depends in many ways on our decisions. Ultimately it will not depend on technology and economics but on what we —people— decide."

CHRIS LUEBKEMAN
Energy Manual: Sustainable Architecture. Stark, T., Manfred Hegger, Matthias Fuchs, and Martin Zeumer. Birkhäuser, 2012.

EARTH "Today's global sustainability crisis would certainly be worse without the spread of environmentalism since the 1965. More than a thousand multi-lateral environmental agreements are in place, and across the world governments have set up environmental protection agencies. Wildlife sanctuaries and ocean parks are multiplying; municipal water and sewage management are improving; and markets for products certified as 'sustainable' are growing rapidly. Energy productivity is increasing, as is recycling. And corporations are making real efforts to reduce waste and improve environmental efficiencies. [...] Less understood, however, is what has been happening to the nature of environmentalism as the crisis intensifies. Over the past two decades environmentalism in both rich and poor countries has been losing its critical edge—and thus much of its power as a counter narrative to consumer capitalism."

PETER DAUVERGNE
Environmentalism of the Rich.
MIT Press, 2016.

AIR "Adaptation planning must be flexible—the understanding of future climate change can only be given in terms of range because of various uncertainties, including the climate sensitivity because of feedbacks in the climate system and how future emissions related to human activities will change."

DONALD J. WUEBBLES
Engineering response to climate change. Watts, Robert G., ed. Boca Raton: CRC Press, 2013.

AIR — "Climate change represents an enormous challenge, but humans have the capacity to respond to avoid the worst of the changes and to adapt to those that cannot be avoided. Because the climate is already changing because of human activities and some amount of additional change is inevitable, adapting to higher temperatures and to trends in severe is an essential (and complementary) strategy to reduce emissions. For each adaptation measure considered, policy makers and managers must carefully assess the potential barriers, costs, and unintended social and environmental consequences."

DONALD J. WUEBBLES
Engineering response to climate change. Watts, Robert G., ed. Boca Raton: CRC Press, 2013.

RECYCLING — "The real environmental and economical problem of the 20th century is that scientific and technological developments have increased the human capacity to extract resources from nature, process them, and use them, but have not offered parallel and similar insight into how these resources can be returned to their environmental origin or how they could be entered into a new cycle of extraction, processing, and use. Much of the resources extracted from nature are used in unsustainable activities and end up as waste. This can be described as a cradle-to-grave scenario in which the resources have a 'lifetime' and are disposed of after they are used, ending up in a 'grave' (a landfill, for example). If this were to continue unabated, we may end up completely depleting our natural resources. The only way to evade this dead end is to develop newer production and processing techniques that use up resources in an alternative cradle-to-cradle scenario."

SALAH EL HAGGAR
Sustainable industrial design and waste management: cradle-to-cradle for sustainable development. Amsterdam: Academic Press, 2007.

RECYCLING — "From the point of view of environmental science urban environment can be considered as a highly condensed anthropogenic system, which is organized for the efficient flow of water, energy and information. This extremely dynamic super organism can efficiently provide the services required by society, such as safe drinking water, efficient sanitation and mitigation of floods which is fundamental due to very high population density. However, increases in society's education and environmental awareness raises the public demand for improvement of the quality of life. Therefore other expectation, depending to a great extent on proper ecosystem functioning, arise. These include ecosystem services like those determining human health and quality of life, based on water quality improvement by self-purification and clean air, as well as those fulfilling materialistic and spiritual aspirations. Such as high-quality living spaces, recreational areas and aesthetic value."

IWONA WAGNER, MACIEJ ZALEWSKI
Aquatic habitats in sustainable urban water management: science policy and practice. London: Taylor & Francis, 2008.

WATER "Water is a habitat, a life supporting resource, a means of production and transport, and a commodity. Water flows, it has geographic mobility.

Changes in water quality or flow at one end of a catchment can impact river characteristics downstream; resulting in the translation and transmission of attributes across time and space. Water is international, national, regional and local. The complexity and interdependence of the water environment network presents particular problems for management."

PAUL JEFFREY
Integrated urban water resources management.
Hlavinek, Petr, Jiri Marsalek, Tamara Kukharchyk, and Ivana Mahrikova, eds. Dordrecht: Springer, 2006.

WATER "It is important to note that the shadow value of water in a given location does not generally equal the direct cost of providing it there. Consider a limited water source whose pumping costs are zero. If demand for water from that source is sufficiently high, the shadow value of that water will not be zero; benefits to water users would be increased if the capacity of the source were greater. Equivalently, buyers will be willing to pay a non-zero price for water in short supply, even though its direct costs are zero.

A proper view of costs accommodates this phenomenon. When demand at the source exceeds capacity, it is not costless to provide a particular user with an additional unit of water. That water can only be provided by depriving some other user of the benefits of the water; that loss of benefits represents an opportunity cost." In other words, scarce resources have positive values and positive prices even if their direct cost of production is zero. Such a positive value—the shadow value of the water in situ—is called a "scarcity rent." Where direct costs are zero, the shadow value of the resource involved consists entirely of scarcity rent."

FRANKLIN. M. FISHER
Water trading and global water scarcity: international experiences.
Maestu, Josefina, ed. Abingdon, Oxon: RFF Press, 2013.

AIR "As an atmospheric force, whether through disaster or not, dust not only represents a counter form of nature. It produces a new milieu, a new environment through the colonization of earth and air. Dust, from demolition and construction, blocks the sun, lowering the temperature of the spaces immediately beneath it by several degrees. It transforms the odor and, most disturbingly, the pH balance of air. And the dust produced from demolishing buildings contains alkali levels rivaling some the most powerful industrial cleaners.

But in addition to all of these chemical and climatic aspects, dust is most often associated with dirt, soiling the surfaces and windows of buildings and coming inside through openings and passages."

DAVID GISSEN
Subnature: Architecture's Other Environments. Princeton Architectural Press, 2009.

AIR "As much as we try to control it, dust pervades us, and as much as it remains a nuisance-as a conveyor of destruction, hygienic obsessiveness, and historical change-dust in architecture contains a certain type of material and intellectual power that might be engage, even as we try to wash it away. Such an engagement with dust might produce a negotiation that neither relinquishes space to dust nor rejects its prominence in urban life. By addressing dust, we can confront its particular physical and emotional power, its connotations as a historical register, and its existence as a form of matter that moves with calamities and in the most banal moments of time."

DAVID GISSEN
Subnature: Architecture's Other Environments. Princeton Architectural Press, 2009.

WATER "Our cities' water systems were conceived in a different historical moment, in an era where recources seemed unlimited. Deep changes are taking part today. Our collective vision of the world is different from the one our predecessors had when designing the urban systems we live in. Further changes are expected with climate change: rising global temperature are expected to deepen water scarcity problems that already exist throughout the globe. Today's urban metabolisms have increasing resources needs and produce more and more excreta. We need to radically change the way we need to conceive our urban systems in order to keep our urban ecosystem resource needs within renewable source limits."

M. GOMEZ-GALVARRIATO FREER
Urban water II.
Mambretti, Stefano, and Carlos Alberto Brebbia, eds. Southampton: WIT Press, 2012.

EARTH "In combination the different dimensions of ecology have great potential to alter the outlook of designers, deepen their understanding of landscape and environment and assist in the development of an integrative and dynamic design methodology. While ecological sciences provide a holistic, dynamic and evolutionary understanding of landscape, ecology the idea inspires through its search for connecting patterns a search for ethical and spiritual dimensions, both of which have been increasingly absent from current design and planning approaches."

JALA MAKHZOUMI AND GLORIA PUNGETTI
Ecological landscape design and planning. London: Taylor & Francis, 2016.

FIRE "Rather than boosting efficiency as one effort in practice or more successfully managing the necessary information and documentation of its realization as a separate effort. Thermally active surfaces integrate material, energy, and practice by reducing by the number of layers and systems in a structure and thereby reduce the organizational complexity of building production."

KIEL MOE
Thermally active surfaces in architecture.
New York: Princeton Architectural Press, 2010.

FIRE "Architecture can no longer sustain its focus on the visual formation of objects alone anymore that its can sustain its incomplete and inadequate focus on the conservation, efficiency and optimization of energy. For decades, if not centuries, the question of architectural formation has rested on elaborately developed, but incomplete object compositions. The discipline of architecture has evolved such that the formation of buildings is taught and practice in ways that largely preclude engagement with buildings as actual formation of matter and energy.

Architecture's formations have been reduced to visual preoccupations and energy to mere quantities to optimize."

KIEL MOE
Architecture and energy: performance and style. Braham, William W., and Daniel Willis. ed. London: Routledge, 2013.

FIRE "Any analysis of the role played by energy in architecture is faced with serious limitations due to the lack of studies in the architectural bibliography, especially studies of popular architecture. An awareness of these limitations will allow us to understand better why architects have paid little attention to the interaction of form and energy, and to the bioclimatic approach in contemporary architecture in general.

The first limitation stems from the very essence of bioclimatic analysis; energy is immaterial, difficult to represent in images, changing in time and wrongfully left out of the architectural literature. This is why it is difficult to find a basic knowledge of the functional aesthetic possibilities of bioclimatism in the culture experience of present-day architect."

HELENA COCH ROURA
Architecture: comfort and energy. Gallo, Cettina, A. M. M Sayigh, and Marco Sala, ed. New York: Elsevier Science, 1998.

FIRE

BJARKE INGELS TALK
Hedonistic Sustainability
urbanNext.net

FIRE "A vast range of policy issues are raised by the effort to limit climate change, including perhaps the most basic of them all: how far are growth and sustainability (however that problematic term is defined) compatible? I shall offer a few comments on three areas only: what should be the role of green taxation; how far green taxes are compatible with preserving or enhancing social justice; and what are the implications of the overlap between climate change and energy policy."

ANTHONY GIDDENS
The politics of climate change. Cambridge (UK): Polity Press, 2012.

FIRE "When energy is released, whether heat and light from a burning piece of wood, sound waves from a speaker, light from a flashlight, or steam from a hot cup of coffee, that energy seeks to dissipate into its surroundings. "Energy spontaneously disperses from being localized to becoming spread out if it is not hindered from doing so," states the second law of thermodynamics. The rate at which that energy spreads is based on the parameters of its surroundings, including existing temperature, light levels, humidity, and air velocity. For this reason, the shape of an architecture made of energy cannot have an unwavering and consistent form due to one primary feature; instead, it manifests the feedback between the energy exerted to create a physical space and the context of atmospheric conditions that interact with that energy. Such architectural shape is a boundary that represents the relationship between material energies and existing climate conditions.

These two factors interact and exchange forms of energy that influence not only the architecture's initial shape but also the degree to which it can fluctuate over time, as external atmospheric conditions change. Architectural shape will therefore always be in a feedback loop between the existing environment and the system an architect produces.

This feedback goes beyond the external forces acting on its shape to include those that enter the architecture. There is an "energy balance equation" in which anything that crosses that boundary (additional people—their body temperature, physical mass, or supporting objects) affects the energy system, that is, the architecture."

SEAN LALLY
Projective ecologies.
Cambridge, MA: Harvard University Graduate School of Design, 2014.

FIRE "All of these biogeophysical processes require energy and it is a grave thermodynamic and ecological error to presume, as other forms of energy analysis do, that these bio-geophysical resources are an infinite reserve of available forms of captured energy. Indeed, the notion that raw materials for building construction are plentiful and can be extracted at will for free from Earth's geo-biosphere —and that these materials do not undergo any degradation or related deterioration in energy performance while in use— is alarming and entirely inaccurate.

The flow of solar energy through these manifold biogeophysical processes must further temper our understanding of the energy and materials that presuppose our buildings and cities."

RAVI SRINIVASAN, KIEL MOE
The hierarchy of energy in architecture: energy analysis.
London: Routledge, 2015.

FIRE	"Apparently, our future is dark: oil and gas are not going to last so much - at present low prices - because of the depletion of the low cost reserves; coal is not an option clue to its high carbon emission per unit of energy (neither is carbon sequestration a safe, sustainable and cheap answer); nuclear energy faces insurmountable problems such as the depletion of affordable uranium reserves, the unsolved issue of radioactive wastes and security against terrorism; renewable energy sources cannot have any significant role in the present energy system because the large amount of energy needed to keep the system running cannot be provided by them, due to their low density, territorial distribution, and availability."	**FEDERICO BUTTER** *Urban Energy Transition: From Fossil Fuels to Renewable Power.* ed. Droege, Peter. Oxford: Elsevier, 2008.
FIRE	"This relationship 'in between' urbanism and energy is mediated by governance capacity and capability to act. It is how this capacity and the capability to act is organized in this space 'in between' that is critical to understanding the consequences of action in relation to urban energy. It is in this space that new 'intermediary' organizations seek to mediate between the priorities, purpose, targets and objectives of those social interests that provide its 'membership' and their 'implementation' in communities, organizations, buildings, households and so on."	**MICHAEL HODSON, SIMON MARVIN AND HARRIET BULKELEY** *Renewable energy and the public: from NIMBY to participation.* Devine-Wright, Patrick. ed. London: Earthscan, 2010.
RECIYCLING	"The reasons for seeking a state of zero waste are dear in terms of reducing costs and environmental load and achieving a closed-loop material flow by means of resource recovery. The design and specification of buildings need to be precise and integrated with the construction process to encourage waste minimization. Greater off-site manufacturing of building components will assist this process. To encourage the reuse of buildings at the end of their life, the design and construction process should be undertaken with ease of disassembly as an objective. These considerations indicate that pursuing and achieving a state of zero waste lie squarely among the responsibilities of construction management."	**NICHOLAS CHILESHE, JIAN ZUE, STEPHEN PULLEN AND GEORGE ZILLANTE** *Designing for Zero Waste: Consumption, Technologies and the Built Environment.* Lehmann, Steffen, and Robert Crocker. ed., Florence: Taylor and Francis, 2013.
FIRE	"No other concept has disturbed and disfigured our understanding of energy more than the seemingly innocent idea of isolation. Further, no other material practice in architecture has systematically reinforced this errant idea than insulation. In too many cases, architects and engineers treat buildings as increasingly 'efficient' isolated systems without any regard for the larger energy hierarchies of a building. This is the exact opposite of how architects should engage energy."	**KIEL MOE** *Insulating modernism: isolated and non-isolated thermodynamics in architecture.* Basel: Birkhäuser, 2014.

MOVING "Transport is a key to sustainability because it can either be used to accelerate resource depletion and global atmospheric damage or it can be the focus of living arrangements that can be serviced by environmentally tolerable practices such as walking and cycling. However, reducing dependence on motorised transport and changing the organization of land uses and activities are obstructed by the persistence among decision makers of the view that transport investment is an essential prerequisite to economic growth which is itself essential to development."

RODNEY TOLLEY, BRIAN JOHN TURTON
Transport Systems, Policy and Planning: A Geographical Approach, S.l.: Routledge, 2016.

MOVING "The present relationship between cities and automobiles represent, in short, one of those jokes that history sometimes plays on progress. The interval of the automobile's development as everyday transportation has corresponded precisely with the interval during which the ideal of the suburbanized anti-city was developed architecturally, sociologically, legislatively and financially."

JANE JACKOBS
The death and life of great American cities. New York: Vintage books, 1961.

MOVING "Why would anyone want to 'own' and maintain an automobile when they could "access" a driverless vehicle from a car-sharing service at a moment's notice from their cell phone and have it ferry them effortlessly with GPS guidance to their destination, paying only for the precise time they are using the vehicle? If ever proof were needed that the capitalist era, wedded to the exchange of property in markets, is ceding ground to the access of services in the Collaborative Commons, the changing relationship to the automobile is prima facie evidence of the great transformation at hand."

JEREMY RIFKIN
The zero marginal cost society: the internet of things, the collaborative commons, and the eclipse of capitalism. New York: Palgrave Macmillan, 2014.

MOVING "We are thus in a new era that has come much faster than we had predicted: the end of automobile dependence. The planning paradigm that enabled cities to be built around the car is now virtually dead; a different kind of city can now envisaged and each day sees more evidence of its reality being implemented for economic, environmental, and social reasons."

PETER NEWMAN, JEFFREY KENWORTHY
The end of automobile dependence: how cities are moving beyond car-based planning. Newman, Peter, and Jeffrey R. Kenworthy. Washington, DC: Island Press, 2015.

MOVING "Sustainable development applied to transport system requires the promotion of linkages between environmental protection, economic efficiency and social progress. Under the environmental dimension, the objective consists in understanding reciprocal influences of the physical environment and the practices of the industry and that environmental issues are addressed by all aspects of the transport. industry."

JEAN-PAUL RODRIGUEZ, CLAUDE COMTOIS
The geography of transport systems. London: Routledge, 2009.

AIR "Today, we know that moving forward in a sustainable manner requires more than simply building new energy-efficient buildings or increasing the number of hybrid cars on our roads. We must make significant, demonstrable changes to our existing city landscape, altering not only how our city looks but how it works. An urban ecosystem relies on the true integration of each of a city's elements. Smart buildings rely on smart transit networks; smart energy systems rely on the creation of smart infrastructure. The process of DeCarbonization aims to improve the performance of every major metropolitan system to create a healthier, more sustainable, more livable city."

ADRIAN DEVAUN SMITH, GORDON N. GILL
Toward zero carbon: The Chicago central area decarbonization plan. Australia: Images Publishing, 2011.

FIRE "Ultimately the prospect of a survivable future hinges on energy and how rapidly societies shift from fossil fuel dependence to near carbon neutral energy. The case for renewable energy is being strengthened by increasing anxiety over the alleged gap between new discoveries of reserves of fossil fuels and rising demand, especially from China and India. Rapid economic growth in the developing world means that predicted energy demand under the high emissions CO_2 scenario is outpacing gains in energy efficiency and could reach over three times the current level of primary energy demand by the end of the century. [...] Renewables can rescue the world from energy starvation. But quality of life will only be sustained with massive cuts in the demand for energy."

PETER F. SMITH
Building for a changing climate: the challenge for construction, planning and energy. London: Routledge, 2016.

MOVING "Electric vehicles do not only replace regular cars but also bikes and pedestrian traffic. Public transport is not affected by electric vehicles, especially not for commuting. For short distances of 10 km or less Pedelecs are an alternative to non-electric motorized vehicles. Even though most respondents have an overall positive attitude towards electromobility. Only a few would consider buying an electric car due to the high costs of purchase. However, certain incentives, such as tax reduction and free parking would change peoples' minds."

PETRA K. SCHAEFER, KATHRIN SCHMIDT AND DENNIS KNESE
Evolutionary Paths Towards the Mobility Patterns of the Future. Hülsmann, Michael, and Dirk Fornahl. Berlin, Heidelberg: Springer Berlin Heidelberg, 2014.

MOVING "Electro mobility is considered to be a pioneering trend in the field of road traffic to reduce the emissions of greenhouse gases. Because of technical restrictions, which limit the range and loading capacity of vehicles, electro mobility is mostly discussed with regard to passenger cars. However, recent developments raise the question whether electro mobility can be also used promisingly for local height traffics of the so-called city logistics, interesting are especially transports on the 'first' and 'last mile' of supply chains with combined transports."

SABANA CRIES, CHRISTIAN ME LIEN! HEWING AND STEPHAN ZELEWSKI
Innovative methods in logistics and supply chain management current issues and emerging practices. Blecker, Thorsten. Berlin: Epubli, 2015.

WATER — "Although water is part of a global system, how it is used and managed locally and regionally is what really counts. Unlike oil, wheat, and most other important commodities, water is needed in quantities too large to make it practical to transport long distances. No global water crisis is likely to shake the world the way the energy crisis of the seventies did. But with key crop-producing regions and numerous metropolitan areas showing signs of water scarcity and depletion, global food supplies and economic health are in jeopardy. Moreover, global warming from the buildup of greenhouse gases could greatly complicate regional water problems by shifting the patterns of rainfall and runoff that agriculture and urban water systems are geared to.

Without question, water development has been a key to raising living standards, and it needs to be extended to the one fifth of humanity who have largely missed out on its benefits."

SANDRA POSTEL
The Last oasis: facing water scarcity. London: Earth scan, 1992.

FIRE — "Energy is a constantly fought over commodity, but Free Energy City demonstrates that by rationalizing a city's immediate hinterland, whether rooftops, rivers, estuaries or even derelict realm, and developing urban energy farms, such a prolific amount of electricity and heat can be developed that it becomes a clean and 'free-to-use' asset.

By running cities autonomously on decentralized independent networks, current alternatives like nuclear are completely redundant not only on efficiency and production grounds, but also on ecological terms."

GREG KEEFFE
Sustainable energy landscapes: designing, planning, and development. Dobbelsteen, Andy Van den., and Sven Stremke. ed. Boca Raton, FL: CRC Press, 2013.

FIRE — "The fields and disciplines that architects have to interact with have grown so much in complexity and breadth that comprehensive expertise is impossible. This has led to increased dependence on technical consultants, but also to a retraction from the basic intuition about energy potentials that influence all areas of design. The experience of designing the thermoheliodome convinces me that real innovation is possible when architects can experience the differences among energy potentials directly. Whether that knowledge stems from theoretical descriptions, the origins of the theory, or from concrete analogies and examples, the objective is to build an intuitive relationship with energy.

Architects don't have to become experts in thermodynamics or energy systems. It is as simple as accepting the abstract energy potentials that both we as organisms and buildings as systems contain."

FORREST MEGGERS
Energy accounts: architectural representations of energy, climate, and the future. Willis, Daniel, William W. Braham, Katsuhiko Muramoto, and Michael E. Mann. London: Routledge, 2017.

MAKING "Architecture is creating new challenges as computing moves into everyday life. As hardware components become smaller, faster and cheaper, computational devices are becoming embedded in building elements such as doors, walls, floors, and furniture. These devices are largely invisible and linked together through wireless network. Buildings would largely contain smart spaces and appliances that provide access to computational resources at any place and time. Architecture becomes an interaction interfaces between human and computers. A key problem in developing for such ubiquitous smart spaces is to map physical spaces to the underlying computing infrastructure and the corresponding patterns of situated interaction in everyday life. Many ubiquitos smart spaces projects have emphasized the computational capabilities, with less concern for the *logical mapping* between user experiences, digital infrastructures and physical interfaces in a broader context of design."

TAYSHENG JENG
Design computing and cognition '04. Gero, John S. ed., Dordrecht: Springer, 2011.

AIR "If architecture is, ultimately, solid, here we have to interact explicitly with the gassy, kinetic conditions of the medium. We have to reflect on its consistency, over and above the need to protect and enclose. More than providing protection, totally closed off from the environment, we must try to develop a more positive relationship by introducing a form or organism that somehow creates a continuation of these facts."

JOSEP LLUIS MATEO, FLORIAN SAUTER
Earth, water, air, fire. The four elements and architecture. New York: Actar, 2015.

AIR "Buildings today have much shorter load changes and have to fulfill much closer comfort requirements. But even then convective or radiation exchange accessible thermal mass by ceilings or walls can provide an important buffer effect to reduce peak load demands and improve occupants' comfort. Activating this thermal capacity is typically done by natural or forced night ventilation. which partially raises questions in respect to security and air loads such as dust and insects. In addition these systems need motorized facade openings with a control taking into account the inside temperature and outside rain and storm events. For forced night ventilation the fan energy should be minimized and recalculated into primary energy and compared with cooling savings."

MATTHIAS SCHULER
Thermally active surfaces in architecture. Moe, Kiel. New York: Princeton Architectural Press, 2010.

AIR "Understanding the systems of radiant interactions between the material of bodies and buildings form the basis of radiation design, which increase air quality, reduce noise pollution in indoor space, redefines the concept of comfort, reduces non-essential/tectonic components of the building, and engages material as a total thermodynamic regulator. In short, it establishes a symbiotic dialogue between body and architecture, with sensorial, somatic implications in addition to their traditional purely visual or phenomenological relations."

DANIEL WILLIS, WILLIAM W. BRAHAM, KATSUHIKO MURAMOTO, DANIEL A. BARBER
Energy Accounts: Architectural representations of energy, climate, and the future. London: Routledge, Taylor & Francis Group, 1995.

EARTH — "Global change cannot be understood in terms of a simple cause-effect paradigm. Human-driven changes cause multiple effects that cascade through the Earth System in complex ways. These effects interact with each other and with local and regional-scale changes in multidimensional patterns that are difficult to understand and even more difficult to predict. Surprises abound. Earth System dynamics are characterized by critical thresholds and abrupt changes. Human activities could inadvertently trigger such changes with severe consequences for Earth's environment and inhabitants."

ANDREW S. GOUDIE
The human impact on the natural environment: past, present, and future. Oxford: Wiley-Blackwell, 2013.

EARTH — "The smallest meaningful unit of sustainability is probably the city-state, or the city and its surrounding region, though with contemporary trade and commerce the extent of regions has literally become global. Romantic proposals for solitary, sustainable buildings in the landscape are dream-images or, at best, experimental laboratories for the real work of reckoning with regional arrangements of production and consumption."

DAN WILLIS, WILLIAM W. BRAHAM, KATSUHIKO MURAMOTO, DANIEL A. BARBER
Energy accounts: architectural representations of energy, climate, and the future. London: Routledge, 2016.

COMMUNICATING — "Spatially, all developments can lead to two different scenarios that can occur simultaneously. On the one hand, urban media can be deployed to reinforce the spatial boundaries of a parochial domain: electronic access gates, dynamic pricing mechanisms or camera monitoring can exclude or, more subtly, make a place less attractive for those who are not considered part of a parochial district or do not comply with the applicable protocol. Digital media can thus strengthen the clear boundaries between the domains of different urban groups."

MARTIJN DE WAAL
The City as Interface: How New Media Are Changing the City. Rotterdam: NAI 010 Publishers, 2014.

MAKING — "Digital fabrication will usher in an era defined by individual control. The factory of the future will focus on mass customization and may look more like those weavers´ cottage that Ford´s assembly line."

CARLO RATTI, MATTHEW CLAUDEL
The city of tomorrow: sensors, networks, hackers, and the future of urban life. New Haven; London: Yale university press, 2016.

EARTH — "The emergent topic of urban adaptation to the effects of climate change is among the more pressing areas of research for those engaged in the built environment. While it was not entirely clear how the mitigation of climate change implicated the disciplines of architecture, urban design, or planning, the more recent focus on adaptation to ongoing effects of anthropogenic climate change puts those fields at the center of the conversation."

CHARLES WALDHEIM
South Florida and Sea Level: Adaptive Strategies for Green Infrastructure, Landscape Ecology, and Cultural Heritage, GSD, 2016.

COMMUNICATING | "Thanks to the exploitation of "tele-communications," the City today, to a greater degree than ever before, actually is those data sets and is those networks of public equipment through which the data circulates. Our rapidly disarticulating city is increasingly reconstituting itself in vitro as a dynamic archive, where the latter term is understood as a massive depository of local and global knowledges that, in the manner of any natural ecology, provide a maximally flexible, 'satisficing' ('suffice' plus 'satisfy') infrastructure for life." | **SANFORD KWINTER, DANIELA FABRICIOUS**
Mutations. Barcelona: Actar and arc en rêve, 2000.

SENSING

CARLO RATTI TALK
Digital Technology & Physical Space
urbanNext.net

COMMUNICATING | "When people talk about smart cities, they often cast a wide net that pulls in every new public-service innovation from bike sharing to top-up parks. The broad view is important since cites must be viewed holistically. Simply installing some new technology, no matter how elegant or powerful, cannot solve a city's problems in isolation. But there really is something going on here—information technology is clearly going to be a big part of the solution. It deserves treatment on its own." | **ANTHONY M. TOWNSEND**
Smart Cities: Big data, civic hackers, and the quest for a new utopia. New York: WW Norton & Co, 2014.

COMMUNICATING | "The city is a complex text and a permanent broadcast. Therefore, our ambition as architects and urban designers must be to spatially unfold more simultaneous choices of communicative situations in dense, perceptually palpable, and legible arrangements. The visual field must be dense with offerings and information about what lies behind the immediate field of vision. The parametricist logics of rule-based variation, differentiation, and correlation establish order within the built environment, giving those who must navigate it the crucial possibility of making inferences." | **PATRIK SCHUMACHER**
Paradigms in computing: Making, machines, and models for design agency. Evolo, 2014.

SENSING | "In Reality, technology displays a significant degree of social and political indeterminacy. In the case of the smart city, the indeterminacy is expressed through the existence of another model than that of the technologically managed cyborg-city. In contrast to neo-cybernetic temptation are the desires and experiences of spontaneity and collaboration that are just as present in the contemporary landscape." | **ANTOINE PICON**
Smart cities: a spatialised intelligence. Chichester: Wiley, 2015.

HEARTH

"Urban design—that is, the creative spatial organization of places—is a growing planning concern that presents many opportunities for improving sustainability. The form and character of places within cities should work well for both people and the environment, and many twentieth century locales do neither. Too often, the design of communities requires residents to drive everywhere fails to provide walkable and human-scaled public spaces, requires high levels of water and energy use, and destroys or fragments wildlife habitat. Good urban design matters—particularly as cities become more compact and higher density."

S. M. WHEELER
Metropolitan sustainability: understanding and improving the urban environment. Sawston, Cambridge, UK: Woodhead Pub., 2012.

SENSING

"Intuitively, environmental sensing can be viewed as a procedure to distinguish and learn the complex condition of the environment. Moreover, environmental sensing not only requires the collection of the information from a group of the sensors, but also it is desired to process it and discover the pattern of its internal behavior. Fortunately, image fusion offers an improved comprehension on the underlying structure or behavior of the environment. It can integrate pertinent geometrical information into a single informative image, e.g.. a combination of high spatial and spectral or spatial-temporal information. This technology can be categorize into three classes broadly, i.e., pixel-level, feature level and decision-level."

ZHONGLIANG JING, HAN PANG, GANG XIAO
Intelligent Environmental Sensing. Lung, Henry, Subhas Chandra Mukhopadhyay. ed., Springer International PU, 2016.

SENSING

"Within smart urbanism the use of distributed sensing technologies and the potential coupling of mobile technologies, urban infrastructures and environmental sensors has been championed as a possible exemplar strategy for the achievement of both environmental security and urban sustainability for example via air quality sensors embedded across networks of personal mobile devices."

SIMON MARVIN, ANDRÉS LUQUE-AYALA, COLIN MCFARLANE
Smart urbanism: utopian vision or false dawn? London: Routledge, 2016.

SENSING

"It is true that some, if not many, smart city texts mention the important role of people. Often, however, it seems like a second thought, which was added because someone had noticed that it had been omitted. Even when the text is present, the parts about citizen engagement are not always incorporated by the governments that purchase the advice and technological development from the smart city vendors. The smart city expectation that 'data' is sufficient for city infrastructure management ignores the fact that social science 'data' is not absolute, non-negotiable. without politics, or unequivocally and discreetly translatable into something else."

DOUGLAS SCHULER
Human smart cities: rethinking the interplay between design and planning. Concilio, Grazia, and Francesca Rizzo. Switzerland: Springer, 2016.

SENSING

"There is a real need for cities to encourage more of the ideal sharing of the underutilized resources and that smart cities may actually be the ones that do regulate sharing enterprises instead of let them operate free of restrictions."

BOYD DEREK COHEN, PABLO MUNOZ
The emergence of the urban entrepreneur. Santa Barbara, CA: Praeger, an imprint of ABC-CLIO, LLC, 2016.

COMMUNICATING

"To improve our understanding of the recursive interactions between cities and telecommunications, we must leave behind the myths of determinism, both technological and social. The assumption that telecommunications impact in some simple, universal and linear way on cities is still common; the stress that they simply reflect some abstract capitalist political economy is still prevalent in some critical literatures. Both, we argue, are unhelpful. An integrated perspective of cities and telecommunications teaches us that social action shapes telecommunications applications in cities in diverse and contingent ways, even if this goes on against the backcloth of broader political economic trends.

New telecommunications technologies bring new options and capabilities within which urban processes can be shaped."

STEPHEN GRAHAM, SIMON MORVIN
Telecommunications and the city: electronic spaces, urban places. London: Routledge, 1996

MOVING

"The City, as seen through the medium of that face, oozes with living data to be touched and rewritten all over again. It doesn't only represent its world, but affects it as well; interaction is recursive, as a single User action is itself also new information aggregated into a living whole, informing what everyone else sees as their map.

This recursion can cause one person to change his path and decisions in accordance with the actions of another User as indexed by the App, which is itself read as a real physical event, happening as part of the urban fabric, not floating 'on top of it.' In this way, the virtual envelope of the mobile apparatus is, as much as the architectural envelope, a real circuit of movement primary to the City layer. But that equivalence also complicates programming strategies."

BENJAMIN BRATTON
The Stack—On Software and Sovereignty. Massachusetts: MIT Press, 2016.

COMMUNICATING

"There is a disconnect between the stories and promises associated with the technology and what the urban space is actually doing. Both urban space and telecommunications are technologies and mediums of information.

Fiber-optic cable buried in the ground gives land a new value much like a high-way or railroad. Mobile telephony, while atomized and airborne, must nevertheless tap into that physical broadband network, and at these or any other switching points, a bottleneck or monopoly can develop. The position of the fiber in the urban and rural areas or the character of new enclaves and roads are all spatial factors with the power to either amplify or diminish the access to information."

KELLER EASTERLING
Extrastatecraft: The Power of Infrastructure Space. London, Brooklyn: Verso. 2014.

SENSING "The current debate about Smart Cities is strongly influenced by technological and application-oriented "hard" perspectives that predominantly materialize through the insertion of smart infrastructures into existing urban systems. Citizens (as individuals) and urban societies (as bodies) remain passive beneficiaries, end users or consumers–or at least are not regarded as the "software" that runs the city and gives Vitality to the (smart) "hardware". Not surprisingly, the smartification of the urban is contrasted by increasing demands made by civil society and urban social movements towards greater inclusion in decision-making: New urban actors acquire new agency through local knowledge, expertise, creativity, social networking skills and collaborative capabilities, or social entrepreneurship. We can–and must–question the perception of the Smart City as an operationalized version of 'sustainability', but must also extract and interlink the empowering aspects within smart technology–especially regarding the role of people."

ALBERTO VANOLO, SASKIA SASSEN, MARK DEAKIN
Beware of smart people! redefining the smart city paradigm towards inclusive urbanism: symposium proceedings, Berlin, June 19th to 20th, 2015. Berlin: Universitätsverlag der TU Berlin, 2016.

SENSING "In our rush to build smart cities on a foundation of technologies for sensing and control of the world around us, should we be at all surprised when they are turned around to control us?"

ANTHONY M. TOWNSEND
Smart Cities: Big data, civic hackers, and the quest for a new utopia. New York: WW Norton & Co, 2014.

AIR "The ecological crisis, and the large-scale destruction of biodiversity, can threaten the very existence of the human species. The baneful consequences of an irresponsible mismanagement of the global economy, guided only by ambition for wealth and power, must serve as a summons to a forthright reflection on man: man is not only a freedom which he creates for himself. Man does not create himself. He is spirit and will, but also nature."

POPE FRANCIS
Transcript of the Pope's speech to the United Nations, 2015.

EARTH "Rapid global population growth, escalating pollution and waste generation, environmental degradation, and a form of economic growth that was rather profligate if not downright destructive with respect to the use of non-renewable as well as renewable resources have created a whole series of global concerns. Add to that the recognition that widespread (sometimes global) ecological consequences could be produced by small-scale activities (such as the local use of various pesticides like DDT) or that the burgeoning scale of fossil fuel use has been exacerbating climate change, and that losses of habitats and of biodiversity have been accelerating, and it is clear that the environmental issue will assume prominence in global concerns in ways that have not broadly been experienced before. There is, as it were, a translation of traditional environmental concerns (about, say, clean air and water, landscape conservation, and healthy living environments) from a rather local (often urban or regional) to a more global scale."

DAVID HARVEY
Spaces of hope. Berkeley: University of California Press, 2008.

MAKING

"The true ambition of the Metropolis is to create a world totally fabricated by man, i.e., to live inside fantasy. The responsibilities of a specifically Metropolitan architecture have increased correspondingly: to design those hermetic enclaves—bloated private realms—that comprise the Metropolis. Such an architecture not only creates the "sets" of everyday life, but it also defines its contents with all possible means and disciplines such as literature, psychology, etc. Through the magical arrangement of human activities on all possible levels, it writes a scenario for the scriptless Metropolitan extras."

REM KOOLHAAS
Architecture theory since 1968. Hays, K. Michael, ed. Cambridge, MA: The MIT Press, 2000.

RECYCLING

"Now that the bulk of humanity has chosen to in urbanized area, waste management needs a radical revision. What kind of effort is required to reuse the landfills´ bountiful contents? For hundred of years we designed cities to generate waste. Now it is time that we begin to design waste to regenerate our cities. What are the possibilities for urban environments when our aged infrastructure has been recalibrated? how can urban intensification and waste mixed?"

MITCHELL JOACHIM
Building from waste: recovered materials in architecture and construction. Hebel, Dirk E., Marta H. Wisniewska, and Felix Heisel. Basel: Birkhäuser, 2014.

COMMUNICATING

"The global city and the network of these cities is a space that is both place centered in that it is embedded in particular and strategic locations; and it is transterritorial because it connects sites that are not geographically proximate yet are intensely connected to each other. If we consider that global cities concentrate both the leading sectors of global capital and a growing share of disadvantaged populations (immigrants, many of the disadvantaged women, people of color generally, and, in the megacities of developing countries, masses of shanty dwellers) then we can see that cities have become a strategic terrain for a whole series of conflicts and contradictions."

SASKIA SASSEN
Shanghai rising: state power and local transformations in a global megacity. Chen, Xiangming, and Zhenhua Zhou. Minneapolis: University of Minnesota Press, 2009.

MOVING

"Growth will only take place where conditions are actually already evident and transport investment may increase the rate of growth, but only in already vibrant local economies. If this is the case, then transport investment may contribute to greater variation in local economic growth. It may increase regional and local disparities rather than reduce them. However, if this is the case, how can new locations evolve or develop? The understanding of the dynamics of the development process and the role that transport might have as an agent to accelerate or slow it down is not well known. The effects may lie in the subjective psychology of perception, rather than in objective, measurable cost reductions. The image of a particular area may form an important part of the decision to locate."

PETER HALL AND DAVID BANISTER
Transport and urban development. London: Routledge, 2011.

COMMUNICATING

"Mobility, valued economically as a vector for growth, is also a fact of life for employees whose companies demand that they be mobile. What is more it takes on new forms that combine telecommunications, transportation and residential aspirations, utterly disrupting the temporalities of daily life and destabilizing the institutional infrastructure by calling for the reform of decision-making bodies at their very core and ultimately casting a doubt on the governability of urban areas in so doing."

VINCENT KAUFMANN
Rethinking the city: urban dynamics and motility.
Lausanne: EPFL Press, 2011.

AIR

"Public opinion and consumer demand will force the government to take actions that may have once seemed unimaginable. It is more than a pollution issue: if left uni-addressed, social stability could be threatened. And this is why the central government has put significant political capital behind an economic reform program that is also meant to more vigorously tackle pollution and environmental challenges."

MA JUN, DAMIEN MA, AND BERNARD CLEARY
The economics of air pollution in China: achieving better and cleaner growth. New York: Columbia University Press, 2016.

MAKING

"Post-industrial manufacturing systems that allow a high level of user involvement in the co-creation of objects do in fact hold the key to the reduction of global product consumption for many types of goods in a sustainable future."

PAUL ATKINSON, JUSTIN MARSHALL, ERTU UNVER, LIONEL T. DEAN
Fabvolution: development in digital fabrication. Malé-Alemany, Marta. Barcelona: Ajuntament de Barcelona, 2010.

MOVING

"There is a deep symbiosis between city and transport, with each of them affecting the other, and it is in the rapidly growing cities in developing countries that these tensions are most apparent. The choice is clear, namely that there are many innovations in terms of restraint on the use of the car, effective pricing policies, designation of priority users and uses of scarce urban space, the substitution of travel by tele activities, and a range of existing new modes of transport. But equally, there is a strong desire to produce and sell cars to new consumer markets and to provide employment in those same cities. The economic imperative has never been greater, but nor have the social and environmental consequences. The balance between the three main Wars of sustainable development and transport has never been more severely tested."

DAVID BANISTER
Unsustainable transport: city transport in the new century.
London: Routledge, 2007.

RECYCLING

"There are diverse opportunities to add value through simple design interventions and aesthetically pleasing WtE (Waste-to-Energy) plants. These interventions can go a long way toward changing public perception, creating a scenario where people will embrace WtE facilities as a viable source of energy and beneficial community amenities."

ANDREAS GEORGOULIAS
Architecture and waste: a replanned obsolescence.
Cambridge, MA: Harvard University Graduate School of Design: Actar, 2017.

EARTH — "It has become conventional to think of urbanism and landscape as opposing one another—or to think of landscape as merely providing temporary relief from urban life as shaped by buildings and infrastructure. But, driven in part by environmental concerns, landscape has recently emerged as a model and medium for the city, with some theorists arguing that landscape architects are the urbanists of our age. [...] With populations decentralizing and cities sprawling ever-outward, twenty-first-century urban planners are challenged by the need to organize not just people but space itself. Hence a new architectural discourse has emerged: landscape urbanism."

CHARLES WALDHEIM
Landscape as urbanism a general theory. Princeton: Princeton University Press, 2016.

COMMUNICATING — "The evidence available suggests that to include e-participation procedures in the normal activities of the institution, avoiding the use of additional resources, improves the outcomes of these participatory processes. The use of different e-participation tools for different targets and the political commitment by those responsible for the e-participation process within the institution has also a positive effect. To provide clear evidence that the contribution offered by participants, citizens and other stakeholders, is indeed taken into consideration in the formulation of urban policies and in its implementation is also seen as an important factor for the sustainability of the participatory process."

CARLOS NUNES SILVA
Citizen e-participation in urban governance: crowdsourcing and collaborative creativity. Hershey, PA: Information Science Reference, 2013.

RECYCLING

MARKUS BADER TALK
Recycling Architecture
urbanNext.net

RECYCLING — "The problem of waste and the history of architecture seems to have become intertwined at the latest from this moment onward. A similar mindset and the ensuring designs are to be found around the world until today. Following the strategy that uses architecture to form barriers or borders to separate human beings from their own waste."

DIRK E. HEBEL, MARTA H. WISNIEWSKA, FELIX HEISEL
Building from waste: recovered materials in architecture and construction. Basel: Birkhäuser, 2014.

RECYCLING — "Within this emerging aesthetic of antiseptic urban consumption, growing legal constraints on urban scrounging and scrap accumulation accomplish two related purposes: the protection of upscale consumption zones and upscale communities from symbolic intrusion by ragtag urban scroungers, and the rationalized control of waste that these consumers and communities predictably spawn."

JEFF FERRELL
Empire of scrounge inside the urban underground of dumpster diving, trash picking, and street scavenging. New York: New York University Press, 2006.

COMMUNICATING — "If such a city-as-platform can be created and then replicated around the world, cities would be able to interrogate each others´ data directly and easily. The benefits could be enormous: city governments would be able to learn from one another with enormous speed and efficiency. It would lower the barriers created by siloed agency operations, as city halls around the world no longer answered basic urban governance questions: How do I best target emergency services during dangerous weather? How do I target health service interventions so so that they will have the greatest impact?"

STEPHEN GOLDSMITH, SUSAN CRAWFORD
The responsive city: engaging communities through data-smart governance. San Francisco, CA: Jossey-Bass, a Wiley Brand, 2014.

COMMUNICATING — "The recent bout of globalization has significantly diminished the monopoly protections given historically by high transport and communications costs, while the removal of institutional barriers to trade (protectionism) has likewise diminished the monopoly rents to be procured by keeping foreign competition out. But capitalism cannot do without monopoly powers, and craves means to assemble them."

DAVID HARVEY
Rebel cities: from the right to the city to the urban revolution. London: Verso, 2013.

COMMUNICATING — "For a new cadre of civic leaders, smart technology isn't just way to do more or less. It´s a historic opportunity to relink and reinvents government on a more open, transparent, democratic, and responsive model. They are deploying social media to create more responsive channels of communication with citizens. Publishing vast troves of government data on the Web and sharing real-time feeds on the location of everything from subways to snowplows.

There's also a huge economic opportunity. By unlocking public databases and building broadband infrastructure, many cities hope to spawn homegrown inventions that others will want to buy and attract highly mobile entrepreneurs and creative talent. Looking smart perhaps even more than actually being smart, is crucial to competing today´s global economy."

ANTHONY M. TOWNSEND
Smart Cities: Big data, civic hackers, and the quest for a new utopia. New York: WW Norton & Co, 2014.

EARTH — "A proper representation of a city's system boundary is essential for allocating appropriate responsibility for city carbon management, for policy making and for devising the effective carbon mitigation regimes. Comparing cities for their carbon emissions, activities and policies need a very detailed and careful look. A comparative perspective provides important insights but is often challenging, especially in case of cities where information is scarce and unconsolidated."

M. ROHINTON EMMANUEL, KEITH BAKER
Carbon management in the built environment. London: Routledge, 2012.

WATER

"Water trading can probably work only in properly working economic systems. In effect, water markets do not exist in isolation, and water is but one (although a very important one) among the many inputs used in the economy. In the same sense, we cannot expect to have an efficient use of water in an economy in which inefficiency is pervasive.

When, for instance, the exchange rate is overpriced, this will distort the economy and the use of all natural resources, including water. Interest rates lower than the opportunity cost of capital, artificially maintained by lax monetary policies and increasing external borrowing, will also boost the derived demand of water in the overall economy. Even in the presence of model water institutions, we cannot expect an efficient allocation of water if the agricultural sector is driven by price-distorting subsidies."

CARLOS MARIO GÓMEZ
Water trading and global water scarcity: international experiences. Maestu, Josefina, ed. Abingdon, Oxon: RFF Press, 2013.

WATER

"Conflicts involving land use and water are complicated even where lines of authority are dear. They evoke competing visions of community identity and disagreement about how to manage scientific uncertainty and local fiscal limitations. Participants enter these disputes with conflicting goals and different ideas about the meaning and value of water itself. Developers seek to harness and direct water so it can meet the demands of homeowners and promote economic prosperity."

MEGAN MULLIN
Governing the tap: special district governance and the new local politics of water. Cambridge, MA: MIT Press, 2009.

RECYCLING

"The pursuit of sustainable waste management as we enter the 21st century must be placed within the context of diverse pressures on public policy from sources such as the revolution in information technology, the restructuring of the global economy, mass movements of people in search of a better quality of life, fluidity and uncertainty in political developments, and the difficulties facing the post-war Keynesian welfare state as an ageing population and intense fiscal pressures force a constant re-evaluation of the relative roles of the state and the market in modem capitalist societies."

MATTHEW GANDY
Recycling and the politics of urban waste. London: Routledge, 2014.

RECYCLING

"Considering waste within regimes of power and practice that link modes of government, policy, institutions and agents (including the architectural profession and architects) moves it beyond the status of the by-product or the unintended consequence of discrete events. Wasting becomes an arena of deliberate action intertwined with collective mode of disposal, conservation and reuse in both material and conceptual terms."

C. GREIG CRYSLER
Consuming architecture: on the occupation, appropriation and interpretation of buildings. Maudlin, Daniel, Vellinga, Marcel. ed., London: Routledge, 2014.

COMMUNICATING

"In fact, globalization has been accompanied by the creation of new legal regimes and practices and the expansion and renovation of some older forms that bypass national legal systems. Globalization and governmental deregulation have not meant the absence of regulatory regimes and institutions for the governance of international economic relations. Among the most important in the private sector today are international commercial arbitration and the variety of institutions that fulfill the rating and advisory functions that have become essential for the operation of the global economy."

SASKIA SASSEN
Losing control: Sovereignty in an age of globalization.
New York: Columbia University Press, 1995.

WATER

"Water demand throughout the world is increasing as a consequence of population growth, changing diets, and economic growth. Moreover, since the 1975 environmental awareness and values have gained currency and recreational demand for water has grown. In the future these influences will continue to increase demand, while increases in supply will be limited due to the predicted impact of climate change and limited opportunities for new major water supply infrastructure within sustainable, economic, environmental and political constraints. As a consequence water scarcity will increase, especially within semi-arid and arid regions. Failing to manage these growing demands will have significant environmental, social and economic implications, especially within low to middle-income countries and communities where water is a key factor to reduce poverty and improve public health.

Reflecting these developments and concerns, there has been a major shift in water policy away from supply management; that is, meeting new demand with increased supply, to demand management; that is, meeting new demand by using existing supply more efficiently and reallocating water from existing to new users. This shift has also changed how water is perceived, from being a social good to being an economic good that should be allocated according to market forces. An important element of the new paradigm is the use of market instruments such as full cost recovery prices, private property rights, water markets, and privatization."

HENNING BJORNLUND, SARAH WHEELER, PETER ROSSINI
Water trading and global water scarcity: international experiences.
Maestu, Josefina, ed.
Abingdon, Oxon: RFF Press, 2013.

RECYCLING

"Urban infill is on the rise. The practice of reusing rundown buildings in urban cores, urban infill is the salvaging of complete structures. In situationalizing urban infill and creating financial incentives that reward reuse over demolition help reduce architectural waste and revitalize, rather than gentrifying, blighted urban areas."

JESSICA KELLNER
Housing reclaimed sustainable homes for next to nothing.
Gabriola: New Society Publishers, 2011.

MOVING

"Points fixed on the ground are akin to members that have momentarily stopped moving. Fixed points connect to create a constantly moving chain of mobility. Permanence lies not in buildings or the earth but in the fact that the world is constantly moving."

YOUNG JUNE LEE
Machine Critique,
Seoul: Hyeonsilmunhwa
Yeongu, 2006.

COMMUNICATING

"Who could be opposed to the idea of collaborative consumption and a sharing economy? These new economic models seem so benign. Sharing represents the best part of human nature. Reducing addictive consumption, optimizing frugality, and fostering a more sustainable way of life is not only laudable, but essential if we are to ensure our survival. But even here, there are winners and losers. The still-dominant capitalist system believes it can find value in the collaborative economy by leveraging aspects of the sharing culture toward new revenue-generating streams. Still, whatever profit it can squeeze out of the growing networked Commons will pale in comparison to the ground it loses."

JEREMY RIFKIN
The zero marginal cost society:
the internet of things, the
collaborative commons, and the
eclipse of capitalism. New York:
Palgrave Macmillan, 2014.

FIRE

"Another explanation of the non-decreasing energy demand in the household sector is that decreased energy use is often rhetorically connected with changing people' current lifestyles to ones that are less comfortable and convenient. But is it 50s? How can we know that reduced energy use in a household does not rather contribute to the good life of its members? To draw any conclusions about how energy conservation will affect a household we must know more about how energy use contributes to everyday life today, which is the focus of this article. Visualization strategies can help us to understand household occupants' energy consumption when striving for sustainability. To gain new knowledge in this area we need to know how life is lived today, not just in specific households but also in households at the aggregate level."

**KAJSA ELLEGAARD AND
JENNY PALM**
Energy accounts: architectural
representations of energy,
climate, and the future.
Willis, Daniel, William W.
Braham, Katsuhiko Muramoto,
and Michael E. Mann. London:
Routledge, 2017.

RECYCLING

"Recycling is better—I won't write 'good'—for the environment. But without economics—without supply and demand of raw materials—recycling is nothing more than a meaningless exercise in glorifying garbage. No doubt it's better than throwing something into an incinerator, and worse than fixing something that can be refurbished. It's what you do if you can't bear to see something landfilled. Placing a box or a can or a bottle in a recycling bin doesn't mean you've recycled anything, and it doesn't make you a better, greener person: it just means you've outsourced your problem. Sometimes that outsourcing is near home; and sometimes it's overseas. But wherever it goes, the global market and demand for raw materials is the ultimate arbiter. Fortunately, if that realization leaves you feeling bad, there's always the alternative: stop buying so much crap in the first place."

ADAM MINTER
Junkyard planet: travels in the
billion-dollar trash trade.
New York: Bloomsbury, 2015.

FIRE — "Energy consumption is part of an essential basket of consumption goods that every household should be able to afford in order to have a 'normal' standard of living, with the benefit of household heating and service appliances. A household is said to face an affordability issue if its energy budget share exceeds a critical threshold, determined—more or less arbitrarily by policy makers. Such a household would then be considered as part of the target population of policy aimed at reducing energy poverty."

RAFFAELE MINIACI, CARLO SCARPA, AND PAOLA VALBONESI
The economics and political economy of energy subsidies. Strand, Jon. ed. Cambridge, MA: MIT Press, 2016.

WATER — "There should be a relationship between the underlying structures of topography and hydrology and the major structuring elements of urban form, such as the use of catchments as the basis for physical planning and regulation. There is an obvious synergy between the need to create networks for open space to serve social needs and new approaches to open systems of urban water management."

ELIZABETH MOSSOP
The Landscape urbanism reader. New York (N.Y.): Princeton Architectural Press, 2006.

WATER

SASKIA SASSEN TALK
Dead Land, Dead Water
urbanNext.net

COMMUNICATING — "The reasons behind considering active participation of the community as an essential premise are connected both to the use of large amounts of public resources to realise smart cities (the same resources that may be used to develop other social, cultural projects, etc.), and to the need for the various stakeholders to become coproducers of public services precisely due to the diffusion of technological solutions linked to the implementation of smart projects. For involving the local government stakeholders is necessary the implementation of a performance measurement system, specifically projected for the smart city, in order to plan the activities to put in place and the goals to achieve, monitor their progress and be accountable for the results achieved."

BASTIAAN BACCARNE, PETER MECHANT AND DIMITRI SCHUURMAN
Smart city: how to create public and economic value with high technology in urban space. Cham: Springer, 2014.

RECYCLING — "Waste is not the 'dark, shameful secret of all production'. How can there be anything 'dark' or 'shameful' about the inevitable generation of debris and detritus? Waste can only be grasped as a reprehensible material form if it is construed as the accidental or callous by-product of something else."

MARTIN O'BRIEN
A crisis of waste?: understanding the rubbish society. London: Routledge, 2008.

RECYCLING

"Architecture and design currently play a minor role in the design and construction of industrial building types, especially waste-to-energy facilities. Through comparing the well-established waste-to-energy industries in Sweden with less established engagements in the northeast of the United States, opportunities and lessons are revealed. Architects have a role to play in integrating waste-to-energy plants physically and programmatically within their urban or suburban contexts, as well as potentially lessening the generally negative perception of energy recovery plants."

HANIF KARA
Architecture and waste: a replanned obsolescence. Cambridge, MA: Harvard University Graduate School of Design: Actar, 2017.

COMMUNICATING

"The wider explosion of e-commerce mediated by Internet or telephone transactions, and underpinned by advanced logistics systems distributing goods to customers, is leading to the proliferating of a second type of classic 'glocal' network spaces where connections elsewhere are far more important than links to the local urban landscape.

Across the western world, in fact, declining warehouse parks are being gradually reconstituted as "virtual" warehouses, automated spaces, close to major mail and highway hubs that are linked seamlessly into the just-in-time logistics systems designed to serve national and even continental markets for Internet-sold goods."

STEPHEN GRAHAM
Urban mutations: periodization, scale, mobility. Nielsen, Tom, Niels Albertsen, and Peter Hemmersam. Kobenhavn: Arkitektens Forlag, 2004.

MAKING

"Our work aims to minimize electronic actuation and sensing by producing pure material-actuation and dynamic systems that increase performance, minimize weight, and tune aerodynamics. The convergence of these applications demonstrates new capabilities that can produce material response, self-assembly, energy efficiency, and new manufacturing techniques.

These rapidly developing capabilities, both basic and applied, demonstrate the convergence of our physical and digital worlds. These techniques will expand our capabilities for inventing new materials, fabrication processes, and design tools while creating novel solutions for industry and government challenges. This future world is dependent. on the programmability and interaction of our materials and the energy in our environment now."

SKYLAR TIBBITS
Self-Assembly Lab: experiments in programming matter. New York, NY: Routledge, 2017.

MAKING

"We would like to speak of a 'reconceptualization', whereby through the robot the central role of the design is strengthened and the inherent capacities of materials—sometimes lost in the information age—now confidently remerge within an evocative diverse and tangible encounter."

FABIO GRAMAZIO, MATTHIAS KOHLER, JAN WILLMANN
The robotic touch: how robots change architecture. Zurich: Park Books, 2014

SENSING

"The sensing citizen should be seen to be an expression of the idea mode of citizen participation in smart-city visions, rather than a resisting agent to them. Sensing citizens are the necessary participants in smart cities—where the smart cities are the foregone conclusion." Dumb citizens in smart cities would be a totalitarian overshoot, since they would be entities subject to monitoring without participating in the flow of information. The smart city raises additional questions about the politics of urban exclusion, about who is able to be a participating citizen in a city that is powered through access to digital devices.

JENNIFER GABRYS
Smart urbanism: utopian vision or false dawn?
Marvin, Simon, Andres Luque-Ayala, and Colin McFarlane. London: Routledge, 2016.

SENSING

"Individuals are becoming agents of data collection, and at the scale of an urban population, we all constitute a vast trove of crowdsourced information. As Gordon Bell's experiment recedes into the past, society is moving from 'life-logging' to 'city-logging'. We are all enmeshed in a distributed sensing ecosystem."

CARLO RATTI, MATTHEW CLAUDEL
The city of tomorrow: sensors, networks, hackers, and the future of urban life.
New Haven; London: Yale university press, 2016.

COMMUNICATING

"Rather than legitimizing austerity, co-production processes could widen (and deepen) the participation of city inhabitants in the development, management and use of their everyday environments by encouraging connectivity, communication, knowledge-sharing and peer-to-peer learning.

Within such processes, collaborative technology platforms offer opportunities for new forms of urban governance, opening up the city and its infrastructures so that ordinary inhabitants are not mere 'users' or 'consumers' but active (and reflective) co-producers of knowledge and actions for a more resilient city together with the decision-makers."

CORELIA E. BAIBARAC
Enriching urban spaces with ambient computing, the internet of things, and smart city design.
Konomi, Shin'ichi, and George Roussos. Hershey: Engineering Science Reference, 2017.

COMMUNICATING

"Once the internet of things is rolled out, we are at the real takeoff point of the information economy. From then on, the key principle is to create democratic social control over aggregated information, and to prevent its monopolization or misuse by states and corporations. The internet of things will complete a vast social 'machine.' Its analytical power alone could optimize resources on a scale that significantly reduces the use of carbon, raw material and labour.

Making the energy grid the road network and tax system 'intelligent' are just the most obvious things on the task list. But the power of this emerging vast machine does not lie solely in its ability to monitor and feedback. By socializing knowledge, it also has the power to amplify the result of collective action."

PAUL MASON
Postcapitalism: a guide to our future. New York: Farrar, Straus & Giroux, 2015.

MAKING

"It is important to point out that the implementation of the Human Smart Cities concept can be made through the use of frugal technology and does not always require sophisticated and complex infrastructures. This fact is relevant essentially in what concerns the scalability of the solution. Simple and creative solutions can emerge from the local communities, which allow, as an example, big cities to extend their strategies and include broad metropolitan areas or small cities to integrate new strategies.

This is an important advantage for the city administration that has the potential to enable the creation of humanly smart services without having to make significant investments. Another significant advantage of this concept, from the governance point of view, is the fact that the codesign and coproduction of solutions take out the 'burden' of the city administration processes that become lighter and more transparent."

ALVARO DUARTE DE OLIVEIRA

Human smart cities: rethinking the interplay between design and planning. Concilio, Grazia, and Francesca Rizzo. Switzerland: Springer, 2016.

RECYCLING

"Designer and artists rethink (rather than reapply) recycling, reconsider people's relations to the material dimension of things and places, and when allowed reexamine recycling and reuse facilities in terms of how they express and enhance culture."

MIRA E. ENGLER

Designing America's Waste Landscapes. The Johns Hopkins University Press, 2006.

COMMUNICATING

"The use of geolocalization and tracing technologies by some groups of artists is all the more interesting, as its focus is not the concept of communication (or community) as a whole, but connection itself. Working on connections implies finding opportunities to link rather than oppose —the local and the global, the practice of places and the formalization of space, the construction of situations, and the representation of urban form as a totality.

As far as interface is concerned, the idea is to install distance communication technologies within a given context and, by the same token, to critically engage with the multilayered nature of spacetime, focusing on the superposition of 'real' space, the space of immediate co-presence, and of a virtual space that is the locus of interlocality and connection. In the end, the issue is to manage to link not only the local and the global, but also the real and the virtual, with a view to the process of urban form as such."

ELIE DURING

Cognitive architecture: from bio-politics to noo-politics: architecture & mind in the age of communication & information. Hauptmann, Deborah. Rotterdam: 010 Publishers, 2011.

COMMUNICATING

"We need smart cities. But without a vigorous, aware, ubiquitous, and diverse contingent of smart citizens. We will not develop the civic intelligence that is desperately needed. The equation in the title would not balance. To address the problems we are facing, we will need creativity, dedication, humor, reason, and compassion. Fortunately, the potential is there because people often have these talents. Remember that governance is not solely a technological matter. The market or side effects will not solve our problems for us. But citizen engagement is not 'one size fits all.'

Different contexts require different approaches. We cannot define a single, uniform, "silver bullet" that is guaranteed to work everywhere.

The informed contribution of citizens is an indispensable element of governance. Citizen engagement ideally provides both impetus for social change when it is needed and a bulwark against tyranny and oppression when that becomes necessary. These are absolutely key roles and their importance highlights the need for civic intelligence.

Without strong, engaged citizenry, we will not be able to address our problems. With strong, engaged citizenry, we may be able to address our problems."

DOUGLAS SCHULER
Human smart cities: rethinking the interplay between design and planning. Concilio, Grazia, and Francesca Rizzo. Switzerland: Springer, 2016.

COMMUNICATING

"Idensity is a composite term, combining the word 'density'—of real (urban) and 'virtual' (media) communication spaces (density of connections)—and the word 'identity.' Idensity integrates the concept of 'density' (density of connections, density of physical and digital infrastructure, density of communication spaces, etcetera) with the concept of 'identity' (image policies, urban brands, and so forth). Idensity addresses therefore the logics of today's expanding economy of attention.

It can, for example, help in understanding the processes of spatial segregation and distinction between urban fragments that have qualities of 'global' performance and that can be seen as part of a 'global urban condition,' such as airports or front office locations, and those other, sometimes neighboring (parts of) cities that lose in relevance and disappear from (global) mental maps. It can therefore be implemented as an operative tool to steer the processes of urban development.

But it is not a mere summation of the concepts of 'density' and 'identity.' It is instead a fusion, as it inverts 'identity,' linking it to communication, 'identity' being defined by connectivity."

ELIZABETH SIKIARIDI & FRANS VOGELAAR
Cognitive architecture: from bio-politics to noo-politics: architecture & mind in the age of communication & information. Hauptmann, Deborah. Rotterdam: 010 Publishers, 2011.

COMMUNICATING

"Economic globalization and telecommunications have contributed to produce a spatiality for the urban that pivots on cross-border networks and territorial locations with massive concentration of resources. This is not a completely new feature. Over the centuries cities have been at the crossroad of major often worldwide processes.

What is different today is the intensity, complexity and global span of these networks, the extent to which significant portions of economies are now dematerialized and digitalized and hence the extent to which they can travel at great speeds through some of these networks operating at vast geographic scales."

SASKIA SASSEN
Cities in transition power, environment, society.
Ding, Wowo, Arie Graafland, and Andong Lu. Rotterdam: Nai 010 Publ., 2001.

COMMUNICATING

"The effects of telecommunications within cities are therefore complex and ambivalent. They allow urban infrastructures and transport systems actually to extend their capacities, so removing barriers to further urban growth and concentration. Telecommunications are supporting environmentally damaging increases in transport flows as well as promising assistance in the drive towards sustainable cities through telecommuting and reduced transport flows. Telecommunications assist the globalisation of the economy in which city economies are being fragmented as nodes on the global telecommunications network of transnational corporations. They also provide new policy tools of urban management at the local level through which the public, civic face of cities can be strengthened and local economic and social cohesion supported."

STEPHEN GRAHAM, SIMON MORVIN
Telecommunications and the city: electronic spaces, urban places.
London: Routledge, 1996.

COMMUNICATING

"The mission architects have in contemporary society goes beyond making sure we get spatial proportions right, developing innovative artistic concepts or guaranteeing environmentally and economically efficient building processes.

More than ever, architects also need to play a prominent role in the social and political debate on the way we read, plan, design and build the environments we inhabit and play this game at all scales simultaneously. At the same time, the needed architectural innovation needs to start from rethinking different ways of sharing space and from creating novel programmatic adjacencies, as nowadays it seems like separating mechanisms win from inclusive ones, individual aspirations overtake collective strategies of using space and creating monocultures increasingly dominate making heterogeneous environments based on multiplicity."

KRIS SCHEERLINCK
Doing it the Belgian Way.
Amsterdam: Volume Magazine, num. 40, 2016.

COMMUNICATING

"Communication spaces where citizens can learn to manipulate their own languages, codes, signs, and symbols empowering them to name the world in their own terms. Citizens' media trigger processes that allow citizens to recodify their contexts and themselves. These processes ultimately give citizens the opportunity to restructure their identities into empowered subjectivities strongly connected to local cultures and driven by well-defined, achievable utopias. Citizens' media are the media citizens use to activate communication processes that shape their local communities."

CLEMENCIA RODRIGUEZ
Citizens' media against armed conflict disrupting violence in Colombia.
Minneapolis: University of Minnesota Press, 2011.

COMMUNICATING

"The current sharing trend must understood and developed politically and culturally, not just technologically and behaviorally, if we are to get more just, inclusive, and environmentally sustainable sharing. Rebuilding social capital in sharing could also help rebuild the public square of collective politics. Without this, extending sharing city action to the infrastructures, urban commons, and public realm of the city would be difficult. But the ways in which social capital can be rebuilt (and cultural norms shifted) by sharing with justice reveal another virtuous cycle: as the public square of collective politics is strengthened, so investments in sharing infrastructures are more easily agreed, and those investments in turn lead to more sharing and even stronger social capital. The domains of sharing and support for sharing can expand hand in hand until they encompass the urban commons and indeed the whole city."

DUNCAN MCLAREN, JULIAN AGYEMAN
Sharing cities a case for truly smart and sustainable cities.
Cambridge, MA: MIT Press, 2017.

MAKING

"It is precisely by looking at these unclassifiable architectural creatures whose meaning is always suspended between celebration and fragility that we can understand the 'lasting' power of 'ephemeral events' such as revolts and their avatars, festivals. Even if the fate of revolts is to be vanquished, their attempt to halt "normal time" forever subverts the experience of the city, its sense of both physical and symbolic orientation. Facing the ever-present possibility of social disorder, power can not recompose space as if nothing has happened."

PIER VITTORIO AURELI
Atlas of Political Cliches,
Journal Quaderns d'Arquitectura i Urbanisme, 2015.

EARTH

"We don't mean that we need more traditional capitalism masked as sharing economy, like Uber, but rather we expect, and hope, the cities will be the birth of economic and noneconomic sharing models that will allow a more efficient use of finite global resources. As far as we are aware, there is only one planet that has been proven to the inhabitable by humans, and that is planet Earth. If we are to retain, or even improve the quality of life for the growing global and urban population, cities and urbanpreneurs must lead us to a more sustainable, circular, and sharing economic. While some of the solutions will certainly rely on technology and virtual platforms, others may be decidedly low-tech and local."

BOYD DEREK COHEN, PABLO MUÑOZ
The emergence of the urban entrepreneur: how the growth of cities and the sharing economy are driving a new breed of innovators. Santa Barbara, CA: Praeger, an imprint of ABC-CLIO, LLC, 2016.

EARTH — "We need to view the fragility of the planet and its resources as an opportunity for speculative design innovations rather than as a form of technical legitimation for promoting conventional solutions. By extension, the problems confronting our cities and regions would then become opportunities to define a new approach. Imagining an urbanism that is other than the status quo requires a new sensibility—one that has the capacity to incorporate and accommodate the inherent conflictual conditions between ecology and urbanism. This is the territory of ecological urbanism."

MOHSEN MOSTAFAVI AND GARETH DOHERTY
Ecological urbanism.
Zürich, Switzerland: Lars Müller Publishers, 2016.

COMMUNICATING — "Why can´t open sourcing, a methodology that commands almost limitless potential in the digital world (proven time and again by the likes of Mozilla, Airbnb, and the Internet itself), and which has existed throughout the history of architecture, have the same transformative effect on contemporary design and building practice? Where is the linux of homes or offices or libraries? page through any design magazine—you won't find a building without signature. The world of architecture circles on its well-worn orbit, seemingly, outside the gravitational pull of networked participation."

CARLO RATTI WITH MATTHEW CLAUDEL
Open source architecture.
NY: Thames & Hudson, 2015.

MAKING — "Architecture must seek multidisciplinary codes, networking mechanisms, knowledge transfer methods and skills exchange protocols. This higher degree of communication is a constitutive aspect of contemporary architecture. The Renaissance signs have been replaced by data, by information. Design has become information. Of course, this sustains our ambition to discuss contemporary architectural paradigms, for example whether digitality equals representation/simulation/narratives or production/ fabrication/ processes and to initiate a debate on design research theory."

MARJAN COLLETTI
Digital poetics an open theory of design-research in architecture.
Farnham: Ashgate Publ., 2013.

SENSING — "The coupling of geo-referencing and time-based landscape sensing provide opportunities to understand the landscape through different timescale, recognized trends and make predictions. This has applications and implications for how we manipulate landscape processes, ultimately informing decision making. [...] Data that is gathered and reapplied to interpret histories is projected and manipulated to understand or find new futures."

BRADLEY E CANTRELL, JUSTINE HOLZMAN
Responsive landscapes: strategies for responsive technologies in landscape architecture.
London: Routledge, 2016.

RECYCLING — "The Anthropocene mix of human history and natural history also demands a new historical consciousness. The division of intellectual labor that, until now has consigned geological, species-level thinking to science, and human history to the humanities, must go. For, if we are to draw other lins, we must learn to see the lines that draw us and, with them, learn to imagine and to visualize previously unthinkable change."

REINHOLD MARTIN
The Underdome guide to energy reform. Kim, Janette, and Erik Carver, ed. New York: Princeton Architectural Press, 2015.

FIRE

"Similarly, most people who heard that the unfolding global warming would be unprecedented in its rapidity knew nothing about actual CO_2 emission factors or about the relative decarbonization of the global energy supply. Understanding complex energy matters, formulating informed arguments, and making sensible choices can be done only on the basis of a quantitative understanding that must be both relatively broad and sufficiently deep. There is a natural progression in this understanding, from simple quantities to rates that relate those variables to basic physical attributes, to time and space."

VACLAV SMIL
Power Density: A Key to Understanding Energy Sources and Uses. Cambridge, MA: MIT Press, 2016.

COMMUNICATING

"The fragmentation of systems of local governance has been accentuated by particular changes in the national contextual circumstances within which individual cities are located, and cross-national generalizations about the emergence of a new local governance are dangerous. Nevertheless it is possible to identify a number of features of European urban life which provide a common backdrop against which to look at the specificities of particular cities. Within a general process of globalization a number of features combine to homogenize the city-the revolution in communications technologies, the growth of the knowledge economy, the collapse of the command economies of eastern Europe, and the emergence of individual and group life styles which challenge traditional attitudes and behaviours."

MURRAY STEWART
Urban governance and democracy: leadership and community involvement. Haus, Michael, ed. London: Routledge, 2007.

COMMUNICATING

"A truly sustainable society is one where wider questions of social needs and welfare, and economic opportunity, are integrally connected to environmental concerns. This emphasis upon steams equity as a desirable and just social goal, intimately linked to a recognition that, unless society strives for a greater level of social and economic equity, both within and between nations, the long-term objective of a more sustainable world is unlikely to be secured.

The basis for this view is that sustainability implies a more careful use of scarce resources and, in all probability, a change to the high-consumption lifestyles experienced by the affluent and aspired to by others. It will not be easy to achieve these changes in behaviour, not least because this demands acting against short term self-interest in favour of unborn generation and 'unseen others' who may live on the other side of the globe. The altruism demanded here will be difficult to secure and will probably be impossible if there is not some measure of perceived equality in terms of sharing common future and fates."

JULIAN AGYEMAN ROBERT D BULLARD AND BOB EVANS
Just sustainabilities: development in an unequal world. London: Earthscan, 2006.

COMMUNICATING — "As the global reaches into the urban and urbanization spreads around the globe, new movements are emerging that are likely to affect local efforts to deal with urban poverty and inequality. Struggles over environmental issues and poverty become simultaneously local, urban, metropolitan, regional, national, supranational and global issues. They include the rise of what some call global civil society, global or cosmopolitan citizenship and identity, and the global justice movement."

EDWARD W. SOJA, J. MIGUEL KANAI
Implosions/Explosions: Toward a Study of Planetary Urbanization. Brenner, Neil. Berlin: Jovis, 2014.

MAKING — "From Jane Jacobs to Stanford Anderson, from William Whyte to Donald Appleyard, Jan Gehl, Aldo Rossi to Lefebvre: all authors share this vision of streetscapes becoming happy places, void of conflict and danger, allowing their inhabitants or visitors to share these spaces of social cohesion. Nevertheless, the poetics of 'streetscapes of making' also refer to a different kind of urban fabric: the ones that are not necessary conflict-proof or entail a certain harshness but nevertheless have an as structural role in our environment and society: manufacturing streetscapes. Here, people work: productive areas include a wide range of users, requirements, needs and routines, not always avoiding a more bold appropriation (or even misappropriation) of the city's real streetscapes."

KRIS SCHEERLINCK, HANNES VAN DAMME
Productive Sidewalks in New York City. In Productive and Resilient City:
Vol. 5 (1) University of San Francisco, 2016.

MAKING

TERESA CALDEIRA TALK
Aestheticization of Street Culture
urbanNext.net

COMMUNICATING — "The system where a piece of land or a building is allotted a certain price is made possible because there is always a neighbor. Consider the fact that real estate value is determined not by itself but within the context of the city. Then the value of the city as a whole is always determined as a relation. Let us confirm that my value is created by my neighbors; that all space in the city is an intimately inter-connected product of the commons."

GUYON CHUNG
People, Architecture,
Seoul: Hyeonsilmunhwa Yeongu, 2008.

FIRE — The interconnection between the environment and its climate, its built structures and the human body requires overlying architecture with other disciplines such as meteorology, thermodynamics or physiology to engage them in a holistic way."

JAVIER GARCÍA-GERMÁN
Thermodynamic interactions. An exploration into material, physiological and territorial atmospheres.
New York: Actar, 2015.

FIRE — "Achieving a sustainable energy future must include measuring public responses to the imposition of energy facility on the landscape, identifying acceptable renewable energy development goals, and managing the landscapes that reaching this goal will create. Of the several resources that may play a role, wind, solar, and to a much lesser degree geothermal energy development each creates landscape-siting issues. All three of them have intrinsic characteristics that will strongly influence the appearance of the landscape, public reactions to the associated generation facilities, and how we can assess their visual impacts. Each produces its own unique landscape signature."

MARTIN PASQUALETTI, RICHARD SMARDON
The renewable energy landscape preserving scenic values in our sustainable future. Apostal, Dean, James Palmer, Martin J. Pasqualetti, Richard C. Smardon, and Robert Sullivan. ed. London: Routledge, 2017.

EARTH — "Given that 'the environment' includes the entire biosphere, a system was needed to organize these services in a manner that transcended technology. The categories were found by looking back into human history, back to the beginnings of western civilization. Not because western civilization was in fact the beginning, but rather it presented a simple and enduring description of the human environment at the dawn of urbanization. Empedocles was one of the first to identify the natural elements (air, water, earth, fire) and while we have since learned that matter is much more complex, these concepts prove resilient when viewed through the perspective of human needs.

These four elements provide a suitable lens through which the services that nature provides can be viewed as well as a rough division for discussing the challenges of sustainability. In a sense, they are fundamental. We need air to breath, water to drink, earth to grow our food and fire to keep us warm. Expanding fire to include all forms of energy, we include the larger challenges facing humanity. The metropolitan perspective on these four services is unique in the sense that it must import virtually all of them individually and, by conservation of mass, discharge an equivalent amount usually in mixed streams over a much smaller area."

FRANK ZEMAN
Metropolitan sustainability: understanding and improving the urban environment. Sawston, Cambridge, UK: Woodhead Pub., 2012.

EARTH — "Peace and the survival of life on earth as we know it are threaten by human activities which lack a commitment to humanitarian values. Destruction of nature and natural resources results from ignorance, greed and lack of respect for the earth's living things. This lack of respect extends even to earth's human descendants, the future generations who will inherit a vastly degraded planet if world peace does not become a reality, and if destruction of the natural environment continues at the present rate. […] it is essential that we re-examine ethically what we have inherited, what we are responsible for, and what we will pass on to coming generations."

DALAI LAMA
The Dalai Lama, a policy of kindness: an anthology of writings by and about the Dalai Lama. Bstan-'dzin-rgya-mtsho, and Sidney D. Piburn. Ithaca, NY: Snow Lion, 1998.

MUMBAI by Ibay Rigby

SHARING AND THE URBAN COMMONS

Duncan McLaren and Julian Agyeman

INTRODUCTION

Cities have always been shared spaces, urban commons co-created and sustained by their citizens.[1] In the modern world, cities are also places where difference is most starkly exhibited as different cultures and races share the same spaces and infrastructures, and as rich and poor live, work, and subsist cheek by jowl. If we are to live together and flourish in cosmopolitan cities, humanity has to reinvent sharing for the modern age and rebuild an inclusive urban commons. In this essay, we argue that modern intermediated sharing offers that possibility, but to deliver its potential, we will need new approaches to governance, infrastructure, and urban design that recognize humans' potential as relational, connected, sharing beings, rather than treating people as the autonomous, selfish individuals of neo-liberal economic theory and commercial practice

INTERDEPENDENCE

In modern cities, humans are more deeply interdependent on one another in greater numbers than ever. Yet, leading politicians across the Western world pander to a perverse populism that emphasizes individual choice, but resists recognition of genuine difference; a populism that lauds individual autonomy, but seeks to build walls to keep out anyone whose ethnicity, culture, or politics doesn't match those of the wealthy elite; a populism that fetishizes equality of opportunity even as it widens the inequalities of outcome between the haves and the have-nots. In all these ways, contemporary political culture, especially in the West, resists and rejects the reality of human interdependence in a world whose environmental resilience is being pushed to the breaking point.

---

1. David Harvey, *Rebel Cities: From the Right to the City to the Urban Revolution* (New York and London: Verso, 2012).

Sharing is our species' evolved response to interdependence. Humans evolved both biologically and culturally as collaborators and sharers: today under the right conditions, we still choose to share.[2] We rely on mutuality and shared relationships for our lives, our happiness, and our ability to flourish. We share a wide range of things in a remarkable diversity of ways. In all its forms, sharing is a product of our evolved nature as social animals. But it is as much cultural as biological, rooted in our ability to cooperate in tribes and to trust and reciprocate with others in our social groups. This underlies socio-cultural traditions of sharing that persist to this day.

FROM TRADITIONAL TO INTERMEDIATED SHARING

The traditional "sharing economy" is huge, and includes most domestic labour. In large parts of the world, traditional sharing in extended families remains the norm, and across local communities, gift economies based in reciprocal social obligations underpin the basics of life—water, shelter, food, clothing, and care. But such traditional communities typically have social downsides: they can be heavily gendered, oblivious to difference, and oppressive of minorities. In other words, our instincts to share can too easily be limited to those who look and think like us. Cities have long been places where people go to escape the strictures and oppression of traditional communities, to lose and to find themselves, and to reweave the narratives of their identities. The German proverb that "city air brings freedom" may have originated in feudal times, but it still rings true for millions of migrants, such as those protected in "sanctuary cities" in the United States today, or the Syrian refugees welcomed into some Canadian and European cities. And today, the significance of cities for the expression and recognition of social difference—from ethnicity to sexuality—is ever more critical to the modern age's great challenge: how humanity lives together on a crowded planet.

Whatever their motivations for moving, newcomers to cities have rarely behaved purely as autonomous individuals. Waves of migrants have formed new communities in which sharing and shared identities have remained central to their lives. But traditional forms of sharing are being undermined by the characteristic practices of neo-liberal capitalism: the social

---

2. See, for example, Mark Pagel, *Wired for Culture: The Natural History of Human Cooperation* (London: Allen Lane, 2012).

Little libraries: modern communal sharing at its best

fragmentation resulting from labour flexibility and mobility, the commercialization of the public realm by private shopping malls and ubiquitous advertising hoardings, and the privatisation of shared infrastructures and services. Essential urban commons—community support structures and collective capabilities to support health, learning, and our needs for social affiliation and interaction—are all threatened. Despite their many freedoms, individualist markets simply cannot meet these critical needs, however hard advertisers and brand managers try to persuade us otherwise. The very fabric of society is under stress.

Cities are on the sharp end of this challenge. The breakdown of community and trust that is triggering political withdrawal and wall-building is also seen in growing anomie, violence, and segregation in cities; yet, without sharing, cities simply cannot function. Increasingly, modern cities face a dilemma: traditional sharing is exclusive, limited to communities of "people like us," and declining; yet, neo-liberal capitalism is being consumed by a self-defeating pursuit of individual autonomy and cannot revive critical urban commons. This is why the emergence of new peer-to-peer and intermediated forms of sharing at the intersection of cities' highly networked physical and cyber-spaces is so exciting. Intermediated sharing supports the cosmopolitan potential of markets while reviving the communal solidarity of traditional sharing.

SHARING CITIES
The pilot lights offered by emerging "sharing cities"—led by Seoul—are therefore one of the most hopeful signs of the contemporary age; not because they improve environmental efficiency or stimulate a vibrant economy—although they can do both of these, and more—but because they point the way to a rediscovered and reinvented humanity. By focusing on shared urban commons, they enable residents to connect as commoners with shared interests, rights, ownership, and generative agency, rather than competing as autonomous and separated individuals. As the world's first official "sharing city," Seoul demonstrates that it is possible to show political leadership—shaping sharing culture, policies, plans, and practices—and to blend the cosmopolitanism of web platforms with the communitarianism of civic and communal sharing.

The Cheonggyecheon stream is symbolic of modern Seoul and its approach to sharing (Figure 2). In 2005 Seoul closed a major highway, successfully slashing traffic levels and pollution throughout the district, and replaced the road with a new, shared public space, restoring the Cheonggyecheon stream. More generally, under Mayor Park Won Soon, Seoul is actively working to cultivate an inclusive sharing culture—both at the public or civic level and by building public trust in sharing enterprises and organisations—through the city-funded Sharing City project. This initiative aims to expand physical and digital sharing infrastructure, incubate and support sharing economy startups, and put idle public resources to better use. Sharing in Seoul also reflects the Korean cultural concept of *jeong*, a collective solidarity which motivates kindness between strangers. To make sharing initiatives more socially inclusive, the city provides free second-hand smartphones to the elderly and disadvantaged so they can access the same sharing services, apps, and commons as others.

By enabling and co-constructing a new digital commons—including commercial sharing platforms and intermediaries, as well as civic, communal, and charitable ones—cities like Seoul are inviting a new recognition of the underlying urban commons that emerge from the cooperative interactions of citizens and public bodies: the commons of public spaces; of civility and social norms; of green and grey infrastructures for transport, water, sewerage, healthcare, education, and leisure; of social facilities and community support; the public square of shared political debate; and more. They also highlight the long-standing expertise of public service administrators and citizen users in managing shared commons and sharing services such as libraries and public transit. It's no coincidence that one of the most widespread emanations of the new sharing paradigm is the city bike-share scheme, which brings together public service management skills with new "smart" digital technologies for coordination and monitoring.

The Cheonggyecheon stream, Seoul: genuinely shared space

Cities such as Angers, France, have long experience in managing public transit

SHARING IS THE REAL "SMART"

But unlike so-called smart cities, which too often simply seek to impose technological and commercial "solutions" and "apps" on social and political problems, sharing cities apply their experience with public spaces and services to make sharing sustainable and equitable. They recognize it as political, and therefore understand the need to regulate the emerging commercial sharing economy, even as they enable and facilitate it.

Where cities focus only on technology not people, allow commercial motives to dominate sharing practices, and fail to engage with the politics of sharing, smart can become socially dumb and divisive. There's no app to replace collective action. Yet, sharing cities do not eschew smart technology—they combine it with civic leadership to enable inclusive community sharing and solidarity. They use modern technology to build an urban commons of civic sharing of *public* facilities and *private* resources—and to help citizens share more, more often, and more widely. But they also find many other ways to revive their urban commons. Colombia's second city, Medellín, for example, has pioneered the philosophy of social urbanism. Library parks such as Parque Biblioteca España have been constructed in marginalized parts of the city, providing free access to computer and information technology and educational classes, as well as space for cultural activities and recreation. The city has also invested heavily in shared public transit and infrastructure—including bus rapid transit, nine cable car links, and a huge outdoor escalator—to connect the poor hillside comunas with the centre. Public facilities such as health centers and schools have been developed at the cable-car stations. These major projects have been funded with revenue from the city's public services company, Empresas Públicas de Medellín (EPM), and developed through a participatory planning process with the community.

Shared bikes in Copenhagen: complete with GPS and handlebar tablets

SHARING FAIRLY

The social dimension demonstrated in Medellín is critical to any Sharing City initiative worthy of the name. The value of sharing lies in its potential to enhance equality and inclusion. And to support justice, a "sharing paradigm" that transcends the sharing economy is essential. To see sharing as just an economic activity misses so much. Being human is about more than what we buy—it's about the empathetic and interdependent relationships we have with other people. And in sharing practices, such relationships are recognized and reinforced. When commercial sharing replaces communal sharing, it can therefore be socially damaging; yet, if the same commercial sharing replaces commercial market transactions, it reinforces interdependent relationships, helping us engage with people as peers, rather than as employees or salespersons.[3] In other words, daily experience and practice, social norms and behaviours, policies and marketing can either constantly reinforce sharing … or undermine it.

The dominant ideology of neo-liberalism threatens sharing by promoting a false individualism. The sharing paradigm instead sees people as interdependent social beings, more than as autonomous individuals, and sharing as relational more than transactional. It offers changes in behaviour, norms, and identities. Even in commercial forms like "Rent the Runway"—which makes elite brands available to anyone—sharing reorientates our identities away from what we consume and towards our shared relationships. Like other sharing platforms, Rent the Runway creates a

3. Cameron Tonkinwise, "Sharing You Can Believe In," *Medium*, 1 July 2014.

The Parque Biblioteca España overlooks Medellín, Colombia, from Comuna Popular

shared equal-access commons (of clothing, in this case). Such commons change our relationship to things themselves (not just to brands): by seeing them as shared, durable, less constitutive of our identities, we replace our attachments to multiple possessions with a stronger and more sustainable attachment to the shared commons and our relationship with other commoners.

Most sharing platforms were started with social (or environmental) purposes in mind. But commercial drivers—particularly the demands of venture capital in its quest for $1 billion "unicorns"—have pushed these purposes into second place (or eliminated them altogether). The commercial model exemplified by Uber, Airbnb, and TaskRabbit—utilising technology and software from Silicon Valley and business models underpinned by risk-hungry venture capital funds—has seen the communal spirit of ride-sharing, couch-surfing, and skill-sharing sidelined in favour of sweating assets, casualizing labour, and taking socially useful resources (such as rental housing) out of the reach of the poorest by shifting them into the sharing economy. Yet, commercialised sharing can still bring benefits as well as risks. It is most socially useful when it draws existing but *socially underused* resources into the market. And in already market-dominated societies, it helps renew trust and community values in inclusive or "cosmopolitan" ways. For sharing to be fair, it needs the guidance and regulation that public authorities—such as cities—can bring.

Self-built home in Christiania, Copenhagen

SHARING POLITICS

While even commercial sharing can help shift values, sharing is most transformative where it gives voice to the powerless and access to the excluded. Commercial sharing is often not as egalitarian as it appears: it does more to reduce friction in the lives of the elite than it offers new access to the marginalized, enabling the asset-rich to monetize their second homes, cars, and yachts. Sharing cities must therefore promote policies, regulations, and norms that favour collective commons over commercial sharing. This might mean providing investment and support, such as premises, to communal initiatives, or underwriting citizens' reputations to enable their access to commercial platforms. It also demands more radical thinking—for example, enabling squatters to improve unused buildings, as happened in Christiania in Copenhagen.

Practically autonomous for many years, the "Freetown" of Christiania comprises a disused military district in central Copenhagen that has been squatted since 1971. Initial motivations for the squat included the lack of affordable housing elsewhere in the city. Since 1994, Christiania's 900 or so residents have paid taxes and fees for utility services, and in 2012 they struck a deal—as a residents' collective—with the Danish government to purchase the site for substantially below market value—raising the money through a form of crowd-funding. In the intervening years, residents have successfully established an alternative local currency, restored the buildings, built new homes, and regulated the socially and ethnically diverse district according to collective anarchist governance models.

Squatters are symbolic for sharing cities, in the same ways that *online* countercultures are transforming sharing societies. Online norms regarding music and software have shifted rapidly, as forms of "piracy" have become widespread, challenging consumerism, establishing new commons, and redefining identity for those involved, especially among the millennial generation. Urban piracy in the form of direct seizure of land and buildings by squatters is typically less widely welcomed. But we concur with urbanist Miguel Martinez that squats should "be recognized and supported for what they are: vibrant social centers at the very heart of the 'commons,' actively including the excluded."[4]

Countercultural commoning behaviors like squatting and graffiti begin in autonomous spaces beyond the reach of the powers that be. As a result, they can be, as in Christiania, the birthplace of more far-reaching approaches to social transformation. Sharing offers a bottom-up—simultaneously *countercultural* and *intercultural*—redefinition of consumption as a collaborative, shared, identity-redefining, co-production of services and products supplying fundamental needs.

4. Miguel Martinez, "Squatting for Jústice," *ROARmag*, 13 May 2014.

In Bogotá, Colombia, murals and graffiti are central to the urban commons, as at this market in San Victorino

This understanding of sharing has dramatic implications for urban planning and design, and infrastructures. It means enabling bottom-up, emergent provisions, not providing top-down master plans. Sharing means involving citizens in delivery, not just consulting them on proposals; and facilitating self-building of homes and co-production of shared infrastructures—not just in the developing world, but everywhere. Architects and planners can seek inspiration in informal,

pop-up, experimental developments and methods,[5] ranging from the occupation and transformation of the Torre David in Caracas to the informal sewerage installations in the Orangi squatter camps of Karachi; and from the guerilla transformation of parking lots into gardens on "Park[ing] day" to the pop-up cafes of "restaurant day". Governance that encourages experimentation but ensures accountability—for example through open data and user evaluation—is an important part of the sharing paradigm, and allows cities to impose and flex limits on commercial sharing to maximize its benefits. Cities such as Amsterdam limit Airbnb and similar rentals to a specific number of nights per year to ensure that there is no incentive for landlords to remove property from the local rental market and turn homes into informal hotels.

5. See, for example, Justin McGuirk, *Radical Cities: Across Latin America in Search of a New Architecture* (New York and London: Verso, 2014).

Torre David, Caracas, Venezuela: the world's highest squat

Park[ing] Day has spread around the world: here, activists claim street space in Munich

In such ways, sharing cities "repurpose" the tools of commercial sharing to build civic sharing communities. Communal-commercial sharing hybrids in the Amsterdam model show a third way between state and market. Sharing on platforms like Kiva City, Freecycle, and Peerby, and in community gardens, maker spaces, and repair cafés renews social capital, builds capabilities, and reweaves the web of community.

Real sharing cities share power too, with open government, co-produced services and citizen participation. They weave together the distributed and fragmented autonomy of communities and NGOs. For example, in Seoul, sharing extends to governance: in addition to open government and participatory budgeting initiatives, co-production between the state and the third sector helps deliver a wide range of public services including childcare, healthcare, library services, and waste management. The Occupy movement and its precursors across the Arab world and southern Europe, such as Los Indignados in Spain, have also generated new sharing institutions, including alternative currencies and integrated cooperatives, and have even stimulated new political expressions of sharing and solidarity (Figure 10). Amsterdam's move to adopt sharing city status was even led by activists, who built alliances with sharing economy businesses and city administrators.

CONCLUSION

Healthy sharing builds empathy and more open, inclusive, and "sharing" communities. It also grows with—and encourages—increased social investment in public goods and the urban commons. Thus, it renews the conditions and drivers of desperately needed collective democratic political action for the public good. Sharing the whole city can and should become the guiding purpose of the future city.

Sharing cities offer more than a revival of traditional collective politics. They offer reconfigured models of governance rooted in the transformation of institutions and norms that only arises when previously unheard and marginalized groups gain voice and inclusion in city politics. They suggest a genuinely intercultural form of cosmopolitanism that transcends the liberal paternalist "melting pot" that sought to flatten difference and offered inclusion only on the terms of the dominant majority. This is a new politics of recognition and inclusion, capable of sustaining sharing cities through the environmental and social challenges of the emerging Anthropocene.

Next double page: Democracy in action: *Indignados* in Gijon indicate agreement

LIVE PROJECTS SEOUL:
PRODUCTION CITY

Curatorial Statement by
Jie-Eun Hwang, SoA, and Hyungmin Pai

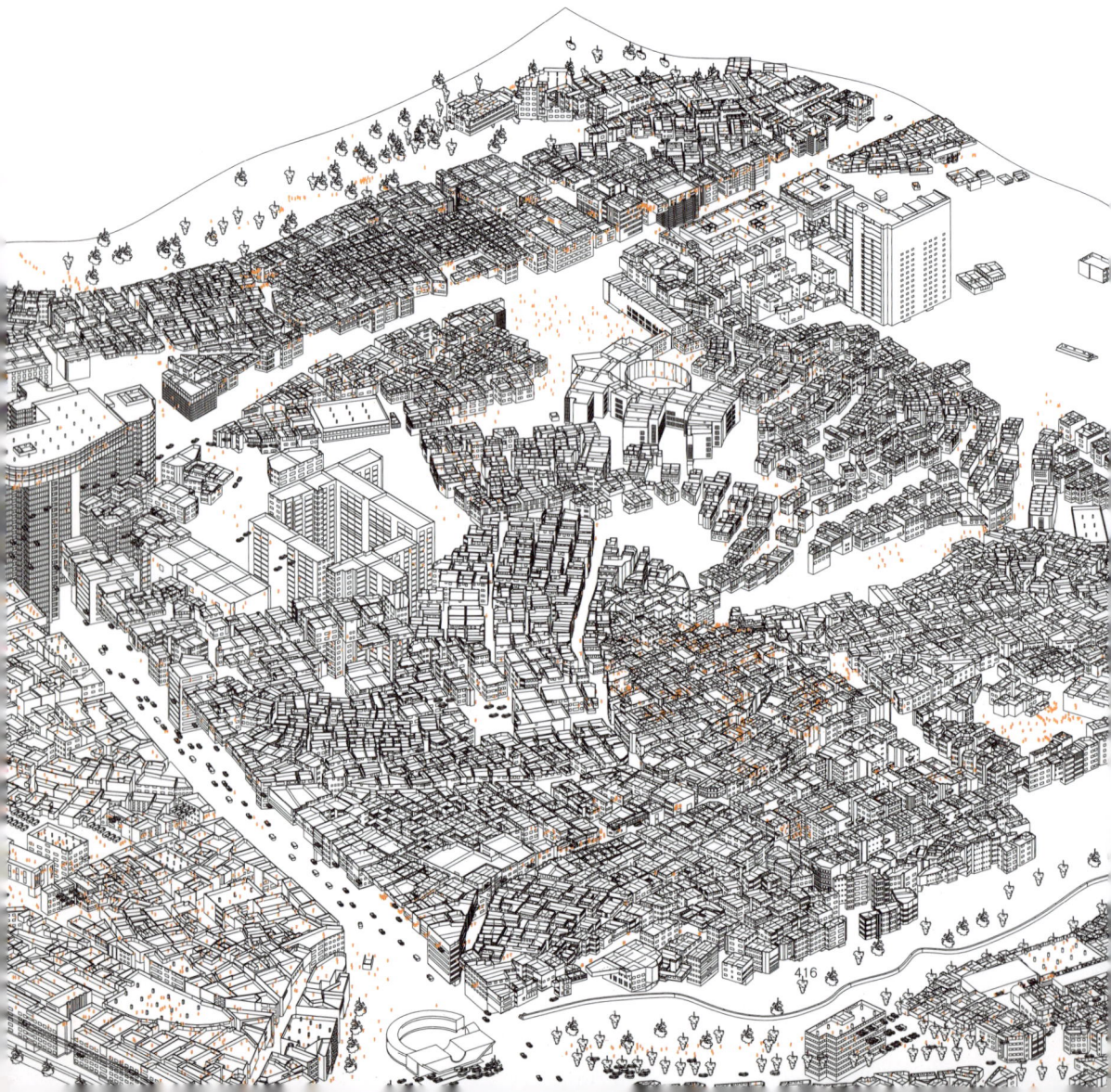

The Seoul Biennale of Architecture and Urbanism 2017 highlights production as an essential and imminent common of the evolving contemporary city. In the modern era of mass production, industrial infrastructure expanded beyond the borders of cities and nations and became part of a global network. Modern industry was no longer a viable function within the city as the metropolis became the center of consumption and real estate investment. However, as we now confront the limits of growth and inequality, the industrial system is being reorganized across a vast social, spatial, and ecological landscape. The scales and networks of production and consumption are being readjusted to the entire lifecycle of a city. Within this evolving value chain, mass customization and the urban fabric become inseparable. If mass production gave birth to the modern city, new modes of production in the twenty-first century are giving rise to a new kind of value network that challenges the contemporary city to reorganize itself as a sustainable social, economic, and political entity.

Unlike most major metropolises, central Seoul has retained manufacturing as a key component. Since the latter half of the twentieth century, the historical center of Seoul has become a battlefield of the forces of real estate development, historic preservation, and industrial clusters. This dynamic is an essential part of the evolving identity of Seoul and provides the conditions for innovative urban renewal and a healthy social ecology.

Production City delivers live projects which engage in the current in-situ phenomenon of central Seoul. Production City consists of four thematic sections: Anatomy of Things, Local Standards, Recycling Networks, Neo Manufacturing, and Seoul Apparel. The diverse projects and exhibition installations developed from these sections will be located in the garment and fashion district of the Changsin-Shindang-Dongdaemun area, the metal and machinery district of Euljiro, and the electronics district of the Sewoon Sangga complex.

ANATOMY OF THINGS

"Anatomy of Things" forms the central project on the value chain of urban manufacturing. It seeks an analytical and creative overview of the geography of resource networks centered in the fashion and garment cluster of the Dongdaemun area and the metal, machine, and electronics cluster of the Euljiro and Sewoon Sangga areas. If the role of the city in the production chain is to be understood, things must be disassembled and located, and then relocated and reassembled. It is a geography of both the micro-neighborhood scale and the global scale that reveals the way the production processes and commodity chains are interwoven with the urban fabric and its human resource networks. Focusing on field research, artists, designers, engineers, and architects from around the world are invited to experiment and hack the existing network to both articulate its capacities and discover new possibilities.

LOCAL STANDARDS

The "standard" is the essential modern concept that seemingly overrides industrial production across the globe. However, a closer look at the industries in the inner city of Seoul shows that, intertwined with the global industrial standard, it has sustained a set of its own legitimate standards. These local standards were developed and adopted by ceaseless and ever-changing demands from the different local factors of material supply and distribution. In the imminent era of mass customization, digital fabrication, and the prosumer, the local standard becomes an increasingly important condition of urban production. "Local Standards" investigates these standards to reveal the communal norm of production.

RECYCLING NETWORKS

Recycling can no longer be limited to the issue of waste but must become an integral part of the design and production process. It must take into account the wide spectrum of issues in manufacturing—from the lack of natural resources to the ethics of industrial production. Recycling has been a longstanding issue in the global fast fashion and electronic industries, and an essential part of the solution must be found in the local modes of production. Based on intimate understanding of local conditions, "Recycling Networks" seeks not merely to insert an additional procedure at the tail-end of production but to bring innovation to the overall system. These proposals will discover and bring in new kinds of production values, values that are expected to reorganize the current framework of production and benefit the producer community.

NEO MANUFACTURING

New technology changes society. It offers innovative opportunities that challenge existing socio-economic systems. It is again the central issue in an era when the end of work is at stake. While youth unemployment is at an all-time high, the manufacturing sector of Seoul struggles with declining labor supply. "Neo Manufacturing" proposes that new technologies can bring young labor and sustainable work back into the city. Rather than accepting the logic that seeks to replace human work with machines, "Neo Manufacturing" envisions machines working with humans to create new modes of production and consumption. A series of workshops is organized to introduce and integrate new technologies with the traditional mastery of the diverse fields of manufacturing, thus closing the generation gap between the old and young, between analogue and digital technologies. Scientists, engineers, artists, designers, and architects working in the field of artificial intelligence, robotics, 3D printing, and digital fabrication will be invited to explore hybrid approaches that can thrive in the inner city.

Pages 416 and 419: Erik L'Heureux, Gregory Barber, et al. Washington University in St. Louis

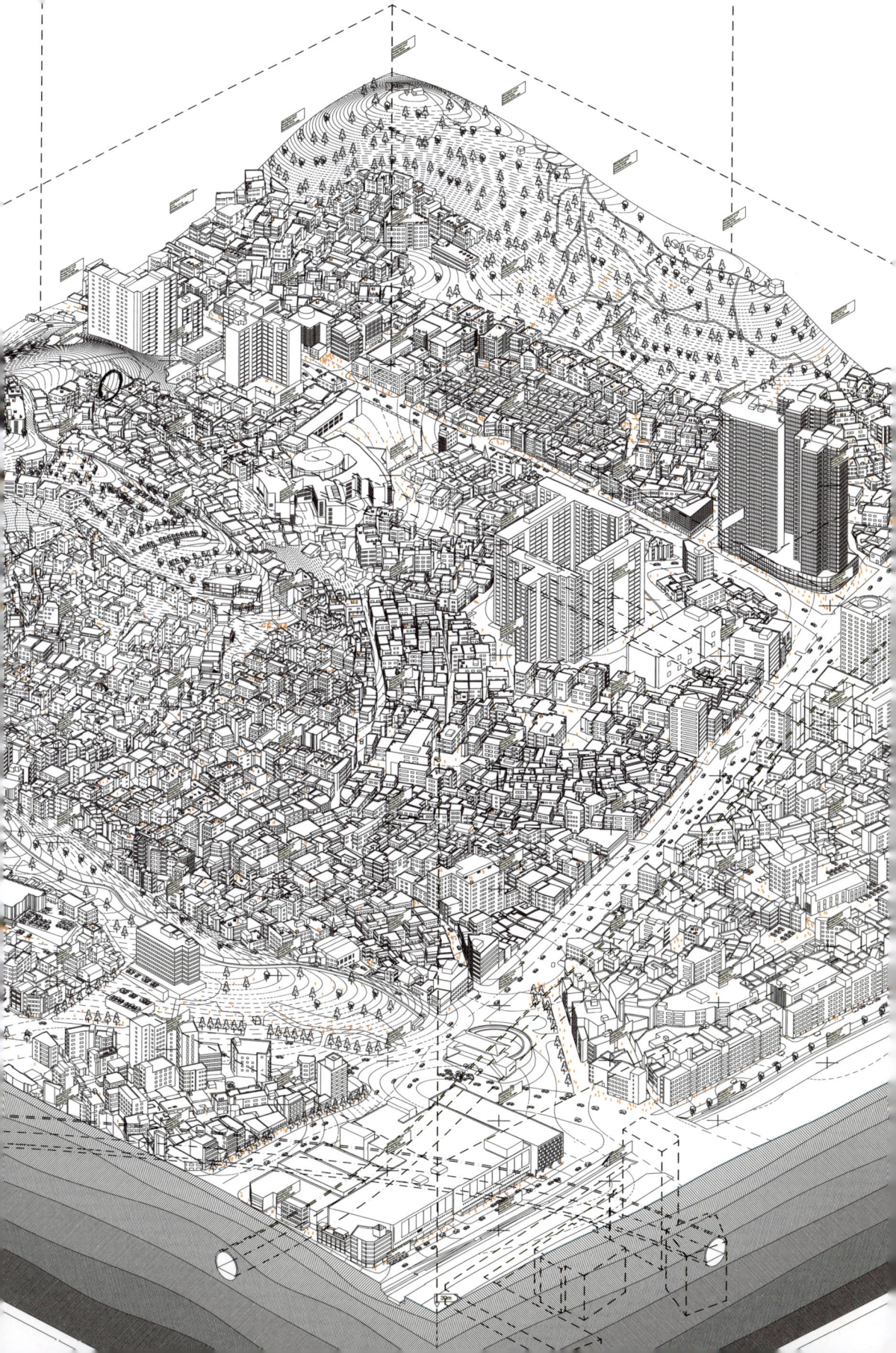

LIVE PROJECTS SEOUL:
URBAN FOODSHED

Curatorial Statement by
Hyewon Lee

Since the start of the twenty-first century, we have witnessed a series of global food security disasters, from the worldwide bee colony collapse (2006), to the wheat failure in Eastern Europe (2012), and the most recent bird flu outbreaks in Europe and Asia (2016). In South Korea alone, the bird flu resulted in 27 million poultry being culled. We have further entered the age of *peak food*—peak corn (1985), peak rice (1988), peak fish (1988), peak wheat (2004), and peak chicken (2006).[1] Borrowed from the concept of "peak oil," the point in time when the maximum amount of production is reached followed by a plateau or terminal decline, peak food highlights the high inputs of water and energy that go into agricultural production (over 70% of global water consumption is used for agriculture) as related to the downward inflections of these major food crops. Moreover, as peak food leads to generalized food insecurity, volatile food markets and food shortages ensue, affecting the poorest populations. At the same time, we have witnessed the rise of new "water barons," as top multinational investment banks and multibillionaires race to buy up land around important water sources worldwide.[2]

Set against this background, *Urban Foodshed* seeks to provide a vision for alternative urban food systems based on the sustainable use of land, water, and energy. A *foodshed* constitutes the geographical area and the resource flows that produce food for a particular population. Adapting the term "watershed" to the socio-economic context of food production, food ecologists and urban geographers have introduced the term to "facilitate critical thought on where our food is coming from and how it is getting to us" as well as to restore a sense of place to our food system.[3] A foodshed involves an ensemble of leading actors that include organic farmers and permaculturalists, beekeepers, environmental activists, and a diverse group of scientists—soil biologists, botanists, mycologists, entomologists, ornithologists, oceanographers, meteorologists, and toxicologists. *Urban Foodshed* will raise awareness of the geography of food production, distribution, and consumption in the everyday life of the city.

THE RESTAURANT
The restaurant forms the heart of the *Urban Foodshed*, functioning as the main platform for daily meals, food events, and debates focused on the global food and resource crises. The daily component of the Restaurant is a South Indian *thali* lunch served as a platter-per-person menu.

1. See, for example, Alastair Bland, "The World Hit 'Peak Chicken' in 2006," *Smithsonian.com*, 27 January 2015, http://www.smithsonianmag.com/science-nature/world-hit-peak-chicken-2006-180954037/; and Federica Cocco, "Peak Chicken' Was 2006 – How Food Production Isn't Keeping Pace with Population," *Mirror*, 28 January 28 2015, http://www.mirror.co.uk/news/ampp3d/chick-chick-chick-chick-chicken-5056318, accessed 20 December 2016.

2. Shiney Varghese, "The Global Water Grab," Institute for Agriculture & Trade Policy, 18 January 2013, http://www.iatp.org/blog/201301/the-global-water-grab, accessed 20 December 2016.

3. Jack Kloppenburg Jr., John Hendrickson, and G. W. Stevenson, "Coming in to the Foodshed," *Agriculture and Human Values* 13(3) (Summer 1996): 33.

Pyeongtaek, South Korea, 2015 by Suyeon Yun and Hyungyu Kim

This format will bring attention to the remarkable intercultural connections and transnational currents that have historically linked Korea and the south Indian region. The restaurant will also host a dozen different themed dinners—over-fishing and desertification of the ocean (Sea Shepherd), biodiversity and seed sovereignty (Heirloom Gala), GMO and global agribusiness (Multinational Dinner), food and energy consumption (Solar Cooking), food legacies of U.S. militarism and security alliances in Asia (Spam Commons), food refugees (Arabian Nights), food recycling and distribution (Salvaged Dinner), Bee Colony Collapse Disorder and peak food (Honey, Honey), etc.—spread throughout the biennial period. As part of the project's comprehensive strategy to spread awareness of the connections between food sustainability, consumption habits, the global waste crisis, and today's overwhelming nutrition challenges, the Restaurant adopts an anti-food-waste policy. Accordingly, any leftover or surplus food will be recycled as compost back into the Restaurant's own food system at the onsite gardens or its offsite farm locations.

SEED LIBRARY
The dining tables of the restaurant will have a dual purpose, and will be designed to showcase a horizontal Seed Library where an assortment of diverse seed samples will be exhibited. Each unique dining table will house a seed display with specimens including traditional or heirloom seeds, colorfully coated hybrid seeds produced and distributed by global agro-businesses, wild beans and seeds of edible weeds as future food resources, and samples of GMO crops that Korea typically imports from abroad.

ONSITE GARDENS, OFFSITE FARMS, AND FOOD FORAGING
Forming a pivot of the food ecosystem of *Urban Foodshed*, onsite gardens and offsite farms in various regions across Korea will supply essential foodstuffs for the restaurant. The restaurant rooftop features an onsite garden consisting of an aquaponic system, beehives, vegetable boxes, and compost bins. The courtyard of the restaurant grows lettuce, string beans, tomatoes, chili peppers, etc. The main water source for this fresh produce will be rainwater stored in rain-harvesting drums connected to the gutters of the restaurant building. Botanist-led food-foraging trips will be organized to call attention to edible weeds, wild beans, and mushrooms as future food resources, and will guide urban dwellers to develop food-crisis survival skills by learning how to identify edible plants and mushrooms.

WATER BAR
The Water Bar will invite customers to make a personal decision on the water source for one's beverage, thus raising awareness about the origin, treatment processes, and transportation of the various water sources leading up to consumption. To supplement their individual water selection, customers can also interact with the Seoul metro water-route map, download a Water Bar app to track the source of his or her bottled water, and operate a water deposit kiosk that deals with drought-stricken regions.

FUTURE MART
The Future Mart stocks two sets of goods for purchase: first, foodstuffs from the global food system, accompanied by labels revealing the environmental impact and health risks related to its production and consumption; and second, fresh produce from the onsite gardens and offsite farms of the *Urban Foodshed*, labeled with information about where, how, and by whom the food was grown. Future Mart counteracts a global food system that evades transparency and access to information about the growing and transportation of food and its destructive impact on natural and social environments.

EM/MENA PROJECT
In a region with one of the fastest-growing populations in the world, the ever-increasing and extreme pressures on the sustainable use of freshwater supply, energy production, and food resources have already exceeded societal and environmental thresholds. The EM/MENA (Eastern Mediterranean, Middle East, and North Africa) Project will present practical knowledge and innovative examples of how to regenerate living systems—water, land, soil, and food production—as a basis for long-term rehabilitation of ecosystems. Discarding conventional and industrial farming practices, these methods empower people anywhere to restore their natural environments, sequester carbon, increase soil organic matter, re-establish biodiversity, mitigate against flooding, and increase drought-resistance. These methods of combating climate change will create resilient and productive food systems that will ensure future food security.

LIVE PROJECTS SEOUL:
WALKING THE COMMONS

Curatorial Statement by
Soo-in Yang, Kyung Jae Kim, and Hyungmin Pai

Technology is the answer, but what was the question?
—Cedric Price, 1966

Walking is the most basic means of moving from one point to another. As a practical activity, it serves the role of connecting each means of transportation within a multimodal traffic system. In the near future, with the spread of smart mobility, there will be a fundamental change to walking. Personal mobility is currently growing at an exponential pace. In 2015, the global market for personal mobility devices amounted to 6.5 billion U.S. dollars and by 2023 is expected to reach 12.8 billion U.S. dollars.[1] The advent of autonomous vehicles and smart connections will have a profound impact on our walking patterns. With the development of various modes of transportation responsible for the last mile, walking will become unnecessary even when traveling short distances. The smooth and seamless connection between different means of transportation minimizes the distance and time traveled from one mode to another. Furthermore, autonomous driving technology will maximize transportation efficiency as personalized public transport will provide pick-up services in front of the home. Once out the door, it is more efficient not to walk. Why walk, then? In the imminent age of smart mobility, in the age of the digital sensorium, what constitutes the motivation and experience of walking?

Walking is a culture. Whether we are alone or with friends or in the streets of Seoul or Paris, taking a walk is less an act of necessity and more a type of play in our daily lives. Walking is a sensorial act of constant contact. In addition to the physical movement of arms and legs, we use all the sensory organs, constantly communicating with the surrounding physical environment. We look with our eyes, smell with our noses, feel the humidity and temperature of the air through our skin, and check the condition of the ground with our feet. Walking enables communication with the environment and becomes a process of discovery. We might discover something that was already there but not noticed, and now see and feel it in a new way. It could be the smell of a street vendor, the paving of the sidewalk, the history that permeates a neighborhood, or a process of enlightenment and spirituality. The stroll of Aristotle and his peripatetics in the School of Athens, the pilgrimage to Santiago de Compostela, the philosopher's path in Kyoto, the monk's trek towards the mountain temple of Chiang Mai: these are just a few of the most prominent examples of walking as discovery. During the nineteenth century, the physical environment of the city evolved to allow more contact between cities and the people. With better shoes, street pavement, sanitation, artificial lighting, better air quality, and later on, traffic signals, the modern flaneur was born. In the modern age, walking became a commons because pedestrians came in daily contact with the physical and nonphysical environment of plazas, arcades, and streets. As much as the train, the automobile, and the plane became the essential mechanisms of modernity, walking was an essential mode of discovery and play.

1. Credence Research, "Global Personal Mobility Devices Market—Growth, Future Prospects, Competitive Analysis, and Forecast, 2016–2024," 2017.

Page 424: Soo-in Yang and Kyung Jae Kim, The Four Walking Levels of Seoul (Drawing by Kyung Jae Kim), 2017

The meaning of walking is evolving. If discovery and communication are the precious gifts of walking, then smart mobility brings new dimensions to this process. Personal mobility is granular in nature; its devices operate independently in their own judgment, without being controlled by a large common flow, ideally coming into harmony as part of a moving commons. As smart mobility becomes pervasive, when walking becomes part of an expansive network of information, as augmented sensing and communication become imbedded in the experience of mobility, the walking commons expands beyond the realm of direct physical contact to new forms of collective environmental consciousness. Pedestrian-based neural networks will soon be integrated with AI-based, vehicle-centered traffic control in the transition to a new infrastructure and traffic system. If it is clear that we are moving towards machine-oriented mobility, the question remains why we will want to walk.

EXPERIMENTS IN THE WALKING COMMONS OF SEOUL
After decades of rapid modernist development, Seoul became a city inhospitable to walking and almost devoid of pedestrian plazas. A more recent shift in Seoul Metropolitan Government policy has given birth to various mobility sharing programs, the regeneration of infrastructure, the excavation and recovery of urban walking routes, and the continuous improvement of public transportation systems, all seeking to reinvent Seoul into a walking city. The regeneration of Sewoon Sangga, the Seoul Station area, and Seoullo; the establishment of Gyeongui Line Green Park; the Jongno BRT project; and plans for the reuse of obsolete underground passageways are just a few of the major projects that seek to transform Seoul's existing modern infrastructure into part of a pedestrian-based mobility network. In contrast to previous redevelopment projects in Seoul—based on transportation nodes and large-scale, insular interior spaces—these projects engage history, culture, economic incentive, and technology in a multidimensional experiential and information network. Through projects such as Playable City, Musicity, Brain Flaneur, and Soundline, and in partnership with a variety of mobility projects in Seoul, Walking the Commons intervenes into the fabric of the city to explore the possibilities of an evolving walkable city.

Appropriating infrastructure and smart city technologies to create new connections by injecting play and creativity into the everyday urban fabric, these interactive, participatory installations bring citizens into a social dialogue with their city. In Musicity, for example, pedestrians with GPS applications installed in their personal mobile devices listen to music as they reach a certain area within the city. Musicians are commissioned to compose original tracks in response to a particular building or urban landscape. As part of their walking experience, citizens are inspired to explore the city, musically and architecturally. The Brainwave Flaneur is a project that tracks pedestrian brainwaves in real time. The vast brainwave data generated in particular walking environments are recorded, archived, analyzed, and displayed. Whereas in the past the quality of the walking environment was evaluated with limited data such as sidewalk measurements, the number of building openings, and the density of greenery, it is now possible to use the psychological responses of pedestrians to understand the walking environment.

SEOUL by Erik Gerard L'Heureux

BIOGRAPHIES

HYUNGMIN PAI is a historian, critic, and curator. He studied architecture and urban design at Seoul National University and received his Ph.D from the History, Theory, and Criticism of Architecture program at MIT. He has taught at the Rhode Island School of Design and Washington University (St Louis) and is presently professor at the University of Seoul. Twice a Fulbright Scholar, he was a research fellow at the Seoul Institute and visiting scholar at MIT and London Metropolitan University. He is author of *The Portfolio and the Diagram* (MIT Press, 2002), required reading in core courses at Harvard University, Columbia University and the AA School; *Sensuous Plan: The Architecture of Seung H-Sang* (Dongnyok, 2007); and *The Key Concepts of Korean Architecture* (Dongnyok, 2012). For the Venice Biennale, he was curator for the Korean Pavilion in 2008 and 2014 (awarded the Golden Lion for best national participation), and a participant in the Common Pavilions project (2012). He was Visiting Director of the Asia Culture Complex (2014–15), Head Curator for the Gwangju Design Biennale (2010–11), and guest curator at the Aedes Gallery (Berlin), the Tophane Amire Gallery (Istanbul), The Cass Gallery (London), and Plateau, Samsung Museum of Art (Seoul). He presently serves on the Presidential Committee for the Hub City of Asian Culture, on the Mayor's Committee for the Future of Seoul, and as Chair of the Mokchon Architecture Archive.

ALEJANDRO ZAERA-POLO is an accomplished contemporary architect. His work has consistently merged the practice of architecture with theoretical practice, deftly integrating architecture, urban design and landscape architecture in his projects. His practice has produced critically acclaimed and award winning projects for the public and private sector on an international scale. He trained at the Escuela Técnica Superior de Arquitectura de Madrid, graduating with Honors, and went on to do a Master in Architecture (MARCH II) at the Graduate School of Design, Harvard University, USA, where he graduated with Distinction. He worked at OMA in Rotterdam between 1991 and 1993, prior to establishing Foreign Office Architects in 1993, and AZPML in 2011. Alejandro Zaera-Polo has also had an extensive involvement in education at an international level since 1993. He was the Dean of Princeton SoA 2012-2014 and of the Berlage Institute in Rotterdam from 2000-2005 where he held the Berlage Chair at the Technical University in Delft, the Netherlands. He was the inaugural recipient of the Norman Foster professorship at Yale University School of Architecture between 2010 and 2011, and has been a Visiting Critic at Columbia GSAPP and UCLA School of Architecture. He led a Diploma Unit between 1993 and 1999 years at the Architectural Association in London. He is a tenured professor at Princeton SoA. In addition to his professional and academic roles, Alejandro Zaera-Polo is recognized as an original theorist and thinker of contemporary architecture, with a sharp capacity to identify social and political trends and translate them into the architectural discourse. His texts can be found in many professional publications such as El Croquis, Quaderns, A+U, Arch+, Log, AD and Harvard Design Magazine.

IÑAKI ÁBALOS is a Ph.D. in Architecture and Chaired Professor of Architectural Design at the ETSAM since 2002. He was Kenzo Tange Professor (2009), Design Critic in Architecture (2010-2012), and since 2013 Professor in Residence and Chair of the Department of Architecture at Harvard University Graduate School of Design. In association with Renata Sentkiewicz, he is a founding member of Abalos+Sentkiewicz AS+ since 2006. The firm last published monograph is "*Essays on Thermodynamics, Architecture and Beauty*" Actar (2015).

JULIAN AGYEMAN is a Professor of Urban and Environmental Policy and Planning at Tufts University in Medford, MA. He is a critical urban studies and environmental social science scholar whose work focuses on the possibility of *just sustainabilities*.

DANIELE BELLERI is a design journalist and communication consultant, working as head of communications and editor at Carlo Ratti Associati office. As a writer, his works have appeared on international media including *Wired Italia, Domus, Volume, Reuters*. He runs a course in Storymaking and Strategic Communication at the MA Advanced Urban Design, a joint program of the Higher School of Economics and the Strelka Institute for Media, Architecture and Design in Moscow.

LINDSAY BREMNER is the director of Architectural Research in the Faculty of Architecture and the Built Environment at the University of Westminster. She was previously Professor and Chair of Architecture in the Tyler School of Art at Temple University in Philadelphia and Chair of Architecture at the University of the Witwatersrand in Johannesburg. She is an award-winning architect and writer and published, lectured and exhibited widely on the transformation of Johannesburg after the end of apartheid. She is currently Principal Investigator on the European Research Council funded project Monsoon Assemblages that is investigating changing monsoon climates in Chennai, Delhi and Dhaka. She holds M. Arch and DSc. Arch degrees from the University of the Witwatersrand, and a B.Arch degree from the University of Cape Town.

NEREA CALVILLO is an architect, researcher and curator, Assistant Professor at the Centre for Interdisciplinary Methodologies (University of Warwick) and unit master at the Architectural Association. She studied at the ETSAM, was awarded the Fulbright grant to pursue studies at Columbia University (MsAAD), and she received her doctorate in 2014 with the thesis Sensing Aerópolis. The work produced at her office, C+ arquitectos, and her environmental visualization projects like In the Air have been presented, exhibited and published at international venues. She is a Poiesis Fellow (NYU) and was a post-doc researcher at Citizen Sense (Goldsmiths). Her research investigates the material, technological, political and social dimensions of environmental pollution working at the intersection between architecture, science and technology and feminist studies, new materialisms and urban political ecologies.

MARIO CARPO, Reyner Banham Professor of Architectural Theory and History, the Bartlett, University College London. Carpo's research and publications focus on the relationship among architectural theory, cultural history, and the history of media and information technology. His *Architecture in the Age of Printing* (2001) has been translated into several languages. His most recent books are *The Alphabet and the Algorithm*, a history of digital design theory (2011); and *The Digital Turn in Architecture, 1992-2012*, an AD Reader. His next monograph, *The Second Digital Turn: Design Beyond Intelligence* is forthcoming with the MIT Press in the fall of 2017.

GRAHAM FLOATER is a former advisor to the UK Prime Minister and senior official at HM Treasury. His areas of expertise include international trade and sustainable finance. He currently directs the cities and finance programme for the Global Commission on the Economy and Climate. His varied roles have included deputy director and senior advisor to the Prime Minister on energy and climate finance, Head of European Economic Negotiations at HM Treasury, Private Secretary to a Cabinet Minister, and EU trade negotiator at the European Commission and WTO. He holds a BA(Hons) 1st class in natural science from the University of Oxford, a postgraduate degree in economics from the University of Cambridge, and a PhD in population modelling.

DAVID GISSEN is a historian, theorist, curator and critic whose work examines histories and theories of architecture, landscapes, environments and cities, primarily in the 19th and 20th century. His recent work focuses on developing experimental forms of historical practice, writing, and translation to depict the spaces, environments, and landscapes of the past.
David lectures on his work internationally, including recent invited talks at the Canadian Centre for Architecture, Milan Polytechnic, Berlage Institute, Harvard University, Yale University, Princeton University, The Royal Melbourne Institute of Technology, and The Royal Danish Academy of Art. He is currently teaching at California College of Art (CCA), David is a visiting professor in the program in the History, Theory and Criticism of Art and Architectural History at the Massachusetts Institute of Technology and has led workshops on his work at several international universities.

FABIO GRAMAZIO is an architect with multi-disciplinary interests ranging from computational design and robotic fabrication to material innovation. In 2000, he founded the architecture practice Gramazio & Kohler in conjunction with his partner Matthias Kohler, where numerous award-wining designs have been realised. Current projects include the design of the Empa NEST research platform, a future living and working laboratory for sustainable building construction. Opening also the world's first architectural robotic laboratory at ETH Zurich, Gramazio & Kohler's research has been formative in the field of digital architecture, setting precedence and de facto creating a new research field merging advanced architectural design and additive fabrication processes through the customised use of industrial robots. This ranges from 1:1 prototype installations to the design of robotically fabricated high-rises. The recent research is outlined and theoretically framed in the book *The Robotic Touch: How Robots Change Architecture* (Park Books, 2014).

ADAM GREENFIELD was previously a rock critic, bike messenger and psychological operations specialist in the US Army, he spent over a decade working in the design and development of networked digital information technologies, for consultancy Razorfish, phone manufacturer Nokia and his own practice Urbanscale. Selected in 2013 as Senior Urban Fellow at the LSE Cities centre of the London School of Economics, he has taught in the Urban Design program of the Bartlett, University College London, and in New York University's Interactive Telecommunications Program. His books include *Everyware: The Dawning Age of Ubiquitous Computing* (2006), *Urban Computing and its Discontents* (2007), and the #1 bestselling "Against the smart city" (2013). He lives in London with his partner, the filmmaker Nurri Kim.

DIRK E. HEBEL is Professor of Sustainable Construction at the Karlsruhe Institute of Technology (KIT) in Germany, as well as the Future Cities Laboratory (FCL) in Singapore. He previously held the position of Assistant Professor of Architecture and Construction at the Department of Architecture of ETH Zürich in Switzerland; he was the Founding Scientific Director of the Ethiopian Institute of Architecture, Building Construction and City Development in Addis Ababa. Between 2002 and 2009, he taught at the Department of Architecture at ETH Zürich, held a guest professorship at Syracuse University and taught as a guest lecturer at Princeton University, USA. Work resulting from his teaching and research has been published in numerous books and academic journals, lately SUDU–The Sustainable Urban Dwelling Unit (Ruby Press, 2015) and Cities of Change–Addis Ababa (with Marc Angélil, second and revised edition, Birkhäuser, 2016). His research concentrates on a metabolic understanding of resources and investigates alternative building materials and construction techniques and their applications in developed as well as developing territories.

FELIX HEISEL is an architect currently working as Head of Research and PhD candidate at the Professorship of Sustainable Construction Dirk E. Hebel at the Karlsruhe Institute of Technology (KIT) in Germany, as well as the Future Cities Laboratory (FCL) in Singapore. He previously held the position of Research Coordinator at the Professorship of Architecture and

Construction at ETH Zürich. He has taught and lectured at the ETH Zürich and the Future Cities Laboratory in Singapore, as well as the Ethiopian Institute of Architecture, Building Construction and City Development in Addis Ababa, the Berlage Institute in Rotterdam, and the Berlin University of the Arts. His teaching and research has been published in books and academic journals including *Building from Waste* (with Dirk E. Hebel and Marta H. Wisniewska, Birkhäuser, 2014). His interest in informal processes led him to establish the documentary movie series _ Spaces in 2011, which is published online and as the book Lessons of Informality (with Bisrat Kifle, Birkhäuser, 2016). His research work is focused on the phenomena of informality in connection and dependency on the establishment of (alternative) building materials in developing territories.

CHRISTIAN HUBERT is an educator, architect and writer based in lower Manhattan, whose work walks the border between art and architecture in the exploration of space, light, and material. He is currently an Associate Professor at Parsons the New School of Design. He is the founder of Christian Hubert Studio, which specializes in the design of gallery spaces, artist residences, and art and culture institutions. During the early 1980's he taught at the Institute for Architecture and Urban Studies in New York and was elected to the fellowship of the Institute in 1982. During the same period, he designed lofts for artists including David Salle and Francesco Clemente, as well as several exhibitions at the Whitney Museum. From 1986 to 1995, Mr. Hubert worked and taught in Los Angeles, where he was president of the Los Angeles Forum for Architecture and Urban Design. He has taught extensively on the East and West Coasts of the U.S., as well as in Canada, and his lower Manhattan office serves as an outpost of the PhD Architecture program at the University of Delft. Mr. Hubert received a B.A from Columbia and a M.Arch. from the Harvard Graduate School of Design.

JIE-EUN HWANG is an associate professor at University of Seoul. Her research interests include spatial information representation, digital tectonics, design media and interface, open data. As an educator, new media experiment and alternative education are also recent challenges. She pursued various research projects, including: developing participatory mobile augmented reality contents, developing a spatio-temporal timeline system for monitoring public space, developing index system for monitoring UNESCO heritage. Art galleries: Gallery Factory, Gwangju Design Biennale, Culture Station Seoul 284, and Kumho Gallery, have invited her for media art installations that represent social commons.

ALEX IVANČIĆ is a mechanical engineer, holds a PhD in Thermal Science. The main area of his professional interest is focused on energy systems in built environment. Alex is equally committed to researching, practicing and teaching. He currently works with Aiguasol Engineering (Barcelona, Spain) as Senior Consuntat. Alex is an elected member of the Scientific Society of Serbia and Member of the International Keio Institute for Architecture and Urbanism, Keio University, Tokyo. He has taught at Barcelona Institute of Architecture and Universitat Politècnica de Catalunya, among others. As invited lecturer he visited Université de Genève, Universita della Svizzera Italiana, Princeton University, New Delhi Schoolo of Planning and Architecture, Aalto University, etc. Alex published over sixty scientific and technical publications on great variety of energy related topics, including the book *EnergyScapes*, 2010, Gustavo Gili.

MITCHELL JOACHIM, Ph.D. is the Co-Founder of Terreform ONE and an Associate Professor of Practice at NYU. Formerly, he was an architect at the offices of Frank Gehry and I.M. Pei. He as been awarded a Fulbright Scholarship and fellowships with TED, Moshe Safdie, and Martin Society for Sustainability. He was chosen by *Wired* magazine for "The Smart List" and selected by *Rolling Stone* for "The 100 People Who Are Changing America". Mitchell won many honors including; AIA New York Urban Design Merit Award, 1st Place International Architecture Award, Victor Papanek Social Design Award, Zumtobel Group Award for Sustainability, History Channel Infiniti Award for City of the Future, and *Time* magazine's Best Invention with MIT. He's featured as

"The NOW 99" in *Dwell* magazine and "50 Under 50 Innovators of the 21st Century" by Images Publishers. He co-authored the books, "XXL-XS: New Directions in Ecological Design," "Super Cells: Building with Biology" and "Global Design: Elsewhere Envisioned". His design work has been exhibited at MoMA and the Venice Biennale. He earned: PhD at Massachusetts Institute of Technology, MAUD Harvard University, MArch Columbia University.

KYUNG JAE KIM is a registered architect in New York, and the founder of Atelier KJ and co-founder of Common Pracrice, an architect activist group in New York City. His expertise is in architecture, urbanism, and art. Kyung Jae Kim studied Urban Planning and Design at Yonsei University and received his Master of Architecture from the Graduate School of Architecture, Planning, and Preservation at Columbia University. He also participated in developing the master plans for Maritime Complex in Doha, Qatar and Moscow Airport.

MATTHIAS KOHLER is an architect with multi-disciplinary interests ranging from computational design and robotic fabrication to material innovation. In 2000, he founded the architecture practice Gramazio & Kohler in conjunction with his partner Fabio Gramazio, where numerous award-wining designs have been realised. Current projects include the design of the Empa NEST research platform, a future living and working laboratory for sustainable building construction. Opening also the world's first architectural robotic laboratory at ETH Zurich, Gramazio & Kohler's research has been formative in the field of digital architecture, setting precedence and de facto creating a new research field merging advanced architectural design and additive fabrication processes through the customised use of industrial robots. This ranges from 1:1 prototype installations to the design of robotically fabricated high-rises. His recent research is outlined and theoretically framed in the book *The Robotic Touch: How Robots Change Architecture* (Park Books, 2014). Since 2014, Matthias Kohler is also director of the new National Centre of Competence in Research (NCCR) Digital Fabrication.

MAIDER LLAGUNO-MUNITXA co-founded the London and New York based architecture office AZPML in 2011, after having worked for Foreign Office Architects in London since 2006. Maider is currently Adjunct Assistant Professor at Columbia GSAPP and postdoctoral researcher at the Civil and Environmental Engineering department at Princeton University. Her fields of knowledge include urban physics; building physics, environmental modelling, analysis and visualization, and computational design. In 2016 Maider Llaguno-Munitxa completed her Ph.D. from the Institute of Technology in Architecture at the ETH in Zurich. Her Ph.D. topic focused on the study of the interaction of architecture, urban microclimate and its dynamics of flow and transport. Before initiating her Ph.D. studies, Maider graduated from ETSASS/ETSAB with Honors in 2006 and from Columbia GSAPP with Excellence in Design in 2010. Maider has taught at different universities such as the Barnard College and Columbia GSAPP in New York, the ETH in Zurich and the Yale School of Architecture in New Haven. The work of Maider Llaguno-Munitxa has been published in various international architectural periodicals and newsletters as well as in scientific journals focused on the topics of environmental sciences and design computation.

JESSE LECAVALIER is an award-winning designer, writer, and educator whose work explores the architectural and urban implications of contemporary logistics. LeCavalier is an assistant professor of architecture at the New Jersey Institute of Technology where he coordinates the Special Topics and Integrated Studio sequence. In 2015, he was the recipient of the New Faculty Teaching Award from the Association of the Collegiate Schools of Architecture (ACSA). He was the 2010–11 Sanders Fellow at the University of Michigan, a Poiesis Fellow at the Institute for Public Knowledge at NYU, and a researcher at the Singapore-ETH Future Cities Laboratory. His research has been supported by the Graham Foundation, the New York State Council for the Arts, and the BMW Foundation.

HYEWON LEE is Professor of Art History at Daejin University. Her curatorial projects include *Water*

Preppers at DDP, *Water Line* at I:Project Space in Beijing, *Waterscapes: the Politics of Water* at Kumho Museum of Art and *Water Bodies* at SPACES, Chennai. She also curated *A Room of His Own: Masculinities in Korea and the Middle East* at Art Sonje Center and Up in the Air: From Yeoido to Incheon, an exhibition of various objects and artifacts that South Koreans brought home from their overseas travels from the time of Vietnam War to the first decade of the 21st century.

DUNCAN MCLAREN is currently a freelance researcher, and part-time PhD student at Lancaster University, UK. Previously he worked for many years in environmental research and advocacy, most recently as Chief Executive of Friends of the Earth Scotland from 2003 until 2011.

GUNTER PAULI graduated as "Licencié en Sciences Economiques" from St. Ignatius Loyola University in Antwerp,Belgium and obtained his masters in business administration at INSEAD, in Fontainebleau, France. He was the founder of a dozen companies, and as Chairman and President of Ecover he created the first ecological factory building that aimed for zero emissions. A building made out of wood with a large grass roof. In 1994 he was invited as, a senior advisor to the Rector of the United Nations University in Tokyo (Japan) to lead a think tank preparing for the Kyoto Protocol. His entrepreneurial activities span business, culture, science, politics and the environment. He founded the "Zero Emissions Research and Initiatives" (ZERI) at the United Nations University in Tokyo, and subsequently established The Global ZERI Network as a foundation, redesigning production and consumption into clusters of industries inspired by natural systems. He has been visiting lecturer and professor at universities in on all continents, and Member of the Board of NGOs and private companies. He has advised governments, entrepreneurs and industry leaders on how to implement breakthrough innovations that permits society to better respond to the basic needs of all, starting with water, food, housing, health and energy. He works with what is locally available, focuses on the generation of value." He has implemented over 200 projects, mobilized $5 billion in investments and created 3 million jobs. Each successfu.l initiative is translated into a children's fable of which by 2017 some 144 have been distributed to schools by the Chinese Government

JENNIFER GABRYS is currently Reader in the Department of Sociology at Goldsmiths, University of London. She is also Principal Investigator on the European Research Council (ERC) project, "Citizen Sense," which investigates the use of environmental sensors for new modes of citizen involvement in environmental issues. Prior to joining the Department of Sociology, She was Senior Lecturer and Convenor of the MA in Design and Environment in the Department of Design at Goldsmiths, University of London. She completed a PhD in Communication Studies at McGill University in Montreal, during which time she was engaged as a research fellow on the Culture of Cities and Digital Cities / Mobile Digital Commons projects. This work drew on her interest in the intersections of environments and communication technologies, which she had developed through working in the field of landscape architecture and urban design in Minneapolis (at Coen + Partners) and Los Angeles (at Rios Clementi Hale Studios). Jennifer Gabrys research investigates environments, material processes and communication technologies through theoretical and practice-based work. Projects within this area include a recently published study on citizen sensing and environmental practice, *Program Earth: Environmental Sensing Technology and the Making of a Computational Planet* (University of Minnesota Press, 2016); and *Digital Rubbish: A Natural History of Electronics* (University of Michigan Press, 2011), which examines the materialities of electronic waste.

CARLO RATTI. Director, MIT Senseable City Lab. Founding Partner, Carlo Ratti Associati
An architect and engineer by training, Professor Carlo Ratti teaches at MIT, where he directs the Senseable City Lab. He is also a founding partner of the international design and innovation office Carlo Ratti Associati. His work has been exhibited in several venues worldwide, including the Venice Biennale, New York's MoMA, London's Science Museum, and Barcelona's Design Museum. Two of his projects–the Digital Water Pavilion and the Copenhagen Wheel–were hailed by *Time* Magazine as 'Best Inventions of the Year'. He

has been included in *Blueprint* Magazine's '25 People who will Change the World of Design' and in *Wired* Magazine's 'Smart List: 50 people who will change the world'. He was curator for the Future Food District at Expo Milano 2015, and is currently serving as co-chair of the World Economic Forum Global Future Council on the Future of Cities and Urbanization.

PHILIPP RODE is Executive Director of LSE Cities and Associate Professorial Research Fellow at the London School of Economics and Political Science. As researcher, consultant and advisor he has been directing interdisciplinary projects comprising urban governance, transport, city planning and urban design at the LSE since 2003. The focus of his current work is on institutional structures and governance capacities of cities and on sustainable urban development, transport and mobility. He is co-directing the cities workstream of the Global Commission on the Economy and Climate and has co-led the United Nations Habitat III Policy Unit on Urban Governance. He has previously led the coordination of the chapters on Green Cities and Green Buildings for the United Nations Environment Programme's Green Economy Report. Rode is Executive Director of the Urban Age Programme and since 2005 organised Urban Age conferences in over a dozen world cities bringing together political leaders, city mayors, urban practitioners, private sector representatives and academic experts. He manages the Urban Age research efforts and recently co-authored 'Towards New Urban Mobility: The case of London and Berlin' (2015), 'Cities and Energy: Urban morphology and heat energy demand' (2014), 'Going Green: How cities are leading the green economy' (2012) and 'Transforming Urban Economies' (2013). He has previously worked on several multidisciplinary research and consultancy projects in New York and Berlin and was awarded the Schinkel Urban Design Prize 2000. He holds a PhD in Cities and MSc in City Design and Social Science from the LSE and a Graduate Engineering Degree in Transport Planning and Management from Technical University Berlin.

RENATA SENTKIEWICZ is an Architect, Master of Sciences by the Polytechnic of Cracow. She is the founder and co-director of Abalos+Sentkiewicz, AS+, with offices in Madrid, Shanghai and Cambridge. She combines this activity with research and academia. Renata is currently a Design Critic at Harvard GSD, and Associate Professor of Architectural Design at ETSAM. Her work has been internationally recognized in 15 solo exhibitions, multiple collective shows, 18 prizes to built work and 45 other prizes to her joint research and design work with Iñaki Ábalos.

SOA (SOCIETY OF ARCHITECTURE) Yerin Kang, Chihoon Lee, Jaewoen Lee are the partners of SoA (Society of Architecture), an architectural firm, who are working on building environments of various scales through analysis of social conditions of city and architecture. It critically interprets the multi-cultural context of city-architecture and aims at architecture that works universally in the Korean society. To this end, it explores urban planning as a social technology, architecture as materials–part of industrial structure– and technology, collaborates with various genres within and outside architecture such as urban sociology, politics, geography, history and art.

CHARLES WALDHEIM is a North American architect, urbanist, and educator. Waldheim's research examines the relations between landscape, ecology, and contemporary urbanism. He coined the term 'landscape urbanism' to describe the emergent discourse and practices of landscape in relation to design culture and contemporary urbanization. On these topics he is author of *Landscape as Urbanism: A General Theory* and editor of *The Landscape Urbanism Reader*. Waldheim is John E. Irving Professor at Harvard University's Graduate School of Design where he directs the School's Office for Urbanization. He is recipient of the Rome Prize Fellowship from the American Academy in Rome; the Visiting Scholar Research Fellowship at the Study Centre of the Canadian Centre for Architecture; the Cullinan Chair at Rice University; and the Sanders Fellowship at the University of Michigan.

JAN WILLMANN is Professor of the Theory and History of Design at the Bauhaus-Universität Weimar. After studying architecture and theory in Oxford, he served as Scientific and Teaching Assistant at the Institute of Architectural Theory at Innsbruck University, where he also earned his Ph.D. (with distinction), and was Senior

Assistant of Gramazio Kohler Research at the Swiss Federal Institute of Technology (ETH) in Zurich. Jan Willmann's research and publications focus on the relationship between the theory and history of design, cultural history, and the history of media and information technology. He has lectured worldwide and collaborated with numerous renowned international design institutions and research agencies, and is regularly invited as an expert and design critic. His essays and articles have been published in various journals and magazines, including *AD/Architectural Design, GAM, Arquitectura Viva, 3D Printing and Additive Manufacturing, The Architectural Review, T&A, IEEE, Elsevier Automation & Construction, IJAC* and *DETAIL*.

MARTA H. WISNIEWSKA is an architect and co-principal of Heisel Architekten in Germany. She previously worked as a researcher and teaching assistant at the Assistant Professorship of Architecture and Construction at the ETH Zürich and the Future Cities Laboratory in Singapore. Prior to her engagement at ETH Zurich, she lectured and acted as 1st year architectural program coordinator at the Ethiopian Institute of Architecture, Building Construction and City Development in Addis Ababa. In 2011, the EiABC Student Council recognized her commitment with a 'Best Teaching' award. In 2014, Marta has published 'Building from Waste: Recovered Materials in Architecture and Construction' (2014, Birkhäuser, with Dirk E. Hebel and Felix Heisel), based on her Waste Research. Apart from that she has contributed texts to such entities as 'ETH Intranet' (2014), 'Architektura i Biznes' (2012, 2013), 'Construction Ahead' (2012), or 'Building Ethiopia: Sustainability and Innovation in Architecture and Design' (2012, EiABC). Marta's research focuses on the paradigm shift of activating waste as a future resource for an industrial use in construction.

SOO-IN YANG is an architect and the director of Lifethings, an architectural firm. After graduating from the Columbia Graduate School of Architecture, Planning and Preservation, Soo-in Yang has served as an adjunct professor at Ewha Womans University and Columbia University. Soo-in Yang won the Architectural League of New York's Young Architects Forum and was selected as one of the Next Generation Design Leaders of Korea.

IMAGE CREDITS

31: Yonsei University Museum

42: ©Ibay Rigby

46-47: Getty Image

60 (Left): https://www.youtube.com/watch?v=Rh6NGNfBy8o

60 (Right): Everett/REX/Shutterslock

61 (Left): http://imgur.com/gallery/hEsGaNS, Emojitracker.com, accessed in 2015

61 (Right): http://imgur.com/gallery/hEsGaNS, Emojitracker.com, accessed in 2015

63 (Left): http://www.illienglobal.com/international-day-of-happiness-earth-day-model/

63 (Right): United Nations

64 (Right) Screenshot of Whitehouse Youtube Channel

64 (Left): cnbc interview video screenshot

65 (Table): European Comission: http://ec.europa.eu/environment/air/quality/standards.htm

These data has been compiled from various sources:
-Australian Government Department of Environment and Energy, url: http://www.environment.gov.au/protection/air-quality/air-quality-standards accessed in March 2016
-China Government air quality standards, url: http://transportpolicy.net/index.php?title=China:_Air_Quality_Standards accessed in March 2016
-Canada Government air quality standards, url: http://www.ec.gc.ca/default.asp?lang=En&n=-56D4043B-1&news=A4B-2C28A-2DFB-4BF4-8777-ADF-29B4360BD accessed in March 2016

-United States air quality standards https://www.epa.gov/criteria-air-pollutants/naaqs-table accessed in March 2016
-Europe air quality standards, url: http://ec.europa.eu/environment/air/quality/standards.htm accessed in march 2016
-World health organization, url: http://www.who.int/mediacentre/factsheets/fs313/en/ accessed in march 2016

WHO: http://www.who.int/mediacentre/factsheets/fs313/en/

69 (Left): http://www.messynessychic.com/2015/01/27/building-mr-eiffels-penthouse-apartment-the-tower-under-construction/

75: http://www.opensense.ethz.ch/trac/

76: http://aqicn.org/city/beijing (accessed in April 2017)

78-79: https://commons.wikimedia.org/wiki/Category:Makoko#/media/File:2010_Boats_Makoko_Lagos_Nigeria_5342610737.jpg

90: Haughton (1964), Geological Society of South Africa

91: ©Lindsay Bremner

93 (Top): William Cullen Library, University of the Witwatersrand, Johannesburg

93 (Bottom): Johannesburg Public Library

94: Johannesburg Public Library

96: ©Lindsay Bremner

94: ©Lindsay Bremner

108: Ivanka Milenkovic ©2017

110: Colombia ©2016

133: Menloparkmuseum: http://www.menloparkmuseum.org/wp-content/uploads/2014/07/Bulb-Post-Card1.jpg

134: Tesla Motor: http://www.

twinkletoesengineering.info/induction_motor.htm

135: ©Ford

136: http://www.williscarrier.com/images/slide_sample_03.jpg

137: Précisions sur un état présent de l'architecture et de l'urbanisme

138: City of Melbourne

140: https://setis.ec.europa.eu/related-jrc-activities/jrc-setis-reports/cost-maps-unsubsidised-photovoltaic-electricity Cost Maps for Unsubsidised Photovoltaic Electricity

141: ©Alex Ivancic

142: http://cullinanstudio.com/project/bunhill-2-energy-centre

143: Islington Council, Ninety90

153: ©AIZAR RALDES/AFP/Getty Images

154: ©Bruno Braquehais/BHVP/Roger-Viollet: Wikimedia

155: World War I barricade at Porte Maillot, Paris, ca. 1914–15: Wikimedia

160: ©Jeff Pachoud/AFP

163: ©Charles Waldheim

169: ©Charles Waldheim

170-171: http://designmind.frogdesign.com/2014/05/unseen-sensors-constantly-sensing-rarely-seen/

176-177: ©Studio Jinc

183: MIT Senseable City Lab

184: MIT Senseable City Lab

186: MIT Senseable City Lab

188: MIT Senseable City Lab

191: MIT Senseable City Lab

193: Universal History Archive/Getty Images

194: ©Fondation Le Corbusier

195: Peter Phipp/Travelshots.com / Alamy Stock Photo

197: ©John Horner Photography

199: MIT Senseable City Lab

204-205: Masai Tribesman with cell phone, Kenya. © Svin Torfinn. Image courtesy of Verso Books.

209: http://rhubarbes.com/post/159598197381/via-b-o-n-%E3%83%9C%E3%83%B3

218-219: ©Katie Brinn: Wikimedia

241: LSE Cities 2014 based on ADB 2009 and Hickman and Banister 2014

242: LSE Cities 2014 (concept and information design based on Sorensen and Hess 2007)

246: Newman and Kenworthy 2015

247 (Right): Kenworthy and Laube 2001

247 (Left): LSE Cities 2014 based on STF 2014

248: Angel 2012

250-251: ISEGS: Ivanpah Solar Electric Generating System tower

253 (Top): Wagner 2013

253 (Bottom): IEA (2012)

254: Arze del Granado, Coady et al. 2012

255: Office of National Statistics (ONS) (2010)

256: Heck and Rogers 2014

257: LMC automotive data, reproduced in OECD (2013a)

260 (Appendix): Litman (2014b)

268 (Left): "I'm Young and Healthy," http://youtu.be/mSvQtAnh_CI , accessed July 15, 2012.

268 (Right): "Logistics: Live in Beijing," http://youtu.be/YvTrMaLi1cs, accessed July 15, 2012.

269: U.P.C. Symbol Specification, (Washington, DC: Distribution Number Bank), May 1973, http://www.idhistory.com/standards/UPCSymbolSpecificationMay1973.pdf, accessed March 03, 2012.

270: Image created by author from illustration in Lawrence Hicks, The Universal Product Code, 1975.

272: Alfred Chandler, Jr., The Visible Hand: The Managerial Revolution in American Business (Cambridge: Harvard University Press, 1977).

273: Charles B. Einstein, "Modeling the Wholesale Logistics Base," Army Logistician (November-December, 1983), 19.

274-275: various Dematic case study brochures, http://www.dematic.com/na/case-studies, accessed July 15, 2012.

276: DeVita et al., "Wrist-mounted Optical Scanning and Pointing Systems," USPTO Patent No. 5898161, April 27, 1999.

278: David C. Weston and Adrian Arnott, "Stacker Crane System," USPTO Patent No. 3606039, September 20, 1971.

279: Mountz et al., "Method and System for Replenishing Inventory Items," USPTO Patent No. 7894932, February 22, 2011.

280 (Left): http://openlibrary.org/books/OL24191484M/Choregraphie_ou_L'art_de_d%C3%A9crire_la_dance_par_caracteres_figures_et_signes_d%C3%A9monstratifs, accessed July 15, 2012;

280 (right): USPTO Patent No. 7912574, March 22, 2011.

281: USPTO Patent No. 6950722 B2, September 27, 2005.

288: ©Dominik Raskin: https://dominikraskin.com/

296: © François Lauginie

298: © Gramazio Kohler Research, ETH Zurich

301: © Gramazio Kohler Research, ETH Zurich

317: Filippo Romano

328: Terreform ONE

329: Terreform ONE

330-331: Terreform ONE

332-333: Terreform ONE

338: Sophie Nash, Dirk E. Hebel and Felix Heisel

342: Albert Vecerka/Esto

343: Albert Vecerka/Esto

346: This image was originally posted to Flickr by Kentaro IEMOTO@Tokyo at http://flickr.com/photos/28573791@N08/12691254574

405: Valdis Dunis (via Wikimedia Commons) [CC BY-SA 4.0]

407 (Top): Smiley.toerist (via Wikimedia Commons) [CC BY-SA 4.0]

407 (Bottom): Smiley.toerist (via Wikimedia Commons) [CC BY-SA 3.0]

408: ©Duncan McLaren

409: Paco Godoy (via Wikimedia Commons) [CC BY-SA 3.0]

410: Pelle Sten (via Wikimedia Commons) [CC BY 2.0]

411: Peter Angritt, from Wikimedia Commons [CC BY-SA 4.0]

412 (Top): Saúl Briceño [CC-BY-2.0]

412 (Bottom): Sandra Wallner (via Wikimedia Commons) [CC-BY-SA-3.0]

SEOUL BIENNALE OF
ARCHITECTURE
AND URBANISM 2017:
IMMINENT COMMONS

HOSTED BY
Seoul Metropolitan Government
Seoul Design Foundation

CO-DIRECTORS
Hyungmin Pai
Alejandro Zaera-Polo

SEOUL BIENNALE OF
ARCHITECTURE
AND URBANISM DIVISION,
SEOUL DESIGN FOUNDATION

DIVISION DIRECTOR
Soik Jung

PROJECT MANAGERS
Nayeon Kim
Hye Seong Park
Myungcheol Shin
Myeongju Keum
Suna Lee
Green Kim
Ri Jin Yoo
Jina Lee
Sunjae Kim
Sobaek Oh
Junyoung Lee

BOOK 1:
IMMINENT COMMONS:
URBAN QUESTIONS FOR
THE NEAR FUTURE

PUBLISHED BY
Actar Publishers and the Seoul
Biennale of Architecture and
Urbanism

EDITED BY
Alejandro Zaera-Polo
Hyungmin Pai
Ramon Prat Homs
Jeffrey S. Anderson

With the collaboration of
Ricardo Devesa
Mahgol Motalebi

COPY-EDITING
Paula Woolley

PROOF-READING
Daniel Collins

GRAPHIC DESIGN OF THE BOOK
Ramon Prat Homs

GRAPHIC IDENTITY OF
THE SEOUL BIENNALE
Sulki and Min

DISTRIBUTED BY
Actar Publishers
440 Park Avenue South, 17th Floor
New York, NY 10016
T +1 212 966 2207
F +1 212 966 2214
salesnewyork@actar-d.com

Barcelona
Roca i Batlle 2-4
08023 Barcelona
T +34 933 282 183
salesbarcelona@actar-d.com
eurosales@actar-d.com

COPYRIGHT
© 2017 Actar Publishers and the
Seoul Biennale of Architecture
and Urbanism
© Text and images by the authors

All rights reserved. No part of this
publication may be reproduced, stored
in a retrieval system, or transmitted in
any form or by any means, electronic,
mechanical, photocopyng, recording,
or otherwise, without prior written
consent of the publishers, except in the
context of reviews.

The editors have made every effort to
contact and acknowledge copyright
owners. If there are instances where
proper credit is not given, the publisher
will make necessary changes in
subsequent editions.

ISBN 978-1-945150-51-7
Library of Congress Control
Number: 2017944657
A CIP catalogue record for this
book is available from the Library of
Congress, Washington D.C., USA.